INSIDE AMERICA

THE GREAT AMERICAN INDUSTRIAL TOUR GUIDE

1,000 Free Industrial Tours
Open to the Public
Covering More than 300 Different Industries

By Authors
Jack & Eunice Berger

Heritage Publishing
Peabody, Massachusetts

INSIDE AMERICA - THE GREAT AMERICAN INDUSTRIAL TOUR GUIDE
Printed in the United States of America
Set in Times New Roman

First printing November 1996
Second printing November 1997

For your convenience, an order form can be found at the back of this book.

Library of Congress Catalog Card Number: 96-95115

ISBN 0-9655306-1-2

Heritage Publishing
P.O. Box 4320
Peabody, MA 01961-4320
978-532-3993
800-624-4961

Copyright © 1997 by Jack Berger

Graphics and cover design by Donna Berger
Desktop publishing support by Bruce Berger

Our thanks to everyone whose help, encouragement and patience were essential toward making this book a reality. We extend a deep debt of gratitude and appreciation to the many thousands of workers who make the industries of this wonderful country the success that it is.

TABLE OF CONTENTS

Introduction

Cultural tourism is the fastest growing segment of the travel and tourism industry which, in the United States alone, represents expenditures of more than 400 billion dollars annually. Tourism creates jobs, supports businesses, and brings new money into local economies. In addition, tourism helps promote a cultural exchange with visitors and serves to enhance a community's "sense of place" through the development of attractions that celebrate local resources. It is this cultural exchange that INSIDE AMERICA focuses upon. Industrial plant visits have always been an attraction to both local residents and travelers for two main reasons. First, plant visits can be a valuable educational experience for the visitor, young and old, and is usually an interesting way to spend free time, either at home or away. Secondly, for the manufacturer, plant visits provide an ideal opportunity to "show-off" their products and to promote goodwill. Equally important, is the opportunity to provide the consumer with a chance to get a closer look at the manufacturer and how products are made.

INSIDE AMERICA - The Great American Industrial Tour Guide is a specialized tourist information book which contains a listing of industrial facilities, including manufacturers, that offer tours to the interested public. The emphasis in the book is on attractions that are free or less than $5.00. Nearly 1,000 tour attractions are listed in alphabetical order by state and city. The listings include the company name, address, telephone number, contact person, tour description, directions, disability access information and the Standard Industrial Classification Code (SIC Code) for that industry.

It is our hope that this book will appeal to and provide enjoyment for all people including families, with and without children, domestic and foreign travelers, and the educational field trip programs of school systems throughout the country. The tour attractions that are listed have been carefully selected for their interesting and unique nature. Although many are of the more common types, a significant number of the listings are one of a kind. To assist the truly focused reader, an index by industry and an index by SIC Code information is provided at the end of the book to help in the selection of specific industries.

Readers' Notes

The best way to use this book is to check the tour locations in the areas where you expect to be. From the information listed, decide which facilities you might want to visit. Remember that tour availability may vary with seasons of the year, as well as times and days of the week. Even though all of the information was current when published, companies may have changed their hours, may have moved without letting us know, and some may have gone out of business. Confirmation of the tour information has been received from each listing prior to adding them to our book. When advance notice is indicated, <u>calling ahead to confirm</u> is the best safeguard to cover your plans. <u>This cannot be overemphasized</u>. Understanding that tour programs are an expense to the industries involved, please keep in mind that the visitor has a responsibility to follow whatever rules are posted or explained.

Heritage Publishing is committed to keeping this and future editions of this book accurate and up-to-date.

At time of publication, many telephone area codes within the country were in the process of being changed. Please accept the authors apology for any errors in this regard.

If you would like to have your facility listed or if you know of a unique tour that has not been included in this book and would like it to be considered for printing in the next edition, please send us the information. We will extend a credit toward your next book purchase if the information is used.

About the Authors

The working career of Jack Berger has been as a manager in private industry and as a Colonel in the military. During much of this time, travel has played a key role for both professional and vacationing purposes. In fact, travel was usually more of a highlight than a task. Jack and his wife Eunice visited many areas of the United States and along the way, they always took time to learn about the uniqueness of local cultures and industries. They also took advantage of the many opportunities to visit manufacturing plants and facilities during their travels.

At this time, their major work commitments have lessened and they finally have the opportunity to do the things that have truly interested them. One such aim has been to produce this book, **Inside America - The Great American Industrial Tour Guide** with the hope that it will serve people well and provide many enjoyable experiences.

Jack's writing career has consisted mostly of professional articles and occasional personal interest works that have been published in journals, magazines and newspapers.

Eunice Berger's working career has been in the Human Resource area and most recently she has been involved in the legal field. Over the years, she has developed a strong talent for both writing and proofreading correspondence and documents of all types.

Robinson Iron Corporation (metal works)   SIC Code: 3499
Robinson Road
Alexander City, AL 35010
Tel: 334-329-8486   Contact: W. Wayne Fuller

Plan to tour the fabrication shop and the pattern manufacturing area of this metal works company. **DIRECTIONS:** Hwy 280 east to Hwy 22. Take left, turn left on Washington St and proceed for one and one-half miles to Robinson Rd.

Hours: 8:00 am - 4:00 pm   Days: Tuesday - Friday
Advance Notice: Yes   Fee: No   HP Access: Yes

Birmingham Brewery (brewery)   SIC Code: 2082
3118 3rd Avenue South
Birmingham, AL 35233
Tel: 205-326-6677   Contact: John Zanteson

A walk through of this newly opened microbrewery will have a detailed explanation of the brewing process of their Red Mountain Beer. **NOTE:** Free samples for those over age 21. **DIRECTIONS:** From Rt 65 take exit 260 to the center of the city.

Hours: By appointment only   Fee: No   HP Access: Yes

Southern Research Institute (research)   SIC Code: 8731
2000 Ninth Avenue
Birmingham, AL 35255
Tel: 205-581-2317   Contact: Barbara Caspar

A 90 - minute tour begins with a slide presentation, then a walk through the laboratory build-ings where scientists are involved in cancer research, developing new medical devices, solving air pollution problems, contributing to the space program, and developing new drugs. **DIRECTIONS:** Located on Ninth Ave south between 20th and 21st Sts (parking available).

Hours: 2:30 pm   Days: Friday
Advance Notice: Yes   Fee: No   HP Access: Yes

Kyumlga Grist Mill (corn mill)   SIC Code: 2041
County Road 46 and 36
Childersburg, AL 35044
Tel: 334-378-7436   Contact: Staff

Grist mill operates on three large turbines with 2 - 800 lb. grinding stones. Corn is still ground on these stones. **NOTE:** Mill is open April - September. **DIRECTIONS:** Located on County Rd 46 and 36 between Childersburg and Talladega. The mill is located next to the Kymulga Covered Bridge over Talladega Creek.

Hours: 9:00 am - 5:00 pm   Days: Monday - Saturday
Advance Notice: No   Fee: $2.00   HP Access: No

Butler's Mill (corn mill)   SIC Code: 2041
County Road 92
Graham, AL 36263
Tel: 205-568-3030   Contact: Manager

Now a functioning grist mill, this two-story frame structure was built in 1881 to combine sawmill, grist mill, cotton gin, and feed mill in one operation. **DIRECTIONS:** Between AL 48 and US 431, four miles west of Graham on County Road 92.

Hours: 8:00 am - 4:00 pm   Days: Saturday
Advance Notice: No   Fee: No   HP Access: Yes

Punta Clara Kitchen (candy mfr)   SIC Code: 2064
US 98
Point Clear, AL 36564
Tel: 334-928-8477   Contact: Manager

Watch the process of making candies and confections, pralines, fudges, English toffee, pecan butter crunch, preserves and pickles. **NOTE:** Free samples. **DIRECTIONS:** Located on scenic US Hwy 98 about 20 miles southeast of Mobile. Punta Clara Kitchen is approximately one mile south of the Grand Hotel.

Hours: 9:00 am - 5:00 pm   Days: Monday - Saturday
Advance Notice: No   Fee: No   HP Access: Yes

Fox Mountain Trout Farm (preserve)   SIC Code: 0971
RR 1
Valley Head, AL 35989
Tel: 205-632-3194   Contact: Manager

Plan to tour here where trout are raised for your fishing pleasure. Fishing poles, bait, bagging and icing of the fish you catch are all included in the small fee. **NOTE:** The Trout Farm is closed on Mondays. **DIRECTIONS:** North of Valley Head, two miles off I - 59. Take Rising Fawn, GA exit, turn west.

Schedule: March 1 - November 1
Advance Notice: No   Fee: $2.00   HP Access: Yes

Sonoita Vineyards (winery)   SIC Code: 2084
H.C.R. Box 33
Elgin, AZ 85611
520-455-5893   Contact: Karen Robbins

You are invited to take a 30 - 60 minute tour to the rolling grasslands of this winery and enjoy the warm days and cool nights at an elevation of 5,000 feet. You can enjoy an outing by packing a picnic lunch and sample their international award winning wines which include Cabernet Sauvignon, Chardonnay, Fume Blanc, Merlot as well as many other estate wines. **NOTE:** Reservations are taken for groups larger than 10. Closed major holidays. **DIRECTIONS:** Located 12 miles southeast of Sonoita, 65 miles southeast of Tucson.

Hours: 10:00 am - 4:00 pm   Days: Monday - Friday
Advance Notice: No   Fee: $1.00   HP Access: Limited

Megafoods Stores Inc. (grocer)   SIC Code: 5411
1455 South Stapley Drive
Mesa, AZ 85204
520-926-1087   Contact: Eden Higgins

Take a one hour tour of one of the largest retail groceries which includes behind the scenes of receiving, sorting and stocking of fresh foods. **DIRECTIONS:** Superstitution Fwy to Stapley (north) to southern SE corner.

Hours: Call for hours   Days: Monday - Sunday
Advance Notice: Yes   Fee: No   HP Access: Yes

Phelps Dodge Corporation (copper mine)   SIC Code: 1021
4521 US Highway 191
Morenci, AZ 85540
520-865-4521   Contact: Arlene Boling

Three and one-half hour tour by van into the second largest open pit copper mine in the world. Tour also goes into the Concentrator and around by the copper dock. **NOTE:** Cameras are allowed, but no camcorders. Very little or no walking. Closed holidays. You may be able to pick up rock samples. **DIRECTIONS:** From the south, stay on US 191, across the street from the Fire Department.

Hours: 8:30 am and 1:15 pm   Days: Monday - Friday
Advance Notice: Yes   Fee: No   HP Access: Yes

America West Airlines (airline)   SIC Code: 4512
4000 East Sky Harbor Boulevard
Phoenix, AZ 85034
602-693-5748   Contact: Tara Galvin

You will have an opportunity to tour the terminal and the Technical Support Facility. Tours are limited in quantity and are given only during the school year. **NOTE:** Tour the terminal on Wednesday and Saturday at 11:30 am and the hangar on Tuesday, Wednesday and Thursday between 1:00 - 3:30 pm. **DIRECTIONS:** Located at Phoenix International Airport.

Hours: 11:30 am   Days: Wednesday and Saturday (terminal)
        1:00 and 3:30 pm   Tuesday - Thursday (hangar)
Advance Notice: Yes   Fee: No   HP Access: Yes

Karsten Manufacturing Corp. (sporting goods)   SIC Code: 3949
2201 West Desert Cove
Phoenix, AZ 85068
602-870-5000 (800-474-6434)   Contact: Chuck Renner

Tour this manufacturing plant where they make golf equipment including irons, putters and woods. **NOTE:** Please request reservations as far in advance as possible. **DIRECTIONS:** One-half mile north of Peoria Ave on 21st Ave.

Hours: Call for schedule   Days: Tuesday and Thursday
Advance Notice: Yes   Fee: No   HP Access: Yes

The Arizona Republic (newspaper)   SIC Code: 2711
22600 North 19th Avenue
Phoenix, AZ 85027
602-780-7090   Contact: Julie Rodolico

On the one and one-half hour walking tour of this facility you will have an opportunity to learn how a newspaper printing plant works. You will see a video, receive hands-on samples and get a comprehensive tour of the printing center. **NOTE:** No children under 10. Please book your tour at least two months in advance. **DIRECTIONS:** Plant is located approximately 1/4 mile north of Deer Valley Rd on 19th Ave to Deer Valley Center on your left.

Hours: By appointment only
Advance Notice: Yes   Fee: No   HP Access: Yes

The Peanut Patch (nuts)   SIC Code: 0173
4322 East County 13th Street
Yuma, AZ 85365
520-726-6292   Contact: Lorie Honeycutt or Cecil Pratt

This tour begins with a description of the farming of the peanuts. You will see a slide presentation and then you will be taken through the sheller, cleaner and processing plant. The tour concludes with a visit to the kitchens and packing room. Finale of tour is the retail store. **DIRECTIONS:** I - 8 to Ave 3 east, south to County 13th St, turn left one and 1/4 miles.

Hours: 10:00 am   Days: Wednesday or Saturday
Advance Notice: Yes   Fee: No   HP Access: Yes

Mount Bethel Winery (winery)   SIC Code: 2084
Highway 64 East
Altus, AR 72821
Tel: 501-468-2444   Contact: Peggy Post

The winery is in an historic cellar built in the 1800's which houses a bottling room, and storage and fermenting areas. The storage area includes a 7,000 gallon redwood tank and 200 American white oak barrels. **NOTE:** Free wine tasting in the cellar. Open every day except Christmas. **DIRECTIONS:** From I - 40, take exit 55 west at Clarksville (Coal Hill-Hartman). Winery is located 1/4 mile east of Altus on Hwy 64. Winery is located approximately 13 miles west of I - 40 exit 55.

Hours: 9:00 am - 7:00 pm   Days: Monday - Saturday
Advance Notice: No   Fee: No   HP Access: Yes

Post Familie Winery (winery)   SIC Code: 2084
Route 1 and Highway 186
Altus, AR 72821
Tel: 501-468-2741   Contact: Paul J. Post

A walking tour through the entire winery will demonstrate the process from crushing to bottling. You will tour the cold storage facility/packing shed ending with the retail sales outlet and tasting of the wines. **NOTE:** Vineyard tour by appointment only. **DIRECTIONS:** I - 40, exit 41, six miles south on Hwy 186 or one block north of Hwy 64 on Hwy I - 86.

Hours: 11:00 am - 4:00 pm   Days: Monday - Saturday
        12:00 noon - 5:00 pm   Sunday
Advance Notice: Yes   Fee: No   HP Access: Yes

Lephiew Gin Company (cotton gin)   SIC Code: 0724
117 North Freeman Street
Dermott, AR 71638
501-538-5288   Contact: Lephiew Dennington

Family owned and operated since 1886, the gin and warehouse is open for tours during the fall harvest season. **DIRECTIONS:** Located approximately 100 miles south of Little Rock, take Hwy 165, which is about five miles south of McGehee, AR. Continue on Hwy 165 and turn right on Hwy 35. Mill is about two miles on the left.

Hours: Call for schedule
Advance Notice: No   Fee: No   HP Access: No

Terra Studios (pottery products)   SIC Code: 3269
12103 Hazel Valley Road
Fayetteville, AR 72701
501-643-3185   Contact: Ronda Downey

At this glass studio you will have an opportunity to watch bluebirds being made by highly skilled Ozark pottery craftsmen. The artisans also create a wide variety of art and utilitarian stoneware pottery. **DIRECTIONS:** Rt 16 southeast of Fayetteville and Durham to studio. Call for specific directions.

Hours: 9:00 am - 5:00 pm   Days: Monday - Sunday
Advance Notice: No   Fee: No   HP Access: Yes

Mountain Valley Spring Water (bottled water)   SIC Code: 2086
150 Central Avenue
Hot Springs, AR 71901
870-623-6671   Contact: Ron Cheek

This self-guided tour includes displays depicting Mountain Valley's historical exhibits of natural spring water. Every drop of Mountain Valley Spring Water is packaged with stringent quality control procedures. Since 1871, Mountain Valley has truly developed a superior reputation among bottled waters. **NOTE:** Free samples. Advance notice for large groups. **DIRECTIONS:** I - 40 to I - 30, head west. Take exit 111 (Hot Spring National Park) Rt 270 to Hot Springs. Continue to Central Ave (Rt 7 north). Take a right at signal light at intersection and continue into town. Company is on the left.

Hours: 9:00 am - 5:00 pm   Days: Monday - Friday
Advance Notice: No   Fee: No   HP Access: Yes

Joe Hogan State Fish Hatchery (hatchery)   SIC Code: 0921
P.O.Box 178
Lonoke, AR 72086
870-676-6963   Contact: Berry Beavers

On this tour you will see an indoor exhibit of aquaria, fish, mounted mammal, bird, and fish species. Catfish, large-mouth bass, crappie, striped bass and hybrid striped bass are all produced at one of the largest hatcheries in the U. S. Outdoor exhibits of ponds and native wildlife and fish. **DIRECTIONS:** Hwy 70 and Fish Hatchery Rd.

Hours: 8:00 am - 4:00 pm   Days: Monday - Friday
Advance Notice: No   Fee: No   HP Access: Yes

Cowie Wine Cellars (winery)   SIC Code: 2084
101 North Carbon City Road
Paris, AR 72855
501-963-3990   Contact: Robert Cowie

When you tour this family-owned and operated winery you will visit the wine cellars where the wine is fermented and aged. You will observe the wine making operations and learn how wine is made and stored for aging. **NOTE:** Free samples. **DIRECTIONS:** 14 miles south, then three miles east of Ozark, AR at Carbon City.

Hours: 10:00 am - 5:00 pm   Days: Monday - Saturday
Advance Notice: Yes   Fee: No   HP Access: Yes

Heifer Project International (livestock breeder)   SIC Code: 0751
RR 2 (Box 33)
Perryville, AR 72126
501-889-5124   Contact: Bill and Jeanne Chappell

The tours begin with a short video and a brief discussion of the project map. This will be followed by a 45 - minute van or hayride which will show you the 1200 acre educational center and ranch that demonstrates the techniques taught to poverty families throughout the world. You will also see how life is lived in developing countries. Tour of Guatemala Hillside Farm. **NOTE:** Hay rides or van tours. Self-guided walking trail. Video and Gift Shop. **DIRECTIONS:** Hwy 9 & 10, two miles south of Perryville. Located 45 miles northwest of Little Rock, 16 miles south of I - 40.

Hours: 10:00-1:00, 3:00 pm   Days: Monday - Saturday
          1:00 and 3:00 pm   Sunday
Advance Notice: Yes   Fee: $1.50   HP Access: Yes

Chase's Olive Barrel (olives)   SIC Code: 0191
1127 Mesa View Drive
Arroyo Grande, CA 93420
805-481-5450 (800-733-3026)   Contact: William or Lana Majors

Touring this gourmet olive and chocolate factory you will see how olives are grown and processed and see how the chocolates are made. **DIRECTIONS**: On Old Hwy 1 on the Nipoma Mesa.

Hours: 11:00 am - 5:00 pm   Days: Monday - Friday
Advance Notice: Yes   Fee: No   HP Access: Yes

Bakersfield Processing & Dist. Center (postal)   SIC Code: 4311
3400 Pegasus Drive
Bakersfield, CA 93380-8000
805-392-6158   Contact: JoAnne Rowles

A one hour tour of the U. S. Postal Processing & Distribution Center where you will be shown how the mail is processed for delivery. **DIRECTIONS**: Located in the center of town near the intersection of Rts 99 and 53.

Hours: Mornings only   Days: Tuesday - Thursday
Advance Notice: Yes   Fee: No   HP Access: Yes

KBAK-TV-Channel 29 (TV broadcast)   SIC Code: 4833
1901 Westwind Drive
Bakersfield, CA 93301
805-327-7955   Contact: Laura Kershner

You will have an opportunity to tour the Graphics Department, the Master Control Room, the Studio, the Edit Bays, the Weather Office and the Newsroom of this TV station.
DIRECTIONS: Go north on Fwy 99, turn right on Rosedale Hwy. Go to the first light which is Oak St and take a right. At the next light (21st St) take a right. Take a left at the first light (Westwind Dr). Continue on Westwind until you see a building on the right with a "29" Cube.

Hours: Call for appointment
Advance Notice: Yes   Fee: No   HP Access: Yes

NBC Studio (KNBC TV) (TV broadcast)   SIC Code: 4833
3000 West Alameda
Burbank, CA 91523
818-840-3537   Contact: Ronilyn Reilly

Learn some of the fascinating secrets of TV production as you take a 75 - minute walking tour of this large broadcasting complex. You will have an opportunity to see the 'Tonight Show' set, wardrobe, video demonstration on makeup, an NBC Sports Presentation set, and construction and production studios. You will also experience the Special Effects and Sound Effects sets. **DIRECTIONS:** Located five minutes from the Hollywood Ventura & Golden State Freeways; 10 minutes from Hollywood.

Hours: 9:00 am - 3:00 pm   Days: Monday - Friday
Advance Notice: Yes   Fee: $5.00 Adults   HP Access: Yes

Larkmead Cellar/Kornell Champagne (vineyard)   SIC Code: 0172
1091 Larkmead Lane
Calistoga, CA 94515
707-942-0859   Contact: Dennis Zablosky

Take a 20 - minute walking tour of this winery in the best wine producing areas of the world. **NOTE:** Complimentary wine tasting. **DIRECTIONS:** Four and 2/10 miles north of St. Helena on Hwy 29.

Hours: 10:15 am - 4:00 pm   Days: Monday - Sunday
Advance Notice: Yes   Fee: No   HP Access: Yes

Stewart Orchids (floriculture)   SIC Code: 0181
3376 Foothill Road
Carpinteria, CA 93014
805-684-5448 (800-621-2450)   Contact: Ned or Peter

On this self-guided brief tour of a two acre orchid growing facility you will learn how orchid history has been made with cattleya hybridizing, cymbidiums, phalaenopsis and paphiopedilums as well as contributions to orchid literature. **NOTE:** Two weeks advance notice. Guided tours available for groups of 15 or more. **DIRECTIONS:** From Santa Barbara, exit Padero Ln off Rt 101 south and left at stop sign. At Via Real take a right and go one-half mile to Nidever, take a left. The nursery is on the right side across from the condos.

Hours: Call for times   Days: Monday - Friday
Advance Notice: Yes   Fee: No   HP Access: No

NASA Ames-Dryden Flight Res Facility(space research) SIC Code: 9661
Lilly Drive - Building 4800
Edwards, CA 93523-0273
805-258-3446   Contact: Ronnie

The 90 - minute guided tour begins with a film about the Center. You will be escorted
through a hangar where you will view aircraft, an aerospace laboratory, the world's largest
wind tunnel, centrifuge operations, research aircraft, and flight simulation facilities. **NOTE:**
No tours during shuttle landing. Children must be accompanied by adults. **DIRECTIONS:**
From Los Angeles, Rt 5 north to Rt 14 to Rosamond/Edwards AFB cutoff. Follow signs.

Hours: 10:15 am and 1:15 pm   Days: Monday - Friday
Advance Notice: Yes   Fee: No   HP Access: Yes

Orfila Vineyards (winery)   SIC Code: 2084
13455 San Pasqual Road
Escondido, CA 92025
619-738-6500   Contact: Manager

On this 20 - minute guided tour, you will be introduced to the entire wine making process
from grape to bottle. Self-guided tours are also available. **NOTE:** There is no charge for
non-tour groups. **DIRECTIONS:** I - 15 to Via Rancho Pkwy. Right onto San Pasqual Rd
for one mile, entrance on right side.

Hours: 11:30,1:30,3:00,4:00   Days: Monday - Friday
Advance Notice: Yes   Fee: $5.00 groups   HP Access: Yes

Herman Goelitz Candy Co., Inc. (candy mfr)   SIC Code: 2064
2400 North Watney Way
Fairfield, CA 94533
707-428-2838 (800-522-3267)   Contact: Cynthia Dale

The manufacturers of 'Jelly Belly' jelly beans and other fine confectionery products will take
you on a guided tour along an elevated walkway above the production floor where you will
get a birds eye view of hundreds of thousands of pounds of candy in the making.
DIRECTIONS: Take I - 80 north to Fairfield. Exit freeway at Hwy 12/Chadbourne Rd, and
exit at Chadbourne. Turn right at stop sign, left onto Courage Dr. Turn left onto North
Watney.

Hours: 9:00 am - 2:00 pm   Days: Monday - Friday
Advance Notice: No   Fee: No   HP Access: Yes

Fall River Wild Rice (rice farm)   SIC Code: 0112
HC-01 Osprey Drive
Fall River Mills, CA 96028
530-336-5222   Contact: Todd

A visit to this ranch nestled in the mountains of northeastern CA between the Sierra Nevada and Cascade ranges will show their fertile soils, clean air, spring waters, and a crisp climate for producing wild rice. After the tour, you will be invited into their store to see the many products produced from wild rice. **DIRECTIONS:** Located about 75 miles east of Redding, CA on Hwy 299 east. Call for more specific directions.

Hours: 8:00 am - 4:30 pm   Days: Monday - Friday
Advance Notice: No   Fee: No   HP Access: Yes

Gekkeikan Sake, USA (winery)   SIC Code: 2084
1136 Sibley Street
Folsom, CA 95630
916-985-3111   Contact: Jackie Fogg

On this self-guided tour, you will visit the Japanese gardens, koi pond and tasting room. You will also tour the unique sake brewery with complimentary tasting of original and draft sake as well as plum wine. **DIRECTIONS:** From Sacramento, take Hwy 50 east to Pacific City Rd. Go north on this road and continue going straight until it becomes Sibley St.

Hours: 10:00 am - 4:300 pm   Days: Monday - Sunday
Advance Notice: No   Fee: No   HP Access: Yes

Goldsmith Seeds, Inc. (seeds)   SIC Code: 0181
2280 Hecker Pass Highway
Gilroy, CA 95020
408-847-7333   Contact: Keith Muraoka

Take a one hour guided tour which offers a behind-the-scenes look at how hybrid flower seeds are developed, including visits inside greenhouses, labs and flower fields. **NOTE:** Self-guided tours are also available year round from dawn to dusk. Tours must be scheduled at least two weeks in advance. The best time to visit is June through August when the fields are blooming. **DIRECTIONS:** Located on Hwy 101 about 25 miles southeast of San Jose.

Hours: By appointment   Days: Monday and Wednesday
Advance Notice: Yes   Fee: No   HP Access: No

Hendry Telephone Products (communications)   SIC Code: 4899
55 Castilian Drive
Goleta, CA 93117
805-968-5511   Contact: Karen Faulkner

A tour of this telephone manufacturing plant will show you the various processes and departments, welding, paint, sheet metal, etc., including the high speed turret punch presses, electronic laser cutting center, a welding robot and an efficient powder paint coating and conveyor baking system. **DIRECTIONS:** North on Hwy 101 from Santa Barbara, exit Los Carneros, left over Fwy, right on Castilian.

Hours: Call for times   Days: Monday - Friday
Advance Notice: Yes   Fee: No   HP Access: Yes

Monterey Vineyard (winery)   SIC Code: 2084
800 South Alta Street
Gonzales, CA 93926
408-675-2316   Contact: Lorraine Worthy

The 30 - minute tour includes the complete winemaking process from grape to finished wine. A wine tasting concludes the tour with a selection of four - six wines ranging from bone dry to slightly sweet. **DIRECTIONS:** Located 20 minutes south of Salinas just off Hwy 101 on the south edge of the City of Gonzales. From Monterey, it is recommended you take the scenic drive - River Rd south from Hwy 68.

Hours: 10:00 am - 5:00 pm   Days: Monday - Friday
Advance Notice: Yes   Fee: $3.00   HP Access: Yes

Apples of Gold (fruits)   SIC Code: 0175
13739 Old Westside Road
Grenada, CA 96038
916-436-2610   Contact: Willis or Claudia Thompson

Included in the tour of this apple processing plant will be a visit to the cold storage facilities
and cider manufacturing area. You will see fresh apple cider made 2 - 3 times per week during the months of September through December. In addition you can enjoy the magnificent
view of the Shasta Valley and Mount Shasta. Future plans include a commercial kitchen to
process jams, jellies and syrups. **NOTE:** A beautiful time to visit is Blossom Time in April.
DIRECTIONS: Eight miles south of Yreka, CA, two and one-half miles south on old Hwy
99, then one and 6/10 miles on Old Westside Rd.

Hours: By appointment   Days: Monday - Friday
Advance Notice: Yes   Fee: No   HP Access: Yes

Hilmar Cheese Company (cheese processor)   SIC Code: 2022
9001 Lander Avenue
Hilmar, CA 95324
209-667-0865   Contact: Lori Bill

From viewing windows, you will see Monterey Jack Cheese and Mild Cheddar Cheese being
made. This company produces approximately 25% of the Monterey Jack consumed in California. **NOTE:** Cheese tasting. You must call in advance for reservations. **DIRECTIONS:**
Take Rt 99 from Sacramento into Turlock. Take the Lander-Los Banos exit, go right on
Lander for three miles (also known as Rt 165).

Hours: Call for schedule   Days: Monday - Friday
Advance Notice: Yes   Fee: No   HP Access: No

Iron Gate Salmon/Steelhead Hatchery (hatchery)   SIC Code: 0921
8638 Lakeview Road
Hornbrook, CA 96044
916-475-3420   Contact: Kim Rushton

Visit this hatchery which spawns and rears chinook (king) salmon, coho (silver) salmon and steelhead trout. The hatchery produces 275,000 steelhead and coho yearlings and is operated by the California Department of Fish and Games Resource Agency. Best time to visit is October when there are adult salmon. **DIRECTIONS:** Take Henley/Hornbrook exit off I - 5, about 15 miles north of Yreka. Go right (east) on Copco Rd for approximately eight miles to hatchery.

Hours: 7:00 am - dusk   Days: Monday - Sunday
Advance Notice: No   Fee: No   HP Access: No

Sun Empire Foods (candy mfr)   SIC Code: 2064
1220 South Madera Avenue
Kerman, CA 93630
209-846-8208 (800-252-4786)   Contact: Sandra Dee

Take a 30 - minute tour of this candy manufacturing plant and see the chocolate coated raisins and nuts process. You will also have an opportunity to view the machine packaging demonstration. **NOTE:** Free tasting. Tours are only given from January through September. **DIRECTIONS:** 15 miles west of Fresno on Madera Ave, also known as Hwy 145.

Hours: 9:00 am - 3:00 pm   Days: Monday - Saturday
Advance Notice: Yes   Fee: No   HP Access: Yes

Salk Institute for Biological Study (research)   SIC Code: 8731
10010 North Torrey Pines Road
La Jolla, CA 92037
619-453-4100   Contact: Wendy Laver

Plan to take a docent-led tour in one of the world's foremost independent non-profit institutions conducting basic science research dedicated to the improvement of human health. **DIRECTIONS:** I - 5 to Genesee west, continuing to the first stoplight. Turn right past Institute. Turn left into the main Salk Institute parking lot. Reception area is located at the courtyard level in the south building.

Hours: 10:00,11:00, noon   Days: Monday - Friday
Advance Notice: Yes   Fee: No   HP Access: Yes

Scripps Institute of Oceanography (research)   SIC Code: 8731
2300 Expedition Way
La Jolla, CA 92037
619-534-3474   Contact: Cindy Clark

This is a wonderful opportunity to visit one of the oldest, largest and most important centers for marine science research, education and public service. You will see more than thirty aquarium tanks teaming with live marine life, oceanographic museum, and a man-made tide pool all serving as the public education center. **NOTE:** Closed Thanksgiving and Christmas Day. **DIRECTIONS:** Exit I - 5 at La Jolla Village Dr, west one mile. Left onto Expedition Way.

Hours: 9:00 am - 5:00 pm   Days: Monday - Sunday
Advance Notice: Yes   Fee: $6.00   HP Access: Yes

KUZZ-Radio, Inc., AM/FM (radio broadcast)   SIC Code: 4832
4120 Barlow Drive
Lake Isabella, CA 93240
760-379-3648   Contact; Jim Ridenour

Tour studio, transmitter and tower site including endangered Mariposa Lily field where the transmitter is located. **DIRECTIONS:** Take egress off St Hwy I - 78 at Lake Isabella and turn left 200' to Barlow Dr.

Hours: Call for appointment
Advance Notice: Yes   Fee: No   HP Access: No

Los Angeles Times (newspaper)   SIC Code: 2711
202 West 1st Street
Los Angeles, CA 90053
213-237-5000   Contact: Tour Department

On this 35 - minute tour of The Times, you will pass through the editorial offices, where news from the city and around the world is gathered, written and edited; the composing room, where the news stories and advertisements are assembled into page form; the library and photography departments and the test kitchen, where recipes are tested for The Times' Food Section. **NOTE:** Children must be at least 10 years old or in the fifth grade. Group tours must be booked at least 30 days in advance. **DIRECTIONS:** Located next to City Hall.

Hours: 11:15 am and 3:00 pm   Days: Monday - Friday
Advance Notice: Yes   Fee: No   HP Access: Yes

Los Angeles Times Olympic Plant (newspaper)   SIC Code: 2711
2000 East 8th Street
Los Angeles, CA 90053
213-237-5555   Contact: Tour Director

On the tour of the Olympic Plant, you will pass through the state-of-the-art pressroom, the newsprint storage area where robot-like automated guidance vehicles carry rolls of newsprint weighing 2,500 pounds; platemaking, where newspaper pages are converted from photographic negatives to aluminum printing plates, and the distribution center. **NOTE:** Children must be 10 years old. Please arrange for your tour at least 30 days in advance.
DIRECTIONS: Located at intersection of East 8th St and Alameda.

Hours: 9:45 and 10:00 am   Days: Tuesday and Thursday
Advance Notice: Yes   Fee: No   HP Access: Yes

Marysville Processing & Dist. Center (postal)   SIC Code: 4311
407 C Street
Marysville, CA 95901-9998
916-742-2331   Contact: Debora Arnold

Take a one hour tour of this U.S. Postal Distribution & Processing Center where you will observe the letter sorting machines and other automated equipment with explanations of mail flow of normal letters and packages. **DIRECTIONS:** Take Hwy 5/99 east out of Sacramento. Marysville is about 50 miles northeast of Sacramento.

Hours: 10:00 am   Days: Tuesday and Wednesday
Advance Notice: Yes   Fee: No   HP Access: Yes

BFI Recyclery (recycling center)   SIC Code: 5093
1601 Dixon Landing Road
Milpitas, CA 95035
408-432-1234   Contact: Cheryl Golden

Visit the Materials Recovery Facility (MRF) and see how recyclables are sorted, baled and then shipped out to be sold. You will also visit the Education Center and see the 100 foot long "Wall of Garbage". Also there are interactive electronic displays such as "Shoot the Loot" laser gun, Magnetic Fishing, and a video tour of the landfill and compost site. Fun for the whole family. **DIRECTIONS:** North of San Jose on I - 880. Dixon Landing Rd west exit.

Hours: 9:00 am - 4:00 pm   Days: Tuesday and Thursday
Advance Notice: Yes   Fee: No   HP Access: Yes

Ames Research Center (NASA) (space research)   SIC Code: 9661
Moffett Field, CA 94035-1000
650-604-6497   Contact: Tour Office

This is a two hour guided tour of a field installation of the National Aeronautics and Space Administration which provides vital research and technology for the US space program, the aeronautics industry and national security. Some of the tour stops include the world's largest wind tunnel, research aircraft, a centrifuge and flight simulation facilities. Actual tour stops vary depending on daily research activities. **NOTE:** The walking tour is canceled in the event of rain. Children must be nine years old. Please call in advance for reservations. **DIRECTIONS:** Take the Moffett Field exit from Hwy 101, left at Main Gate, follow signs.

Hours: 8:00 am - 4:30 pm   Days: Monday - Friday
Advance Notice: Yes   Fee: No   HP Access: No

Mount Shasta Hatchery (hatchery)   SIC Code: 0921
3 North Old Stage Road - Interstate 5
Mount Shasta, CA 96067
916-926-2215   Contact: Manager

This is the oldest operating fish hatchery west of the Mississippi. It presently spawns brown and two strains of rainbow trout. You will see high numbers of fish in all stages of growth and enjoy feeding them with food provided on site. **DIRECTIONS:** One-half mile west of I - 5 in the town of Mount Shasta..

Hours: 8:00 am - 4:00 pm   Days: Monday -Friday
Advance Notice: No   Fee: No   HP Access: Yes

Carneros Alambic Distillery (winery)   SIC Code: 2084
1250 Cuttings Wharf Road
Napa, CA 94559-9738
707-253-9055   Contact: Lindsay Randolph

Resembling the romantic Brandy houses that dot the French countryside, on this tour you will visit the still house with its cathedral ceiling and exotic alambic stills and the barrel house where nearly 4,000 barrels of aging brandy. This distillery, a departure from the standard wine country experience, has the largest stock of aging alambic brandy in North America. **DIRECTIONS:** Off Hwy 121 (west of Hwy 29) one mile on Cuttings Wharf Rd.

Hours: 10:30 am - 4:30 pm   Days: Monday - Sunday
Advance Notice: No   Fee: No   HP Access: Yes

Graber Olive House (canning)   SIC Code: 2033
315 East 4th Street
Ontario, CA 91764
909-983-1761 (800-996-5483)   Contact: Manager

A tour of the historic canning facilities where you will see the processing, canning and labeling of world famous Graber Olives which has taken place since 1894. During the fall harvest, visitors are welcome to view the activities of grading, curing and canning of their famous olives. **NOTE:** Scenic picnic area. Free samples. **DIRECTIONS:** Take I - 10 (San Bernardino Fwy) to the Euclid Ave and south to 4th. Turn left.

Hours: 9:00 am - 4:30 pm   Days: Monday - Friday
Advance Notice: Yes   Fee: No   HP Access: No

Renaissance Vineyard & Winery (winery)   SIC Code: 2084
12585 Rices Crossing Road
Oregon House, CA 95962
916-692-3104   Contact: Alisanne Frew

This extended tour includes the terraced vineyard of 365 acres using drip irrigation. Grapes for the Sauvignon Blanc, White Riesling and Cabernet Sauvignon wines are picked, processed, bottled, labeled and shipped from this, the largest mountain estate-bottled vineyard in America. **NOTE:** Free tasting. **DIRECTIONS:** From Sacramento, Hwy 80 north to Hwy 99/70 north to Hwy 20 towards Grass Valley and left on Rt E 21 past Collins Lake. Right on E 20 to Oregon House for two miles and right on Rices Crossing Rd.

Hours: 10:30 am   Days: Wednesday - Sunday
Advance Notice: Yes   Fee: No   HP Access: No

Pasadena Processing & Dist. Center (postal)   SIC Code: 4311
600 North Lincoln Avenue
Pasadena, CA 91109-9998
818-304-7231   Contact: Judy Paggett

The U.S. Postal Processing & Distribution Center tour will explain the entire processing of mail sorting, and show you how hundreds of thousands of pieces of mail are processed daily. **DIRECTIONS:** 210 Freeway, exit Fair Oaks.

Hours: 12 noon - 9:00 pm   Days: Monday - Friday
Advance Notice: Yes   Fee: No   HP Access: Yes

Creamery Store (cheese processor)   SIC Code: 2022
711 Western Avenue
Petaluma, CA 94952
707-778-1234   Contact: Betsy Penn

After a 10 - minute video highlighting past and current products made at their plants, you will walk to the cheese plant and look through a viewing window at the cheesemaking process as the tour guide explains what is happening. **NOTE:** Cheese samples. **DIRECTIONS:** From Hwy 101, go west on Washington, south on Petaluma Blvd, northwest on Western Ave.

Hours: 11:00 am - 3:00 pm.   Days: Monday - Saturday
Advance Notice: Yes   Fee: No   HP Access: No

North Bay Processing & Dist. Center (postal)   SIC Code: 4311
1150 North McDowell Street
Petaluma, CA 94999-9998
707-778-5300   Contact: Debra Houweling

A tour of the U. S. Postal Processing & Distribution Center will demonstrate the latest in mail processing equipment and procedures utilizing the latest on mail handling equipment. **DIRECTIONS:** US Hwy 101 north, exit on Old Redwood Hwy.

Hours: 8:00 am - 8:00 pm   Days: Monday - Friday
Advance Notice: Yes   Fee: No   HP Access: Yes

Nimbus Fish Hatcheries (hatchery)   SIC Code: 0921
Department of Fish and Game
2001 Nimbus Road
Rancho Cordova, CA 95670
916-355-0666

Most of the yearly catch of King Salmon and Steelhead begin here. See aquariums with local species of fish. This facility is used for the production of salmon, steelhead trout and striped bass. In this self-guided tour you will visit the raceway ponds, the fish weir and ladder entrance, the holding pond entrances, the sorting and spawning area and the nursery ponds. **DIRECTIONS:** Take Rt 50 west of Sacramento to Hazel Ave exit towards Orangevale. Follow Hazel Ave to Gold County Rd to Nimbus Rd.

Hours: 8:00 am - 4:00 pm   Days: Monday - Sunday
Advance Notice: No   Fee: No   HP Access: Yes

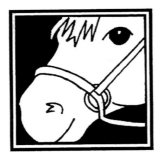

Murieta Equine Complex (horses)   SIC Code: 0272
7200 Lone Pine Drive
Rancho Murieta, CA 95683
916-985-7334   Contact: Kelly Bess

Visit this thoroughbred horse farm and training facility and you will have an opportunity to see the breeding operation. **NOTE:** Please check with office for type of horse event in progress and calendar of events. **DIRECTIONS:** East on Jackson Hwy 16 to Lone Pine Dr. Right turn past first mailbox.

Hours: Call for schedule   Days: Monday - Friday
Advance Notice: Yes   Fee: No   HP Access: Yes

KMS Research, Inc. (beauty salon equip)   SIC Code: 5087
4712 Mountain Lakes Boulevard
Redding, CA 96003
916-244-6000   Contact: Lana Deppen

A tour of the KMS Healthcare hair products manufacturing plant will include the customer service department, research and development lab, manufacturing, receiving, shipping and packaging areas, and marketing and sales departments. **NOTE:** Tours are limited to organized groups of not less than 10 and no more than 30. **DIRECTIONS:** Located on US Rt 5, north of Sacramento.

Hours: 8:00 am - 5:00 pm   Days: Monday - Friday
Advance Notice: Yes   Fee: No   HP Access: Yes

San Bernardino Processing Center (postal)   SIC Code: 4311
1900 West Redlands Boulevard
Redlands, CA 92373
0909-335-4303   Contact: Julie Robledo

A one and one-half hour tour of this U. S. Postal Processing & Distribution Center will include a 20 - minute video and a floor tour of the modern mail processing equipment. **DIRECTIONS:** Fwy 10, California exit/south to Redlands Blvd east.

Hours: 10:30 am - 12 noon   Days: Tuesday - Friday
Advance notice: Yes   Fee: No   HP Access: Yes

Exotic Feline Breeding, Inc. (zoo)   SIC Code: 8422
Rosamond & Tropico Roads
Rosamond, CA 93560
805-256-3793   Contact: Sandy Masek

An interesting place to visit and bring the family for an on-site guided tour where over 50 endangered or threatened exotic cats, representing 16 different species, are on exhibit. **NOTE:** Closed Wednesdays and Christmas Day. **DIRECTIONS:** Five miles west of Hwy 14 near the Tropico Gold Mine and Willow Springs Raceway.

Hours: 10:00 am - 4:00 pm   Days: Monday - Friday
Advance Notice: No   Fee: No   HP Access: yes

Fiddyment Farms Inc. (nuts)   SIC Code: 0173
5000 Fiddyment Road
Roseville, CA 95747
916-771-0800 (800-859-4038)   Contact: Saundra Festa

Visit this 40 - acre pistachio farm and see how one of the most popular nuts is grown.
NOTE: After the tour, you can browse in their country store. **DIRECTIONS:** Located on US Rt 80, about 10 miles northeast of Sacramento.

Hours: 10:00 am - 4:00 pm   Days: Monday - Friday
Advance Notice: Yes   Fee: No   HP Access: No

Mumm Napa Valley (winery)   SIC Code: 2084
8445 Silverado Trail
Rutherford, CA 94573
707-942-3434   Contact: Jim O'Shea

Well trained tour guides will lead you through the winery where you will receive a clear look at each step of the complex methode champenoise process used to produce sparkling wines.
DIRECTIONS: From Napa take 29 north, right on Rutherford Crossroad, right on Silverado Trail for two miles.

Hours: 11:00 am - 3:00 pm   Days: Monday - Sunday
Advance Notice: No   Fee: No   HP Access: Yes

St. Supery Vineyards & Winery (winery)   SIC Code: 2084
8440 North St. Helena Highway
Rutherford, CA 94573
707-963-4507   Contact: Lili Thomas/Jack Bittner

A beautiful facility where you can experience everything the wine country has to offer at one location. This recently discovered microclimate creates a fascinating character for which St. Supery wines are known. **DIRECTIONS:** In the middle of the Napa Valley on Hwy 29 in the Pope Valley at the Dollarhide Ranch.

Hours: 9:30 am - 4:30 pm   Days: Monday - Friday
Advance Notice: Yes   Fee: No   HP Access: Yes

Safety Center, Inc. (school)   SIC Code: 8299
3909 Bradshaw Road
Sacramento, CA 95827
916-366-7233   Contact: Terry Polvado

A one hour walk through a miniature American town built at 1/3 scale where children will learn everyday skills including safety skills for Preschool Kids through 6th grade. **NOTE:** Ideal for children age four through the third grade. **DIRECTIONS:** Hwy 50 east to Bradshaw Rd exit, go south about one mile.

Hours: 8:45 am - 3:30 pm   Days: Monday - Friday (Saturday, a.m.)
Advance Notice: Yes   Fee: $1.00/child   HP Access: Yes

Witter Ranch Historic Farm (ranch)   SIC Code: 0291
3480 Witter Way
Sacramento, CA 95834
916-927-4116   Contact: Ed Witter/Charlene Williams

You will have a first hand view of a ranch that represents the 1915-50 era of farming, including an escorted walk through the old stable, a conducted walk through the crop area, the farm garden and handling of farm animals, a tour of the beautifully-designed Spanish-style ranch house and a demonstration of modern agricultural practices during certain seasons. **NOTE:** Farm has elementary school childrens' program as its main reason for existence.
DIRECTIONS: Convenient freeway access to the ranch via West El Camino interchanges on I - 80 or I - 5. About five miles north of the State Capitol in Sacramento.

Hours: By appointment only
Advance Notice: Yes   Fee: $1.00   HP Access: Limited

KGTV Channel 10 (TV broadcast)   SIC Code: 4833
4600 Air Way (Hwy 94 & 47th)
San Diego, CA 92102
619-237-1010   Contact: Sofia Salgado

The 45 - 90 minute tour of the television studio encompasses viewing the entire television process. **DIRECTIONS:** From Rt 5 north or south take Rt 94 going east and get off at the Home Ave offramp, take left to first light, right on Federal Blvd, right on 47th St, go about 200 yards, take right on Air Way.

Hours: 1:00 or 2:30 pm   Days: Wednesdays
Advance Notice: Yes   Fee: No   HP Access: Yes

M. L. Sellers Processing & Dist. Center (postal)   SIC Code: 4311
11251 Rancho Carmel Drive
San Diego, CA 92199-9997
619-674-0109   Contact: Maureen

A one hour tour of the U. S. Postal Processing and Distribution Center handling hundreds of thousands of mail of all sizes will include a 15 - minute video and a tour of the plant's very large mail processing operation. **DIRECTIONS:** I - 15 to Carmel Mountain Rd, east to Rancho Carmel Dr, north to facility.

Hours: 8:00 am - 5:00 pm   Days: Monday - Friday
Advance Notice: Yes   Fee: No   HP Access: Yes

Basic Brown Bears (stuffed toys)   SIC Code 3944
444 De Haro Street
San Francisco, CA 94107
415-626-0781   Contact: Victoria Adams

Plan to tour this teddy bear factory where small family groups of no more than five - six children can visit. **NOTE:** Tours can be set up for larger groups with advance notice. **DIRECTIONS:** Hwy 101 north to Vermont St exit. Cross over Vermont St to Mariposa St to De Haro St, company is on left.

Hours: Call for schedule   Days: Sunday - Saturday
Advance Notice: No   Fee: No   HP Access: Yes

Federal Reserve Bank/San Francisco (bank)   SIC Code: 6021
101 Market Street
San Francisco, CA 94105
415-974-3252   Contact: Amy Westphal/Carla Gomez

This 90 - minute tour begins in the Bank's Interpretive Center with a videotape presentatation which will familiarize you with Federal Reserve history and operations. Following this, a tour guide will lead you through the major operational areas of the Bank. Check processing procedures are explained as you go to another area of the Bank where checks are sorted at an average rate of 140,000/hr, 24 hours a day. **NOTE:** Tours are by appointment only and can accommodate up to 30 people per tour. **DIRECTIONS:** Located downtown.

Hours: 12:30 pm   Days: Monday - Thursday
Advance Notice: Yes   Fee: No   HP Access: Yes

San Jose Processing & Dist. Center (postal)   SIC Code 4311
1750 Lundy Avenue
San Jose, CA 95101-8000
408-437-6609   Contact: Joe Flores

A tour of the U. S. Postal Processing & Distribution Center will show the automation equipment and the manual and mechanized operations of the workroom floor. **DIRECTIONS:** Corner of Lundy Ave and Hostetter Rd in North San Jose.

Hours: 8:00 am - 8:00 pm   Days: Wednesdays
Advance Notice: Yes   Fee: No   HP Access: No

Santa Barbara Orchid Estate (floriculture)   SIC Code: 0181
1250 Orchid Drive
Santa Barbara, CA 93111
805-967-1284 (800-553-3387)   Contact: May

This is a self-guided tour, located just 500 feet from the Pacific Ocean, where you will see over 100 varieties of orchids displayed on two acres of estate. This family owned business is one of the world's foremost collectors and propagators of orchid species and hybrids.
DIRECTIONS: From Los Angeles, take Fwy 101 north to Santa Barbara. Get off Fwy 101 at Patterson Avenue and follow signs.

Advance Notice: Yes   Fee: No   HP Access: Yes

Santa Barbara Winery (winery)   SIC Code 2084
202 Anacapa Street
Santa Barbara, CA 93101
805-963-3646 (800-225-3633)   Contact: Laila Rashid

This tour includes inspection of wine production, facility barrel room, bottling line and tasting of some of the featured wines, Chardonnay, Sauvignon Blanc, Chenin Blanc, Riesling, White Zinfandel, Pinot Noir, and Cabernet Sauvignon. **DIRECTIONS:** 101 Fwy to Garden St exit. Turn right on Yanonali. Winery is on the corner of Yanonali and Anacapa, just two blocks from the beach.

Hours: 11:30 am and 3:30 pm   Days: Monday - Friday
Advance Notice: No   Fee: No   HP Access: Yes

Santa Barbara Olive Company, Inc. (olives)   SIC Code: 0191
3280 Calzada Avenue
Santa Ynez, CA 93460
805-688-9917   Contact: Craig Makela

A tour of this farm where olives are grown and processed will include tasting and a short talk about the growth and harvest of olives. **NOTE:** Tour must be scheduled in advance.
DIRECTIONS: Take Fwy 101 to Hwy 154 to Roblar to Calzada.

Hours: By appointment
Advance Notice: Yes   Fee: No   HP Access: No

KCBQ Radio (radio broadcast)   SIC Code: 4832
9416 Mission Gorge Road
Santee, CA 92071
619-570-1170   Contact: Lisa Ashby

A 20 - 30 minute informal tour in which you will see how a major market radio station operates day to day. The building that houses KCBQ is the only building in San Diego that was actually built to be a radio station, so there's lots to see. **DIRECTIONS:** Located on Hwy 52 near junction at Rt 67, north of El Cajon.

Hours: By appointment
Advance Notice: Yes   Fee: No   HP Access: No

Seiad Valley Vineyards (winery)   SIC Code: 2084
45011 Highway 96
Seiad Valley, CA 96086
916-496-3325   Contact: Brian Helsaple

Learn the history of the gold dredge that left Seiad's fertile soils covered with river rocks in 1940. Sample the wine made in the German style from vines rooted on their own rootstocks extracting characten from the gold that early miners missed. See home made machines accomplish tasks that large wineries spend thousands of dollars to do. **DIRECTIONS:** From I - 5 go 53 miles west on Hwy 96 to yellow bulldozer with "Winery" on the blade.

Hours: By appointment   Days: Monday - Friday
Advance Notice: Yes   Fee: No   HP Access: Yes

Rowdy Creek Fish Hatchery (hatchery)   SIC Code: 0921
255 South Fred Haight Drive
Smith River, CA 95567
707-487-3443   Contact: Robert D. Will

Tour this public fish hatchery located on the Smith River which is noted for huge steelhead (up to 30 lbs) and chinook salmon (up to 100 lbs). **DIRECTIONS:** Located on US 101 in the northwestern corner of the state. Located behind the Post Office.

Hours: 9:00 am - 4:30 pm   Days: Monday - Sunday
Advance Notice: No   Fee: No   HP Access: Yes Gloria Ferrer

Gloria Ferrer Champagne Caves (winery)   SIC Code: 2084
23555 State Highway 121
Sonoma, CA 95476
707-996-7256   Contact: Tom Scott

A 30 - minute walk through of this state-of-the-art wine making facility where you will see their detailed method of making champagne and the wine making process. You will also have an opportunity to walk through man-made caves which are used for the aging process. **DIRECTIONS:** Fwy 101 north of the Golden Gate Bridge to Hwy 37 to Hwy 121, six miles from Sears Point Raceway.

Hours: 11:00 am - 4:00 pm   Days: Monday - Sunday
Advance Notice: No   Fee: No   HP Access: Yes

Sonoma Cheese Factory (cheese processor)   SIC Code: 2022
2 Spain Street (On the Plaza)
Sonoma, CA 95476
707-996-1000 (800-535-2855)   Contact: David Viviani or Lou Biaggi

See the cheesemaking process from a viewing window and enjoy the self-activated slide presentation describing the process as well. **DIRECTIONS:** 44 miles from Golden Gate Bridge in the heart of Sonoma's Wine & Cheese Country.

Hours: 9:00 am - 5:00 pm   Days: Monday - Sunday
Advance Notice: No   Fee: No   HP Access: Yes

Beringer Vineyards (winery)   SIC Code: 2084
200 Main Street (Highway 29)
St. Helena, CA 94574
707-963-4812   Contact: Ann Williams

Guided tour of an 1877 winery which includes a discussion of the vineyard and winemaking processes. **NOTE:** Complimentary tasting of award-winning wines and discussion of each. **DIRECTIONS:** On Hwy 29 north of St. Helena (in the heart of the Napa Valley).

Hours: 9:30 am - 5:00 pm   Days: Monday - Sunday
Advance Notice: No   Fee: No   HP Access: Yes

Charles Krug Winery (winery)   SIC Code: 2084
2800 Main Street (Hwy 29)
St. Helena, CA 94574
707-967-2245   Contact: Karen Hakim

A one - hour historical and production tour of this oldest winery in the Napa Valley including wine tasting. The Winery produces Cabernet Sauvignon, Chardonnay, Merlot, Pinot Noir and White Zinfandel along with many other fine wines. **NOTE:** There will be about 40 - 45 minutes of walking and standing. Closed Wednesdays and special holidays. **DIRECTIONS:** The winery is located just north of St. Helena on Hwy 29 in the heart of the Napa Valley.

Hours: Call for times   Days: Monday - Sunday
Advance Notice: No   Fee: No   HP Access: Yes

Merryvale Vineyards (winery)   SIC Code: 2084
1000 Main Street
St. Helena, CA 94574
707-963-2225   Contact: Jacqui Norman

You will have a view of the historic cask room with a brief history of the Napa Valley and Merryvale, an overview of the winemaking process with a special emphasis on their philosophy. You will then taste unparalleled wines in a unique setting of Merryvale, the mandatory stop in the Napa Valley. **DIRECTIONS:** Located at the southern entrance to St. Helena off Hwy 29.

Hours: By appointment only
Advance Notice: Yes   Fee: $3.00   HP Access: Yes

Stanford Linear Accelerator Center (research)   SIC Code: 8731
2575 Sand Hill Road
Stanford, CA 94309
415-926-2204   Contact: Pauline Wellington

This two hour tour of the facility begins with an orientation meeting and slide presentation followed by a guided bus tour of the 426 - acre facility. **NOTE:** Tours should be scheduled at least one week in advance. Children must be at least 11 years old. **DIRECTIONS:** Located adjacent to Menlo Park, west of the Stanford campus, east of Hwy 280.

Hours: 9:00 am or 1:00 pm   Days: Monday - Saturday
Advance Notice: Yes   Fee: No   HP Access: Yes

Stockton Processing & Dist. Center (postal)   SIC Code: 4311
3131 Arch-Airport Road
Stockton, CA 95213-9998
209-983-637   Contact: Ron Brooks

On the tour of the U. S. Postal Processing & Distribution Center, you will see the workroom floor and dock area where many of the operations take place. In addition, you will visit the cancellation, automation, mechanization and manual processing operations as well. **DIRECTIONS:** At exit off Hwy 99, between Stockton & Manteca.

Hours: 24 hours/day   Days: Monday - Sunday
Advance Notice: Yes   Fee: No   HP Access: Yes

Thornton Winery (winery)   SIC Code: 2084
32575 Rancho California Road
Temecula, CA 92591
909-699-0099   Contact: Edy Church

Touring this facility will include showing of the tanks and caves where thousands of bottles are aging. Thornton Winery produces Culbertson sparkling wines and Brindiamo still wines. **NOTE:** Wine tasting of four wines, two sparkling and two still wines for $6.00 per person. **DIRECTIONS:** I - 15 east on Rancho California Rd for four miles. Located on right side.

Hours: 9:00 am - 4:00 pm   Days: Saturday - Sunday
Advance Notice: No   Fee: No   HP Access: Yes

Aspen Cellars (winery)   SIC Code: 2084
Route 2 (Box 3966)
Trinity Center, CA 96091
530-266-3363   Contact: Mark or Keith Groves

This tour is a must, due to the combination of high elevation and favorable microclimate which proves to be the ideal conditions for growing early maturing vinifera grapes such as White Riesling, Gewurztraminer, Chardonnay and Pinot Noir, the four varieties to which the ranch vineyard is planted. **NOTE:** Free wine tasting. Retail store. **DIRECTIONS:** Trinity Center is located approximately 25 miles north of Weaverville on Rt 299 between Eureka and Redding. Watch for signs.

Hours: By appointment   Days: Monday - Friday
Advance Notice: Yes   Fee: No   HP Access: No

Medic Alert Foundation (metal goods mfr)   SIC Code: 3499
2323 Colorado Avenue
Turlock, CA 95380
209-668-3333   Contact: Kathleen Feuerstein

This 30 - minute tour begins with a video presentation. You will visit the Information Technology Center, the 24 hour Emergency Response Center and the Manufacturing Department where the engraving process is explained. **NOTE:** 24 hour advance notice is appreciated for groups larger than eight. **DIRECTIONS:** From Hwy 99 take Monte Vista Ave east, past CSU Stanislaus, take a right on Colorado Ave.

Hours: 8:00 am - 3:00 pm   Days: Monday - Friday
Advance Notice: No   Fee: No   HP Access: Yes

Dreyer's Grand & Edy's Grand Ice Cream (ice cream)   SIC Code: 2024
1250 Whipple Road
Union City, CA 94587
510-471-6622   Contact: Michelle Heitman or Susan Biegelow

A one to one and one-half hour tour will include a brief video on the manufacturing of ice cream. You will be taken upstairs to "Rocky Road Lane" where you will look at the production floor through viewing windows onto the manufacturing floor. You will also taste fresh ice cream right off the line and will be taken into the chilly 30 degree below zero "cold box". At the end of the tour, you will be taken back into the "Double Scoop Depot" where you will enjoy a scoop of ice cream. **NOTE:** You must make arrangements at least two months in advance. No cameras, closed-toed shoes only. Please bring a sweater or coat for the walk through freezer. Gift shop. **DIRECTIONS:** 30 minutes from San Francisco. Take Bay Bridge to Hwy 980 south to Hwy 880 south. Exit at Whipple/Dyer. Go east on Whipple.

Hours: 9:15,11:15,2:00   Days: Monday - Friday
Advance Notice: Yes   Fee: $2.00   HP Access: Limited

Bates Nut Farm (nuts)   SIC Code: 0173
15954 Woods Valley Road
Valley Center, CA 92082
619-749-3333   Contact: Carol Hughes or Peggy Rogers

Visit this farm and smell the lingering fragrance of fresh peanut butter, see rows and rows of your favorite nuts and dried fruits and candies. **NOTE:** This eight acre farm has beautiful trees and park grounds, excellent for picnicking. **DIRECTIONS:** Take I-15 to 78 east into the city of Escondido. Freeway will come to an end at Broadway. Cross Broadway and continue on to Ash, turn right to Valley Pkwy. Turn left and continue nine miles to Woods Valley Rd. Stay on this road for three and one-half miles to the farm, which is on the left.

Hours: 9:15,11:15, 2:00 pm   Days: Monday - Friday
Advance Notice: Yes   Fee: No   HP Access: Yes

Domaine Chandon Winery (winery)   SIC Code: 2084
One California Drive
Yountville, CA 94599
707-944-2280   Contact: Judy Gee

Each 30 - minute tour is conducted by a knowledgeable staff member trained in all aspects of
the methode champenoise. You will visit the demonstration vineyard where Chardonnay,
Pinot Blanc, Pinot Noir and Pinot Meunier vines are planted in the style of Champagne. In
the winery, you will see an impressive array of tanks containing still wines. The tour ends in
the bottling room where the wines are disgorged and dressed for market. **NOTE:**
Champagne tasting is available. Advance notice is necessary for large groups.
DIRECTIONS: In the Napa Valley take exit Hwy 29 at Yountville-Veterans Home and turn
west toward the Veterans Home. After the railroad tracks, turn right.

Hours: 11:00 am - 6:00 pm   Days: Monday - Sunday
Advance Notice: No   Fee: No   HP Access: Yes

Celestial Seasonings Inc. (tea)   SIC Code: 5149
4600 Sleepytime Drive
Boulder, CO 80301
970-581-1202   Contact: Steve Spencer

On this one-hour tour you can see, taste and smell the world of tea. You will visit the Art Department and see their famous packaging in the making; in the Research and Development Labs you will learn how herbs and spices are blended to make the world's best tea; in the factory you will stroll through their rock and roll plant and see how they get all the herbs and spices into those tiny tea bags. **NOTE:** Ages five and older for children is a must. Flat-soled shoes recommended. Tea Shop and Cafe. **DIRECTIONS:** Take US 36, Boulder Tnpk, to the Foothills Pkwy which becomes the Diagonal Hwy, to Jay Rd, turn right and continue one mile east to Spine. Left on Spine one-half mile and left on Sleepytime Dr.

Hours: 10:00 am - 3:00 pm   Days: Monday - Saturday
Advance Notice: Yes   Fee: No   HP Access: Yes

Eco-Cycle (recycling center)   SIC Code: 5093
5030 Pearl Street
Boulder, CO 80301
970-444-6634   Contact: Zita Lynn

This is a 45 - minute tour of a recycling process center where you will see what happens to recyclables after they are collected from the curb or drop-off center. You will visit the sorting, baling and shipping departments as materials are prepared to be sent to remanufacturing facilities. **NOTE:** This is an outdoor facility so you should be prepared for current weather conditions. Closed-toed shoes are required. Groups of six or more adults (children must be over age 10) should schedule appointment one week in advance. **DIRECTIONS:** From Denver, north on I - 25 to Hwy 36 north to Foothills Pkwy. East on Pearl Pkwy to 49th St, and east on Pearl St to Eco-Cycle's mail box. Park in Visitors Parking area.

Hours: 9:30 am - 3:30 pm   Days: Tuesday - Friday
Advance Notice: Yes   Fee: No   HP Access: No

Colorado Springs Processing & Dist. Center (postal)   SIC Code: 4311
3655 East Fountain Boulevard
Colorado Springs, CO 80910-9998
719-570-5372   Contact: Sandra Claus

On the U. S. Postal Processing & Distribution Center tour, you will see a 19 - minute film, "An Adventure of a Letter", followed by a walk-through of the plant and carrier section with an explanation of each area. **DIRECTIONS:** Located on the corner of South Academy Blvd and East Fountain Blvd.

Hours: 6:00 am - 1:00 pm   Days: Tuesday - Saturday
Advance Notice: Yes   Fee: No   HP Access: Yes

Patsy's Candies (candy mfr)   SIC Code: 2064
1540 South 21st Street
Colorado Springs, CO 80904
719-633-7215   Contact: Annette

On this 30 - minute tour of a confectionery plant you will visit the exciting world of chocolates and confections and see them made on the premises. **NOTE:** Generous samples. Call for times except during June - August. **DIRECTIONS:** From I - 25, take exit 141, head west. Turn left on 21st St.

Hours: 2:00 pm   Days: Tuesday (June - August)
Advance Notice: No   Fee: No   HP Access:

Van Briggle Art Pottery (pottery products)   SIC Code: 3269
600 South 21st Street
Colorado Springs, CO 80904
719-633-4080   Contact: Craig Stevenson,

The tour takes you through the studios where artisans create distinctive art pottery, including a demonstration of throwing the potter's wheel, one of the oldest art forms in history. You will also watch the various steps involved in the creation of fine art pottery including glazing and firing. These creations include figurines, American Indian busts and distinctive lamp shades, bowls, vases and lamps. **NOTE:** Gift shop. **DIRECTIONS:** From Denver, go south on I - 25, exit at US 24, go west to 21st.

Hours: 8:00 am - 4:30 pm   Days: Monday - Saturday
Advance Notice: No   Fee: No   HP Access: Yes

Denver Processing & Dist. Center (postal)   SIC Code: 4311
7500 East 53rd Place
Denver, CO 80266-9997
303-297-6489   Contact: Carol Petersen

At this U. S. Postal Processing & Distribution Center, you will get an overview of the processing of mail and how it gets from the mail box to the customer. **NOTE:** Please call at least 24 hours prior to your visit. **DIRECTIONS:** Located off I - 70 and Quebec in the center of the city.

Hours: 10:00 am - 7:00 pm   Days: Tuesday - Friday
Advance Notice: Yes   Fee: No   HP Access: Yes

KMGH-TV (TV broadcast)   SIC Code: 4833
123 Speer Boulevard
Denver, CO 80203
303-832-0247   Contact: Emilie Leman

The tour of this television studio, an affiliate of CBS, will include the production and news areas where you will see the behind-the-scenes activities of a large network studio.
DIRECTIONS: From US Rt 70, follow US RT 25 south. Exit on Colfax Ave and go east to Spear Blvd.

Hours: 11:00 am - 12:30 pm   Days: Monday - Thursday
Advance Notice: Yes   Fee: No   HP Access: Yes

Rocky Mountain News (newspaper)   SIC Code: 2711
400 West Colfax Avenue
Denver, CO 80204
303-892-2756   Contact: Marilyn Hershberger

On this one hour tour of the Colfax Facility, you will see how the paper is designed, incorporating advertising and editorial through sophisticated technology. You will see the production area and learn how the paper is produced through the use of robots. You will also see five new Gross Colorliner presses and the high technology inserting systems. **NOTE:** Tour is for third graders and older. **DIRECTIONS:** Spier Blvd to Colfax east.

Hours: 8:00 am - 5:00 pm   Days: Monday - Thursday
Advance Notice: Yes   Fee: No   HP Access: Yes

Anheuser-Busch Brewery (brewery)   SIC Code: 2082
2351 Busch Drive
Fort Collins, CO 80524
970-490-4694   Contact: Tour Department

In this 90 - minute guided tour, you will walk to the Brew Hall viewing area overlooking the state-of-the-art brewing control room. Then you will watch the amazing high-speed packaging lines at work, which will be followed by a chance to visit the lager cellar. **NOTE:** Complimentary samples. Soft drinks for the kids. The tour's grand finale is a visit to the Budweiser Clydesdale Hamlet, where those enormous horses are housed. **DIRECTIONS:** Take I - 25 to Mountain Vista Dr (exit 271), turn right onto Busch Dr.

Hours: 10:00 am - 4:00 pm   Days: Wednesday - Sunday (November - Apr)
Advance Notice: Yes   Fee: No   HP Access: Yes

Coors Brewing Company (brewery)   SIC Code: 2082
13th & Ford Streets
Golden, CO 80401
970-227-2337   Contact: Lynette Gomes

Take a 30 - minute walking tour of this famous brewing plant and see their unique brewing methods and learn about the finest natural ingredients used to create their superior quality products. The entire tour, including free tasting (non-alcoholic drinks are available) takes about one and one-half hours. **DIRECTIONS:** Take Sixth Ave west to 19th St in Golden, turn right and follow 19th St to the third light, which is Ford St. Turn left to 13th St. Parking lot is on right.

Hours: 10:00 am - 4:00 pm   Days: Monday - Saturday
Advance Notice: No   Fee: No   HP Access: Yes

Hakushika Sake USA Corp (brewery)   SIC Code: 2082
4414 Table Mountain Drive
Golden, CO 80403
970-279-7253   Contact: Nori Robinson

On this one hour tour of a Japanese Sake Brewery you will learn about the over 330 years of history of sake which came to Colorado in 1992. You will visit the Guest House where you will enjoy a large collection of Japanese wood cut prints. **NOTE:** Reservations are required. **DIRECTIONS:** From Denver, take I - 70 west to exit 265. At McIntyre go right over 44th Ave and railroad tracks and left at Service Dr to stop sign. Look for the brewery on the left.

Hours: 10:00 am - 4:00 pm   Days: Monday - Friday
Advance Notice: Yes   Fee: No   HP Access: Limited

Eco-Cycle (recycling center)   SIC Code: 5093
111 South Martin Street
Longmont, CO 80501
970-772-7300   Contact: Kat Bennett

The approximate one hour tour of this recycling drop-off center and material processing facility will enable you to see the sorting of commingled glass, cans and plastics for respective markets. Tour may include hands-on sorting, if desired and planned in advance. **NOTE:** Groups of children need one adult per three children. All tours must be scheduled in advance. This is an outdoor facility so be prepared for the weather. Closed-toe shoes required. Dress casual. **DIRECTIONS:** From Denver north on I - 25 to Hwy 119 exit and west into Longmont. After first traffic light, take first left. Two blocks south. Beige building.

Hours: 8:00 am - 4:00 pm   Days: Monday - Saturday
Advance Notice: Yes   Fee: No   HP Access: Yes

Grande River Vineyard and Winery (winery)   SIC Code: 2084
787 Elberta Avenue
Palisade, CO 81526-0129
970-464-5867   Contact: Marlien Weller

This is a 15 - 30 minute tour of the winemaking facility which has won many national and international awards for their 100% premium Colorado grown wines from grapes grown in their own vineyards (estate bottled). **NOTE:** Free samples. **DIRECTIONS:** Located off I - 70 at exit 42 (Palisade), or Hwy 6 turn north at Elberta Ave (37.3 Rd) for one mile.

Hours: 10:00 am -6:00 pm   Days: Monday - Sunday
Advance Notice: Yes   Fee: No   HP Access: Yes

Nutmeg Vineyard (winery)   SIC Code: 2084
800 Bunker Hill Road
Andover, CT 06232-0146
860-742-8402   Contact: Tony Maulucci

A self-guided tour of the vineyards and wine tasting where a new family of grapes of European-American ancestry have made wine growing possible in certain micro-climates when combined with the proper varieties.   Some of their wines include Seyval Blanc, Baco Noir, Raspberry, Strawberry and Angel Wings. **DIRECTIONS:** Located about 20 minutes east of Manchester. Rt 84 to Rt 384 to Rt 6 east. Bunker Hill Rd is on the left just beyond the traffic lights in Andover.

Hours: 11:00 am - 5:00 pm   Days: Saturday - Sunday
Advance Notice: No   Fee: No   HP Access: No

Arteffects (signs)   SIC Code: 3993
27 Britton Drive
Bloomfield, CT 06002
860-242-0031   Contact: Lawrin D. Rosen

Take an approximate one hour tour of this facility where you will see all kinds of award-winning signs being made. You will visit the neon and sign letters gallery, see computer layouts, the Arts Department, and the Shop. **DIRECTIONS:** Exit 35B off Rt 91. Cottage Grove Rd off of Blue Hills Ave, end of Britton Dr.

Hours: 9:00 am - 4:00 pm   Days: Tuesday - Friday
Advance Notice: Yes   Fee: No   HP Access: Yes

DiGrazia Vineyards (winery)   SIC Code 2084
131 Tower Road
Brookfield, CT 06804
800-852-6961   Contact: Mark Langford

Guided tour of winery in which you will view automated bottling line and a modern plant facility in a small environment. This winery makes fifteen styles of premium table and dessert wines, including Anastasia's Blush, Yankee Frost and Magnolia.. **DIRECTIONS:** Exit 9 off I - 84, go north on Rt 25, follow wine trail.

Hours: 11:00 am - 5:00 pm   Days: Wednesday-Sunday (May-December)
Advance Notice: No   Fee: No   HP Access: Yes

Wright's Mill Tree Farm (trees)   SIC Code: 5261
63 Creasy Road
Canterbury, CT 06331
860-774-1455   Contact: Debbie or Al

The tours may focus on Christmas Tree culture, scenic beauty, nature or bird watching. You will learn the history of the use of water power at this site from earliest settlement times. The tour may touch on a bit of everything, depending upon season. **NOTE:** Self-guided tours at any time with no charge. Guided tours by appointment only and there is a small fee. **DIRECTIONS:** Rt 6 to Brooklyn Rd, or Rt 160 or Rt 14 to Canterbury and follow the signs.

Hours: By appointment
Advance Notice: Yes   Fee: No   HP Access: Yes

Quinebaug Valley Trout Hatchery (hatchery)   SIC Code: 0921
Trout Hatchery Road
Central Village, CT 06332
860-564-7542   Contact: Manager

This is a 30 - minute self-guided tour of one of the largest hatcheries in the East. This hatchery produces 280,000 pounds of trout annually. You will be able to see the hatchery through a glass wall. **NOTE:** Guided tours with advance reservations. Minimum group is 12. **DIRECTIONS:** From I - 395, take exit 89. Follow signs.

Hours: 8:30 am - 5:00 pm   Days: Monday - Friday
Advance Notice: No   Fee: No   HP Access: Yes

Old New-Gate Prison/Copper Mine (copper mine)   SIC Code: 1021
Newgate Road
East Granby, CT 06026
860-653-3563   Contact: Manager

A guided tour of America's first chartered copper mine and Connecticut's first state prison used by the Continental Congress to house Loyalist prisoners. Tour the copper mine's underground caverns and learn about Early American mining of this rich mineral. **NOTE:** Minimum group is 10. Open Mid-May - October 31. **DIRECTIONS:** From I - 91, take exit 40. Look for signs.

Hours: 10:00 am - 4:30 pm   Days: Wednesday - Sunday
Advance Notice: No   Fee: $1.50   HP Access: Yes

Connecticut Yankee Information/Science Ctr (utility)   SIC Code: 5093
362 Injun Hollow Road
Haddam Neck, CT 06424
203-267-9279   Contact: Anthony E. Nericcio

You are welcome to tour through the center's exhibit area and see planned energy programs, play energy computer games, displays and hands-on exhibits which explain basic energy, electricity and nuclear concepts. **DIRECTIONS:** Located on the east bank of the Connecticut River about 25 minutes from Middletown. Follow Rt 151 to Haddam Neck Rd. Bear right at the fork and proceed down a steep hill for 3/4 mile. At the fork, turn left.

Hours: 9:00 am - 4:00 pm   Days: Monday - Friday,
            10:00 am - 4:00 pm   Saturday
Advance Notice: Yes   Fee: No   HP Access: Yes

Channel 13 Television (TV broadcast)   SIC Code: 4833
886 Maple Avenue
Hartford, CT 061114
860-956-1303   Contact: Lucco Ruzzier, Sr.

A tour of this television station includes a visit to the television and radio broadcasting studios, control room, and editing facilities. Watch live and behind the scenes activities to get a full appreciation of the broadcast medium. **DIRECTIONS:** Exit 27 from Rt 91 to Airport Rd to Maple Ave.

Hours: 9-:00 am - 5:00 pm   Days: Monday - Friday
Advance Notice: Yes   Fee: No   HP Access: Yes

Mid-CT Regional Recycling Center (recycling center)   SIC Code: 5093
211 Murphy Road
Hartford, CT 06114
860-247-4280   Contact: Cheryl L. Burke

The tour begins at the "Temple of Trash" which will show the old way and the new way of recycling. There are games to help you understand the recycling importance. You will see the Container Processing Facility where items are crushed or baled to make them ready to become new products. **DIRECTIONS:** Take I - 91 to exit 27, Airport Rd, bear right. Turn left on Murphy Rd, approximately 1/4 mile.

Hours   10:00 am - 4:00 pm   Days: Tuesday - Saturday (July - August)
            12 noon - 4:00 pm   Wednesday-Friday (September-June)
Advance Notice: Yes   Fee: No   HP Access: Yes

The Hartford Courant (newspaper)   SIC Code: 2711
285 Broad Street
Hartford, CT 06115
860-241-6431   Contact: Lievanna Gore

A one hour general tour of the newspaper plant including the newsroom, the photography department, the pre-press area, graphics and layout, and then to the press corridor where, through a glass window, you can view the presses at work. **NOTE:** Children must be above the third grade. Presses are usually in operation Tuesday - Friday between 9:00 and 11:00 am. If you are interested in seeing the newsroom when it is busy, it is best to schedule your tour later in the day, when many of the reporters are filing their stories. **DIRECTIONS:** From the east, take I - 84 west to Hartford. Take the Asylum St exit. At light, bear right and then left at fork. Continue straight on Farmington Ave to first light. Take left onto Broad St. The facility is on the right just beyond the bridge. The visitor's parking lot is just after M & M Travel.

Hours: 9:00 am - 5:00 pm   Days: Tuesday - Friday
Advance Notice: Yes   Fee: No   HP Access: Yes

Heritage Vineyards (winery)   SIC Code: 2084
291 North Burnham Highway
Lisbon, CT 06351
203-376-0659   Contact: Diane M. Powell

After touring the six acres of vineyards, you will proceed to the winery where you will view the actual winemaking process and visit the large tasting room. **DIRECTIONS:** Exit 83A on I - 395 (north); left at stop sign, winery is three miles on left, or exit 84 on I - 395 (south); right on Rt 12, left on Rt 138, right on Rt 169, winery is two miles on left.

Hours: By appointment only   Days: Monday, Thursday - Sunday
Advance Notice: Yes   Fee: No   HP Access: No

Haight Vineyard, Inc. (winery)   SIC Code: 2084
29 Chestnut Hill Road
Litchfield, CT 06759
860-567-4045 (800-325-5567)   Contact: Wayne Stitzer

This is a 20 - minute guided tour of the wine making process of wines featuring Seyval Blanc, Chardonnay, Riesling, and Matechal Foch. **NOTE:** Continual free tastings.
DIRECTIONS: One mile from Litchfield, off Rt 118. See state highway sign.

Hours: 10:30 am - 5:00 pm   Days: Monday - Saturday
        12:00 noon - 5:00 pm   Sunday
Advance Notice: Yes   Fee: No   HP Access: Yes

Cox Cable, Inc. (TV cable svcs)   SIC Code: 4841
801 Parker Street
Manchester, CT 06040
860-646-6289   Contact: Dan McNamara

Take this interesting tour and learn about the daily operations of cable television including a look at a full television production studio. **DIRECTIONS:** I - 84 east from Hartford to exit 63, left off ramp, first right.

Hours: 9:00 am - 4:00 pm   Days: Monday - Friday
Advance Notice: Yes   Fee: No   HP Access: Yes

Wesleyan Potters (pottery products)   SIC Code: 3269
350 South Main Street
Middletown, CT 06457
860-347-5925   Contact: Melissa

A one hour guided tour of this prestigious craft gallery will show you handcrafted items on exhibit, including jewelry, as well as the pottery and weaving studios. **NOTE:** Gift Shop.
DIRECTIONS: Located in downtown Middletown. Call for specific directions.

Hours: 11:00 am - 5:00 pm   Days: Tuesday - Saturday
Advance Notice: No   Fee: No   HP Access: Yes

New Haven Brewing Company (brewery)   SIC Code: 2082
458 Grand Avenue
New Haven, CT 06513
203-772-2739 (800-356-2489)   Contact: Michael Gettings

A 45 - minute tour of the Elm City Ales & Blackwell Stout brewery, where you will receive
an overview of how beer is made, packaged and sold. **NOTE:** Free samples.
DIRECTIONS: Rt 91 south to exit 2 (Hamilton St). Take left at end of ramp, (East St) and
right at first light (Grand Ave). Brewery is located 2/10 mile on right.

Hours: 11:00 a.m.   Days: Saturday only
Advance Notice: Yes   Fee: No   HP Access: Yes

Shubert Performing Arts Center (theater)   SIC Code: 7922
247 College Street
New Haven, CT 06510
203-624-1825   Contact: Joanna Spencer

Take a tour of the entire theatre backstage, including the prop and makeup areas, costumes,
and much more. **NOTE:** Tours are by appointment only. **DIRECTIONS:** From I - 95,
take exit 47 (downtown New Haven) to Rt 34 Connector. Get off at exit 1. At the light. take
a right onto Church St. At third light, take a left onto Chapel St. At second light, take a left
onto College St.

Hours/Days: By appointment only
Advance Notice: Yes   Fee: No   HP Access: Yes

Hopkins Vineyard & Winery (winery)   SIC Code: 2084
25 Hopkins Road
New Preston, CT 06777
860-868-7954   Contact: Jennifer Corrigan

A self-guided tour of the 30 - acre vineyard and winery which overlooks beautiful Lake
Watamaug. This vineyard grows both vinefera and French-American Hybrid grapes,
producing an impressive and varied list of award winning wines which have won many gold
and silver medals in national and international competitions. **DIRECTIONS:** From New
Haven, follow Rt 67 north to Rt 202 east at New Milford. Follow Rt 202 to New Preston.
Right on Rt 45 north for two and one-half miles, first left after passing lake, and then second
right on Hopkins.

Hours: 10:00 am - 5:00 pm   Days: Monday-Sunday
Advance Notice: No   Fee: No   HP Access: Yes

Northeast Utilities System (utility)   SIC Code: 4939
Mill Stone Power Station
278 Main Street
Niantic, CT 06357
203-444-4234   Contact: Tony Spinelli

Tour the Millstone Nuclear Power Station, Nature Trail, Simulator Training Building, Plant
Turbine Hall, and the Environmental Lab. You will learn how a nuclear power plant works,
energy from the sun and the wind, food preservation and radiation and radioactive waste.
NOTE: Call two weeks in advance. **DIRECTIONS:** From New Haven and points west,
take I - 95 north to exit 72 (Rocky Neck Connector). Left to Rt 156 and proceed eastbound to
Niantic Center.

Hours/Days: Call for appointment
Advance Notice: Yes   Fee: No   HP Access: Yes

Catnip Acres Herb Nursery (herbs)   SIC Code: 0181
67 Christian Street
Oxford,CT 06478
203-888-5649   Contact: Manager

This is a 20 - minute guided tour where you will see over 400 varieties of herb plants and
scented geraniums. You will visit the formal and informal herb gardens and the greenhouse.
NOTE: Minimum group is 20. Closed January 15 - March 1 and holidays. **DIRECTIONS:**
I - 84 to exit 15, then follow Rt 8 to exit 22. Look for signs.

Hours: 10:00 am - 5:00 pm   Days: Monday - Saturday
Advance Notice: No   Fee: $1.00   HP Access: Yes

McLaughlin Vineyards (winery)   SIC Code: 2084
Alberts Hill Road
Sandy Hook, CT 06482
203-426-1533   Contact: Morgen McLaughlin

This tour of a winery with tastings of current wines is located along the banks of the
Housatonic River. This 100+ acre estate includes over 18 acres of vines, hiking trails and
plenty of room to sit back and absorb the natural beauty of the land. **NOTE:** Free samples.
DIRECTIONS: Exit 10 off I - 84 toward Sandy Hook. Left onto Walnut Tree Hill Rd, keep
bearing right for two miles. At island in the road, bear left.

Hours/Days: By appointment   Days: Monday - Sunday
Advance Notice: Yes   Fee: No   HP Access: No

Warren Corporation (woolen mill)   SIC Code: 2231
8&29 Furnace Avenue
Stafford Springs, CT 06076
860-684-2766   Contact: Michele Parrett

A two hour walking tour of a high quality apparel manufacturing facility which produces cashmere, camel hair, and worsted wool. You will tour the entire manufacturing process, from raw stock into finish bulk of fabric of high quality apparel fabric. **NOTE:** Many stairs involved! **DIRECTIONS:** Exit 70 off I - 84, Rt 32 north four miles, straight through the intersection.

Hours: By appointment only.   Days: Last Friday of month only
Advance Notice: Yes   Fee: No   HP Access: No

Stonington Vineyards (winery)   SIC Code: 2084
523 Taugwonk Road
Stonington, CT 06378
860-535-1222   Contact: Nick Smith

Guided tour of a working farm winery where you will learn how wine is processed from grapes to finished bottle. **NOTE:** Group tours by appointment only. There is a charge for groups. **DIRECTIONS:** Take exit 91 on I - 95, then west on Rt 184 to Taugwonk Rd.

Hours: 2:00 pm,   Days: Monday - Sunday
Advance Notice: Yes   Fee: No   HP Access: No

Comstock, Ferre & Co. (seeds)   SIC Code: 0181
263 Main Street
Wethersfield, CT 06109
860-571-6590   Contact: Roger Willard

Tour the nation's oldest continuously operating seed company (since 1720) and visit the outside gardens (seasonal), main store area, seed storage and seed packing areas. **NOTE:** Handicap accessible to main store only. Seed tour is mostly upstairs. **DIRECTIONS:** Rt 91 south, exit 26, follow signs to Main St.

Hours: 9:00 am - 3:00 pm   Days: Monday - Friday
Advance Notice: Yes   Fee: No   HP Access: No

Nanticoke Homes, Inc. (home construction)   SIC Code: 1521
Route 13 - P.O.Box F
Greenwood, DE 19950-0506
302-349-4561 (800-777-4561)   Contact: Tonda Parks/Ann Bunting

A walking tour of an in-plant home construction company where you will learn how homes
are built in six days and are 85% complete when delivered to the homeowners lot. **NOTE:**
You will be required to wear safety glasses and hard hats. Comfortable shoes and long pants
are recommended. Children must be accompanied by a responsible adult at all times. For
groups of 10 or more, one week advance notice is required. **DIRECTIONS:** Rt 13
southbound to Greenwood. Greenwood is 22 miles south of Dover and approximately 30
miles north of Salisbury, MD.

Hours: 8:00-11:00 /1:00-3:00   Days: Monday - Friday
Advance Notice: Yes   Fee: No   HP Access: No

The Washington Post (newspaper)   SIC Code: 2711
1150 15th Street NW
Washington, DC 20071
202-334-7969   Contact: Public Relations

This is a 45 - minute general tour of a newspaper plant which will show the process of how the newspaper is put together. **NOTE:** Children must be in fifth grade or 11 years old. Closed holidays. **DIRECTIONS:** 15th St at L St.

Hours:10:00,11:00,1:00,2:00   Days: Monday
Advance Notice: Yes   Fee: No   HP Access: Yes

Washington DC Processing & Dist. Center (postal)   SIC Code: 4311
900 Brentwood Road NE
Washington, DC 20066-9998
202-636-1200   Contact: LuVenia Broussard

This general tour of the U S. Postal Processing & Distribution Center will demonstrate how the new automated equipment works in handling hundreds of thousands of pieces of mail being processed daily. **DIRECTIONS:** Follow New York Ave northeast from the White House. Go over railroad tracks and turn left on 9th St to Brentwood.

Hours: 8:00 am - 5:00 pm   Days: Monday - Friday
Advance Notice: Yes   Fee: No   HP Access: Yes

Kerlu Tree Farm (trees)   SIC Code: 5261
9590 Boynton Beach Boulevard
Boynton Beach, FL 33437
561-732-7256   Contact: Scott Niebel

Visit one of Florida's largest tropical tree farms where you will see over 10,000 palm trees growing on 60 acres. Many varieties are grown from seedlings and grow over 25 feet tall. The most popular trees grown here are the coconut palm and the royal palm trees. **NOTE:** By appointment only. **DIRECTIONS:** Rt 95 to Boynton Beach Blvd west. Located on the left just beyond Hagen Ranch Rd.

Hours: By appointment only
Advance Notice: Yes   Fee: No   HP Access: Yes

Tropical World (floriculture)   SIC Code: 0181
7281 Hagen Ranch Road
Boynton Beach, FL 33437
561-732-8813   Contact: Bruce Pearson

On this tour you will see cacti, orchids, tropical foliage, aquatic and unusual plants growing in a natural environment and are being cultured in a natural habitat. **NOTE:** Gift shop.
DIRECTIONS: Located on Hagen Ranch Rd between Boynton Beach Blvd and Atlantic Ave, Delray Beach.

Hours: 9:00 am - 5:00 pm   Days: Monday - Saturday
Advance Notice: No   Fee: No   HP Access: Yes

Knollwood Groves (fruit farm)   SIC Code: 0175
8053 Lawrence Road
Boynton Beach, FL 33436
561-734-4800   Contact: Tour Manager

On this 45 - minute tour of one of Palm Beach County's oldest producing citrus groves, you will get a rare step back into Florida's natural and native past. You will take a tram ride through the grove and tropical hammock area where you will have an opportunity to explore the Seminole Village and stop at the alligator pit where you can say hello to 'Big Joe' and his family. **DIRECTIONS:** Exit at Rt 95 on Boynton Beach Blvd and head west to Lawrence Rd. Go north on Lawrence Rd for approximately one mile and the grove will be on your left.

Hours: 9:00 am - 5:00 pm   Days: Monday - Sunday
Advance Notice: No   Fee: $1.00 for tram   HP Access: Yes

Mixon Fruit Farm (fruit farm)   SIC Code: 0175
2712 26th Avenue, East
Bradenton, FL 34208
941-748-5829 (800-608-2525)   Contact: Wendy Mixon

Take a 45 - minute tour of this 350 acre orange grove where you can walk among the fruit trees and enjoy the beauty. The beautiful fruit is a sight to behold. **NOTE:** Free samples of fruit juice and fudge. Gift shop. Groups of 25 or more must make reservations in advance. **DIRECTIONS:** I - 75 to exit 42 (Rt 64) west to 27th St east. Look for signs.

Hours: 8:30 am - 5:30 pm   Days: Monday - Saturday (November - April)
Advance Notice: No   Fee: No   HP Access: Yes

Triple "R" Ranch (ostrich farm)   SIC Code: 0291
8210 County Road 630
Bushnell, FL 33513
352-793-3385   Contact: Esther Ronstrom

This one hour tour of an ostrich and emu farm begins in the incubation hatching facility, then on to the chick rearing facility, the grow out area, and to the breeder's pens. The tour will include an explanation of all phases of the ranch from the incubating to the end products of raising ostrich and emus. **NOTE:** Advance reservations only. See the unusual egg exhibit. **DIRECTIONS:** I - 75 to Webster exit 476B (National Cemetery exit). Follow Road 476B west to Road 476. County Road 630, turn left and the ranch is the third on the right.

Hours: By appointment
Advance Notice: Yes   Fee: $2.50   HP Access: Limited

Lakeridge Winery & Vineyards (winery)   SIC Code: 2084
19239 US 27 North
Clermont, FL 34711
904-394-8627 (800-768-9463)   Contact: Claudia Del Pino

You will see a 15 - minute video of the working farm winery which is followed by a guided
walking tour through the winery where you will view the vineyard production. The tour ends
in the gift shop with a tasting of five different wines. **DIRECTIONS**: Located west of
Orlando, three miles south of the Florida Tpk at exit 285, south on Rt 27, three miles on right.

Hours: 10:00 am - 5:00 pm   Days: Monday - Saturday
            12 noon - 5: 00 pm   Sunday
Advance Notice: Yes   Fee: No   HP Access: Yes

Sun-Sentinel Company (newspaper)   SIC Code: 2711
333 SW 12th Avenue
Deerfield Beach, FL 33442
954-425-1076   Contact: Megan M. Holcombe

A one hour walking tour through a state-of-the-art newspaper production facility. From
videos to robots to thundering presses, the excitement is non-stop as you discover the wonders
of daily newspaper printing. **DIRECTIONS**: I - 95 to Hillsboro Blvd west, turn left at 12th
Ave.

Hours: 9:00 am - 4:00 pm   Days: Tuesday - Friday (selected Saturdays)
Advance Notice: Yes   Fee: No   HP Access: Yes

J.E.M. Orchids (floriculture)   SIC Code: 0181
6595 Morikami Park Road
Delray Beach, FL 33446
561-498-4308   Contact: Jean or Gene Monnier

A visit to this family owned business will include a walking tour of the greenhouses and seedling area where you may see as many as 10,000 orchid plants growing. You will learn how the microscopic seeds, under sterile conditions, are transferred to glass bottles in a controlled environment. The seedlings spend as much as four years before they are transplanted into pots. **NOTE:** Tour by appointment only. **DIRECTIONS:** I - 95 to Linton Blvd west to Jog Rd south to Morikami Park Rd. Take right.

Hours: 8:30 am - 5:00 pm   Days: Monday - Saturday
Advance Notice: Yes   Fee: No   HP Access: Yes

Gainesville Processing & Dist. Center (postal)   SIC Code: 4311
4600 SW 34th Street
Gainesville, FL 32608-9997
352-334-1840   Contact: Norma Fancher/Cheryl Bevel

On this tour you will get an overview of the U. S. Postal Processing & Distribution Facility as you follow the path of a letter as it moves through the facility. **DIRECTIONS:** I - 75 to exit 74. Head east 1/4 mile to 34th St. At SW 34th St take a left and the facility will be 1/4 mile on the left.

Hours: 1:00 - 4:00 pm   Days: Tuesday - Thursday
Advance Notice: Yes   Fee: No   HP Access: Yes

Hoffman's Chocolate Shoppe (candy mfr)   SIC Code: 2064
5190 Lake Worth Road
Greenacres City, FL 33463
561-967-2213   Contact: Tour Department

You will be able to watch the chefs create chocolate magic through the full-view windows of the kitchens and processing areas. You'll see bubbling chocolate in the huge copper kettles hand crafted into all of the wonderful taste delights. Also be sure to visit their colorful gardens. **NOTE:** Bus groups are welcome. **DIRECTIONS:** I - 95 to Lake Worth Rd west. Located between Military Trail and Jog Rd.

Hours: 9:00 am - 5:00 pm   Days: Monday - Sunday
Advance Notice: No   Fee: No   HP Access: Yes

Anheuser-Busch Brewery (brewery)   SIC Code: 2082
111 Busch Drive
Jacksonville, FL 32218
904-751-8118   Contact: Tour Department

In just 90 minutes, you will visit the Brew Hall viewing area for an eye-opening look at the century-old brewing process. You will also see two different types of lager tanks used for the primary and secondary fermentation. Before you see the amazing high-speed packaging operations in action, you will have an opportunity to relax in the Hospitality Room and enjoy complimentary samples of beer, soft drinks and snacks. **DIRECTIONS:** Take I - 95 to Busch Dr exit, located between downtown Jacksonville and the airport.

Hours: 9:00 am - 4:00 pm   Days: Monday - Saturday
Advance Notice: Yes   Fee: No   HP Access: Yes

Lakeland Processing & Dist. Center (postal)   SIC Code: 4311
2800 Lakeland Hills Boulevard
Lakeland, FL 33805-9997
813-682-1772   Contact: Jim Meyer

A guided tour of the U. S. Postal Processing & Distribution Center will demonstrate the computerized operation of the facility as well as track a letter or magazine from entry into the plant to exit, ready for delivery. **DIRECTIONS:** Approximately one mile south of I - 4, exit 19.

Hours: 9:00 am - 1:00 pm   Days: Tuesday - Friday
Advance Notice: Yes   Fee: No   HP Access: Yes

Chariot Eagle, Inc. (mobile home mfr)   SIC Code: 2451
931 NW 37th Avenue
Ocala, FL 34475
904-629-7007   Contact: Public Relations

A 20 - 30 minute walking tour of an 18-station, 70,000 square foot facility showing the manufacturing process of mobile homes from start of floor, including the state-of-the-art cabinet shop, to the final finish of unit. **NOTE:** Closed holidays. **DIRECTIONS:** I - 75 to exit 70, go east approximately one mile, right on NW 30th Ave (500A), immediate right on NW 10th St to 37th Ave, left to front of building.

Hours: 10:00 am & 2:00 pm   Days: Monday - Friday
Advance Notice: Yes   Fee: No   HP Access: No

St. Petersburg Processing & Dist. Center (postal)   SIC Code: 4311
3135 First Avenue North
St. Petersburg, FL 33730-9997
813-323-6533   Contact: Cindy Beierlein

On this tour of the U. S. Postal Processing and Distribution Center, you will see the box section, the loading dock, the motor vehicle section, the carrier section, and the automated and mechanized equipment including: parcel sorter, bar code sorter, flat sorter, letter sorter, optical character reader and the facer/canceller. **DIRECTIONS:** Follow I - 275 southbound to exit 11, 5th Ave, north. Go east to 31st St north, and turn.

Hours: 10:00 am - 3:00 pm   Days: Monday - Friday
Advance Notice: Yes   Fee: No   HP Access: Yes

Tallahassee Democrat (newspaper)   SIC Code: 2711
277 North Magnolia Drive
Tallahassee, FL 32301-0990
904-599-2134   Contact: Peggy Durham

A tour of the newspaper will include the production process and seeing the printing presses at work. **NOTE:** When calling for appointment, please let them know if special accommodations for the handicapped are needed. **DIRECTIONS:** From US Rt 27 go south at the State Capital Building (Rt 265) to Magnolia Dr.

Hours: By appointment   Days: Monday - Friday
Advance Notice: Yes   Fee: No   HP Access: Yes

Zephyrhills Bottled Water (bottled water)   SIC Code: 2086
4330 20th Street
Zephyrhills, FL 33540
813-783-1959   Contact: Billy Smith

This one hour tour of a bottled water company will show you the entire process of spring water being packaged for distribution. You will watch containers being made and filled using the latest in high-tech equipment. This facility has a total output of nearly 15 million containers of water ranging in size from 11 ounces to five gallons. **NOTE:** Free samples. **DIRECTIONS:** Located 15 miles north of Plant City, US Rt 4 exit 14, between Lakeland and Tampa.

Hours: 1:00 pm   Days: Thursday
Advance Notice: Yes   Fee: No   HP Access: Yes

The World of Coca-Cola (soft drinks)   SIC Code: 2086
55 Martin Luther King, Jr. Drive, SW
Atlanta, GA 30303
404-676-5151   Contact: Leslie Breland

On this one-hour self-guided tour you will learn about the century-old worldwide history
through memorabilia, state-of-the-art video technology, including an unforgettable showpiece
soda fountain. **NOTE:** Free samples. Shop from a large collection of Coca-Cola brand merchandise in TradeMart. **DIRECTIONS:** Across from the State Capitol and adjacent to
Underground Atlanta.

Hours: 10:00 am - 8:30 pm   Days: Monday - Saturday
            Noon to 6:00 pm   Sunday
Advance Notice: No   Fee: $2.50 adults   HP Access: Yes

WSB TV/Radio (TV broadcast)   SIC Code: 4833
1601 West Peachtree Street NE
Atlanta, GA 30309
404-897-7369   Contact: Beth Wright

A behind-the-scenes tour of WSB TV, WSB Radio-AM 750 News Talk and1398.5 FM radio
stations. You will visit the newsrooms, studios, and control booth, viewing radio 'On Air'.
NOTE: Reservations are necessary. **DIRECTIONS:** Exit US Rt 75/85 into the center of
town. Call for more specific directions.

Hours: 9:30 and 10:30 am   Days: Tuesday and Thursday
Advance Notice: Yes   Fee: No   HP Access: Yes

G. D. Searle Company (pharmaceutical mfr)   SIC Code: 2834
1750 Lovers Lane
Augusta, GA 30903
706-823-6056   Contact: Pat Tante

This is a walking tour of a pharmaceutical manufacturing facility which will include visiting
the control rooms and the manufacturing floor. **NOTE:** Some areas are not handicap
accessible. **DIRECTIONS:** Located five miles southeast of Augusta.

Hours: By appointment only
Advance Notice: Yes   Fee: No   HP Access: Yes

The Augusta Chronicle (newspaper)   SIC Code: 2711
725 Broad Street
Augusta, GA 30903
706-823-3622   Contact: Camille Hardy

A tour of this newspaper will include explanations of the various phases of the business in addition to a visit to the newsroom and pressroom. **NOTE:** Tours in summer for non-school groups only. **DIRECTIONS:** Take US Rt 20 exit 66 south. Augusta is situated on the Georgia/South Carolina border.

Hours: 9:00 am   Days: Friday
Advance Notice: Yes   Fee: No   HP Access: No

Edwin Hatch Nuclear Plant (utility)   SIC Code: 4939
Route 1 - Box 720
Baxley, GA 31513
912-367-3668   Contact: Debbie Thigpen

This Visitors Center is a showcase for nuclear power, illustrated by animated exhibits, films and special effects. Colorful hands-on exhibits stir the imagination of all ages. **NOTE:** Special programs and tours can be arranged for your school, class, club, bus tour or other group. Weather permitting, plan to bring a picnic lunch and enjoy the view overlooking the Altamaha River. **DIRECTIONS:** 12 miles north of Baxley on US Hwy 1. Enter the main gate to Plant Hatch, turn right at the Visitors Center sign.

Hours: 8:30 am - 5:00 pm   Days: Monday - Friday
Advance Notice: Yes   Fee: No   HP Access: Yes

Chateau Elan Winery (winery)   SIC Code: 2084
7000 Old Winder Highway
Braselton, GA 30517
770-932-0900 (800-233-9463)   Contact: Chris Da Rin

After viewing a video presentation, you will tour the vineyard and production areas and winery. In addition to white and red wines, this winery features summer, autumn blush, winter spice and duncan creek wines. **NOTE:** Wine tasting. Advance notice for groups. Tours are scheduled every 75 minutes starting at 11:00 am. Closed Christmas Day. **DIRECTIONS:** I - 85 at exit 48, 30 minutes north of Atlanta.

Hours: 11:00 am - 4:00 pm   Days: Monday - Friday
Advance Notice: No   Fee: No   HP Access: Yes

Chestnut Mountain Winery (winery)   SIC Code: 2084
Highway 124
Braselton, GA 30517
770-867-6914   Contact: Robert Lyon

Situated on 30 acres of lush trees, lawns, vineyards and colorful roses, you will go on a wine production tour where you will also have an opportunity to taste fine wines. **DIRECTIONS:** I - 85 north to exit 48, turn right and right again on Hwy 124, one-half mile on right.

Hours: Upon request	Days: Tuesday - Sunday	
Advance Notice: No	Fee: No	HP Access: Yes

Babyland General Hospital (doll mfr)   SIC Code: 3942
19 Underwood Street
Cleveland, GA 30528
706-865-2171   Contact: Mari Forquer

Visit the Home of the "Cabbage Patch Kids". Take part in the fantasy and witness the birth of an original, soft-sculptured Cabbage Patch Kid. Doctors and nurses assist in adoption of Kids. **DIRECTIONS:** Located approximately 70 miles north of Atlanta. Take Rt 85 north to Cleveland exit. Follow signs.

Hours: 9:00 am - 5:00 pm	Days: Monday - Saturday	
1:00 - 5:00 pm	Sunday	
Advance Notice: Yes	Fee: No	HP Access: Yes

Kandlestix (candle mfr)   SIC Code: 3999
2653 Highway 129 South
Cleveland, GA 30528
706-865-6131   Contact: Terri Rider

See hundreds of candles of many different shapes, sizes, and colors being made with a live demonstration of the dipping and carving process. **DIRECTIONS:** Cleveland is in the north central part of the state. Hwy 129 south of downtown Cleveland, GA. Follow signs.

Hours: 9:00 am - 4:00 pm	Days: Monday - Saturday	
Advance Notice: yes	Fee: No	HP Access: Yes

Dolly Madison (bakery)   SIC Code: 2051
1969 Victory Drive
Columbus, GA 31901
770-324-6616   Contact: Brenda

This is a 45 - minute tour of a bakery manufacturing plant which will demonstrate how they make their snack foods and cakes. **DIRECTIONS:** Take exit 1 north from US Rt 185.

Hours: 9:30 am   Days: Friday
Advance Notice: Yes   Fee: No   HP Access: Yes

North Metro Processing & Dist. Center (postal) SIC Code: 4311
1605 Boggs Road
Duluth, GA 30159-9000
770-717-3140   Contact: Erin Christiansen

A one hour tour of the 650,000 square foot U. S. Postal Processing and Distribution Center will include seeing all of the mail processing equipment and an explanation of the mail flow. **NOTE:** Reservations required. **DIRECTIONS:** From I - 85 south, take exit 40 and turn left off ramp. Take first left on Breckenridge Dr. Follow to end and take right to first building on left.

Hours: 10:00 am - 7:00 pm   Days: Tuesday - Thursday
Advance Notice: Yes   Fee: No   HP Access: Yes

Coachmen Recreational Vehicle Co. (trailer mfr)   SIC Code: 3792
Northside Industrial Park (US 319)
Fitzgerald, GA 31750
912-423-5471   Contact: Lawton Tinley

On this escorted tour you will visit the travel trailer and fifth wheel production facilities. **DIRECTIONS:** Located in south Georgia, approximately 45 miles west of I - 75 from the Ashburn exit.

Hours: 9:00 am - 2:00 pm   Days: Monday - Friday
Advance Notice: Yes   Fee: No   HP Access: No

Easterling Farms (farm)   SIC Code: 0191
Route 3 - Box 15
Glennville, GA 30427
912-654-4054 (800-664-6676)   Contact: Betty Jean or India Easterling

Tour the Vidalia Sweet Onion facility during May, June and July where you will see Vidalia sweet onions harvested, graded and packed. **NOTE:** Country store on premises featuring Vidalia sweet onion products. **DIRECTIONS:** On I - 95, take exit 15 and continue on Rt 144 west for 40 miles. Look for signs.

Hours: 9:00 am - 3:00 pm	Days: Monday - Friday	
Advance Notice: Yes	Fee: No	HP Access: Yes

Dickey's Peach Farm (fruit farm)   SIC Code: 0175
Old Highway 341 North (P.O.Box 10)
Musella, GA 31066
912-836-4362   Contact: Cynde Dickey

Tour is given of the peach packing shed which was built in the 1930's and is still in operation today by a fourth generation owner. Learn the history of the operation as well as facts about growing peaches. **NOTE:** Open mid-May to mid-August. **DIRECTIONS:** Located about 30 miles west of Macon or 30 miles north of Perry, GA.

Hours: Call for schedule	Days: Monday - Friday	
Advance Notice: Yes	Fee: No	HP Access: No

Musella Gin & Cotton Co. (cotton gin)   SIC Code: 0724
Old Highway 341 (P.O.Box 40)
Musella, GA 31066
912-836-3903   Contact: Buddy or Cary IV

This is a guided visit of the oldest continuously operating cotton gin in the United States, built in 1913, bought in 1941 and operated by the same family today. **NOTE:** Tours October, November, December. Since cotton gins are dusty when in operation, dress casually. Closed Christmas and Thanksgiving. Call at least two days in advance. **DIRECTIONS:** Six miles north of Roberta - 20 miles south of Barnesville.

Hours: 7:00 am - 5:00 pm	Days: Monday - Friday	
Advance Notice: Yes	Fee: No	HP Access: Yes

Boise Processing & Dist. Center (postal)   SIC Code: 4311
770 South 13th Street
Boise, ID 83708-9731
208-383-4258   Contact: Frank Nick

This tour of the U. S. Postal Processing & Distribution Center includes the mail processing workroom. See the latest in mail handling equipment and follow pieces of individual mail as it travels through the entire sorting and processing route. **DIRECTIONS:** Call for specific directions.

Hours: 10:00 am - 2:00 pm   Days: Call for schedule
Advance Notice: Yes   Fee: No   HP Access: Yes

Micron Technologies, Inc. (electronics)   SIC Code: 3674
2805 East Columbia Road
Boise, ID 83706
208-368-4400   Contact: Teresa Kirkmire

A tour of this semiconductor plant includes going through the hallways of the facility to see the production areas from fabrication to test. Production areas are visible from the hallways. **NOTE:** Tours are by reservation only. **DIRECTIONS:** Two miles east of Boise; Idaho City/Gowen exit off I - 84.

Hours: 9:00 am - 4:00 pm   Days: Monday - Friday
Advance Notice: Yes   Fee: No   HP Access: Yes

Ste. Chapelle, Inc. (winery)   SIC Code: 2084
14068 Sunny Slope Road
Caldwell, ID 83605
208-459-7222   Contact: Jolyn Green

Tour this winery located on two acres of lawn and trees with a beautiful view overlooking the valley and learn how their vintage wines are made. **NOTE:** Tours are every hour on the hour. Free wine tasting limited to four wines of your choice. **DIRECTIONS:** From Boise, Rt 84 to exit 35, Marsing exit. Take left and follow Hwy 55 to Lowell Rd. Follow signs to winery.

Hours: 10:00 am - 5:00 pm   Days: Monday - Saturday
        Noon - 5:00 pm   Sunday
Advance Notice: Yes   Fee: No   HP Access: Yes

Idaho National Engineering Labs (utility)　　　　SIC Code: 4939
1955 South Fremont Avenue
Idaho Falls, ID 83402
208-526-0050　　　　　　　Contact: Harlin Summers or Nancy Loper

Visit the Experimental Breeder Reactor #1 (EBR-1), the world's first nuclear plant to generate usable amounts of electricity. Three other nuclear reactors are also on the grounds and tours explain their functions. Another nearby reactor lighted Arco, ID, the first city in the world to be lighted by nuclear power. Tours also describe current projects at the INEL, a Department of Energy complex with varied national and international experiments. **NOTE:** Open Memorial Day weekend through Labor Day. **DIRECTIONS:** Eight miles west of Hwy 20/26 intersection or 18 miles east of Arco.

Hours: 8:00 am - 4:00 pm　　　Days: Monday - Sunday
Advance Notice: No　　　　　Fee:　No　　　　　HP Access: Yes

Potlach Corporation (paper mfr)　　　　　　SIC Code: 2621
805 Mill Road
Lewiston, ID 83501
208-799-1795　　　　　　Contact: Judy Kilmer - Public Affairs

This is a three hour tour of a sawmill, tree nursery, pulp and paper mill operation. **NOTE:** Children must be over 10 years old. Walking and stairs involved, and can be very hot in summer. Closed-toed, flat shoes required. No Birkenstocks style shoes. There is no access for visitors who are physically handicapped. **DIRECTIONS**: Call for specific directions.

Hours: 9:00 am - 1:30 pm　　　Days: Monday, Wednesday, Friday
Advance Notice: Yes　　　　Fee:　No　　　　　HP Access: No

SkyStar Aircraft Corp. (aircraft mfr)　　　　SIC Code: 3721
100 North Kings Road
Nampa, ID 83687
208-466-1711　　　　　　Contact: Manager

Tour the producers of affordable kit aircraft that offers flight to everyone. Three different models are manufactured with a wide capacity of options. SkyStar has produced over 2,500 kits for owners living in 42 different countries. **NOTE:** Demonstration flights available. Please call for advance reservations. **DIRECTIONS:** Located at the airport, 13 miles west of Boise off US Rt 84.

Hours: By appointment only
Advance Notice: Yes　　　　Fee:　No　　　　　HP Access: Yes

Fox Valley Processing & Dist. Center (postal)   SIC Code: 4311
3900 Gabrielle Lane
Aurora, IL 60599-9997
630-978-4432   Contact: Ronald Woodall

A tour of the U. S. Postal Processing & Distribution Center will include the dock and work-room floor, the letter sorter machine, the optical character reader, the delivery bar code sorter and the bar code sorter mail sorting machines. **DIRECTIONS:** Take 290 Expressway west to I - 88 Tollway to Rt 59. Go south three miles to New York Ave. Right about one mile to Commons Dr and take right about one-half block down. Take a left on Gabrielle Ln. Follow signs for parking.

Hours: 24 hours/day   Days: Monday - Sunday
Advance Notice: Yes   Fee: No   HP Access: Yes

Beer Nuts, Inc. (nuts)   SIC Code: 2068
103 North Robinson Street
Bloomington, IL 61701
309-827-8580   Contact: Kelly Schroeder

A 15 - minute video is shown of the Beer Nuts plant, the only place in the world where Beer Nuts are manufactured. You will learn how the beer nuts are grown and harvested, as well as how they travel through the plant facilities. **NOTE:** Free samples. Advance notice for large groups only. **DIRECTIONS:** Veterans Pkwy to Washington Ave to Robinson St.

Hours: 8:00 am - 5:00 pm   Days: Monday - Friday
Advance Notice: No   Fee: No   HP Access: No

Kathryn Beich, Inc. (A Nestle Co.) (candy mfr)   SIC Code: 2064
2501 Beich Road
Bloomington, IL 61701
309-829-1031   Contact: Tour Department

This is a 40 - minute tour of the candy factory that produces such classic delights as Katy-dids and Bit-O-Honey. You will see a 20 - minute video presentation and view the actual machines used to make the candy. **NOTE:** Production varies seasonally. No cameras allowed. Free samples. Tours by reservation only. **DIRECTIONS:** I - 55/I - 74 to Veterans Pkwy exit. Take first left at Cabintown Rd, take first right onto service road.

Hours: 9:00-11:00.1:00,2:00   Days: Monday - Friday
Advance Notice: Yes   Fee: No   HP Access: No

Champaign Processing & Dist. Center (postal)   SIC Code: 4311
2001 North Mattis Avenue
Champaign, IL 61821-9998
217-373-6002   Contact: Lisa Hartley

On the tour of the U. S. Postal Processing & Distribution Center, you will see a live demonstration of the high-tech equipment being used. The tour includes the stamped and metered mail areas, the optical character reader, the barcode sorter, the letter and flat sorting machines, and the manual distribution area. **DIRECTIONS:** I - 57 to University Ave exit. Turn left on Mattis and proceed two miles.

Hours: 6:00 - 8:00 pm   Days: Monday - Friday
Advance Notice: Yes   Fee: No   HP Access: Yes

Chicago Sun Times (newspaper)   SIC Code: 2711
401 North Wabash
Chicago, IL 60611
312-321-3251   Contact: Public Information Bureau

On this 45 - minute tour, you will visit the newsroom, composing room, press room and photoengraving area. You will learn about the history of the Chicago Sun Times, as well as fascinating facts about what it takes to publish the most widely read daily paper in Chicago. You will see everything from the reporter's desk to the printing press. **NOTE:** Minimum age for children is eight. **DIRECTIONS:** Call for specific directions.

Hours: 10:30 am   Days: Tuesday - Thursday
Advance Notice: Yes   Fee: No   HP Access: No

Nuclear Information Center (electric company)   SIC Code: 4911
Iowa-Illinois Gas and Electric Company
22511 206th Avenue North
Cordova, IL 61242
319-654-2662   Contact: Dianne Schneider

On this tour you will see interactive displays and interesting videos which allow you to learn about nuclear energy. You will get a birdseye view of the Quad Cities Nuclear Power Station and the Mississippi River from atop the 40 foot observation tower. **DIRECTIONS:** Located north of Cordova, off Hwy 84.

Hours: 9:00 am - 5:00 pm   Days: Tuesday - Saturday
Advance Notice: No   Fee: No   HP Access: Yes

Haeger Potteries (pottery products)   SIC Code: 3269
7 Maiden Lane
Dundee, IL 60118
847-426-3033   Contact: Marilyn Spear

The 40 - minute walking tour includes viewing the Master Potter creating pottery on the wheel, a tour of the factory where slip cast and ram press production methods are seen. **NOTE:** Closed holidays. **DIRECTIONS:** From Chicago, take the I - 90 tollway (Northwest Tollway) west to Rt 25 to Rt 72 west to Van Buren St, then south to Maiden Ln.

Hours: 10:00 am - 1:00 pm   Days: Monday - Friday
Advance Notice: Yes   Fee: No   HP Access: Yes

CASE Corp. (farm equipment mfr)   SIC Code: 3523
1100 Third Street
East Moline, IL 61244
309-752-3369   Contact: Joni Trumpold

A two - three hour walking tour where you will observe the manufacture of combines, cotton pickers, planters and cabs on the assembly lines. **NOTE:** No tours during plant shutdown in August, last two weeks in December or on holidays. Must be age 10. No opened toed shoes, brief tops or shorts. No video cameras or cameras allowed. **DIRECTIONS:** Rt 92 at Moline/ East Moline border on the Mississippi River.

Hours: 8:00, 10:00,1:00 pm   Days: Tuesday and Thursday
Advance Notice: Yes   Fee: No   HP Access: No

John Deere Parts Dist. Ctr (distribution center)   SIC Code: 5083
1600 First Avenue, East
Milan, IL 61264
309-756-1401   Contact: Pag Bauersfeld

Visit this major parts distribution center where 270,000 different parts for John Deere products are shipped to depots and dealers worldwide. **DIRECTIONS:** Take exit 15 from US Rt 280. Milan is in the Quad City area.

Hours: Call for appointment
Advance Notice: Yes   Fee: No   HP Access: Yes

Palatine Processing & Dist. Center (postal)   SIC Code: 4311
1300 East Northwest Highway
Palatine, IL 60095-9997
847-590-6566   Contact: Ken Iversen

This U. S. Postal Processing and Distribution is the mail processing center for 65 Post Offices and their branches where over four million pieces of mail are handled daily. This facility performs outgoing distribution for all of its post offices as well as performs incoming secondary automated operations. On this tour you will see the automation area and see sorting with bar code sorters. **DIRECTIONS:** Located east of Rt 53.

Hours: 11:00 am - 5:00 pm   Days: Monday - Friday
Advance Notice: Yes   Fee: No   HP Access: Yes

Springfield Processing & Dist. Center (postal)   SIC Code: 4311
2015 East Cook Street
Springfield, IL 62703-9997
217-788-7211   Contact: Marlene Bodine

The U. S. Postal Processing & Distribution Center tour will demonstrate how the mail is processed using automated equipment, from the time it enters the facility until it leaves. **NOTE:** You will see more during the evening hours. **DIRECTIONS:** I - 55 to Springfield. Take Clear Lake Ave exit and go to first stop light (Dicksen Pkwy). Turn left to first stop light (Cook St). Turn right to first stop light. Go through intersection to second business on right.

Hours: Call for times   Days: Monday - Friday
Advance Notice: Yes   Fee: No   HP Access: Yes

RAM Graphics, Inc. (screen printing)   SIC Code: 2759
State Road 9 South
Alexandria, IN 46001
765-724-7783   Contact: Troy Jerrils/Heather Ruby North

RAM is the third largest volume shirt printer and embroiderer in the state. The tour will take you through the award-winning Art Department, into the screen room to see how the image is prepared and then on to the printing area to see the three automatic printers actually put the design on the shirt. Then on to Embroidery to see how those stitches are put on so quickly. **NOTE:** Tour ends in the T-shirt Outlet. **DIRECTIONS:** I - 69 to exit 4 (Muncie/ Frankfort). Turn west onto St Rd 128, five miles to St Rd 9, turn one and 1/4 miles on west side of St Rd 9.

Hours: Call for appointment   Days: Monday - Friday
Advance Notice: Yes   Fee: No   HP Access: Yes

Butler Winery (winery)   SIC Code: 2084
1022 North College Avenue
Bloomington, IN 47404
812-339-7233   Contact: Jim Butler

In a relaxed atmosphere of small informal groups, you will hear the basic wine making process described which will include discussions of the wine-making process. **NOTE:** Questions encouraged. Groups must be scheduled one week in advance. **DIRECTIONS:** Southeast corner of 15th & College Ave.

Hours: By appointment only   Days: Tuesday - Friday
Advance Notice: Yes   Fee: No   HP Access: Yes

Dillman Farms, Inc. (canning)   SIC Code: 2033
4955 West State Road 45
Bloomington, IN 47403
812-825-5525   Contact: Sue/Cary

On this tour, you will have an opportunity to look at the room where preserves are made as well as receiving an explanation of where fruit sugar and apples come from and how apple butter is processed. **DIRECTIONS:** One and one-half miles west of Hwy 37 on St Rd 45 south.

Hours: 10:00 am or 1:00 pm   Days: Tuesday - Friday
Advance Notice: Yes   Fee: No   HP Access: Yes

Oliver Winery (winery)   SIC Code: 2084
8024 North State Road 37
Bloomington, IN 47404
812-876-5800   Contact: Kathleen Nossal

When you visit Indiana's oldest and largest winery, located on 15 acres surrounding a small lake, you will learn the history of the Oliver Winery since its beginning in 1972, and then take a 25 - minute tour of the cellar for an informative look at the production process. **NOTE:** Tours for groups can be scheduled by appointment only. Plan to enjoy a picnic on the winery grounds. **DIRECTIONS:** Located seven miles north of Bloomington; 45 miles south of Indianapolis.

Hours: 12 noon - 4:30 pm   Days: Friday - Saturday
          1:00 - 4:30 pm   Sunday
Advance Notice: Yes   Fee: No   HP Access: Yes

Twinrocker Handmade Paper (paper mfr)   SIC Code: 2621
100 East Third Street
Brookston, IN 47923
765-563-3119   Contact: Gail Sutton/Kathryn Clark

This is a 30 - minute tour of a small craft studio which will explain the craft of hand paper making and you will watch craftsmen actually forming sheets of paper by hand. **NOTE:** Paper purchased after the tour is at a 25% discount. Groups over 10 people can schedule in advance any day at their preferred time. **DIRECTIONS:** Located at the intersection of IN St Rd 43 and IN 18.

Hours: 1:30 pm   Days: Tuesday and Thursday
Advance Notice: No   Fee: $4.00   HP Access: Yes

Clay City Pottery, Inc. (pottery products)   SIC Code: 3269
R R #2
Clay City, IN 47841
812-939-2596 (800-776-2596)   Contact: Cheryl Wellman

Tour this 107 year old family operated pottery, featuring reproduction stoneware and garden-ware. This tour will include seeing the pottery being made, the clay being processed, and the kilns. **NOTE:** Retail showroom. **DIRECTIONS:** St Rd 157.

Hours: 9:00-11:00.1:00-4:00   Days: Monday - Friday
Advance Notice: Yes   Fee: No   HP Access: Limited

Zimmerman Art Glass (glass mfr)   SIC Code: 3229
395 Valley Road
Corydon, IN 47112
812-738-2206   Contact: Manager

On this 45 - minute tour of a generations-old and world renowned art glass factory, you will have the opportunity to watch the artists shape paperweights, bowls, lamps, and bottles by hand. **NOTE:** Many of the items are for sale. **DIRECTIONS:** From US Rt 64 take exit south to Rt 62 east. Look for signs.

Hours: 9:00 am - 3:00 pm   Days: Tuesday - Saturday
Advance Notice: Fee: No   HP Access: Yes

House of Glass, Inc. (glass mfr)   SIC Code: 3229
7900 East State Road 28
Elwood, IN 46036
765-552-6841   Contact: Kay, Louise or Lisa

This is an informal, unguided, no-time limit tour of a manufacturer of handmade art glass in which you will have the opportunity to watch the process of glass paperweights, birds, and lamps being made. **NOTE:** No tours allowed 10:00 to 10:30 am, 12 noon - 1:00 pm and 3:00 to 3:30 pm. **DIRECTIONS:** West edge of Elwood on Hwy 28, north side of road.

Hours: 9:00 am - 5:00 pm   Days: Monday - Thursday
        9:00 am - 2:00 pm   Friday
Advance Notice: Yes   Fee: No   HP Access: Yes

Fort Wayne Processing & Dist. Center (postal)   SIC Code: 4311
1501 South Clinton Street
Fort Wayne, IN 46802-9997
219-427-7330   Contact: Diane Huston

On the tour of this U. S. Postal Processing & Distribution Center you will learn the process of mail flow from the point mail arrives in the building until it leaves. The tour also includes a demonstration of some of the equipment used to process the mail. **DIRECTIONS:** Follow US Rt 69, to exit at Northrop St south to Clinton St.

Hours: 9:00 am - 11:30 am   Days: Monday - Friday
Advance Notice: Yes   Fee: No   HP Access: Yes

Abbott's Candy Shop (candy mfr)   SIC Code: 2064
48 East Walnut Street
Hagerstown, IN 47346
765-489-4442   Contact: Manager

A one hour guided tour through the sales room, kitchen, chocolate room with samples along the way. This is a full line candy shop with old-fashioned caramels a specialty. **NOTE:** Sugar free candies are available. No tours other than shopping groups, minimum of 10 people, during November and December. **DIRECTIONS:** Four miles north of I - 70 and SR 1. Take left at SR 38, to junction at Perry St. Go one block south to Walnut, turn right.

Hours: 10:00 am and 2:00 pm   Days: Tuesday, Wednesday, Thursday
Advance Notice: Yes   Fee: No   HP Access: Yes

Indianapolis Processing & Dist. Center (postal)   SIC Code: 4311
125 West South Street
Indianapolis, IN 46206-9997
317-464-6448   Contact: Ann Teipen

On this one and one-half hour tour of the U. S. Postal Processing and Distribution Center you will see the first and second floor mail processing equipment and learn how mail is processed electronically. **NOTE:** Wear comfortable shoes, no cameras, and no children under the age of eight years. No tours during December. **DIRECTIONS:** Located south of downtown Indianapolis between Illinois St (one-way north) and Capital Ave (one-way south) on the south side of South St.

Hours: 9:00 am - 1:00 pm   Days: Tuesday - Friday
Advance Notice: Yes   Fee: No   HP Access: Yes

Scherer Industrial Group, Inc. (repair shop)   SIC Code: 7699
940 South West Street
Indianapolis, IN 46225
317-231-2363 (800-727-0767)   Contact: Kittie Reid

A one hour tour of an industrial electromechanical and hydraulic repair and manufacturing company which repairs motors, electronic components, automotive and power equipment. **DIRECTIONS:** From the split of US Rts 65/70, follow Rt 70 to West St, exit north.

Hours: By appointment only
Advance Notice: Yes   Fee: No   HP Access: Yes

Hillerich & Bradsby Company (sporting goods)   SIC Code: 3949
1525 Charlestown - New Albany Road
Jeffersonville, IN 47131
502-585-5226   Contact: Tour Department

A one hour tour of the Louisville Slugger baseball bat and golf club manufacturer. You will watch a video presentation which describes the history of the company. **NOTE:** Museum and gift shop. **DIRECTIONS:** Located on US Rt 65 north of Louisville (Ky).

Hours: 10:00,11:00,1:00,2:00   Days: Monday - Friday
Advance Notice: Yes   Fee: No   HP Access: Yes

Kokomo Opalescent Glass Company (stained glass)   SIC Code: 3231
1310 South Market Street
Kokomo, IN 46902
765-457-8136   Contact: Manager

See the manufacturing process of sheets of multi-colored stained glass at a company that hasn't changed its way of making glass since 1888. **DIRECTIONS:** Follow US Rt 31 north of Indianapolis to Kokomo. Call for specific directions.

Hours: 10:00 am   Days: Monday - Friday
Advance Notice: Yes   Fee: No   HP Access: Yes

Garwood Orchards (fruit farm)   SIC Code: 0175
5911 West Road 50 S.
La Porte, IN 46350
219-362-4385   Contact: Phyllis Garwood

A one hour tour where you will see demonstrations on apple processing, cider manufacturing and more at one of the biggest orchards in the area. **NOTE:** Cider making during September and October. Open August, September and October. **DIRECTIONS:** Five miles west of LaPorte, off St Rd 2.

Hours: By arrangement
Advance Notice: Yes   Fee: No   HP Access: Yes

Wool for Ewe Farm (woolen mill)   SIC Code: 2231
7989 N 300 E
La Porte, IN 46350
219-778-4472   Contact: Sherry Konya

Step back in time with a visit to this farm where you will see black and natural colored sheep, as well as angora rabbits raised to produce spinning and weaving fibers. You will tour the artists studio and gift shop where you will see spinning and weaving demonstrations. **NOTE:** Open any day during June, July and August. Weekends only September through May. **DIRECTIONS:** Three miles east of LaPorte on Hwy 2 - north on 300 East.

Hours: By arrangement only
Advance Notice: Yes   Fee: No   HP Access: No

Subaru-Isuzu Automotive, Inc. (automobile mfr)   SIC Code: 3711
5500 State Road 38
Lafayette, IN 47903
765-449-6232   Contact: Curtis Smith

The one hour tour is conducted on a catwalk above the production floor of the manufacturing facility. This manufacturing plant is the first joint venture between the two Japanese automobile manufacturing corporations. **NOTE:** Tours are arranged two - three months in advance by written letter and cover a distance of one and 3/4 miles. **DIRECTIONS:** Located 60 miles north of Indianapolis on I - 65 at the intersection of St Rd 38.

Hours: 9:00 am or 1:00 pm   Days: Tuesday and Wednesday
Advance Notice: Yes   Fee: No   HP Access: Yes

Tom's Farms (vegetable farm)   SIC Code: 0161
8542 North Harper Road
Leesburg, IN 46538
219-453-3300   Contact: Kip Tom

A one hour seasonal operation tour of one of Indiana's largest irrigated farm operations, growing seed corn, sweet corn, tomatoes, potatoes, navy beans and traditional midwest crops. **NOTE:** July, detasseling of corn using 200/500 teenagers daily. **DIRECTIONS:** North of Warsaw, on SR 15 to CR 900 east to Harper Rd, then south one-half mile.

Hours: 7:00 am - 5:00 pm   Days: Monday - Friday
Advance Notice: Yes   Fee: No   HP Access: No

Lange's Old Fashioned Meat Market (meat processor)   SIC Code: 2013
218 West 7th Street
Michigan City, IN 46360
219-874-0071   Contact: Peter Lange

This 30 - minute tour will show how old world sausage is made and will discuss smoking and curing of meats. **NOTE:** Questions encouraged. **DIRECTIONS**: I - 94 to US 421 south to 7th St, two blocks due west.

Hours: 9:00 am - 6:00 pm   Days: Monday - Friday
        11:00 am - 4:00 pm   Saturday - Sunday
Advance Notice: Yes   Fee: No   HP Access: Yes

Coachmen Recreational Vehicle Co. (trailer mfr)   SIC Code: 3792
423 North Main Street
Middlebury, IN 46540
219-825-5821   Contact: Lon J. Hoffman

On this escorted tour, you will see the production of travel trailers and fifth wheelers on Monday, Wednesday and Friday at 12:20 pm from May 1 to October 31 and tours for the production of Class A motorhomes on Tuesday and Thursday at 11:50 am from November 1 to April 30. **DIRECTIONS:** Indiana Toll Road (80/90) to exit 107, go south on Hwy 13 to Middlebury. Enter at Visitors Center entrance.

Hours: 11:50 am or 12:20 pm   Days: Monday-Friday
Advance Notice: No   Fee: No   HP Access: No

Deutsch Kase Haus, Inc. (cheese processor)   SIC Code: 2022
11275 CR 250 North
Middlebury, IN 46540
219-825-9511   Contact: Elsie Raber

Visit the cheese factory and watch the Amish cheesemakers at work using their age old process. You will also have the opportunity to sample different types of cheeses. **DIRECTIONS:** East of Middlebury on CR 16, about three miles east of Middlebury.

Hours: 8:00 am - 5:00 pm   Days: Monday - Friday
Advance Notice: No   Fee: No   HP Access: Yes

Jayco, Inc. (trailer mfr)   SIC Code: 3792
58075 State Road 13
Middlebury, IN 46540
219-825-5861   Contact: Michelle Darrenkamp

A 90 - minute tour of a fifth wheel manufacturing and sewing plant in which you will go
through the display area. You will also watch a video of the history of this recreational
vehicle company. **NOTE:** Special tours can be arranged for September - May during the
morning hours. **DIRECTIONS:** Indiana Toll Road (80/90), get off at exit 107. Turn right
on St Rd 13 and go through the intersection of St Rd 120 and continue south through the town
of Middlebury. One mile south of Middlebury is US 20. Cross over and Jayco will be on the
right side of St Rd 13.

Hours: 1:30 pm   Days: Monday - Friday (September-May)
        9:30 am   Monday - Friday (June - August)
Advance Notice: No   Fee: No   HP Access: Yes

Sunburst Stained Glass Company (stained glass)   SIC Code: 3231
20 West Jennings Street
Newburgh, IN 47630
812-853-0460   Contact: Sue or Trish

This is a 45 - minute tour through the production, restoration and custom studios where you
will see stained glass from design to finished windows. **NOTE:** There are some stairs
involved. **DIRECTIONS:** I - 164 to Covert Ave, exit east.

Hours: 9:30 am - 4:30 pm   Days: Monday - Friday
Advance Notice: Yes   Fee: $2.00   HP Access: Yes

Pioneer Hi-Bred Inc. (corn)   SIC Code: 0115
7900 Pine Road
Plymouth, IN 46563
219-936-3243   Contact: Dan Smith

Visit this five year old, state-of-the-art agriculture manufacturing plant which processes three
percent of all seed corn in the U.S. **NOTE:** Best time to tour is September and October. No
tours in July. **DIRECTIONS:** Located one mile west of Plymouth on US 30.

Hours: 8:00 am - 3:00 pm   Days: Monday - Friday
Advance Notice: Yes   Fee: No   HP Access: No

Sechler's Pickles (pickle mfr)   SIC Code: 2035
5686 State Road 1
St. Joe, IN 46785
219-337-5461   Contact: Karen Sechler-Linn

Visit this pickle manufacturer and see pickles made the old fashioned way in large wooden vats. You will see the grading, processing, cutting, sweetening and packing areas. **NOTE:** Retail store open. Tours from April 1 - October 31. **DIRECTIONS:** 20 miles north of Ft Wayne on St Rd 1.

Hours: 9:00,11:00,12:30,3:00   Days: Monday - Friday
Advance Notice: Yes   Fee: No   HP Access: Limited

Terre Haute Processing & Dist. Center (postal)   SIC Code: 4311
1925 South 13th Street
Terre Haute, IN 47802
812-232-2950   Contact: Rod Jones

At this U. S. Postal Processing and Distribution Center you will take a 20 - minute tour to see the BACIS mail flow information and you will receive instructions on the automated systems and addressing equipment. **DIRECTIONS:** From the east, take second exit off of I - 70 (Hwy 41 - 3rd St). Go two miles north to Hulman St. Turn right. Drive nine blocks to 12th St. Turn right and continue for one and one-half blocks. Post Office will be on your left. Visitor parking at the dock.

Hours: 9:00 am - 6:00 pm   Days: Monday - Friday
Advance Notice: Yes   Fee: No   HP Access: Yes

Biomet, Inc. (medical equipment mfr)   SIC Code: 3842
Airport Industrial Park (P.O.Box 587)
Warsaw, IN 46581-0587
219-267-6639   Contact: Carolyn Beatty

Before the one hour tour, you will see a 15 - minute video on the company, and then you will have an opportunity to see artificial knees, hips, and shoulder replacements being made to specifications before your eyes. **DIRECTIONS:** Call for specific directions.

Hours: 9:00 am - 3:00 pm   Days: Monday - Friday
Advance Notice: Yes   Fee: No   HP Access: Yes

Dallas County Brewing Company (brewery)   SIC Code: 2082
301 South 10th Street
Adel, IA 50003
515-993-5064   Contact: Joan Worlan

The home of Old Depot Premium Beers is located in a 1907 historic glove and sunbonnet factory. The brewery features a hospitality room where free samples of beer is available for tasting. **NOTE:** Tours by Al Busch, the Brewmaster, are by appointment only. Without an appointment you will view the Brewery from the Hospitality Room. **DIRECTIONS:** From I - 80, take exit 110 (Adel, DeSoto, Winterset exit). Right on Hwy 169. In Adel, you will come to a stop light (the only one in town). Turn left on Hwy 6. Go one block and turn right..

Hours: 10:00 am - 10:00 pm   Days: Sunday - Thursday
Advance Notice: Yes   Fee: No   HP Access: No

Amana Woolen Mill (woolen mill)   SIC Code: 2231
800 48th Avenue
Amana, IA 52203
319-622-3432 (800-222-6430)   Contact: Donna Trumpold

This 20 - 25 minute self-guided tour of the only operating woolen mill in Iowa includes the warping, weaving and finishing departments. **NOTE:** Guide available upon request. Machines only operate Monday - Friday. Gift shop. Buses welcome. **DIRECTIONS:** 10 miles north of I - 80, exit 225 on Hwy 151.

Hours: 9:00 am - 5:00 pm   Days: Monday - Saturday
        12 noon - 5:00 pm   Sunday
Advance Notice: No   Fee: No   HP Access: Yes

Quad City Times (newspaper)   SIC Code: 2711
500 East 3rd Street
Davenport, IA 52801
319-383-2455   Contact: Vicky

You will have an opportunity to tour every department of this newspaper as well as have contact with the staff. You will see the entire process from start to finished newspaper. **NOTE:** First grade children and older. **DIRECTIONS:** From I - 74 follow State St/River Dr. At 4th St, go to the right. Building is on left.

Hours: 10:00 - 11:30 am   Days: Tuesday and Thursday
Advance Notice: yes   Fee: No   HP Access: Yes

Des Moines Transit Authority (bus line)　　　　SIC Code: 4131
1100 MTA Lane
Des Moines, IA 50309
515-283-8111　　　　　Contact: Elaine Jarvis

You will have a guided 30 - 45 minute tour to see the metropolitan bus maintenance and service departments. **DIRECTIONS:** From US Rt 80, follow Rt I - 235 to downtown exit at SW 9th St.

Hours: 8:00 am - 5:00 pm	Days: Monday - Friday	
Advance Notice: Yes	Fee: No	HP Access: Yes

Norwest Bank Iowa, N.A. (bank)　　　　　SIC Code: 6021
666 Walnut Street
Des Moines, IA 50309
515-245-3169　　　　　Contact: Kimberly Kolbet

A guided 45 - 60 minute tour in which you will see the administrative offices, board room, vault, computer room and safe deposit boxes. **NOTE:** Children must be in fifth grade or above. **DIRECTIONS:** Located near the State Capital Building. Call for specific directions.

Hours: 9:30 am - 3:00 pm	Days: Monday - Friday	
Advance Notice: Yes	Fee: No	HP Access: Yes

The Des Moines Register (newspaper)　　　　SIC Code: 2711
715 Locust Street
Des Moines, IA 50309
515-284-8247　　　　　Contact: Jodi Pieken

You will take a one hour tour of the newsroom and the composition room and see the latest news being processed for publication. **NOTE:** Two weeks advance notice. No tours in the summer. **DIRECTIONS:** Located near the State Capital Building in the center of town.

Hours: 9:00 am - 4:00 pm	Days: Monday - Friday	
Advance Notice: Yes	Fee: No	HP Access: Yes

Triple F Nutrition (animal feed mfr)   SIC Code: 2048
10104 Douglas Avenue
Des Moines, IA 50322
515-254-1200   Contact: Craig Tessau or Bill Hansen

This is a tour of an international agri-business organized to formulate and market nutritional products for livestock and poultry feeders. You will see the processing of soybeans and other products. **DIRECTIONS:** Located in the center of town north of US Rt 235.

Hours: 8:00 am - 4:30 pm   Days: Monday - Friday
Advance Notice: Yes   Fee: No   HP Access: Yes

WHO - TV 13 (TV broadcast)   SIC Code: 4833
1801 Grand Avenue
Des Moines, IA 50309-3362
515-242-3500   Contact: Mary Bracken

On this 45 - minute tour you will follow through the entire operation of television production and Newscenter 13. **NOTE:** Tours are suitable for third grade and older. Groups may be audience members for a local show. **DIRECTIONS:** Rt 235 to Rt 28 south to Grand Ave.

Hours: 8:30-11:00/12:30-4:00   Days: Monday - Friday
Advance Notice: Yes   Fee: No   HP Access: Yes

The Ertl Company, Inc. (toy mfr)   SIC Code: 3944
Highway 20 & 136
Dyersville, IA 52040
319-875-2000   Contact: Tour Department

A 45 - 60 minute tour of the largest farm toy manufacturing company in the world. You will see the pad-printing, bank line, shipping area, picking line, warehouse, injection molding of model kits, vacuum metalizing, model kit line packaging and boxing, steel stamping, paint line and finishing line. **NOTE:** No cameras. Every person must wear safety glasses regardless of age. Closed holidays. **DIRECTIONS:** Hwy 20 west then left on Hwy 136 in Dyersville.

Hours: 10:00-11:00/1:00-2:00   Days: Monday - Friday
Advance Notice: Yes   Fee: No   HP Access: Yes

Danish Windmill Corporation (flour mill)   SIC Code: 2041
4038 Main Street
Elk Horn, IA 51531
712-764-7472 (800-451-7960)   Contact: Lisa Riggs

After a 10 - minute video presentation, you will take a one hour tour of an authentic working Dutch windmill, brought over from Denmark in 1976. You will see the inner workings of the mill, and climb the stairs to the second floor to watch the 66-foot blades turn in the wind. Flour is also ground on the first floor. **NOTE:** Handicap accessibility is on first floor only. **DIRECTIONS:** Located six miles north of I - 80, exit 54, halfway between Des Moines and Omaha.

Hours: 8:00 am - 7:00 pm   Days: Sunday - Saturday (summer/fall)
              9:00 am - 5:00 pm   Sunday - Saturday (winter/spring)
Advance Notice: Yes   Fee: $1.50   HP Access: Yes

Winnebago Industries, Inc. (motor home mfr)   SIC Code: 3716
605 West Crystal Lake Road
Forest City, IA 50436
515-582-6936   Contact: Sharon Nerdig

This is a 90 - minute bus tour, including a video presentation, where you will have the opportunity to see how motor homes are built. You will also visit two assembly plants and actually view the production in the chassis preparation area and in the motor home assembly facility. **NOTE:** Tours are given from 1:00 pm only during November and December. **DIRECTIONS:** Located northeast of Mason City. From US Rt 18 take Rt 69 north. Call for directions.

Hours: 9:00 am - 1:00 pm   Days: Monday - Friday (April - October)
Advance Notice: Yes   Fee: No   HP Access: No

Iowa Public Television (TV broadcast)   SIC Code: 4833
6450 Corporate Place
Johnston, IA 50131
515-281-4500   Contact: Molly Phillips

Take a 30 - minute basic tour of part of the Iowa Communication Network and see viewing machines and satellites. Speak to the program producer (when available). **DIRECTIONS:** US Rt 80 exit 131 north to Johnston.

Hours: 8:00 am - 5:00 pm   Days: Monday - Friday
Advance Notice: Yes   Fee: No   HP Access: Yes

Manchester Trout Hatchery (hatchery)   SIC Code: 0921
Iowa Department of Natural Resources
RR 2 - Box 269
Manchester, IA 52057
319-927-3276   Contact: Secretary/Manager

You will first see a slide/video program on the hatchery production of trout and then tour the hatchery facility. You will have an opportunity to see the fish in raceways and also feed the fish. **NOTE:** No handicap restrooms. **DIRECTIONS:** Two miles east of Manchester, turn south on paved road and drive two miles.

Hours: 8:00 am - 4:00 pm   Days: Monday - Friday
Advance Notice: Yes   Fee: No   HP Access: Yes

KIMT - TV 3 (TV broadcast)   SIC Code: 4833
112 North Pennsylvania Avenue
Mason City, IA 50401
515-423-2540   Contact: Kip Ireland

On this tour you will see where commercials are put together and how they are made. In addition to touring the studio, you will see where they technically direct the news and how the news and weather reports are put together. **NOTE:** No tours February, May, September, or November. **DIRECTIONS:** Located in the north central area of the state at the intersection of US Rts 65 and 18.

Hours: 10:00-11:30/2:30-4:00   Days: Monday - Friday
Advance Notice: Yes   Fee: No   HP Access: Yes

North Iowa Vocational Center (vocational services)   SIC Code: 8331
1225 South Harrison Avenue
Mason City, IA 50401
515-423-3301   Contact: Howard Wilcox

You will tour the various work areas such as the microfilming and custom pallet manufacturing departments, the assembly area and the classroom to see first hand how the rehabilitation training and employment programs are administered for adults with limited vocational abilities. **DIRECTIONS:** Located in Industrial Park in Mason City.

Hours: 8:00 am - 3:00 pm   Days: Monday - Friday
Advance Notice: No   Fee: No   HP Access: Yes

Kopy Kats and Original Dolls (doll mfr)   SIC Code: 3942
412 Main Street
Meservey, IA 50457-0244
515-358-6484   Contact: Karol Johnson

This is a must tour for doll enthusiasts. See how porcelain dolls are created from start to finish by a unique process since no two dolls are alike. **DIRECTIONS:** On Hwy 107 in the middle of Main St.

Hours: 10:30 am - 4:00 pm   Days: Monday - Friday
Advance Notice: Yes   Fee: $1.00   HP Access: Yes

Maytag Dairy Farms, Inc. (cheese processor)   SIC Code: 2022
2282 East 8th Street North
Newton, IA 50308
515-792-1133   Contact: James Stevens

Visit the home of world famous Blue Cheese in the heartland of America. This farm is in the ownership by third and fourth generations of the Maytag family. You will see an 11- minute video presentation. **NOTE:** Free samples. **DIRECTIONS:** I - 80 west of Newton, take exit 164 and follow IA Hwy 14 north for three miles, then follow the signs.

Hours: 9:00 am - 4:00 pm   Days: Monday - Friday
Advance Notice: Yes   Fee: No   HP Access: Yes

Continental Baking Company (bakery)   SIC Code: 2051
325 Commercial
Waterloo, IA 50701
319-234-4447   Contact: Bruce York

This is a complete tour of the baking industry facility. You will take an interesting tour regarding the procedure, outlay of building, products produced and news about upcoming products. **DIRECTIONS:** Located near the Holiday Inn in the center of town.

Hours: Call for schedule   Days: Wednesday
Advance Notice: Yes   Fee: No   HP Access: Yes

John Deere Component Div. (farm equipment mfr)   SIC Code: 3523
400 Westfield Avenue
Waterloo, IA 50704
319-292-7697   Contact: Mary Swehla/Renee Ostrem

A two and one-half hour guided tour of the components parts production area. **NOTE:** Children must be 12 years of age. It is advisable to wear comfortable walking shoes. No open-toed shoes allowed. **DIRECTIONS:** From US Rt 63 exit at Rt 218. Follow signs.

Hours: 9:00 am and 1:00 pm   Days: Monday - Friday
Advance Notice: Yes   Fee: No   HP Access: Yes

John Deere Engine Works (farm equipment mfr)   SIC Code: 3523
3801 Ridgeway Avenue
Waterloo, IA 50704
319-292-7697   Contact: Mary Swehla/Renee Ostrem

A one and one-half hour guided tour which encompasses the complete assembly of an engine. **NOTE:** Children must be 12 years of age. It is advisable to wear comfortable walking shoes and no open-toed shoes allowed. **DIRECTIONS:** From US Rt 63 exit at W. Ridgeway. Look for signs.

Hours: 9:30 am and 1:30 pm   Days: Monday - Friday
Advance Notice: Yes   Fee: No   HP Access: Yes

John Deere Foundry (foundry)   SIC Code: 3322
2000 Westfield Avenue
Waterloo, IA 50704
319-292-7697   Contact: Mary Swehla/Renee Ostrem

A one hour guided tour of the Molds and Casting Foundry. **NOTE:** Hours are flexible. Children must be 12 years of age. It is advisable to wear comfortable walking shoes. No open-toed shoes allowed. **DIRECTIONS:** From US Rt 63 exit at Rt 218 and look for signs.

Hours: Flexible   Days: Flexible
Advance Notice: Yes   Fee: No   HP Access: Yes

John Deere Tractor Works (farm equipment mfg)   SIC Code: 3523
3500 East Donald Street
Waterloo, IA 50704
319-292-7697   Contact: Mary Swehla/Renee Ostrem

This is a two and one-half hour guided tour to see the assembly of tractors 92-400 hp.
NOTE: Children must be 12 years of age. It is advisable to wear comfortable walking shoes.
No open-toed shoes allowed. **DIRECTIONS:** Follow East Donald St from Hwy 63, located
northeast of city.

Hours: 9:00 am and 1:00 pm   Days: Monday - Friday
Advance Notice: Yes   Fee: No   HP Access: Yes

Waterloo Processing & Dist. Center (postal)   SIC Code: 4311
300 Sycamore Street
Waterloo, IA 50701-9997
319-291-7400   Contact: Tom Hagarty

A 45 - minute general tour of the U. S. Postal facility will demonstrate how the mail arrives, is
processed and how it is dispatched. See hundreds of thousands of envelopes and items of
mail being routed through the facility. **DIRECTIONS:** Downtown east side location, next to
river, first street over bridge is Sycamore.

Hours: 9:00 am - 3:00 pm   Days: Monday - Friday
Advance Notice: Yes   Fee: No   HP Access: Yes

Waterloo Water Works (utility)   SIC Code: 4939
325 Sycamore Street
Waterloo, IA 50704
319-232-6280   Contact: Reed G. Craft

You will see a slide show presentation about the workings of the facility and, if time allows,
you will take a short walk through the pumping station. **DIRECTIONS:** Located in the
downtown area on the east side of the Cedar River.

Hours: By appointment
Advance Notice: Yes   Fee: No   HP Access: Yes

Russell Stover Candies (candy mfr)   SIC Code: 2064
1993 Caramel Boulevard
Abilene, KS 67410
913-263-3343   Contact: Shirley Howard

At this 10,000 square foot on-site factory outlet store, you will see a demonstration of how caramels, cherry cordials and toffee are made in their kitchens through a viewing window. **NOTE:** Bus tours are welcome. **DIRECTIONS:** Take the 272 exit, three miles west of Abilene on I - 70. Take a left off of I - 70 coming from the east. Cross over I - 70 and take the first left. Follow the paved road.

Hours: 9:00 am - 6:00 pm   Days: Monday - Saturday
            12:00 - 5:00 pm   Sunday
Advance Notice: Yes   Fee: No   HP Access: Yes

Wolf Creek Nuclear Operating Corp. (electric co)   SIC Code: 4911
1550 Oxen Lane, NE
Burlington, KS 66839
316-364-4162   Contact: John Hicks

This tour consists of a slide show presentation on how a nuclear power plant operates. You will see a geiger counter demonstration and participate in a drive around the plant. **NOTE:** Tours are scheduled on a case-by-case basis. **DIRECTIONS:** 11 miles south of I - 35 (take Hwy 75 south 11 miles).

Hours: 7:30 am - 4:00 pm   Days: Monday - Friday
Advance Notice: Yes   Fee: No   HP Access: Yes

The Puppet Factory (puppet mfr)   SIC Code: 3999
117 East 17th Street
Goodland, KS 67735
913-899-7143   Contact: Martha Bishop

On this 30 - minute tour, you will observe the cutting of materials and the sewing of puppets. You will also be able to see the finished work. **DIRECTIONS:** Exit 19, go left to Cattletrail, right on 17th St. At blinking stop light, building is on left on east end door by the railroad tracks.

Hours: 8:00 am - 4:00 pm   Days: Monday - Friday
Advance Notice: Yes   Fee: No   HP Access: No

US National Weather Service (weather forecast svc)   SIC Code: 8999
920 Armory Road
Goodland, KS 67735-9273
913-899-2360   Contact: Scott Mentzer

On this tour, you will have an opportunity to see the current Doppler Radar Technology used in weather forecasting. **DIRECTIONS:** Located one-half mile east of Fairgrounds.

Hours: 8:00 am - 4:00 pm	Days: Monday - Friday	
Advance Notice: Yes	Fee: No	HP Access: Yes

Training & Evaluation Center (vocational training)   SIC Code: 8331
1300 East Avenue A
Hutchinson, KS 67501
316-663-1596   Contact: Mimi Meredith

On this tour, you will see where clients with disabilities work on a variety of projects including a major recycling processing area. You will tour the Early Education Center where children with special needs are served in an integrated, preschool environment and also receive out-patient therapy services. **DIRECTIONS:** Ave A exit off Hwy 61.

Hours: 8:00 am - 4:00 pm	Days: Monday - Friday	
Advance Notice: Yes	Fee: No	HP Access: Yes

Milford Nature Center & Fish Hatchery (hatchery)   SIC Code: 0921
3115 Hatchery Drive
Junction City, KS 66441
785-238-5323   Contact: Pat Silovsky

This is a tour of a state-owned fish hatchery where you will see the production of fish used to stock state waters from eggs to fry to fingerlings and beyond. **NOTE:** Eggs and fry are best observed during the month of April. Scheduled tours are from mid-April to October. Other times by appointment. **DIRECTIONS:** Go five miles north on Hwy 77 from I - 70 (exit 295), then two miles west on Hwy 57. The Center is located near the spillway of Milford Dam.

Hours: 1:00 pm	Days: Saturday - Sunday	
Advance Notice: Yes	Fee: No	HP Access: Yes

Kansas City Bulk Mail Center (postal)   SIC Code: 4311
4900 Speaker Road
Kansas City, KS 66106-1042
913-573-2620   Contact: Regina Wofford

On the tour of this U. S. Postal Processing and Distribution Center, which processes over 300,000 pieces of mail a day, you will see the various operations used to sort parcel post and bulk business mail. **DIRECTIONS:** From the north, take I - 635 to Kansas Ave exit. Turn right and continue one block to 51st St, turn right and go north two blocks and then turn right on Speaker Rd. From the south, take I - 635 to Kansas Ave exit, turn right on Kansas Ave and continue one-half block to 42nd St, turn right and go north two blocks, turn left on Speaker Rd.

Hours: 24 hours   Days: Monday - Sunday
Advance Notice: Yes   Fee: No   HP Access: No

Kaw Valley Asparagus Farm (vegetable farm)   SIC Code: 0161
1446 East 1850 Road
Lawrence, KS 66011
913-843-1409   Contact: John or Karen Pendleton

The best time to tour is mid-April to the end of May as this is asparagus harvest time. Also raised is hydroporin tomatoes, peonies, bedding plants and other spring produce. **NOTE:** There are no tours August - December. **DIRECTIONS:** Three miles east of Lawrence and one mile north of Hwy 10.

Hours: Flexible   Days: Monday - Friday
Advance Notice: Yes   Fee: No   HP Access: No

La Superior Food Products, Inc. (foods)   SIC Code: 2099
4307 Merriam Drive
Overland Park, KS 66203
913-432-4933   Contact: Adriana Hernandez

On this 30 - 45 minute tour, you will have an opportunity to see how flour and corn tortillas are made. **DIRECTIONS:** Exit at Merriam Dr off I - 635. Turn right (west) on Merriam. Turn left (south) into the driveway between the yellow and a beige building.

Hours: 10:30 am   Days: Tuesday - Thursday
Advance Notice: Yes   Fee: No   HP Access: Yes

Wichita Processing & Dist. Center (postal)   SIC Code: 4311
7117 West Harry Street
Wichita, KS 67276-9997
316-946-4641   Contact: Joanne Lehr

On the 45 - minute tour of the U. S. Postal Processing and Distribution Center, you will see the mail flow along with the current state-of-the-art equipment, including letter and flat mail processing. **DIRECTIONS:** Located at Wichita Mid-Continent Airport.

Hours: 12:00 noon - 6:00 pm   Days: Tuesday - Thursday
Advance Notice: Yes   Fee: No   HP Access: Yes

Binney & Smith, Inc. (crayon mfr)   SIC Code: 3952
2000 Liquitex Lane
Winfield, KS 67156-5300
316-221-4200   Contact: Tiffany Schumacher

This 90 - minute tour begins at History Time and then you will travel on a fun-filled journey through Crayola's "Wonderful World of Color" via video. You will then proceed through the crayon marker and paint manufacturing processes. **NOTE:** Tours are conducted from February 1 to November 15. **DIRECTIONS:** From Wichita, take K - 15 east to Hwy 77. Turn south. Follow Hwy 77 through Winfield to 19th St. Turn left and go 20 blocks east. Company is on the north side at the corner of 19th St and Wheat.

Hours: 10;30 and 1:00 pm   Days: Monday - Friday
Advance Notice: Yes   Fee: No   HP Access: Yes

U. S. Postal Processing & Dist. Center (postal)   SIC Code: 4311
5300 Scottsville Road
Bowling Green, KY 42104-9998
502-843-5760   Contact: Plant Manager

At this U. S. Postal Processing and Distribution Center, you will tour the mail processing area where the emphasis is on automation equipment. Follow hundreds of pieces of mail as it goes through the complete processing system. **DIRECTIONS:** One mile east of I - 65 on Hwy 231.

Hours: 12 noon - 2:00 pm   Days: Tuesday - Thursday
Advance Notice: Yes   Fee: No   HP Access: Yes

Campbellsville Cherry Furniture (furniture mfr)   SIC Code: 2519
600 Water Tower Bypass
Campbellsville, KY 42718
502-789-1741   Contact: Linda McMahan

You are invited to tour this small showroom of this family owned business, operated by Eugene McMahan, who has created fine furniture in cherry and walnut in the manner of Early American cabinetmakers since 1965. You will tour the work area and see the craftsmen at work. **DIRECTIONS:** Turn off East Broadway onto Roberts Rd. Continue straight until you reach the water tower - company is located next to it.

Hours: 10:30 am - 12:00 noon   Days: Monday - Friday
Advance Notice: Yes   Fee: No   HP Access: No

Campbellsville Cherry Reproductions (furniture mfr)   SIC Code: 2519
3380 Saloma Road
Campbellsville, KY 42718
502-465-6003   Contact: Alice McMahan

Tour this company that produces fine cherry furniture and watch as craftsmen transform cherry wood into beautiful pieces of furniture. **DIRECTIONS:** Three and one-half miles north of Campbellsville on Hwy 527.

Hours: 10:00 am - 3:00 pm   Days: Monday - Saturday
Advance Notice: Yes   Fee: No   HP Access: No

Teledyne Packaging (packaging products)   SIC Code: 2655
904 Hawkins Street
Carrollton, KY 41008
502-732-4363   Contact: Manager

A one hour tour of the manufacturing area of a company that makes packaging products of aluminum for the pharmaceutical industry. **DIRECTIONS:** From US Rt 71, northeast of Louisville, take Rt 227 into town. Call for more specific directions.

Hours: By appointment
Advance Notice: Yes   Fee: No   HP Access: Yes

Jim Beam's American Outpost (distillery)   SIC Code: 2085
Highway 245
Clermont, KY 40110
502-543-9877   Contact: Tour Manager

A self-guided tour featuring an informative film showing how Jim Beam's bourbon whiskey is made. Visit the Beam Decanter Museum, the Cooperage (barrel-making) Museum and more. **DIRECTIONS:** I - 65 to exit 112.

Hours: 9:00 am - 4:30 pm   Days: Monday - Saturday
Advance Notice: No   Fee: No   HP Access: Yes

Coca-Cola Bottling of Elizabethtown (soft drinks)   SIC Code: 2086
1201 North Dixie Highway
Elizabethtown, KY 42701
502-737-4000   Contact: Jan Schmidt (x222)

You will have an opportunity to move along a gallery to watch the up-to-date bottling and canning procedures. You may visit the Schmidt Museum (Adults $2.00, 50 cents children). **NOTE:** Free ice-cold Coke. **DIRECTIONS:** From the north, take I - 65 south to exit 94. Follow US 62 to US 31 west about one mile.

Hours: 9:00 am - 4:00 pm   Days: Monday - Friday
Advance Notice: No   Fee: No   HP Access: No

Oldenberg Brewing Company (brewery)   SIC Code: 2082
400 Buttermilk Pike
Fort Mitchell, KY 41017
606-341-2802   Contact: Emma Obertate

Guided tour of the state-of-the-art working microbrewery and The American Museum of Brewing History and Arts. **NOTE:** Free samples. **DIRECTIONS:** I - 75 to Buttermilk Pike exit 186.

Hours: 10:00 am - 5:00 pm   Days: Sunday - Saturday
Advance Notice: Yes   Fee: No   HP Access: Yes

Leestown Company, Inc. (distillery)   SIC Code: 2085
1001 Wilkinson Boulevard
Frankfort, KY 40601
502-223-7641   Contact: Janice Collins

The one hour tour begins with a video followed by a visit to the automated bottling house, single barrel bottling house, warehouse and building where bourbon is dumped. **NOTE:** Gift shop. Tours on the hour. **DIRECTIONS:** North of downtown Frankfort on US 421 (Wilkinson Blvd).

Hours: 9:00 am - 2:00 pm   Days: Monday - Friday
Advance Notice: Yes   Fee: No   HP Access: Yes

Rebecca-Ruth Candy (candy mfr)   SIC Code: 2064
112 East Second Street
Frankfort, KY 40601
502-223-7475 (800-444-3766)   Contact: Pat

Visit the museum room, candy kitchen and production area. Highlight of the tour includes "Edna's Table", an 11 foot marble slab used since 1864, named after Edna Robbins, who is still an active employee after 65 years. **NOTE:** Free sample of the world-famous Bourbon Balls. Groups of 10 or more must give advance notice. **DIRECTIONS:** Take I - 64 to Frankfort exit 58 and follow US 60 to the corner of Capitol Ave and Second St and turn left. Company is located one-half block on left.

Hours: 9:00 am - 4:30 pm   Days: Monday - Thursday
Advance Notice: No   Fee: No   HP Access: No

Toyota Motor Manufacturing, USA, (automobile mfr)   SIC Code: 3711
1001 Cherry Blossom Way
Georgetown, KY 40324
502-868-3027 (800-866-4485)   Contact: Plant Manager

This 90 - minute tour begins with a video presentation allowing you the opportunity to discover the pride of the people of Toyota. Following the video, you will board a battery operated tram for a plant tour through the vehicle production plant showing the stamping, body weld and assembly processes. Toyota produces the Camry and Avalon at this facility. **NOTE:** Children must be eight years or older. **DIRECTIONS:** Georgetown is located north of Lexington on Rt 25. Call for more specific directions.

Hours: 10:00,noon,2:00,6:00   Days: Tuesday and Thursday
Advance Notice: Yes   Fee: No   HP Access: Limited

Maker's Mark Distillery, Inc. (distillery)   SIC Code: 2085
3350 Burks Spring Road
Loretto, KY 40037
502-865-2099   Contact: Donna S. Nally

A guided walking tour of the grounds into the stillhouse where you will see the actual processes of making bourbon, then on to the bottling house where you will see the operations. **NOTE:** Advance notice for groups of 25 or more. **DIRECTIONS:** Hwy 52 east from Loretto, 49 south to 52 from Bardstown.

Hours: 10:30 am - 3:30 pm   Days: Monday - Saturday
Advance Notice: No   Fee: No   HP Access: No

American Printing House for Blind (printer)   SIC Code: 2759
1839 Frankfort Avenue
Louisville, KY 40206-0085
502-895-2405 (800-223-1839)   Contact: Sarah Ferguson

The one hour tour offers an informative and fascinating guided tour where you will see the production of braille publications, the recording of talking books, and a demonstration of special educational aids for visually impaired students. **NOTE:** Closed holidays. Reservations for groups of 10 or more. **DIRECTIONS:** Located in the historic Louisville neighborhood of Clifton, with easy access to nearby I - 64, I - 65, and I - 71.

Hours: 10:00 am and 2:00 pm   Days: Monday - Friday
Advance Notice: No   Fee: No   HP Access: Yes

The Courier-Journal (newspaper)   SIC Code: 2711
525 West Broadway
Louisville, KY 40206
502-582-4545   Contact: Readers Service Personnel

A 45 - minute tour and a 10 - minute slide presentation will provide you with a special look at the news, pre-press, press and photography departments. **NOTE:** By reservation only. **DIRECTIONS:** Located at the intersection of 6th and Broadway in downtown Louisville.

Hours: 9:30 - 11:00 am   Days: Monday - Friday
Advance Notice: Yes   Fee: No   HP Access: Yes

Ford Motor Company (truck mfr)   SIC Code: 3711
Kentucky Truck Plant
3001 Chamberlain Lane
Louisville, KY 40232
502-429-2146   Contact: Bill Kellerman

On this tour you will watch where 500 trucks per day are being built (i.e., school bus chassis F Series from F 250 up and the world famous Louisville Series). **DIRECTIONS:** I - 265 to Westport Rd exit.

Hours: By appointment only
Advance Notice: Yes   Fee: No   HP Access: Yes

Louisville Processing and Dist. Center (postal)   SIC Code: 4311
1420 Gardiner Lane
Louisville, KY 40231-9997
502-454-1650   Contact: Consumer Affairs Office

At this U. S. Postal Processing and Distribution Center you will tour all of the mail processing operations where you will watch mail being routed through the automated machines from start to finish. **DIRECTIONS:** Located between Poplar Level and Newburg Rds.

Tours: By appointment only
Advance Notice: Yes   Fee: No   HP Access: Yes

Louisville Stoneware Company (pottery products)   SIC Code: 3269
731 Brent Street
Louisville, KY 40204
502-582-1900   Contact: Charlie Richardson

The 15 - 30 minute tour will show how plates and mugs are created from raw clay on the "Jigger" wheels. You will visit the Art Prep and Art Departments to observe hand painting. Tour will end at the kilns with a return to the factory outlet store. **NOTE:** Advance notice for groups of 10 or more. **DIRECTIONS:** East on Broadway to the L & N Viaduct, right on Brent St.

Hours: 10:30 am and 2:30 pm   Days: Monday - Friday
Advance Notice: No   Fee: No   HP Access: Yes

Palace Theatre (theater)   SIC Code: 7922
629 South Fourth Avenue
Louisville, KY 40202
502-583-4555   Contact: Teresa Whitelaw

On the 45 - minute tour of the theater building built in 1928, you will hear a description of the changes it has gone through over the years including the recent $4+ million restoration. You will see their celebrated ceiling where clouds float across a deep midnight sky and simulated stars twinkle. You will also visit the backstage activities. Originally built for vaudeville and movies, the Palace now serves as a multi-use theatre for concerts, variety and family shows, comedy and all genres inbetween. **NOTE:** Tours depart at 10:00, 10:45, 11:30, 12:15, 1:00 and 2:00. **DIRECTIONS:** Located in downtown Louisville, off I - 65, one block north of Broadway on Fourth.

Hours: 10:00 am - 2:00 pm   Days: Tuesday - Saturday
Advance Notice: No   Fee: $2.00   HP Access: Yes

Hi-Way Wood Products, Inc. (furniture mfr)   SIC Code: 2519
3430 West Highway 76
Russell Springs, KY 42642
502-866-3910   Contact: Don Emerson

On this tour you will be able to observe how raw lumber is made into finished chair components. **DIRECTIONS:** Located four miles north of Russell Springs on Rt 127.

Hours: 8:00 am - 2:00 pm   Days: Monday - Friday
Advance Notice: Yes   Fee: No   HP Access: Yes

Bluegrass Brewing Company (brewery)   SIC Code: 2082
3929 Shelbyville Road
St. Matthews, KY 40207
502-899-7070   Contact: Sarah Ring

Short tour of a microbrewery where they brew five permanent and two seasonal beers which are sold on the premises. **NOTE:** Free beer tasting. **DIRECTIONS:** Located in the incorporated city of St. Matthews which is on the near east end of Louisville, accessible by Fwy from I - 264 or I - 71. Call for more specific directions.

Hours: 1:00 - 5:00 pm   Days: Monday - Friday
Advance Notice: Yes   Fee: No   HP Access: Yes

Ale 8-One Bottling Company (soft drinks)   SIC Code: 2086
25 Carol Road
Winchester, KY 40391
606-744-3484   Contact: Nancy Colonel

This is a 15 - minute walk through a modern bottling room where you will observe the bottles being filled with the popular Ale 8-One soda. **DIRECTIONS:** US Rt 65, take exit 96 south to town. Call for specific directions.

Hours: 10:45 am and 1:00 pm Days: Monday - Thursday
Advance Notice: Yes   Fee: No   HP Access: No

Abita Brewing Company, Inc. (brewery)   SIC Code: 2082
72011 Holly Street
Abita Springs, LA 70420
501-893-3143   Contact: Jim or Kathleen Patton

Tour a family-owned brewery and see the production of a variety of flavorful brews using the artesian waters of Abita Springs. You will tour the plant where the beers are brewed in small batches with grains imported from England, hops from both foreign and domestic suppliers, yeasts from Germany, and water from 2,000 foot artesian wells. **DIRECTIONS:** Located in downtown Abita Springs, one hour from New Orleans.

Hours: 1:00 pm   Days: Saturday
Advance Notice: No   Fee: No   HP Access: Yes

McIlhenny Company - Tabasco Center (sauce mfr)   SIC Code: 2035
LA 329
Avery Island, LA 70513
318-365-8173 (800-634-9599)   Contact: Linda Clausiz

In touring the Tabasco factory, you will view an eight minute film on the history of this well-known sauce. You will then observe the bottling line and finally end the tour in the Country store where you will find a variety of Tabasco logo items as well as local cajun items from around Acadiana. **DIRECTIONS:** From US Rt 10, east of Baton Rouge, take Rt 90. Follow signs to the Jungle Gardens.

Hours: 9:00 am - 4:00 pm   Days: Monday - Friday
       9:00 am - 12:00 noon   Saturday
Advance Notice: No   Fee: No   HP Access: Yes

United States Postal Service (postal)   SIC Code: 4311
8101 Bluebonnet Boulevard
Baton Rouge, LA 70810-9997
504-763-3730   Contact: Adolph Ray

On the tour of the United States Postal Service you will receive a demonstration of the mail processing operations, depending on the time of day the tour is being given and according to the mail volume. **DIRECTIONS:** Go east on I - 10, exit 162, keep right to second red light, cross Perkins Rd. Post Office is on left.

Hours: 9 - 12, 4 - 7pm   Days: Thursday and Friday
Advance Notice: Yes   Fee: No   HP Access: Yes

Center for Advanced Microstructures (research)   SIC Code: 8731
Louisiana State University
3990 West Lakeshore Drive
Baton Rouge, LA 70810
504-388-8887   Contact: Effie Kousoulas

A tour of this high tech research center, located on the Louisiana State University campus, will give you the opportunity to see how CAMD provides equipment, expertise and infra-structure in the areas of microstructures and microdevices. At the heart of CAMD is a high energy particle accelerator. **NOTE:** Tours must be scheduled at least two weeks in advance. **DIRECTIONS:** From US Rt 10 in Baton Rouge, follow Nicholson Dr to campus.

Hours: By reservation only
Advance Notice: Yes   Fee: No   HP Access: Yes

Red River Research Station (research)   SIC Code: 8731
262 Research Station Drive
Bossier City, LA 71112
318-741-7430   Contact: Jere McBride

You will have the opportunity to view field activities associated with the conduct of applied research of agricultural products including cotton, corn, soybean, tomatoes, watermelon, etc. This is a state operated facility, supported by government and industry funds. Emphasis is on improving plant quality so that they are less dependent on chemical fertilizers and pest control products. **DIRECTIONS:** Off Hwy 71 south, one mile past Sligo Rd, turn right at red barn.

Hours: 7:30 am - 4:30 pm   Days: Monday - Friday
Advance Notice: Yes   Fee: No   HP Access: Yes

Bryan's Vineyard (winery)   SIC Code: 2084
1199 Richardson Road
Calhoun, LA 71225
318-644-5238   Contact: Holmes M. Bryan

You will tour four acres of 48 different varieties of muscaline grapes. The vineyard also sells fruit, jelly, juice and wine made from their grapes. **DIRECTIONS:** Exit 103 off I - 20 to Claiborne Rd to Richardson Rd.

Hours: 7:00 am - 7:00 pm   Days: Monday - Saturday
Advance Notice: No   Fee: No   HP Access: Yes

Producer's Mutual Gin Co., Inc. (cotton gin)   SIC Code: 0724
107 Frenchman Street
Cheneyville, LA 71325
318-279-2145   Contact: Juliette D. Linzay

You will listen to the age-old ginning process explained and view the gin in operation (from September - November 15) and then on through the huge warehouse where you will see many bales of cotton. **DIRECTIONS:** Hwy 71 south to city limits of Cheneyville.

Hours: 9:00 am - 3:00 pm   Days: Monday - Friday
Advance Notice: Yes   Fee: No   HP Access: No

Casa De Sue Winery (winery)   SIC Code: 2084
14316 Hatcher Road
Clinton, LA 70722
504-683-5937 (800-683-5937)   Contact: Mac or JoAnn Cazedussus

After watching a 10 - minute video, you will be taken on a tour of this family oriented winery. Some of their wines include Carlos Sweet and Dry, Sterling, Doreen, Magnolia, LaRosa and Miss Blue, muscadine and blueberry wines. **NOTE:** Wine tasting in gift shop. Advance notice for groups of 10 or more. Fee refundable if a purchase is made. **DIRECTIONS:** From Baton Rouge, take Hwy 37 (approximately 27 miles) to Hwy 63 (one and 3/10 miles) onto Hwy 960 (seven miles) to Gilead Rd to Hatcher Rd. Watch for signs.

Hours: 10:00 am - 6:00 pm   Days: Monday - Saturday
Advance Notice: Yes   Fee: $2.00   HP Access: Yes

U-Pick-Um Farm (farm products)   SIC Code: 0191
12088 Marilyn Lane
Hammond, LA 70403
504-294-2393   Contact: Jim or Louise Conerty

On a visit to this farm you will see and pick from 17 different fruits plus Shiitake and Oyster mushrooms. Learn about drip irrigation as an efficient and water conservation watering system. **DIRECTIONS:** Pumpkin Center Rd to Tuttle. 3/4 mile to Marilyn Ln, exit Pumpkin Center on I - 12, exit 35.

Hours: Sunrise - Sunset	Days: Monday - Sunday	
Advance Notice: Yes	Fee: No	HP Access: No

Motivatit Seafoods, Inc. (seafood)   SIC Code: 2092
407 Palm Avenue
Houma, LA 70364
504-868-7191   Contact: Mike Voisin

A tour of the seafood processing plant, featuring oysters, crabs and crawfish, will be followed by a discussion about Louisiana's bountiful seafood harvest and estuaries. **DIRECTIONS:** Hwy 90 west from New Orleans to Houma.

Hours: 7:00 am - 12:00 pm	Days: Monday - Friday	
Advance Notice: Yes	Fee: Yes	HP Access: No

USDA - Sugarcane Research Unit (research)   SIC Code: 8731
800 Little Bayou Black Drive
Houma, LA 70361
504-872-5042   Contact: Ben Legendre/Lois Burton

Tour of a sugarcane research and development complex of the US Department of Agriculture whose goals are to develop varieties that are high yielding and resistant to disease, pets and cold climates. **NOTE:** Two week advance notice required. Tours will be given only if a member of the scientific staff is available on the day that your tour is scheduled. Tour is subject to cancellation without notice if staff member is not available. **DIRECTIONS:** Approximately 50 miles west of New Orleans.

Hours: 7:30 am - 4:00 pm	Days: Monday - Friday	
Advance Notice: Yes	Fee: No	HP Access: No

Lafayette Processing & Dist. Facility (postal)   SIC Code: 4311
1105 Moss Street
Lafayette, LA 70509-9997
318-269-4825   Contact: Alexis O. Herbert

At the U. S. Postal Processing and Distribution Facility, you will go on a tour of the
workroom floor, which will show the process a letter goes through when it is mailed; and
when possible, a mechanic will give a demonstration on how the equipment on the workroom
floor works. **DIRECTIONS:** I - 49 south, make a left turn on Willow, and a right on Moss.

Hours: 10:00 am - 2:00 pm   Days: Monday - Friday
Advance Notice: Yes   Fee: No   HP Access: Yes

PPG Industries, Inc. (chemicals)   SIC Code: 2899
1300 Columbia Southern Road
Lake Charles, LA 70602
318-491-4200   Contact: Chuck Bellon

You will receive a riding tour which will provide you an overview of the chemical complex
where a variety of chemicals are produced that are used in the manufacture of common consumer and industrial goods, including cleaning, foods, plastics and tires. **DIRECTIONS:**
Columbia Southern Rd exit off I - 10.

Hours: On a request basis
Advance Notice: Yes   Fee: No   HP Access: Yes

Panola Pepper Corporation (sauce mfr)   SIC Code: 2035
Highway 65
Lake Providence, LA 71254
318-559-1774   Contact: Manager

You will visit the manufacturer of hot sauces, readi-mixes and seasonings to see how the
process is accomplished. Since different hot sauces are produced each day, you will also be
able to see the production line in progress. **DIRECTIONS:** North of Lake Providence on
Hwy 65. Turn on to black top road at the large 12 foot sign. Plant is located at the end of the
black top road about one - half mile off the highway.

Hours: 9:00 am - 5:00 pm   Days: Monday - Friday
Advance Notice: Yes   Fee: No   HP Access: No

Pender's Pride (winery)   SIC Code: 2084
766 Forest Home Road
Monroe, LA 71202
318-323-7001   Contact: Pat Pender

On this tour you will have an opportunity to walk through the vineyard after which you can sample different varieties of muscadines. **DIRECTIONS:** 18 miles south of Monroe at Besco, follow signs.

Hours: 9:00 am - 11:00 am   Days: Monday - Saturday
Advance Notice: Yes   Fee: $1.00   HP Access: No

Marine Shale Processors, Inc. (recycling center)   SIC Code: 5093
9828 US Highway 90E
Morgan City, LA 70380
504-631-3161 (800-872-6774)   Contact: Maxine Domino

This two hour tour involves a short lecture, video and site tour of the largest recycle, reuse, resource recovery facility of its type in the United States. MSP utilizes hazardous and non-hazardous industrial waste materials as ingredients and fuel in a multi-patented manufacturing process to produce environmentally-safe construction aggregates and to recover grade one steel and limestone. **DIRECTIONS:** From US Rte 10 east of Baton Rouge, follow Rt 90 south to Morgan City.

Hours: Open door policy
Advance Notice: Yes   Fee: No   HP Access: No

Konriko/Conrad Rice Mill (rice mill)   SIC Code: 2044
307 Ann Street
New Iberia, LA 70560
318-394-6462   Contact: Sandra Davis

When you arrive at the mill you will see a 20 - minute slide presentation about the Cajun culture and some history of the rice mill. You will then go on a 20 - minute tour of the rice mill where you will watch rice being packaged and rice cakes being made. **NOTE:** Hours may be flexible. Mill has three steps to climb and is not handicap accessible. **DIRECTIONS:** Follow US Rt 90 to LA 14 (Center St) north. Take a right on St. Peter St and a left on Ann St.

Hours: 10:00,11:00,1:00,2:00   Days: Monday - Saturday
Advance Notice: No   Fee: No   HP Access: No

Creole Foods of Opelousas (food preparation)   SIC Code: 2099
533 North Lombard Street
Opelousas, LA 70570
318-948-4691(800-551-9066)   Contact: Pat McGlothlin

On this tour you will see how creole foods are blended, packaged and shipped in its famous Cajun creole food products packages. **NOTE:** Closed 11:30 am - 1:30 pm daily.
DIRECTIONS: I - 49 north from Lafayette. Exit 19B to Hwy 190 west. At Lombard, turn right and go three blocks. Plant is on left.

 Hours: 9:30 am - 3:30 pm   Days: Monday - Friday
Advance Notice: Yes   Fee: No   HP Access: Yes

Odell Pottery (pottery products)   SIC Code: 3269
1705 West Kentucky Avenue
Ruston, LA 71270
318-251-3145   Contact: Bruce Odell

See all the stages of production of three types of pottery, including forming on the potters wheel, bisque firing, glazing, and often racu-firing. **DIRECTIONS:** Take Tech exit from I - 20 north to four-way stop light to third driveway.

Hours: 10:00 am - 5:00 pm   Days: Monday - Friday
Advance Notice: Yes   Fee: No   HP Access: No

Shreveport Processing & Dist. Center (postal)   SIC Code: 4311
2400 Texas Avenue
Shreveport, LA 71102-9997
318-677-2351   Contact: Jon Carver

At the U. S. Postal Processing and Distribution Center you will take a plant tour and see the mail handling processing equipment and operations of this major mail distribution center.
DIRECTIONS: I - 20 to Greenwood Rd exit. Go east 1/4 mile. Facility is located on the left just past first signal light.

Hours: 10:00 am - 4:00 pm   Days: Tuesday - Thursday
Advance Notice: Yes   Fee: No   HP Access: Yes

Gulf States Utilities (electric company)   SIC Code: 4911
5485 US Highway 61
St. Francisville, LA 70775
504-381-4277   Contact: Kevin Dreher

On this tour you will see an audio-visual presentation, mechanical exhibition, graphic displays and go on a guided tour which will explain the history of electricity, how it is generated, and its many sources including the workings of a nuclear power plant. **DIRECTIONS:** Three miles south of St. Francisville, 25 miles north of Baton Rouge.

Hours: 8:00 am - 4:30 pm   Days: Monday - Friday
Advance Notice: Yes   Fee: No   HP Access: Yes

Plantation Pecan Company (nuts)   SIC Code: 0173
HC-62, Box 139
Waterproof, LA 71375
318-749-5421   Contact: Carol Lee Miller

Tour a very large orchard of pecan trees for which the south is famous. You will learn about the history and processing of the nuts before going to market. You will observe how pecans are used in recipes (which are given out) to make pies, pralines, and fudge products. **NOTE:** Free samples. Gift shop. **DIRECTIONS:** Follow Rt 65 north from Natches, MS to SR 568 to town. Call for specific directions.

Hours: 10:00 am - 5:00 pm   Days: Monday - Friday
Advance Notice: Yes   Fee: No   HP Access: Yes

Vista Chemical Company (chemicals)   SIC Code: 2899
2201 Old Spanish Trail
Westlake, LA 70669
318-494-5301   Contact: Nancy Tower

The tour begins with a 30 - minute presentation with an overview on safety. Depending on time allocated, tour may include a driving tour and stops in the laboratory and/or units. You will learn about the manufacture of alcohols used in cosmetics and detergents, ethylenes, paraffin and vinyl compounds. **NOTE:** Handicap accessible if transportation is provided by group. **DIRECTIONS:** I - 10 to Westlake exit, north on Sampson to first light, west on Old Spanish Trail to Vista entrance on right.

Hours: 8:00 am - 8:00 pm   Days: As requested
Advance Notice: Yes   Fee: No   HP Access: No

The Jackson Laboratory (research & devel. lab)   SIC Code: 8731
600 Main Street
Bar Harbor, ME 04609
207-288-3371   Contact: Dawn Fernald

Tour of the laboratory which specializes in the breeding and raising of special strains of mice for sale to research scientists throughout the country, as well as for genetic research at the facility on human diseases such as multiple sclerosis, cancer and heart. **NOTE:** Tours only June - September. **DIRECTIONS:** From Bangor, take Rt 1A east to Ellsworth and then follow Rt 3 to center of Bar Harbor.

Hours: 3:00 - 4:00 pm   Days: Tuesday and Thursday
Advance Notice: No   Fee: No   HP Access: Yes

Tom's of Maine (toiletries mfr)   SIC Code: 2844
302 Lafayette Center
Kennebunk, ME 04043
207-985-2944   Contact: Regis Park

This one hour factory tour takes you through the production process, from raw materials to mixing to the production line and quality testing. Some products that may be in production are toothpaste, deodorant, mouthwash or shampoo. **NOTE:** Tour not recommended for children under five years of age. Please wear rubber-soled shoes and casual attire. The production area is located on the second floor and is accessed by a flight of stairs. Video tour is available. Toothpaste samples. **DIRECTIONS:** From Rt 95 north/south (Maine Turnpike) take a left off the Kennebunk exit on to Rt 35. At the V in the road, bear right to Storer St, look for Lafayette Center which is the large brick building on your right.

Hours: 11:00 am and 1:00 pm   Days: Tuesday - Friday (June-Labor Day)
          11:00 am   Wednesday (September - May)
Advance Notice: Yes   Fee: No   HP Access: Limited

Gritty McDuff's Brew Pub (brewery)   SIC Code: 2082
396 Fore Street
Portland, ME 04101
207-772-2739   Contact: Tour Manager

This is a 30 - minute tour that will take you through the beer brewing process in their on-site brewery. **NOTE:** Free sampling. **DIRECTIONS:** From Rt 295 south, take exit 7 (Franklin Artery exit), head towards the waterfront to Fore St. Take a right and go three blocks to the end. Brew Pub is on your left.

Hours: 1:00 pm   Days: Saturday - Sunday
Advance Notice: Yes   Fee: No   HP Access: No

Portland Processing & Dist. Center (postal)   SIC Code: 4311
125 Forest Avenue
Portland, ME 04101-9997
207-871-8528   Contact: Sally Higgins

An approximate one hour tour of the U. S. Postal Processing & Distribution Center will show you the automation equipment, the flat sorter machine, the letter sorter machine, the carrier section and the window lobby unit. There is also a 15 - minute video showing the entire process. **DIRECTIONS:** Follow US Rt 95 to exit 6A (Rt 295) into town. Call for specific directions.

Hours: 9:00 am - 1:00 pm   Days: Tuesday, Wednesday, Thursday
Advance Notice: Yes   Fee: No   HP Access: Yes

Harford Systems, Inc. (metal goods mfr)   SIC Code: 3499
2129 Pulaski Highway
Aberdeen, MD 21001
443-272-3400   Contact: Jacqui Bott

This is a 45 - minute tour where you will have an opportunity to see the process involved in manufacturing walk-in freezers and coolers which are used in fast food restaurants, Disney World, stadiums, prisons, and hospitals. **DIRECTIONS:** On Rt 40, between Aberdeen & Havre de Grace.

Hours: 8:00 am - 3:00 pm   Days: Monday - Friday
Advance Notice: Yes   Fee: No   HP Access: No

Jones & Ladd (canvas products)   SIC Code: 2394
Bags by Mimi
326 First Street
Annapolis, MD 21403   Contact: Harry Jones
443-263-6817

On this visit you will see sewing machine operators making canvas bags and screen printing wearables. You will also see the artist making designs for printing. **DIRECTIONS:** From US Rt 50 at intersection of St Rt 70, Rowe Blvd, proceed towards town to Church Circle. Take Duke of Gloucester St off the circle, continuing across draw bridge to Severn Ave (first light). Turn left and continue to Second St. Take left. Go to sea wall. Take left.

Hours: 10:00 am - 2:00 pm   Days: Monday - Friday
Advance Notice: Yes   Fee: No   HP Access: No

Acadia Windows & Doors, Inc. (window mfr)   SIC Code: 3442
9611 Pulaski Park Drive
Baltimore, MD 21220
443-780-9600   Contact: Receptionist

Take this one hour tour of a vinyl window and door manufacturing facility where you will watch the fabrication of units and insulated glass units. **NOTE:** Tours are only available upon request. **DIRECTIONS:** I - 695 to Rt 40 east toward Aberdeen. Continue for three miles on Rt 40. After you pass Middle River Rd, turn right into the industrial park.

Hours: 9:00 am - 12 noon   Days: Monday and Wednesday
Advance Notice: Yes   Fee: No   HP Access: Yes

Baltimore RESCO (recycling center)   SIC Code: 5093
1801 Annapolis Road
Baltimore, MD 21230
443-234-0808   Contact: Steve Tomczewski

Tour this recycling facility where you will see the various aspects of the process of recycling your trash into energy. **DIRECTIONS:** From Washington, DC, take I - 95 north, following signs for downtown Baltimore. Take exit 52, Russell St. Make right turn at bottom of ramp. For more specific directions, please call facility.

Hours: 10:00 am - 5:00 pm   Days: Thursday - Friday
Advance Notice: Yes   Fee: No   HP Access: Yes

General Motors Truck & Bus Group (truck mfr)   SIC Code: 3711
2122 Broening Highway
Baltimore, MD 21224
443-631-2112   Contact: William Guido

A two - hour walking tour of a minivan plant, showing the assembly of the Astro and Safari vans. The tour involves walking approximately two and one-half miles. **NOTE:** Must be age 10. All participants must be able to walk without canes, crutches or wheelchairs. No cameras, tape recorders, open-toe shoes or sandals. Foreign nationals must be pre-approved prior to visit. **DIRECTIONS:** I - 95 north to Boston St exit. Follow signs to Broening Hwy and take left, crossing Holibird Avenue. Parking lot will be on your left. Cross Broening Hwy via pedestrian walkway, and enter at main lobby door.

Hours: 9:00 am and 6:30 pm   Days: Monday - Friday
Advance Notice: Yes   Fee: No   HP Access: No

Metalcraft, Inc. (fire extinguisher mfr)   SIC Code: 3499
718 Debelius Avenue
Baltimore, MD 21205
443-485-0880   Contact: Ernest Ellis

A 30 - minute tour of the manufacturer of fire extinguishers used in home and industry.
DIRECTIONS: Between Erdman Ave and Pulaski Hwy.

Hours: 10:00 am - 3:00 pm   Days: Tuesday - Thursday
Advance Notice: Yes   Fee: No   HP Access: No

Moore's Candies (candy mfr)   SIC Code: 2064
3004 Pinewood Avenue
Baltimore, MD 21214
443-426-2705   Contact: James Heyl

A 30 - 60 minute tour where you will watch the assembly line production of holiday candy
from September to February. At other times of the year you will see the manufacturing of
fine chocolates. **DIRECTIONS:** From Baltimore Beltway, take exit 31A (Rt 147) east for
two miles. Left onto Pinewood Ave, factory is on the left.

Hours: 10:00 am - 1:30 pm   Days: Monday - Friday
Advance Notice: Yes   Fee: No   HP Access: Yes

Pompeian, Inc. (olive oil)   SIC Code: 2076
4201 Pulaski Highway
Baltimore, MD 21224
443-276-6900   Contact: Receptionist

Tour of America's largest and oldest importer, bottler and worldwide distributor of olive oil
and red wine vinegar. You will learn about olive oil from tree to table, and a guided tour of
the underground tanks where 1.5 million gallons of extra virgin olive oil are stored. You will
also visit the warehouse area and an historic olive mill from Spain. **NOTE:** Please call at
least five days in advance for reservations. **DIRECTIONS:** From I - 695 (Beltway) follow
Rt 40 toward Baltimore. Company is on the left of their billboard.

Hours: 10:00,11:30,1:00,1:30   Days: Monday - Friday
Advance Notice: Yes   Fee: No   HP Access: Yes

WBAL-TV (TV broadcast)   SIC Code: 4833
3800 Hooper Avenue
Baltimore, MD 21211
443-467-3000   Contact: Elizabeth Francis

A look behind the scenes of the WBAL-TV 11 News at Noon. You will also tour through the newsroom, news studio, and the control and tape rooms. You will have an opportunity to watch part of the live 12 noon news. **NOTE:** Tours by appointment only. **DIRECTIONS:** Located in downtown Baltimore. Call for specific directions.

Hours: 11:15 am - 12:15 pm   Days: Monday - Friday
Advance Notice: Yes   Fee: No   HP Access: Yes

WJZ TV Channel 13 (TV broadcast)   SIC Code: 4833
3725 Malden Avenue
Baltimore, MD 21211
443-578-7531   Contact: Kallie Amorgeanos

A tour of this TV station includes a visit to the newsroom, two studios and the studio control room. You will then sit in the studio and watch the noon newscast live and behind the scenes in the control room to get a full appreciation of what goes into a news production. Group tours only: minimum - seven people. **DIRECTIONS:** Take exit 9 from US Rt 83 west on Cold Spring Ln. Call for specific directions.

Hours: 11:30 am - 12:45 pm   Days: Monday, Wednesday, Friday
Advance Notice: Yes   Fee: No   HP Access: Yes

USDA ARS National Visitor Center (farm research)   SIC Code: 0762
10300 Baltimore Avenue - Bldg 302
Beltsville, MD 20705-2350
240-504-8483   Contact: Marge Fellows

The 90 - minute tour will vary according to the science and agriculture interests of the group. Experiments on plants, animals, insects, soil and water conservation, and the human diet are featured and tied into information on ARS work nationwide and overseas. Tour begins in the National Visitor Center's Log Lodge on Powder Mill Rd. **DIRECTIONS:** From the south, follow Beltway 495/I - 95 to exit 22 north, turn left on Rt 212 (Powder Mill Rd) and continue for one and one-half miles. Visitor Center is on the left.

Hours: 8:00 am - 4:30 pm   Days: Monday - Friday
Advance Notice: Yes   Fee: No   HP Access: Yes

Brooks Barrel Company, Inc. (wood container)   SIC Code: 2449
5228 Bucktown Road
Cambridge, MD 21613
443-228-0790   Contact: Ken Knox

This is one of only four cooperages left in America and the entire process is still totally hand operated. The plant tour will explain or will show (depending on production schedules) how the barrels and planters are made. **DIRECTIONS:** Located directly across from the airport off Rt 50.

Hours: 9:00 am - 4:00 pm   Days: Monday - Friday
Advance Notice: Yes   Fee: No   HP Access: No

Western Publishing Company (printer)   SIC Code: 2759
806 Woods Road
Cambridge, MD 21613
443-228-4000   Contact: Rusty Hopkins/Al Shepard

A 45 - minute tour of this commercial printing facility will include web offset printing, perfect bindings and saddle stitching. **NOTE:** Minimum five people, maximum 20 people. Tours must be arranged 10 days in advance. **DIRECTIONS:** At Rt 50 & Woods Rd.

Hours: 9:00 am - 4:00 pm   Days: Monday - Friday
Advance Notice: Yes   Fee: No   HP Access: Yes

Wild Goose Brewery (brewery)   SIC Code: 2082
20 Washington Street
Cambridge, MD 21613
443-221-1121   Contact: Marne

Tour this local English style brewery and learn how beer is made. **NOTE:** Free samples. **DIRECTIONS:** Rt 50 east to Crusader Rd, take left and right on Washington St.

Hours: 11:00 am - 3:00 pm   Days: Saturday
Advance Notice: Yes   Fee: No   HP Access: Yes

Southern Maryland Processing & Dist Center (postal)   SIC Code: 4311
9201 Edgeworth Drive
Capitol Heights, MD 20790-9998
240-499-7324   Contact: Gail Corum

A tour of the U. S. Postal Processing & Distribution Center will demonstrate the entire mail processing system. **DIRECTIONS:** Take the Washington Beltway (Rt. 495) to exit 15B, Central Ave, west to Rt 214. After exit move to far left lane of Central Ave. You will be at the intersection of Central Ave and Hampton Park Blvd at light. Turn left and continue straight until you reach Edgeworth Dr. Turn left, facility will be on your right.

Hours: 10:00 am - 4:00 pm   Days: Monday - Friday
Advance Notice: Yes   Fee: No   HP Access: No

Frederick Processing & Distribution Center (postal)   SIC Code: 4311
201 East Patrick Street
Frederick, MD 21701-9998
240-662-2131   Contact: Charles Hall or Howard Huegel

At the U. S. Postal Processing & Distribution Center, depending on the time of day or night, you will see various mail processing machines such as letter sorting machines, bar code sorters, and computerized forwarding of mail, etc. **NOTE:** Night tours have more activity. **DIRECTIONS:** From Baltimore, take I - 70 west and exit on East Patrick St. (first Frederick exit).

Hours: 24 hours a day   Days: Monday - Sunday
Advance Notice: Yes   Fee: No   HP Access: Yes

Suburban MD Processing & Dist Center (postal)   SIC Code: 4311
16501 Shady Grove Road
Gaithersburg, MD 20898-9997
240-670-6000   Contact: Jackie Kretzer/Paul Neff

At this U. S. Postal Distribution and Processing Center you will get an operation-by-operation tour of mail processing from acceptance to dispatch. You will observe the Mechanization, Automation and Manual Sections. **DIRECTIONS:** Capitol Beltway 495 to 270 north, to Shady Grove Rd exit, go east. Proceed two and one-half miles to facility (on right at second traffic light past Rt 355).

Hours: 8:00-11:00, 12-4:00   Days: Monday - Friday
Advance Notice: Yes   Fee: No   HP Access: Yes

Casselwood Furniture Co. (furniture mfr)   SIC Code: 2519
163 River Road
Grantsville, MD 21536
240-895-5069   Contact: Tim Sweitzer

Tour of the showroom and production shop where custom made solid wood Early American
and Country furniture is created. Both showroom and production shop are located in an old
cannery building. **DIRECTIONS:** Exit 19 on I - 68. At the light in Grantsville, turn right
(east on Rt 40). Approximately 2/10 mile east of Penn Alps Restaurant, turn left onto River
Rd, and look for first large building on left.

Hours: 10:00 am - 4:00 pm   Days: Monday - Friday
Advance Notice: Yes   Fee: No   HP Access: No

Jones & Ladd, Inc. (canvas goods mfr)   SIC Code: 2394
140 South Potomac Street
Hagerstown, MD 21740
443-263-6817   Contact: Cecelia Smith

You will see sewing machine operators manufacturing tote bags, luggage, purses and other
items constructed from fabric. **DIRECTIONS:** From I - 70 west to Rt 40 west. Continue to
Potomac St, take left. Go south on Potomac crossing Antiteam St. The factory is on the left.
Take small driveway between the building and a large church.

Hours: 10:00 am - 2:00 pm   Days: Monday - Friday
Advance Notice: Yes   Fee: No   HP Access: No

Boordy Vineyards (winery)   SIC Code: 2084
12820 Long Green Pike Road
Hydes, MD 21082
443-592-5015   Contact: Katrina Farral

You will have an escorted tour of the winemaking and barrel-aging rooms and you will have
an opportunity to stroll through the carefully tended vineyards. **NOTE:** Free wine tasting.
Small charge for groups of 10 or more. **DIRECTIONS:** From the west on Rt 695, take exit
29 (Cromwell Bridge Rd) and go left two and 9/10 miles to the end. Take a left onto Glen
Arm Rd and continue three and 2/10 miles to the intersection with Long Green Pike. Take a
left and go two miles to the winery entrance on the left.

Hours: 10:00 am - 5:00 pm   Days: Monday - Saturday
Advance Notice: Yes   Fee: No   HP Access: No

Windy Meadows Pottery, LTD (pottery products)   SIC Code: 3269
1036 Valley Road
Knoxville, MD 21758
240-663-4115 (800-527-6274)   Contact: Liz or Gail

This approximate one hour tour will show you the company's specialty in the production of miniature collectible cottages. **DIRECTIONS:** Located off Rt 340 west from Frederick, MD.

Hours: 11:00 am - 3:00 pm   Days: Monday - Friday
Advance Notice: Yes   Fee: No   HP Access: No

Westvaco (paper mfr)   SIC Code: 2621
300 Pratt Street
Luke, MD 21540
240-359-3311   Contact: Kelli Hickey

This 90 - minute tour will give you a first-hand look at how pulpwood is converted into high quality, coated white printing paper. See at least two paper machines in operation, the area where coating is applied to the paper and where the product is prepared for shipping. **NOTE:** The tour consists of about one mile of walking, including steps. Closed-toe shoes, hard hat and safety glasses will be provided. Minimum age is 14. **DIRECTIONS:** Take exit 34 from US 68 and follow Rt 36 south to Westernport. Travel west a short distance on Rt 135 to Pratt St.

Hours: 11:00 am and 2:00 pm   Days: Sunday - Saturday
Advance Notice: Yes   Fee: No   HP Access: No

Baltimore Gas & Electric Company (utility)   SIC Code: 4939
1650 Calvert Cliffs Parkway
Lusby, MD 20657
443-260-4083   Contact: Chuck Rayburn

Visit the Visitors/Education Center and learn how nuclear energy is transformed to electrical energy. You will view the turbine/generators, the Chesapeake Bay intake area, the control room simulator and other outside areas. **DIRECTIONS:** Take Rt 4 south from I - 95 (Washington Beltway).

Hours: 9:00 am - 4:00 pm   Days: Wednesday - Friday
Advance Notice: Yes   Fee: No   HP Access: No

Elk Run Vineyards (winery)   SIC Code; 2084
15113 Liberty Road
Mt. Airy, MD 21771
443-775-2513   Contact: Carol Wilson

Tour of winery and vineyard where original settlers from England, France and Germany first made wine as early as the 1700's using fruits such as apples, berries and grapes. You will be able to sample from a large variety of sweet and dry wines. **NOTE:** Picnic grounds. Wine tasting. **DIRECTIONS:** Located midway between Baltimore and Frederick on Rt 26 (Liberty Rd).

Hours: 10:00 am - 5:00 pm   Days: Saturday
Advance Notice: No   Fee: No   HP Access: No

Linganore Wine Cellars (winery)   SIC Code: 2084
13601 Glisans Road
Mt. Airy, MD 21771
240-831-5889   Contact: Lucia Simmons

Complete guided tour through the winery to see the modern fruit processing equipment and learn how it is used. Then on to the aging room in the lower section of a turn-of-the-century barn to see where they cellar and bottle the wines. **DIRECTIONS:** From Baltimore I - 70 to Libertytown exit 62 to Rt 75 north for three miles. Take a right just before concrete bridge.

Hours: 10:00 am - 5:00 pm   Days: Monday - Saturday
Advance Notice: No   Fee   No   HP Access: Yes

Loew Vineyards (winery)   SIC Code: 2084
14001 Liberty Road
Mt. Airy, MD 21771
240-831-5464   Contact: William or Lois Loew

Tour of the vineyards and winery which includes a walk through the orchards where a variety of grapes and fruits are grown. **NOTE:** Sample from many varieties. Must make advance reservations. There is a fee for groups. Picnic grounds available. **DIRECTIONS:** Located on Rt 26 between Baltimore and Frederick, five miles west of Rt 27 or three and one-half miles east of Rt 75 on Rt 26.

Hours: By appointment only   Days: Weekends only
Advance Notice: Yes   Fee: No   HP Access: Yes

Day Basket Factory (baskets)   SIC Code: 2499
110 West High Street
North East, MD 21901
443-287-6100   Contact: Robert McKnight

You will be taken back in time to observe the authentic step-by-step process of how baskets are made. Starting with the cutting of the oak strips used to weave the baskets, the weavers will show how the baskets are put together and finished. The tour ends with a beautiful hand made white oak basket, which is sold in the gift shop. **DIRECTIONS:** I - 95 to exit 100. At 272 south, go one mile straight south on Rt 40 to North East, MD. Take the first right after the light on Rt 40.

Hours: 8:30 am - 5:00   Days: Monday - Friday
Advance Notice: Yes   Fee: No   HP Access: No

Fiore Winery (winery)   SIC Code: 2084
3026 Whiteford Road
Pylesville, MD 21132
443-836-7605   Contact: Rose Fiore

You are invited to experience the Old World Italian traditions at this winery. Stroll through and picnic by the vineyards, and take a tour through the production facilities, and most importantly taste the outstanding variety of wines available at this family winery. **NOTE:** Closed major holidays. **DIRECTIONS:** I - 95 north to exit 77B (Rt 24) to Bel Air. Follow Rt 24 to Rt 136. Turn right at Rt 136 and continue for one mile, the winery is on the right.

Hours: Noon - 6:00 pm   Days: Saturday - Sunday
Advance Notice: Yes   Fee: $2.00   HP Access: No

Salisbury Pewter (pewter ware)   SIC Code: 3914
2611 Salisbury Boulevard (Rt 13 north)
Salisbury, MD 21801
443-546-1188 (800-824-4708)   Contact: Jim Cupp/Judy Bennett

An approximate 10 - 15 minute tour where you will see the art of making pewter by hand, see the pewter spinning shop and the polishing shop. You will also learn the brief history of the company. **DIRECTIONS:** Three miles south of MD - DE line on Rt 13 north.

Hours: 9:00 am - 4:30 pm   Days: Monday - Friday
Advance Notice: Yes   Fee: No   HP Access: Yes

WGBH Public Television (TV broadcast)   SIC Code: 4833
125 Western Avenue
Allston, MA 02134
617-492-2777   Contact: Dianna Moser

A one hour tour of two studios in which you will visit the radio and television control rooms and office. **DIRECTIONS:** Located in the Allston section of Boston. From US Rt 90 east, take exit 18. Follow signs to Western Ave. Via Soldiers Field Rd, go left.

Hours: 9:00 am - 5:00 pm   Days: Monday - Friday
Advance Notice: Yes   Fee: No   HP Access: Limited

Christian Science Publishing (newspaper)   SIC Code: 2711
175 Huntington Avenue
Boston, MA 02115
617-450-3790   Contact: Sharman Brown Reed

Tours of the newsroom of the Christian Science Monitor, the pressroom for periodicals and the bindery. Non-technical tour of radio studios. **NOTE:** Minimum age: eight. No foreign languages available. **DIRECTIONS:** Rt 128 to Rt 9 east (exit 19 or 20). Stay on Rt 9 for approximately 20 miles. Rt 9 turns into Huntington Ave. Stay on Huntington until you get to Massachusetts Ave, take a left. Take a right at The Christian Science Center Plaza. Take another right and follow to the underground garage. Tell security you are going on a tour. Located within walking distance of the Prudential Center.

Hours: 9:30 am - 4:00 pm   Days: Tuesday - Friday
Advance Notice: Yes   Fee: No   HP Access: Yes

Commonwealth Brewing Company (brewery)   SIC Code: 2082
138 Portland Street
Boston, MA 02114
617-523-8383   Contact: Bill Goodwin

On this 20 - minute tour, the Brew Master will start with a history of the brewery, explain the brewing process and will finish with the unique characteristics of their beers. **DIRECTIONS:** Close to the Fleet Center and Faneuil Hall.

Hours: Noon - 4:00 pm   Days: Monday - Sunday
Advance Notice: No   Fee: No   HP Access: No

Federal Reserve Bank of Boston (bank)   SIC Code: 6021
600 Atlantic Avenue
Boston, MA 02106
617-973-3451   Contact: Paul Williams

The 90 - minute tour will begin with a brief slide program that describes the Federal Reserve System and the operations of the Boston Fed. The tour will take you past the Cash Services, Check Collection and Computer Operations Departments. Each department will be explained and questions will be answered. At the end of the tour you will be given free literature about the Federal Reserve. **NOTE:** Minimum age is 13. No briefcases, cameras or packages are allowed. Three to four weeks advance notice is necessary. **DIRECTIONS:** Located close to the waterfront of Boston, across from South Station.

Hours: 10:30 am   Days: Friday
Advance Notice: Yes   Fee: No   HP Access: Yes

Mass Bay Brewing Company (brewery)   SIC Code: 2082
306 Northern Avenue
Boston, MA 02210
617-574-9551   Contact: Fitz Granger

A one hour tour where you will have an opportunity to sample beers from Massachusetts' largest brewery. **NOTE:** Closed some holidays. **DIRECTIONS:** From Rt 93, take exit 22 when coming from the south and exit 34 from the north. Right on Northern Ave. One mile down on the left.

Hours: 1:00 pm   Days: Friday and Saturday
Advance Notice: No   Fee: No   HP Access: No

Morgan Memorial Goodwill Ind. (vocational training)   SIC Code: 8331
1010 Harrison Avenue
Boston, MA 02119
617-445-1010 x 255   Contact: Nancy Cicco

Plan to tour the award-winning rehabilitation center and processing plant which is the birth-place of the Goodwill Industries movement. **DIRECTIONS:** Rt 93 to exit 18, follow exit ramp straight. At the fourth set of lights, get into left-hand turning lane. Take a left onto Harrison Ave and take another left into parking lot.

Hours: By appointment only
Advance Notice: Yes   Fee: No   HP Access: Yes

National Braille Press (printer)   SIC Code: 2759
88 St. Stephens Street
Boston, MA 02115
617-266-6160   Contact: Joanna

This is a 60 - 90 minute tour of both adult and children's books and magazines which are either manually or electrically transcribed onto braille zinc plates, printed, collated, stitched, and then shipped. **NOTE:** Children age six and older. **DIRECTIONS:** I - 93 to Massachusetts Ave exit. Turn right on Massachusetts Ave. At Symphony Hall (on your left) turn left on St. Stephen's St. Building is on your left.

Hours: 10:30 am or 1:00 pm   Days: Monday - Friday
Advance Notice: Yes   Fee: No   HP Access: No

Boston Symphony Orchestra, Inc. (music hall)   SIC Code: 7999
301 Massachusetts Avenue
Boston, MA 02115
617-266-1492   Contact: Sarah Leaf Herrmann

The one and one-half hour tour highlights historical facts related to the orchestra's develop-ment as well as architectural information about Symphony Hall. **NOTE:** Two weeks advance notice. **DIRECTIONS:** From the north, take Rt 93 south to Storrow Dr to the Fenway exit. From the south, Rt 93 to the Massachusetts Ave exit.

Hours: By appointment only   Days: Sunday - Saturday
Advance Notice: Yes   Fee: $4.00   HP Access: Yes

United States Postal Service (postal)   SIC Code: 4311
25 Dorchester Avenue
Boston, MA 02205
617-654-5081   Contact: Mary B. Coyne

On this one hour tour you will see how 6.5 million letters are processed daily at this highly mechanized facility, sorting letters at the rate of 37,500 per hour. Twelve miles of conveyors, canceling machines and sack sorters are part of the maze. **NOTE:** Minimum age is 13.
DIRECTIONS: I - 93 to South Station exit. Take left and first right after South Station.

Hours: Noon - 4:00 pm   Days: Monday - Friday
Advance Notice: Yes   Fee: No   HP Access: Yes

Sydenstricker Galleries (blown glass)   SIC Code: 3229
Route 6A
Brewster, MA 02631
508-385-3272   Contact: Shop Manager

Come and see the unique process of glass crafting featuring their own handcrafted glass. This glass has been collected by embassies and museums and is treasured in private homes. The glass is decorated in a wide range of over 240 colors. **DIRECTIONS:** Located on Rt 6A about five miles from the Sagamore Bridge.

Hours: 10:00 am - 2:00 pm   Days: Tuesday - Saturday
Advance Notice: No   Fee: No   HP Access: Yes

Brewster Pottery (pottery products)   SIC Code: 3269
437 Harwich Road (Route 124)
Brewster, MA 02631
508-896-3587   Contact: Mrs. Eckhardt

On this tour of a small artist's studio and shop, you will have the opportunity to see pottery being made, the throwing of the wheel, handbuilding, glazing, and firing. **DIRECTIONS:** From Rt 6, take exit 10, turn left onto Rt 124.

Hours: 10:00 am - 4:00 pm   Days: Tuesday - Sunday
Advance Notice: Yes   Fee: No   HP Access: Yes

John Harvard's Brew House (brewery)   SIC Code: 2082
33 Dunster Street
Cambridge, MA 02138
617-868-3585   Contact: Tim Morse/Michelle Davis

You will have the opportunity to visit the brewery and beer cellar and learn about the brewing process. **NOTE:** Sorry, no samples. **DIRECTIONS:** MBTA Red Line to Harvard Sq or Massachusetts Ave to Harvard Sq.

Hours: By appointment only   Days: Sunday - Saturday
Advance Notice: Yes   Fee: No   HP Access: Yes

Atlantic Coast Brewing, Ltd. (brewery)   SIC Code: 2082
50 Terminal Street
Charlestown, MA 02129
617-242-6464   Contact: Alex Reveliotty

You will tour a traditional English Brew House with sampling and educational discussions. **DIRECTIONS:** From Charlestown Navy Yard, go to Chelsea St to Terminal St.

Hours: By appointment only   Days: Saturday
Advance Notice: Yes   Fee: No   HP Access: No

Boston Globe (newspaper)   SIC Code: 2711
135 Morrissey Boulevard
Dorchester, MA 02107
617-929-2653   Contact: Dottie or Laura, Tour Department

Your tour will include watching a 12 - minute film and a one hour walking tour of the plant. You will receive an overview of the makings of a daily newspaper. You will see the editorial staff and reporters at work, news machines, see negatives turning into mats, photographs and plates being made and computerized facilities. **NOTE:** Please allow two - three weeks for an appointment. Age 12 and older. **DIRECTIONS:** Southeast Expressway south to exit 15 (Columbia Rd). Go left off ramp. At rotary, take first right onto Morrissey Blvd. The building is just ahead on the right.

Hours: 9:30, 11:00. 2:00 pm   Days: Tuesday and Thursday
Advance Notice: Yes   Fee: No   HP Access: Yes

Massachusetts Port Authority (airport)   SIC Code: 4581
Public Information Department
Boutwell 2 - Logan Airport
East Boston, MA 02128
617-561-1800   Contact: Claude Guiney/Brenda Nocelle

A tour of the field site of the airport, going aboard an airplane (if one is available). **NOTE:** Others areas may be available upon request. 1:00 pm tour available only during the school year. Must make advance reservations at least three weeks in advance. Groups of up to 40. Children must be in third grade or older. **DIRECTIONS:** Located at Logan International Airport.

Hours: 10:00 am and 1:00 pm   Days: Monday - Friday
Advance Notice: yes   Fee: No   HP Access: No

Green Briar Nature Ctr & Jam Kitchen (canning)   SIC Code: 2033
6 Discovery Hill Road
East Sandwich, MA 02537
508-888-6870   Contact: Joan DiPersio

Brief tour provided through the working turn-of-the-century jam kitchen to see jams, jellies and preserves being made as they have been since 1903. Nature Center offers natural history exhibits and nature trails. **DIRECTIONS:** Located off Rt 6A.

Hours: 10:00 am - 3:30 pm   Days: Monday - Saturday
Advance Notice: Yes   Fee: 50 cents   HP Access: yes

Undermountain Weavers (textile mill)   SIC Code: 2399
311 Great Barrington Road
Housatonic, MA 01236
413-274-6565   Contact: Dutch or Anne Pinkston

This is a working mill, weaving cashmere and shetland cloth by hand and selling the cloth and items of clothing they make from the cloth. The selling area is adjacent to where there are two looms in operation. **NOTE:** This is not a museum, but a for profit business. Shop is one step up from ground level. **DIRECTIONS:** Five miles north of Great Barrington or five miles south of West Stockbridge, on Rt 41.

Hours: By appointment only
Advance Notice: Yes   Fee: No   HP Access: Yes

Cape Cod Potato Chip Company (potato chips)   SIC Code: 2096
Independence Park, Breeds Hill Road
Hyannis, MA 02601
508-775-7253   Contact: Sue Sweet

This is a 15 - minute self-guided walking tour through the company in which following signs along the way, you will see production, packaging, sorting and testing of potato chips.
NOTE: Free samples. **DIRECTIONS:** From Sagamore Bridge, take Rt 6 east to exit 6 (Rt 132) south to Independence Park on left (at traffic light).

Hours: 10:00 am - 4:00 pm   Days: Monday - Friday
Advance Notice: No   Fee: No   HP Access: Yes

Ipswich Brewing Co., Ltd. (brewery)   SIC Code: 2082
25 Hayward Street
Ipswich, MA 01938
978-356-3329   Contact: Kat

A tour of the brewery includes an introduction to microbrewing facility including the 7 BBL and 30 BBL system. Brewing is in process during the tour. **DIRECTIONS:** For a scenic ride, take exit 20 from Rt 128. Go north on Rt 1A into town. Call for more specific directions.

Hours: 1:00 and 3:00 pm   Days: Saturday
Advance Notice: No   Fee: No   HP Access: Yes

Boston Beer Company (brewery)   SIC Code: 2082
80 Germania Street
Jamaica Plain, MA 02130
617-522-9080   Contact: Tour Department

On this guided tour, you will see how the beer is made along with learning about the fascinating history and process of brewing. **DIRECTIONS:** Take Rt 93 south to exit 18 (Massachusetts Ave). Bear left off ramp onto Melnea Cass Blvd to 8th stop light. Turn left. Continue straight to 11th stop light. Turn right on Washington St. Take fourth right on Boylston St. Continue straight two blocks and take a left on Bismark St. Watch for "Samuel Adams" signs.

Hours: 2:00 pm   Days: Thursday and Friday
          Noon, 1:00 and 2:00 pm   Saturday
Advance Notice: Yes   Fee: No   HP Access: Yes

U.S. Army Research Command (research)   SIC Code: 8731
Kansas Street
Natick, MA 01760-5012
508-233-4300   Contact: Harvey W. Keene

You will see a video presentation of activities at this research facility and then receive a one hour briefing of product development and engineering done at the installation. This facility plays a major role in developing clothing and other textile products used by the military, NASA, and other specialty governmental agencies. **DIRECTIONS:** Rt 9 to Rt 27 south. Kansas St is 1/4 mile on left.

Hours: 9:30 - 11:30 am   Days: Friday
Advance Notice: Yes   Fee: No   HP Access: Yes

Ould Newbury Brewing Company (brewery)   SIC Code: 2082
50 Parker Street
Newburyport, MA 01950
978-462-1980   Contact: Pam Rolfe

A 45 - minute tour of a small microbrewery in which you will be shown around the brewery and have the brewing process explained. Products available in Massachusetts.
DIRECTIONS: Rt 95 north to exit 56. Take Scotland Rd, two and 8/10 miles to Parker St.

Hours: 1:00 pm   Days: Saturday
Advance Notice: Yes   Fee: No   HP Access: Yes

Middlesex-Essex Processing & Dist. Center (postal)   SIC Code: 4311
76 Main Street
North Reading, MA 01889-7060
978-664-7041   Contact: John M. Lespasio, Jr.

On a tour of this U. S. Postal Processing and Distribution Center, you will get an overview and tour of a medium sized mail processing center. You will receive information on how a first-class letter is processed on state-of-the-art automated equipment. **DIRECTIONS:** Mass Pike to Rt 128 (I - 95) north. At I - 93 go north to exit 39 (Concord St). Turn right at end of ramp and follow to traffic light at Rt 28. Take left at light and go approximately one-half mile on the left.

Hours: 2:00 - 7:00 pm   Days: Monday - Friday
Advance Notice: Yes   Fee: No   HP Access: Yes

Spindrift Pottery (pottery products)   SIC Code: 3269
Route 6A
Orleans, MA 02653
508-255-1404   Contact: Polly Bishop

On this tour you will observe the Potter throwing pots on wheels during gallery hours. You will also have an opportunity to view baskets, watercolors, oils and mirrors. **NOTE:** Open only during June - September. **DIRECTIONS:** Located next to the windmill, right off Orleans Rotary.

Hours: 10:00 am - 6:00 pm   Days: Sunday - Saturday
Advance Notice: Yes   Fee: No   HP Access: Yes

The Berkshire Eagle (newspaper)   SIC Code: 2711
75 South Church Street
Pittsfield, MA 01201
413-447-7311   Contact: Alinda Shank

On this one hour tour, you will have all facets of the newspaper operation explained, including classified ads, circulation, display ads, ad design, newsroom, photos, page composition, camera room, press room and mail room areas. **DIRECTIONS:** Follow Rt 20/7 north from exit 2 on US Rt 90 (Massachusetts Turnpike). Call for specific directions.

Hours: 8:00 am - 5:00 pm   Days: Monday - Friday
Advance Notice: Yes   Fee: No   HP Access: Yes

Cranberry World Visitors Center (berry crops)   SIC Code: 0171
225 Water Street
Plymouth, MA 02360
508-747-2350   Contact: Linda Allan

A 30 - minute tour with a unique exhibit traces the cranberry from colonial times to the present, featuring outdoor working bogs, antique and current harvesting tools, daily cooking demonstrations, and audiovisual presentations. **NOTE:** Sample cranberry beverages. Minimum age is three. **DIRECTIONS:** I - 95 south to Rt 3 south to Rt 44 east. Cross Rt 3A continuing to the waterfront. Turn left around rotary onto Water St.

Hours: 9:30 am - 5:00 pm   Days: Monday - Friday (May - November)
Advance Notice: Yes   Fee: No   HP Access: Yes

Plymouth Colony Winery (winery)   SIC Code: 2084
56 Pinewood Road
Plymouth, MA 02360
508-747-3334   Contact: Lisa Lebeck

In addition to enjoying free wine tasting and a tour of the production area, you are invited to stroll around the bogs for an "up close" look at the life cycle of the cranberry, from the delicate blossoming in late spring, the red ripening of the berries in summer and the spectacularly colorful water harvest in the fall. Some of the wines produced here include Cranberry Grande, Bog Blush, Peach, Raspberry and Bog Blanc. **DIRECTIONS**: From Rt 3 take exit 6, follow Rt 44 west to Pinewood Rd.

Hours: 9:00 am - 5:00 pm   Days: Monday - Saturday (April - December)
Advance Notice: No   Fee: No   HP Access: Yes

Jonathan's Sprouts (vegetable farm)   SIC Code: 0161
384 Vaughan's Hill Road
Rochester, MA 02770
508-763-2577 (800-698-2326)   Contact: Bea Escalante

On this 45 - 60 minute tour of a converted old dairy barn, you will see how sprouts are grown and harvested year round. The tour follows the process from seed to finished product. Separate "wet" growing rooms for Alfalfa and Mung Beansprouts are visited as well. **NOTE:** Samples and recipes. **DIRECTIONS:** Located near Rt 28, exit 21 and US Rt 195.

Hours: 10:00 am - 3:00 pm   Days: Sunday - Friday
Advance Notice: Yes   Fee: No   HP Access: Yes

SEMASS Recovery Facility (recycling center)   SIC Code: 5093
Route 28 - P.O.Box 190
Rochester, MA 02770
508-291-2190   Contact: Susan King

On the tour of this recovery facility, you will see how 1,900 tons of municipal solid waste is converted into electrical energy and recovered materials. The facility demonstrates a resource recovery technology which provides an environmentally sound alternative to land-filling by turning recyclable waste into useful products and turning the remaining waste into fuel to generate energy. **DIRECTIONS:** Rt 28 near exit 21 from US Rt 195. Call for specific directions.

Hours: By appointment only
Advance Notice: Yes   Fee: No   HP Access: Yes

Heifer Project International (animal farm)   SIC Code: 0212
Overlook Farm
216 Wachusett Street
Rutland, MA 01543
508-886-2221   Contact: Pat Stanley

This tour offers you an opportunity to see and learn about the farm's resources first hand. You will see a large variety of animals as well as view Overlook Farm's woodlands, hayfields and pastures. **DIRECTIONS:** From Worcester, follow Rt 122 northwest to Paxton and Rt 56 into Rutland. Call for specific directions.

Hours: 9:00 am - 4:00 pm   Days: Sunday - Saturday
Advance Notice: Yes   Fee: $2.00   HP Access: Yes

Cape Cod Glass Works (blown glass)   SIC Code: 3229
845 Sandwich Road
Sagamore, MA 02561
508-888-9262   Contact: Mark Burchfield

At this glass works company, you will see glassblowing demonstrations making paper-weights, vases, bowls and Christmas ornaments. **DIRECTIONS:** Located behind the Christmas Tree Shops on Rt 6A, next to the Sagamore Bridge.

Hours: 10:00 am - 6:00 pm   Days: Monday - Saturday
Advance Notice: No   Fee: No   HP Access: No

Pairpoint Glass Works (blown glass)   SIC Code: 3229
851 Sandwich Road - Route 6A
Sagamore, MA 02561
508-888-2344 (800-899-0953)   Contact: Joan Kennan

Witness glassblowing from an observation area in the showroom where you can watch as the magic of glassblowing unfolds before your eyes. **DIRECTIONS:** Exit 1 on Rt 6 (Mid-Cape Highway).

Hours: 9:30 am - 4:30 am   Days: Monday - Friday
Advance Notice: No   Fee: No   HP Access: Yes

Harbor Sweets (candy mfr)   SIC Code: 2064
85 Leavitt Street - Palmer Cove
Salem, MA 01970
978-745-7648   Contact: Helen Kozowyk

A tour of this chocolate factory will show you how their distinctive chocolates are made. You will observe the making of chocolate Christmas ornaments, Marblehead mints, Sand Dollars, Sweet Shells as well as Pumpkins, Turkeys, and Salem Witches. **NOTE:** Free samples. Tours are given from September 1 - November 15. **DIRECTIONS:** Rt 114 east to Salem. Turn left onto Leavitt St, last building on left.

Hours: 9:00 and 11:30 am   Days: Monday - Friday
Advance Notice: Yes   Fee: No   HP Access: Yes

Massachusetts Envelope Company (printer)   SIC Code: 2752
30 Cobble Hill Road
Somerville, MA 02143
617-623-8000   Contact: Amy Grossman

This one hour tour will allow you to see where up to two million envelopes a day pass through the 15 offset presses. You will visit the art, printing and graphic departments, darkroom and warehouse, where trucks are waiting at the shipping dock. **DIRECTIONS:** Take Rt 128 and follow to Rt 93 south to Rt 28 in Somerville. Call for specific directions.

Hours: 9:00-Noon/1:30-3:00   Days: Monday - Friday
Advance Notice: Yes   Fee: No   HP Access: Yes

Yankee Candle Company (candle mfr)   SIC Code: 3999
Route 5
South Deerfield, MA 01373
413-665-8306   Contact: Tim O'Brien

You will visit with costumed 1820's candlemakers and learn how candles were handcrafted nearly two centuries ago. These tours are ongoing through the day, but periodically special demonstrations are announced. A self-guided tour of the modern candle making factory is also available daily by following along the 200' wall separating the work area from the store. **NOTE:** Closed Christmas. **DIRECTIONS:** Take exit 24 off I - 91, proceed 1/4 mile north on Rt 5.

Hours: 9:30 am - 6:00 pm   Days: Monday-Friday
Advance Notice: No   Fee: No   HP Access: Yes

Perkins School for the Blind (school)   SIC Code: 8299
175 North Beacon Street
Watertown, MA 02172
617-924-3434   Contact: Judi Cannon

Take a 60 - 90 minute tour of this facility which will include a visit to the Braille library, a museum depicting museum teaching aids as well as learning about current teaching aids. **DIRECTIONS:** From Rt 128 take exit 26. Follow Rt 20 to Watertown. Call for specific directions.

Hours: 9:00 am - 4:00 pm   Days: Tuesday,Wednesday,Thursday
Advance Notice: Yes   Fee: No   HP Access: Yes

Hoffman Pottery (pottery products)   SIC Code: 3269
103 Great Barrington Road
West Stockbridge, MA 01266
413-232-4646   Contact: Elaine Hoffman

Visit this small one-person studio in which you will have an opportunity to watch the creation of works of art at the potter's wheel. **DIRECTIONS:** US Rt 90 (Massachusetts Turnpike) to exit 2, Rt 102 to town. Call for specific directions.

Hours: By appointment only
Advance Notice: Yes   Fee: No   HP Access: No

Amon Orchard (fruit trees)   SIC Code: 0175
8066 US 31 North
Acme, MI 49610
616-938-9530 (800-937-1644)   Contact: Linda Pillsbury

Take a 90 - minute tour of the orchard, known for its luscious blackberries, apricots, apples and cherries. You will hear behind-the-scene information on the operations of a cherry orchard. This is an educational experience in how cherries are grown, harvested and marketed. **NOTE:** Tours are conducted May - October. **DIRECTIONS:** Located on Rt 31, east of Traverse City and north of the Manittee National Forest. Call for specific directions.

Hours: 8:30 am - 5:00 pm   Days: Monday - Saturday
Advance Notice: Yes   Fee: $5.00   HP Access: Yes

Amway Corporation (merchandising)   SIC Code: 5399
7575 Fulton Street East
Ada, MI 49355-0001
616-787-6701   Contact: John Faye

A one hour tour of the world's largest direct selling companies at its World Headquarters. **DIRECTIONS:** Located on M - 21 (Fulton Rd), 12 miles east of downtown Grand Rapids and 11 miles west of the I - 96 Lowell exit.

Hours: 9:00-11:001:00-3:00   Days: Monday - Friday
Advance Notice: Yes   Fee: No   HP Access: Yes

Heart of the Vineyard Winery (winery)   SIC Code: 2084
10981 Hill Road
Baroda, MI 49101
616-422-1617   Contact: Richard Moersch

This is a tour and taste winery with a champagne cave used for storage and aging. This winery is noted for its white and red wines and specialty wines. **NOTE:** Free samples. **DIRECTIONS:** Exit 16 from I - 94 north to Lake/Shawnee Rd. Turn right four miles to Hills Rd, turn right one and one-half miles.

Hours: 9:00 am - 5:00 pm   Days: Monday - Saturday
Advance Notice: No   Fee: No   HP Access: Yes

Chelsea Milling Company (flour mill)   SIC Code: 2041
201 North Street
Chelsea, MI 48118
734-475-1361   Contact: Chris Harrison

The makers of Jiffy Mix offers a one and one-half hour enjoyable and informative tour of their facility showing the processes of making their food product. **NOTE:** Two weeks advance notice (more notice during spring and summer months). There is one flight of stairs (about 16 steps). The length of the plant is approximately one city block. **DIRECTIONS:** Exit 159 off I - 94. Go through Chelsea and after the railroad tracks, turn left on North St.

Hours: 9:30 am - 1:30 pm   Days: Monday - Friday
Advance Notice: Yes   Fee: No   HP Access: Yes

Lionel Trains, Inc. (toy mfr)   SIC Code: 3944
26750 23 Mile Road
Chesterfield, MI 48051-2493
810-949-4100 x 1211   Contact: Sharon Katoch

This one hour tour begins with a fascinating video presentation on the manufacturing process used to make Lionel Trains and the history of the company. You will have access to the large showroom with approximately 40 buttons around the layout enabling you to operate the saw-mill, crossing gate or crane accessory buttons, you may operate your own train or handcar. **NOTE:** Children will receive a paper engineer hat and a small gift. **DIRECTIONS:** From Detroit, take I - 94 at exit 243 (New Baltimore - 23 Mile Rd exit) turn left. At second light, turn left (Russell Schmidt). The parking lot is on right.

Hours: Call for schedule   Days: Wednesday - Sunday
Advance Notice: Yes   Fee: No   HP Access: Yes

Davisburg Candle Factory (candle mfr)   SIC Code: 3999
634 Davisburg Road
Davisburg, MI 48350
248-634-4214   Contact: Mary Tebo

In this 150-year-old building, you will hear a 15 - 20 minute discussion on how candles are manufactured. You will see how tapers and molded candles are made and how the color tank is used. There will be time for questions and answers. **DIRECTIONS:** I - 75 to exit 93 (Dixie Hwy). Go north on Dixie to first traffic light. Go left on Davisburg Rd into town.

Hours: 10:00 am - 4:30 pm   Days: Monday - Saturday
Advance Notice: Yes   Fee: No   HP Access: Limited

Pewabic Pottery (ceramic tile mfr)   SIC Code: 3253
10125 East Jefferson Avenue
Detroit, MI 48214
313-822-0954   Contact: Tour Coordinator

On the self-guided tour of the production facilities, you will get a first-hand exposure to the tile and vessel-making process including clay mixing, glaze making, tile pressing and trimming, mold making, vessel throwing, and kiln operations. **NOTE:** For a guided tour, please call for appointment. Work areas are crowded and narrow. **DIRECTIONS:** From US Rt 94 take exit 219 to Cadillac Blvd to end at Jefferson Ave.

Hours: 10:00 and 12:30   Days: Tuesday - Friday
Advance Notice: Yes   Fee: $3.50   HP Access: No

Fenn Valley Vineyards & Wine Cellar (winery)   SIC Code: 2084
6130 122nd Avenue
Fennville, MI 49408
616-561-2396 (800-432-6265)   Contact: Diana Welsch

A self-guided tour where you will view the wine cellar from an observation deck and watch a video about the wine-making process and the proper use of wine. **NOTE:** Wine samples. **DIRECTIONS:** I - 196 to exit 34, then east three and one-half miles to 62nd St. Go south one mile to 122nd Ave, then east 1/4 mile.

Hours: 10:00 am - 5:00 pm   Days: Monday - Saturday
            pm only   Sunday
Advance Notice: Yes   Fee: No   HP Access: No

AutoAllliance International, Inc. (automobile mfr)   SIC Code: 3711
1 International Drive
Flat Rock, MI 48134-9498
313-783-8200   Contact: Kristie Mosley

This plant tour of the proud producers of the Mazda MX-6, Mazda 626 and Ford Probe will consist of a 30-minute introduction, a 15-minute video presentation, and a 75-minute walking plant tour where you will see the stamping, body assembly, trim/final assembly and a video of the paint process. There will also be time for a question and answer session. **NOTE:** Please wear comfortable, flat shoes. Shorts, sandals and open-toed shoes are strictly prohibited. No cameras. Children must be the ninth grade and above. Plan one - two months in advance. **DIRECTIONS:** From US Rt 75 south of Detroit, take exit 34 south to Flat Rock.

Hours: 8:30 am and 1:00 pm   Days: Thursdays only
Advance Notice: Yes   Fee: No   HP Access: Yes

Frankenmuth Pretzel Co. (pretzel mfr)   SIC Code: 2099
333 Heinlein Strasse
Frankenmuth, MI 48734
517-652-2050   Contact: Linda Trestrail

On this 15 - minute guided factory tour you will learn about the pretzel making process and see the equipment operation from mixing the dough, proofing, baking and the packaging process. **NOTE:** Free samples. Pretzel Twisting School - ($2.00) learn to make a soft pretzel. You will receive a diploma and a hot pretzel. Advance notice is required. Gift shop. **DIRECTIONS:** I - 75 north to exit 136. Follow signs into Frankenmuth. Located south end "Bronners" entrance off Weiss St.

Hours: 11:00 am and 1 :00 pm   Days: Monday - Sunday
Advance Notice: No   Fee: No   HP Access: Yes

Frankenmuth Woolen Mill (woolen mill)   SIC Code: 2231
570 South Main Street
Frankenmuth, MI 48734
517-652-6555   Contact: John M. Ehrlinger

A tour of this woolen mill is like a step back in time. You will learn the complete history of the Mill. You will also see wool processed from raw fleece to finished product through glass windows that divide the store from the mill. **NOTE:** School groups love the hands-on activities. Easy access for bus tours. **DIRECTIONS:** I - 75 to Frankenmuth. Look for the mill under the bright blue awning on Main St. Located two blocks north of Zehnder's.

Hours: 9:00 am - 9:00 pm   Days: Monday - Friday (summer)
         10:00 am - 6:00 pm   Monday - Friday (winter)
Advance Notice: Yes   Fee: No   HP Access: Yes

Zeilinger Wool Co. (woolen mill)   SIC Code: 2231
1130 Weiss Street
Frankenmuth, MI 48734
517-652-2920   Contact: Kathy Zeilinger

This is a one hour tour where you will see wool processed for individual customers from their own sheep. You can watch as wool is processed on vintage textile carding machines. The wool is in the batting stage for quilt making. On the upper level, you may watch the staff create beautiful hand-stitched wool quilts, hand-tied comforters, wool mattress pads and bed pillows. **NOTE:** 15% discount for tourists on any merchandise purchased at time of tour. **DIRECTIONS:** 1/8 mile north of Bronner's Christmas Wonderland on Weiss St.

Hours: 9:00 am - 5:30 pm   Days: Monday - Saturday
Advance Notice: Yes   Fee: No   HP Access: Yes

Original Wooden Shoe Factory (wood products)   SIC Code: 2499
447 US 31 at 16th Street
Holland, MI 49423
616-396-6513   Contact: Sharon Bailey/Celeste Kommer

Opened in 1926, this wooden shoe factory is the oldest such factory in North America and the only factory still using turn-of-the-century, European made wooden shoe-making machines which turn out the shoes one-at-a-time. On this half-hour tour you will smell the Poplar and Aspen used to make the shoes and hear the sounds of these old machines at work. **NOTE:** Gift shop. **DIRECTIONS:** From Grand Rapids take Rt 196 to exit 52 (approximately 25 miles), turn right off exit to entrance two miles ahead on left. From Chicago, take Rt 196 (US 31) north to Holland. Stay on US 31 by-pass towards Mukegon. Factory is one mile north of the Day's Inn Motel.

Hours: 8:00 am - 4:30 pm   Days: Monday - Saturday
Advance Notice: No   Fee: No   HP Access: Yes

Veldheer Tulip Gardens, Inc. (wood products)   SIC Code: 2499
12755 Quincy Street
Holland, MI 49424
616-399-1900   Contact: Jim Veldheer

You will see wooden shoes produced on authentic Dutch production machinery including the only automated production wooden shoe machines in the U.S. This company is also the only delftware factory in this country. You will watch the entire process from pouring the liquid clay into the plaster molds to glazing and firing and finally the hand painting process. In addition, this is a tulip farm which produces over three million blooms and over 200 different varieties. **NOTE:** There is a $3.00 charge for viewing the gardens. **DIRECTIONS:** Located four miles north of Holland on US 31 at Quincy St. Three hours northeast of Chicago - three hours west of Detroit.

Hours: 8:00 am - 5:00 pm   Days: Sunday - Saturday
Advance Notice: No   Fee: No   HP Access: Yes

Iron Mountain Processing & Dist. Center (postal)   SIC Code: 4311
700 West Breitung Avenue
Kingsford, MI 49801-9997
906-774-5111   Contact: Secretary or Manager

A 30 - 60 minute tour of the U. S. Postal Processing and Distribution Center, where you will see the process of sorting mail both manually and with state-of-the-art automation.
DIRECTIONS: Located on Rt 2 in the northwest corner of the state on the Wisconsin border. Call for specific directions.

Hours: 9:00 am - 4:00 pm   Days: Monday - Friday
Advance Notice: Yes   Fee: No   HP Access: Yes

Dow Chemical Company (chemical preparation)   SIC Code: 2899
500 East Lyon
Midland, MI 48667
517-636-8658   Contact: Charlie Reed

This tour is a two and one-half hour visit through the chemical plant with stops at the manufacturing and analytical facilities. On this tour you will see a 5' diameter Saran Bubble! Explanations of displays are available in the Visitors Center. **NOTE:** Must be age 10 or older and in appropriate dress. **DIRECTIONS:** Located south of US Rt 10. Call for specific directions.

Hours: 8:00 am - 4:30 pm   Days: Monday - Friday
Advance Notice: Yes   Fee: No   HP Access: Yes

Simplicity Pattern Co., Inc. (pattern makers)   SIC Code: 3553
901 Wayne Street
Niles, MI 49121-0002
616-683-4100 x 313   Contact: Jo Ann Cabanaw

This one and one-half to two hour tour covers the manufacturing process of paper patterns for home sewing. You will visit the paper mill where the tissue paper is manufactured, the press department where the envelopes, tissue and instructions sheets are printed, the inserting department, and the reorder department where the orders are picked and shipped. **NOTE:** Free sample booklet and pattern. **DIRECTIONS:** Plant is located along Wayne St between railroad tracks east of Eighth St to Twelfth St and along Twelfth St (between Wayne and Sheffield Sts).

Hours: 10:00 am   Days: Monday - Thursday
Advance Notice: Yes   Fee: No   HP Access: Limited

Browning-Ferris Industries (BFI) (recycling center)   SIC Code: 5093
10599 West 5 Mile Road
Northville, MI 48167
810-349-3215   Contact: Education Coordinator

Tour of the Learning Center, Material Recovery Facility and the Arbor Hills Sanitary Landfill which represents the most modern and comprehensive approach to solid waste management yet undertaken. **DIRECTIONS:** Located between Detroit and Ann Arbor at intersection of 5Mile Rd and Napier Rd.

Hours: 8:00 am - 3:30 pm   Days: Monday - Friday
Advance Notice: Yes   Fee: No   HP Access: No

St. Julian Wine Company, Inc. (winery)   SIC Code: 2084
716 South Kalamazoo Street
Paw Paw, MI 49079
616-657-5568   Contact: Manager

Tour Michigan's oldest and largest winery which makes 36 different wines. This facility bottles 1,500 cases a day. View a venerable wood holding vat, which contains more than 26,000 gallons of wine. **NOTE:** Free samples. **DIRECTIONS:** Follow US Rt 94 to exit 60 north. Call for specific directions.

Hours: Call for schedule   Days: Monday - Friday
Advance Notice: Yes   Fee: No   HP Access: Yes

Bachman's Florists (floriculture) SIC Code: 0181
6010 Lyndale Avenue South
Minneapolis, MN 55419
612-861-7692 Contact: Rosemary Kobler

A 45 - minute tour of the greenhouses, nursery and garden center, floral areas and showrooms. Demonstrations available upon request. **NOTE:** Minimum age: Junior high school. Groups of 10 or more by appointment only. No tours the week before major holidays. **DIRECTIONS:** Located in Waterford Plaza on Rt 55, west of intersection.

Hours: 9:00 am - 2:00 pm	Days: Monday - Friday	
Advance Notice: Yes	Fee: No	HP Access: Yes

Guthrie Theater (theater) SIC Code: 7922
725 Vineland Place
Minneapolis, MN 55403
612-347-1111 Contact: Bruce Miller

Backstage tour includes history and description of technical elements of the theater. The one hour tour includes a walking tour through the costume shop, scene shop, prop shop and below and behind stage areas. **NOTE:** Large groups can call for special arrangements. **DIRECTIONS:** From the north, take exit 94 east to the Hennepin - Lyndale exit, go south on Lyndale following the exit, turn right on Vineland Pl at the second stoplight.

Hours: 10:00 am	Days: Saturday	
Advance Notice: Yes	Fee: $3.00	HP Access: No

Minneapolis Processing & Dist. Center (postal) SIC Code: 4311
100 South First Street
Minneapolis, MN 55401-9997
612-349-4900 Contact: Steve Moore

This U. S. Postal Processing & Distribution Center tour will show the mail processing equipment and system. **NOTE:** The tour is for groups only and by appointment only. **DIRECTIONS:** Plant is located in the Minneapolis downtown area, next to the Mississippi River, at the Hennepin Ave bridge.

Hours: By appointment only	Days: Monday - Friday	
Advance Notice Yes	Fee: No	HP Access: Yes

Star Tribune (newspaper)   SIC Code: 2711
800 North First Street
Minneapolis, MN 55401
612-673-4860   Contact: Pat West

A 45 - minute walking tour given by professional guides of the printing plant of this daily
newspaper, includes train delivery of paper, robots, platemaking, printing presses, mail room,
and loading dock. You will also see a twelve minute video "Newton's Apple". **NOTE:** Must
be age 10 and older. **DIRECTIONS:** From Rt 694 to Rt 94 east, take the Broadway exit,
turn left. Go to Second St north, turn right to Eighth ave north and turn left. Located one
mile north of downtown in warehouse district.

Hours: By appointment only   Days: Tuesday - Saturday
Advance Notice: Yes   Fee: No   HP Access: Yes

Champion International Corp. (paper mfr)   SIC Code: 2621
1000 Sartell Street, East
Sartell, MN 56377
320-240-7100   Contact: Mike Sullivan

On this tour, you will see paper in the making from the raw material to the finished product.
NOTE: Free samples. **DIRECTIONS:** Located north of St. Cloud. Call for specific
directions.

Hours: Call for appointment   Days: Monday - Friday
Advance Notice: Yes   Fee: No   HP Access: No

Forester Boats (boat builder)   SIC Code: 3732
180 Industrial Boulevard
Sauk Rapids, MN 56379
320-252-4352   Contact: Robert Menne

A tour of this facility will show you Leisure Island & Forester Pontoons being assembled.
DIRECTIONS: Located north of St. Cloud on the Mississippi River.

Hours: 8:00 am - 4:30 pm   Days: Monday - Friday
Advance Notice: Yes   Fee: No   HP Access: No

DCI Inc. (metal goods mfr)   SIC Code: 3499
600 54th Avenue, North
St. Cloud, MN 56302
320-252-8200   Contact: Tour Department

Tour the fabricator of stainless steel processing equipment for the world wide industries of dairy, food, beverage, pharmaceutical, chemical, biotechnology and original equipment manufacturers. **DIRECTIONS:** Call for specific directions.

Hours: 8:00 am - 5:00 pm   Days: Monday - Friday
Advance Notice: Yes   Fee: No   HP Access: No

Jennings Decoy (wood products)   SIC Code: 2499
601 Franklin Ave, NE
St. Cloud, MN 56304
320-253-2253   Contact: Steve Ree

Tour the wood carving shop and see the making of wood decoys, loons and gallery areas. **DIRECTIONS:** Hwy 10 Frontage Rd - west side.

Hours: By appointment only   Days: Monday - Friday
Advance Notice: Yes   Fee: No   HP Access: Yes

Meridian Aggregates (granite)   SIC Code: 1411
5624 Division Street, West
St. Cloud, MN 56302
320-251-7141   Contact: Don Vry

Tour of a quarry site where granite is mined. **DIRECTIONS:** Call for specific directions.

Hours: Call for schedule
Advance Notice: Yes   Fee: No   HP Access: No

The St. Cloud Times (newspaper)   SIC Code: 2711
3000 7th Street North
St. Cloud, MN 56303
320-255-8700   Contact: Betty Schmit

Tour St. Cloud's daily newspaper where you will walk through the printing process, advertising, production, circulation and editorial departments of the St. Cloud Times and the USA Today newspapers. Watch news being edited and printed as it happens. **DIRECTIONS:** Call for specific directions.

Hours: 9:00 am - 3:30 pm	Days: Monday - Friday	
Advance Notice: Yes	Fee: No	HP Access: Yes

Stone Container Corporation (corrugated boxes)   SIC Code: 2653
655 41st Avenue North
St. Cloud, MN 56303
320-252-3660   Contact: Manager

Tour corrugated packaging manufacturer and see the procedure required to turn a customer order into a manufacturing blueprint through to the shipping area. **DIRECTIONS:** Call for specific directions.

Hours; By appointment only	Days: Monday - Friday	
Advance Notice: Yes	Fee: No	HP Access: No

Webway Incorporated (paper products)   SIC Code: 2678
2815 Clearwater Road
St. Cloud, MN 56301
320-251-3822   Contact: Manager

Tour of the manufacturer of photo albums and related books including diaries, journals, scrapbooks and address books. You will be able to see covers being wrapped, lined and pages being manufactured. **DIRECTIONS:** Call for specific directions.

Hours: Call for appointment	Days: Monday - Thursday	
Advance Notice: Yes	Fee: No	HP Access: Yes

Weeres Industries Corporation (boat builder)   SIC Code: 3732
1045 33rd Street South
St. Cloud, MN 56301
320-251-3551   Contact: Clinton L. Lee

Tour the oldest pontoon boat manufacturer in the world where you will visit the sheet metal shop, assembly shop and furniture manufacture areas. **DIRECTIONS:** Call for specific directions.

Hours: 9:00 am - 3:00 pm	Days: Monday - Friday	
Advance Notice: Yes	Fee: No	HP Access: Yes

Woodcraft Industries, Inc. (wood products)   SIC Code: 2499
525 Lincoln Avenue SE
St. Cloud, MN 56304
320-252-1503   Contact: Tour Department

A 90 - minute tour of the manufacturer of solid hardwood components for kitchen cabinets and the furniture industry. Tour will take you through the entire manufacturing process. **DIRECTIONS:** Call for specific directions.

Hours: 8:00 am - 5:00 pm	Days: Monday - Friday	
Advance Notice: No	Fee: No	HP Access: No

Byerly's (grocer)   SIC Code: 5411
3777 Park Center Boulevard.
St. Louis Park, MN 55416
320-929-2100   Contact: Manager

Walk around Byerly's with a guide and learn about the special features of this facility. You will also have specific services highlighted. **NOTE:** Minimum age: five. **DIRECTIONS:** Call for specific directions.

Hours: 9:00 am - 3:30 pm	Days: Tuesday	
Advance Notice: Yes	Fee: No	HP Access: Yes

Minnesota Brewing Company (brewery)   SIC Code: 2082
882 West 7th Street
St. Paul, MN 55102
612-228-9173   Contact: Tony Tiemann

A one-hour walking tour (with many stairs) of brewhouse, bottling house and fermenting cellar. Producers of various brands of beer, the company is currently the 12th largest brewing operation in the country and has the capacity to increase production by over 1,500,000 barrels making it an excellent partner for contract bottling. **NOTE:** No open shoes. Free samples. **DIRECTIONS:** Rt 5 west to West 7th St at exit 103.

Hours: 10:00 and 1:00 pm   Days: Monday - Friday
Advance Notice: Yes   Fee: No   HP Access: No

Twin Cities Public Television (TV broadcast)   SIC Code: 4833
172 East Fourth Street
St. Paul, MN 55101
612-222-1717   Contact: Ann Sunwall

Visit the studios and control rooms of KTCA/KTCI and learn about the making of television programs and how they travel to your TV screen. **NOTE:** Recommended age, third grade to adult. Tours available October - May. **DIRECTIONS:** From Minneapolis on I - 94, exit eastbound at the Fifth St exit to center of downtown. Turn right at Jackson St, drive one and one-half blocks to the Lowertown ramp. Station is on your left between Fourth and Kellogg.

Hours: 10:00 - 12:00 noon   Days: First Saturday of each month
Advance Notice: No   Fee: No   HP Access: Yes

Winona Knits (apparel)   SIC Code: 2389
215 South Main Street
Stillwater, MN 55082
612-430-1711   Contact: Manager

Tour this privately owned Minnesota-based retail company, specializing in sweaters made in the USA for men, women and children. **NOTE:** All ages welcome. **DIRECTIONS:** Stillwater is a few miles north of US Rt 94 on the Mississippi River. Call for specific directions..

Hours: Call for appointment   Days: Monday - Friday
Advance Notice: Yes   Fee: No   HP Access: No

St. Cloud Processing & Dist. Center (postal)   SIC Code: 4311
517 10th Avenue South
Waite Park, MN 56387-1517
320-654-9658   Contact; Sue Trocke

The U. S. Postal Processing & Distribution Center tour will give you an inside look at the flow of mail and the workings of automated equipment used to move the mail through the system. The tours are best when mail is actually running - between 4:00 pm and midnight. There are also tours during the day. **DIRECTIONS:** Located next to the Waite Park "Smiling Face" Water Tower, just west of St. Cloud.

Hours: 24 hours a day   Days: Monday - Friday
Advance Notice: Yes   Fee: No   HP Access: Yes

Pine Tree Apple Orchard (fruit trees)   SIC Code: 0175
450 Apple Orchard Road
White Bear Lake, MN 55110
612-429-7202   Contact: Tour Director

Tour of a picturesque orchard setting on the shore of Pine Tree Lake, offering a variety of apples, homemade baker/desert products and apple gift items. Guided tours are fun and educational. **NOTE:** Tours available August - October. **DIRECTIONS:** From US Rt 694 take exit 50 into the White Bear Lake Region. Call for specific directions.

Hours: Call for schedule   Days: Monday - Friday
Advance Notice: Yes   Fee: No   HP Access: No

Peavey Electronics Corp. (musical instrument mfr)   SIC Code: 3931
711 A Street
Meridian, MS 39301
228-483-5365   Contact: Becky Holcombe

A 45 - minute tour of a music manufacturer of guitars, sing-a-long instruments and pianos. This is a two story building built in the 1930's by the U.S. Department of Agriculture which houses the Peavey Electronics Corp. Museum of the founder, Hartley Peavey. This is the only music manufacturer visited by President George Bush in 1991. **DIRECTIONS:** Take exit 157B on I - 20/59. Go north on Hwy 45 for approximately 6/10 mile. Exit right to G.V. "Sonny" Montgomery Industrial Park, one and 2/10 miles on right to the Visitors Center.

Hours: 10:00 am - 4:00 pm   Days: Monday - Friday
        1:00 pm - 4:00 pm   Saturday - Sunday
Advance Notice: No   Fee: No   HP Access: Limited

Temple Theatre (theater)   SIC Code: 7922
2320 8th Street
Meridian, MS 39301
228-693-1361   Contact: Margie Stephens

Tour this old movie house which is now used for live plays and performances. This beautiful Moorish designed building was built in 1923. **DIRECTIONS:** Located in the heart of town.

HOURS: 11:00 am - 4:00 pm   Days: Monday - Friday
Advance Notice: Yes   Fee: No   HP Access: Yes

Cooper's Berry Farm (berry crops)   SIC Code: 0171
1011 Rushing Road
Morton, MS 39117
228-732-2412   Contact: Tim Cooper

Visit this farm for an opportunity to see first hand how muscadines, blackberries and blueberries are grown and harvested. You are invited to sample fresh fruit in season.
DIRECTIONS: Take second left south of I - 20 and Hwy 13 intersection and follow signs.

Hours: 7:00 am - 7:00 pm   Days: Monday - Saturday
Advance Notice: Yes   Fee: No   HP Access: Yes

Shearwater Pottery (pottery products)   SIC Code: 3269
102 Shearwater Drive
Ocean Springs, MS 39566
228-875-7320   Contact: Margie Ashby

Plan to tour this family-owned pottery establishment and watch all phases of work being done including wood sculpture, paintings, blockprints and decorated pottery. **DIRECTIONS:** From Hwy 90 turn south on Washington Ave at signal light and cross railroad tracks. Continue straight until you reach the company sign and continue as directed.

Hours: 9:00-11:00 1:00-4:00   Days: Monday - Friday
Advance Notice: Yes   Fee: No   HP Access: No

Mississippi Power Company Plant (utility)   SIC Code: 4939
950 South George Street
Petal, MS 39465
228-582-0909   Contact: Tony Smith/Bill Anderson

Tour consists of a 15 - minute video and a guided tour of Mississippi's first high pressure steam plant which was built in 1945. **DIRECTIONS:** Located on Rt 42, east of Hattiesburg.

Hours: 7:00 am - 3:00 pm   Days: Monday- Friday
Advance Notice: Yes   Fee: No   HP Access: Yes

Pontotoc Blueberry Ridge Farm (berry crops)   SIC Code: 0171
282 Carter Lane
Pontotoc, MS 38863
228-489-8481   Contact: Gerald or Teresa Holifield

You will have an opportunity to see the process that the growth of blueberry bushes go through before they are planted in a field, yard or garden. You will visit two greenhouses as well as two acres of blueberry bushes. **DIRECTIONS:** From New Albany on US Rt 78, take Rt 15 south.

Hours: 8:00 am - 5:00 pm   Days: Friday - Saturday
Advance Notice: Yes   Fee: $1.00   HP Access: Yes

Grand Gulf Nuclear Station (utility)   SIC Code: 4939
Waterloo Road
Port Gibson, MS 39150
228-437-6317   Contact: Valarie Johnson

This 45 - 60 minute tour features hands on displays describing nuclear power, electricity, radia-tion and a simulated control room used for operator training. **DIRECTIONS:** From US Rt 20 in Vicksburg, follow Rt 61 south about 20 miles to Rt 462. Take a right to the Grand Gulf Plant site.

Hours: 8:00 am - 4:00 pm   Days: Monday - Friday
Advance Notice: No   Fee: No   HP Access: Yes

John Allen National Fish Hatchery (hatchery)   SIC Code: 0921
111 Elizabeth Street
Tupelo, MS 38802
228-842-1341   Contact: Hatchery Manager

Tour warm water fish hatchery and see where millions of fish are hatched yearly.
DIRECTIONS: Two blocks south of Tupelo Coliseum.

Hours: 7:00 am - 3:30 pm   Days: Monday - Friday
Advance Notice: Yes   Fee: No   HP Access: Yes

Waterways Experiment Station (engineering svcs)   SIC Code: 8711
U. S. Army Corps of Engineers
3909 Halls Ferry Road
Vicksburg, MS 39180-6199
228-634-2502   Contact: Ann or Felicia

A one and one-half hour tour of the first federal hydraulic research facility which was built to
help the Mississippi River Commission develop and implement a flood control plan for the
lower Mississippi Valley. You will be driving and walking to various points of interest in the
different laboratories. You will also see a display and video depicting WES activities.
NOTE: Closed national holidays. **DIRECTIONS:** Exit 1 - C from I - 20, then south
approximately one mile. Turn left at first flashing yellow light. Park in visitors parking lot.

Hours: 10:00 am and 2:00 pm   Days: Monday - Friday
Advance Notice: No   Fee: No   HP Access: Yes

Mississippi Chemical Corporation (fertilizer mfr)   SIC Code: 2873
Highway 49E
Yazoo City, MS 39194
228-746-4131   Contact: Debra Johnson

A 45 - 60 minute tour of a facility manufacturing a wide variety of plant food fertilizers.
DIRECTIONS: Located on Hwy 49 just north of Yazoo City.

Hours: By appointment   Days: Monday - Sunday
Advance Notice: Yes   Fee: No   HP Access: Yes

Burgers' Smokehouse (meats)   SIC Code: 2013
Highway 87 South
California, MO 65018
573-796-3134 (800-705-2323)   Contact: Dolores Burger

Tour this functioning smokehouse and see the process used for making country-cured meats.
The Visitor's Center features four dioramas of Missouri's seasons. These dioramas were constructed to point out the importance of the changing seasons and how it relates to the process
of curing hams. **NOTE:** Plant tours start every 15 minutes. Large groups are welcome.
DIRECTIONS: Three miles off California, MO on Hwy 87 south, west of Jefferson City.

Hours: 7:30 am - 4:30 pm   Days: Monday - Saturday
Advance Notice: Yes   Fee: No   HP Access: Yes

Monsanto Life Sciences Research Center (research)   SIC Code: 8731
700 Chesterfield Village Parkway
Chesterfield, MO 63017
314-537-6217   Contact: Stacy Soble

Tour the Visitors Center and see a video on Biotechnology Research Programs aimed at
improving the quality and availability of food supplies. **DIRECTIONS:** Located 25 miles
west of downtown St. Louis.

Hours: Call for schedule   Days: Monday - Friday
Advance Notice: Yes   Fee: No   HP Access: Yes

The Examiner (newspaper)   SIC Code: 2711
410 South Liberty
Independence, MO 64050
816-254-8600   Contact: Lou Woods

A 30 - 45 minute tour of the plant which includes a brief description of the background of the
company and assignments. **NOTE:** Ages third grade and older. **DIRECTIONS:** Liberty St
runs north from US Rt 24 in the heart of town.

Hours: 7:00 am - 5:30 pm   Days: Monday - Friday
Advance Notice: Yes   Fee: No   HP Access: Yes

American Telephone & Telegraph (communications)   SIC Code: 4899
1425 Oak Street
Kansas City, MO 64106
816-391-4896   Contact: Jim Nelson

A two hour tour in which you will see the process of long distance switching, operator call servicing, national centers of 1 - 800 and customer data as well as fiber optic equipment preceded by a video presentation. **NOTE:** Ages 13 and older. **DIRECTIONS:** Located near the City Market District north of town.

Hours: 7:30 am - 3:30 pm   Days: Monday - Friday
Advance Notice: Yes   Fee: No   HP Access: Yes

Boulevard Brewing Company (brewery)   SIC Code: 2082
2501 Southwest Boulevard
Kansas City, MO 64108
816-474-7095   Contact: Mary Harrison

A 20 - minute tour of this small, local brewery provides a view of its production facility. **NOTE:** Samples of the brewery's fine ales and lagers are provided for those over age 21. No one admitted under age 12. **DIRECTIONS:** Located near Union Station. Call for specific directions.

Hours: 5:00 - 7:30 pm   Days: Monday - Friday
        1:30 pm   Saturday
Advance Notice: Yes   Fee: No   HP Access: Yes

Federal Reserve Bank of Kansas City (bank)   SIC Code: 6021
925 Grand Avenue
Kansas City, MO 64198
816-881-2000 (800-333-1010)   Contact: Jean Mesnard

This 90 - minute guided tour includes an educational exhibit, and a tour of the Cash Services and Check Collection Departments. You may also visit the mezzanine and the art gallery. **NOTE:** High school age and over. **DIRECTIONS:** Call for specific directions.

Hours: 9:30-10:00,1:00-1:30   Days: Monday - Friday
Advance Notice: Yes   Fee: No   HP Access: Yes

Folly Theater (theater)   SIC Code: 7922
300 West 12th Street
Kansas City, MO 64105
816-474-4444   Contact: Roselle Tyner

A 45 - 75 minute historical tour of this theater will include a backstage visit and slide presentation. **NOTE:** Ages five years - adult. **DIRECTIONS:** 12th St runs north of where US
Rts 70, 35 and 29 meet.

Hours: 10:00 am - 4:00 pm   Days: Monday - Friday
Advance Notice: Yes   Fee: No   HP Access: Yes

Ford Motor Assembly Plant (automobile mfr)   SIC Code: 3711
US Highway 69
Kansas City, MO 64119
816-459-1356   Contact: Gary, Tom or Frank

This 90 - minute walking tour will show the assembly of new automobiles and trucks.
NOTE: Ages six years and older. **DIRECTIONS:** Call for specific directions.

Hours: 9:15 am and 12:15 pm   Days: Friday only
Advance Notice: Yes   Fee: No   HP Access: Yes

HNTB Corporation (engineering company)   SIC Code: 8711
1201 Walnut Street, Suite 700
Kansas City, MO 64106
816-472-1201   Contact: Sharon Hall

A two hour tour of the facility includes a brief history of the company showing the work they do and a demonstration of CADD equipment. **NOTE**: Ages junior high and older. **DIRECTIONS**: Located in the center of town. Call for specific directions.

Hours: 8:00 am - 5:00 pm   Days: Monday - Friday
Advance Notice: Yes   Fee: No   HP Access: Yes

Hallmark Visitors Center (greeting cards)   SIC Code: 2771
2501 McGee Street
Kansas City, MO 64108
816-274-3613   Contact: Gina Pavlich

A one hour tour where you will see the sights and sounds of Hallmark, past and present, through 12 extraordinary exhibits. You are invited to sit on paint jars and view a video where you will learn how original artwork is color separated and turned into an actual product. **DIRECTIONS**: Located in Crown Center Complex. Grand Ave to 25th St.

Hours: 9:00 am - 5:00 pm   Days: Monday - Friday
Advance Notice: Yes   Fee: No   HP Access: Yes

Helping Hand of Goodwill Ind. (vocational training)   SIC Code: 8331
1817 Campbell Street
Kansas City, MO 64108
816-842-7425   Contact: Jeff McCullough

This one hour tour includes a brief history of the facility and a 15 - minute video will gives you a more in-depth history of Goodwill Industries of America. **NOTE**: Ages 18 years and older. **DIRECTIONS**: Located near the Garrison and Columbus Parks. Call for specific directions.

Hours: 8:30 am - 2:00 pm   Days: Monday - Friday
Advance Notice: Yes   Fee: No   HP Access: Yes

KSHB-TV Fox 41 (TV broadcast)   SIC Code: 4833
4720 Oak Street
Kansas City, MO 64112
816-753-4141   Contact: David Zamora

A 20 - 30 minute guided tour through two studios, TV operations and an explanation of how television is brought to the home. **NOTE:** Please bring one canned good (donated to charity). Ages third grade and older. Call for specific hours for tour. **DIRECTIONS:** Located at City Market. Call for specific directions.

Hours: 1:00 pm - 4:00 pm   Days: Tuesday - Friday
Advance Notice: Yes   Fee: No   HP Access: Yes

Kansas City General Mail Facility (postal)   SIC Code: 4311
315 West Pershing Road
Kansas City, MO 64108-9998
816-374-9121   Contact: Postmaster's Secretary

This two hour tour will give you a first hand look at your mail being processed (automation, mechanization and manually). The tour follows the mail flow beginning with letters and packages coming into the docks and ending with mail being shipped out to its final destination. **NOTE:** Evening tours are on Wednesdays at 5:30 pm. Tours are conducted from the 5th through the 25th of every month. **DIRECTIONS:** Located in downtown Kansas City across the street from Union Station. Exit I - 35 south on Broadway.

Hours: 9:30 and 10:30 am   Days: Monday - Friday
Advance Notice: Yes   Fee: No   HP Access: No

Kansas City Royals Baseball (athletic club)   SIC Code: 7941
P.O.Box 419969 - Kauffman Stadium
Kansas City, MO 64141
816-921-2200   Contact: Judy VanMeter

You will receive a panoramic view of the Stadium from inside the Press Box area, Hall of Fame display, playing field, dugout, the indoor batting cage area, the Visitors' Clubhouse and the Stadium Store. **NOTE:** Tour schedule starts first Monday in June and ends last Friday in August. No 2:30 pm tour when the team is in town. Special group tours are given in the month of May. **DIRECTIONS:** Enter the Complex through Gate 1 (located at I - 70 & Blue Ridge Cut-off). Proceed to Gate A of Kauffman Stadium. Park in Lot M.

Hours: 9:30 am - 2:30 pm   Days: Monday - Friday
Advance Notice: Yes   Fee: $2.00 adult   HP Access: Yes

Kansas City Water Plant (water treatment)   SIC Code: 4941
1 NW Briarcliff Road
Kansas City, MO 64116
816-454-6233   Contact: Pam Creswell

This one hour tour consists of a 25 - minute video presentation followed by a walking tour (outdoors) of the water treatment facilities. **NOTE:** Ages seven years and older.
DIRECTIONS: At intersection of Burlington/North Oak and Hwy 9, north of the Missouri River.

Hours: By appointment only   Days: Monday - Friday
Advance Notice: Yes   Fee: No   HP Access: Yes

Marion Merrell Dow Visitors Cnt (pharmaceuticals)   SIC Code; 2834
10236 Marion Park Drive
Kansas City, MO 64137
816-966-7333   Contact: Delite Bowen

A one hour tour will enable you to see exhibits and videos focusing on the pharmaceutical industry, the company and the career of Ewing Kauffman, founder of Marion Laboratories and owner of the Kansas City Royals Baseball Club. **DIRECTIONS:** I - 435 to Hickman Mills Rd. Turn left. Left again on 103rd St and left onto Marion Park Dr.

Hours: 9:00 am - 4:00 pm   Days: Tuesday - Saturday
Advance Notice: Yes   Fee: No   HP Access: Yes

Missouri Repertory Theatre (theater)   SIC Code: 7922
4949 Cherry Street
Kansas City, MO 64110
816-235-2707   Contact: Margot Achterberg

A 45 - 60 minute tour viewing the backstage scene construction, costume construction, on-stage. **NOTE:** Ages 16 years and older. **DIRECTIONS:** Follow Main St south to 27th St to Cherry St.

Hours: 10:am - 3:00 pm   Days: Tuesday - Thursday
Advance Notice: Yes   Fee: No   HP Access: No

National Severe Storms Center (weather forecast svs)   SIC Code: 8999
601 East 12th Street, #1728 Federal. Building
Kansas City, MO 64106
816-426-3427   Contact: Janalee Snyder

A 30 - 45 minute tour of the office responsible for preparing national weather summaries, aviation forecasts and advisories to aircraft inflight, satellite interpretation messages, in addition to forecasts of tornadoes and severe thunderstorms. **NOTE:** Ages eighth grade and older. No tours April - August. **DIRECTIONS:** Downtown district north of US Rt 70.

Hours: 9:00 am & 1:00 pm   Days: Monday - Friday
Advance Notice: Yes   Fee: No   HP Access: Yes

Patricia Stevens Fashion College (school)   SIC Code: 8299
4638 J.C. Nichols Parkway
Kansas City, MO 64112
816-531-3800   Contact: Melissa Stevens

A one hour tour visiting the classrooms where models learn the industry secrets to beauty and self-esteem. **NOTE:** Ages seven years and older. **DIRECTIONS:** Call for specific directions.

Hours: 10:00 am - 4:00 pm   Days: Monday - Friday
Advance Notice: Yes   Fee: No   HP Access: Yes

Simmons Company (bedding mfr)   SIC Code: 2515
1758 North Topping Avenue
Kansas City, MO 64120
816-241-7424   Contact: Ed Spal

A one - two hour tour of the show floor seeing samples of finished mattresses, box springs and flotation beds. Tour of the plant shows the manufacturing from start to finish of all mattresses and box spring products. **DIRECTIONS:** Call for specific directions.

Hours: 8:00 am - 3:00 pm   Days: Monday - Friday
Advance Notice: Yes   Fee: No   HP Access: Yes

Trans World Airlines, Inc. (airline)   SIC Code: 4512
Kansas City International Airport (POBox 20126)
Kansas City, MO 64195
816-842-4000   Contact: Lianne Nichols

A two hour walking tour through TWA's Maintenance and Engineering Center. See commercial passenger aircraft being maintained and repaired. **NOTE:** Ages 12 and older. **DIRECTIONS:** Take exit 13 from US Rt 29, north of the city.

Hours: 9:00 am - 3:30 pm   Days: Monday - Friday
Advance Notice: Yes   Fee: No   HP Access: Yes

Lafayette Work Center, Inc. (vocational training)   SIC Code: 8331
179 Gaywood Drive
Manchester, MO 63021
573-227-5666   Contact: Manager

Visit a sheltered workshop which employs persons who are severely disabled produce light assembly and packaging contract work, using both semi-skilled and unskilled persons. **DIRECTIONS:** From US Rt 270 west of St. Louis, take exit 9, Rt 100 west.

Hours: 9:00 am - 2:00 pm   Days: Monday - Friday
Advance Notice: Yes   Fee: No   HP Access: Yes

Neosho National Fish Hatchery (hatchery)   SIC Code: 0921
East Park Street
Neosho, MO 64850
417-451-0554   Contact: Manager

This oldest fish hatchery in the United States, which features a park-like 15.6 acre setting with picnic area, aquariums and visitors center, raises 200,000 nine - inch rainbow trout and experimentally raises paddlefish and striped bass. **DIRECTIONS:** Located in the southwest corner of the state, off Hwy 86 at East Park St.

Hours: Call for schedule   Days: Monday - Friday
Advance Notice: Yes   Fee: No   HP Access: Yes

KKJO-FM, KSFT-AM (radio broadcast)   SIC Code: 4832
1201 North Woodbine
St. Joseph, MO 64506
816-279-6346   Contact: Chris Michael

Complete tour of the broadcast facility including both AM and FM studios, and the commercial production room. You will have an opportunity to be in the studio while an air
personality is live "on-the-air". **DIRECTIONS:** I - 29 north, Frederick exit, west on
Frederick to Woodbine, north on Woodbine.

Hours: 9:00 am - 3:00 pm   Days: Monday - Friday
Advance Notice: Yes   Fee: No   HP Access: No

Missouri Theater (theater)   SIC Code: 7922
715 Edmond Street
St. Joseph, MO 64501
816-271-4628   Contact: Frank Polleck

Guided tour of the theater building including the backstage, props and costume areas.
DIRECTIONS: Edmond St exit off I - 229.

Hours: 10:00 am - 5:00 pm   Days: By appointment
Advance Notice: Yes   Fee: $1.00   HP Access: Yes

Anheuser-Busch Brewery (brewery)   SIC Code: 2082
12th & Lynch Street - 1 Busch Place
St. Louis, MO 63118
314-577-2153   Contact: Debbie Maguire

Join this fascinating one hour and 45 - minute journey which begins at the new lager cellar where the traditional beechwood-aging takes place. The tour then continues to the Bevo Building, where you will view the brewing video and see the packaging plant. A short trolley ride will take you back to the Tour Center where you will have an opportunity to sample beer. **DIRECTIONS:** Take I - 55 to the Arsenal St exit.

Hours: 9:00 am - 4:00 pm   Days: Monday - Saturday
Advance Notice: Yes   Fee: No   HP Access: Yes

KSDK News Channel 5 (TV broadcast)   SIC Code: 4833
1000 Market Street
St. Louis, MO 63101
314-444-5286   Contact: Lisa Bedian

On this tour you will have an opportunity to visit the newsroom, the engineering facility, the control room and two studios. **NOTE:** Groups must contact station well in advance, in writing, for an appointment. Children must be at least seven years old. **DIRECTIONS:** Hwy 64 to Market St exit, east to 10th & Market.

Hours: 10:00 am and 2:00 pm   Days: Monday -Tuesday, Thursday-Friday
Advance Notice: Yes   Fee: No   HP Access: No

Lambert - St. Louis International Airport (airport)   SIC Code: 4581
10706 Lambert International Drive
St. Louis, MO 63145
314-426-8097   Contact: Sandy Singer

A one hour tour of Lambert's Main Terminal where you will observe the ticket area with an explanation of the baggage service. You will view how the planes are serviced, such as food, fuel and baggage. You will also view the Security Check-Point, the baggage carousels and aviation murals. It may be possible to view the inside of an aircraft. **NOTE:** Tour requires a great deal of walking. **DIRECTIONS:** From US Rt 70 go north of the city. Follow signs.

Hours: 10:00 am - 5:00 pm   Days: Monday - Friday
Advance Notice: Yes   Fee: No   HP Access: Yes

Western Sugar Company (sugar refinery)   SIC Code: 2062
3020 State Street
Billings, MT 59101
406-245-3115   Contact: Tour Department

The tour consists of watching the sugar beets coming in to the factory, seeing the process of making the sugar and seeing the finished product. **DIRECTIONS:** Call for specific directions.

Hours: By appointment only   Days: Monday - Friday
Advance Notice: Yes   Fee: No   HP Access: No

Blackfeet Writing Instruments, Inc. (pens,pencils)   SIC Code: 3952
Blackfeet Industrial Park
Browning, MT 59412
406-338-2535 (800-392-7326)   Contact: Dustin Magee/Marty Meneke

This is a 20 - minute tour of a manufacturing plant where you will observe the process of making pens, pencils and markers. **DIRECTIONS:** One mile southwest off Hwy 2.

Hours: Call for appointment   Days: Monday - Friday
Advance Notice: Yes   Fee: No   HP Access: Yes

Ash Grove Cement Company (cement mfr)   SIC Code: 3241
100 Montana Highway 518
Clancy, MT 59634
406-442-8855   Contact: Denise Kemp

The one hour tour will take you through the cement making process - raw mill, burner floor, control room, lab, finish mill and packhouse. **DIRECTIONS:** Located five miles south of Helena on I - 15, take MT City exit, left on Hwy 518 for one and one-half miles.

Hours: By appointment
Advance Notice: Yes   Fee: No   HP Access: No

Colstrip Visitor Center (coal mine)   SIC Code: 1221
6200 Main Street
Colstrip, MT 59323
406-748-3746   Contact: Manager

This is the Energy Capital of Montana. You will learn the history of this coal mining community, the operation of a coal-fired power plant, and the workings of an open-pit mine. The coal's steam is visible just 25 feet below the surface. The stack is the tallest structure in Montana. **NOTE:** Open Memorial Day - Labor Day. **DIRECTIONS:** Between Forsyth and Custer Battlefield.

Hours: 8:00 am - 5:00 pm   Days: Monday - Friday
Advance Notice: Yes   Fee: No   HP Access: No

Mission Mountain Brewery (brewery)   SIC Code: 2082
US Highway 93, Box 185
Dayton, MT 59914
406-849-5524   Contact: Tom Campbell

A 30 - minute tour of Montana's only winery which offers wines crafted by marrying state-of-the-art equipment with old world, tested techniques of winemaking. **NOTE:** Complimentary wine tasting. Open May 1 - October 31. **DIRECTIONS:** US Hwy 93 on the west shore of Flathead Lake to Dayton. 23 miles north of Polson, MT.

Hours: 10:00 am - 5:00 pm   Days: Sunday - Saturday
Advance Notice: No   Fee: No   HP Access: Yes

Kessler Brewing Company (brewery)   SIC Code: 2082
1439 North Harris Street
Helena, MT 59601
406-449-6214   Contact: Steve Schellhardt

This is a one hour tour where you will learn about the brewing process of beers and ales from the Brewmaster. **NOTE:** Free samples. Tours June 1 - August 31, thereafter by appointment. **DIRECTIONS:** Located at the corner of Harris & Railroad.

Hours: 2:00 and 4:00 pm   Days: Monday - Friday
Advance Notice: Yes   Fee: No   HP Access: Yes

Livingston Rebuild Center, Inc. (railroad equipment)   SIC Code: 3743
704 East Gallatin Street
Livingston, MT 59047
406-222-1200   Contact: Roy Korkalo

On this tour, you will see locomotives and freight cars in all stages of remanufacture. Locomotives and freight cars are from all over the United States, Mexico and Canada. You will also tour the Paint Shop and the Wheel and Axle Shop. **NOTE:** Tours are limited, be sure to call first. **DIRECTIONS:** From US Rt 90, take exit 330.

Hours: Call for schedule
Advance Notice: Yes   Fee: No   HP Access: Yes

A & S Tribal Industries (metal goods mfr)   SIC Code: 3499
Poplar Industrial Park
Poplar, MT 59255
406-768-5151   Contact: Patrick Beauchman

Visit the plant where they manufacture hard ice cream dispensers, energy efficient ceramic cooking ovens, water cooler machines and environmental protecting netting products. This plant has over 185,000 square feet of manufacturing, shipping, receiving and office space. ASTI is wholly owned by the Assinihoine and Sioux tribes of northeast Montana, established 1974. **DIRECTIONS:** Located in the Poplar Industrial Park, south of B.N. train tracks, in the northeast part of the state.

Hours: 8:00 am - 3:30 pm   Days: Monday - Thursday
Advance Notice: No   Fee: No   HP Access: Yes

Pendleton Woolen Mills (woolen mill)   SIC Code: 2231
350 West 23rd Street
Fremont, NE 68025
402-721-6393   Contact: Verna LaRocca

A 30 - 45 minute tour of the women's skirts and slacks production floor which includes the receiving of the cut wool, sewing operations in progress, pressing, inspecting, hanging and bagging of the garments, to the final shipping process. **NOTE:** Five - ten people per group. **DIRECTIONS:** Located on West Hwy 30, one block west at the Broad St and 23rd St intersection stop light.

Hours: 10:00 am & 1:00 p.m.   Days: Monday - Friday
Advance Notice: Yes   Fee: No   HP Access: Limited

MFS/York/Stormor (farm equipment mfr)   SIC Code: 3523
2928 East Highway 30
Grand Island, NE 68802
308-384-9320   Contact: Dan Spindler

This is a 15 - 20 minute walk-through tour showing you the manufacture of steel components for grain bins, grain handling equipment and grain drying equipment. **NOTE:** Call for appointment and schedule. **DIRECTIONS:** From US Rt 80, take exit 312. Call for specific directions.

Advance Notice: Yes   Fee: No   HP Access: No

Christian Record Services, Inc. (printer)   SIC Code: 2759
4444 South 52nd Street
Lincoln, NE 68516
402-488-0981   Contact: Adela Martinez

On this one hour tour, you will learn about writing and reading braille, and take a tour of the production area and library where you will see a demonstration of the braille press and of braille magazines being produced. There will be a brief demonstration on sign language and how the deaf relate in a silent world. **DIRECTIONS:** Exit on Hwy 6, turn left and go two miles to 84th St. Follow 84th St south, pass O St, A St and Van Dorn to Pioneers Blvd. Turn right on Pioneers and go two miles to 52nd St, turn left and building is on the left.

Hours: 8:00 am and 4:00 pm   Days: Monday - Tuesday
Advance Notice: Yes   Fee: No   HP Access: Yes

City Clock Company (clocks)   SIC Code: 3873
110 South 56th Street
Lincoln, NE 68510
402-483-6363   Contact: Deb Burkey

A 30 - 60 minute tour covering the restoration process of antique clocks and watches. You will see the inside works of a grandfather clock and receive an explanation of a cuckoo clock.
DIRECTIONS: I - 80 to 27th St. Go south on 27th to O St. Turn right to 56th St.

Hours: 8:00 am - 4:30 pm   Days: Monday - Friday
Advance Notice: Yes   Fee: No   HP Access: Yes

Cushman, Inc. (farm equipment mfr)   SIC Code: 3523
900 North 21st Street
Lincoln, NE 68501
402-475-9581   Contact: Jerry Ogren

On this one and one-half tour, you will observe a fully integrated manufacturing operation of specialty vehicles and turf maintenance equipment from design to shipment, including the manufacturing of engines and processes such as lasers and robots. **NOTE:** No tennis shoes allowed. **DIRECTIONS:** Corner of 21st and Vine.

Hours: 7:00 am - 3:30 pm   Days: Monday - Friday
Advance Notice: Yes   Fee: No   HP Access: Yes

Journal-Star Printing Company (newspaper)   SIC Code: 2711
926 P Street
Lincoln, NE 68508
402-475-4200   Contact: Marilea Theim

A guided tour showing and explaining the step-by-step process in the production of a newspaper. **NOTE:** Ages fourth grade and up. **DIRECTIONS:** Call for specific directions.

Hours: 8:00 am - 5:00 pm   Days: Monday - Friday
Advance Notice: Yes   Fee: No   HP Access: Yes

KFOR-KFRX Radio (radio broadcast)   SIC Code: 4832
6900 Van Dorn Street
Lincoln, NE 68506
402-483-5100   Contact: J. J. Cook

A tour of the radio station facility will include a demonstration of the broadcast equipment and an explanation of radio broadcast theory. **NOTE:** Schedule your visit to include watching a live broadcast. Fifth grade and older. **DIRECTIONS:** Located near Pioneer Park. Call for directions.

Hours: By appointment only   Days: Monday - Friday
Advance Notice: Yes   Fee: No   HP Access: Yes

KOLN-TV (TV broadcast)   SIC Code: 4833
40th & W Streets
Lincoln, NE 68503
402-467-4321   Contact: Kay Werblow

A complete tour of the technical side of the station, including production, newsroom, main studio, weather center and control room, lasting approximately 30 minutes. **NOTE:** Fourth grade and up. Minimum of five and a maximum of 15 people. **DIRECTIONS:** Call for specific directions.

Hours: 9:00-noon, 2:00-4:00   Days: Monday - Friday
Advance Notice: Yes   Fee: No   HP Access: Yes

Lincoln Telephone Company (communications)   SIC Code: 4899
1440 M Street
Lincoln, NE 68508
402-476-5819   Contact: Lela Kelliher

This one hour tour includes a brief explanation of directory assistance and long distance switchboards. A display of both historical and new telephone equipment can be viewed. **DIRECTIONS:** Call for specific directions.

Hours: 9:00-11:00/2:00-4:00   Days: Tuesday - Friday
Advance Notice: Yes   Fee: No   HP Access: Yes

Sugar Plum Candies (candy mfr)   SIC Code: 2064
333 North Cotner Boulevard
Lincoln, NE 68505
402-466-1236   Contact: Katrinka Schnabel

Take a tour of this chocolate factory and see candy and chocolate being made by hand dipping. You will also view a video tape on the history of chocolate. **NOTE:** Tours must be arranged two weeks in advance. A minimum of six people and a maximum of 15. No tours during Easter Week. **DIRECTIONS:** Located near the Gateway Shopping Center. Call for specific directions.

Hours: 10:30 am - 3:30 pm   Days: Tuesday - Friday
Advance Notice: Yes   Fee: No   HP Access: Yes

Weaver's Potato Chip Company (potato chips)   SIC Code: 2096
1600 Center Park Road
Lincoln, NE 68512
800-456-3445   Contact: Tour Department

See the processing of potatoes as they enter the plant through the potato chip packaging area in this 30 - minute tour. **DIRECTIONS:** From I - 80, take exit at Hwy 2 in Lincoln and follow Hwy 2 west to Rt 77 south. Take the second left and plant is on the left.

Hours: 8:30 - 11:00 am   Days: Monday - Thursday
Advance Notice: Yes   Fee: No   HP Access: Yes

Cranberry World West (berry crops)   SIC Code: 0171
1301 American Pacific Drive
Henderson, NV 89014
702-566-7160   Contact: Tour Department

This 30 - minute tour begins in a 100-seat theater where you will see a brief, but entertaining film featuring Carina the "Cran-Cran" girl. She will take you through the history of cranberries, from the pre-Pilgrim Native Americans, all the way through to the present. You will learn about the various aspects involved in juice processing and you will visit the demonstration kitchen and sample some tasty treats and delicious dishes prepared with cranberries. **NOTE:** Juice drink sampling. Gift shop. **DIRECTIONS:** Gibson Rd south to American Pacific Dr.

Hours: 9:00 am - 5:00 pm   Days: Monday - Friday
Advance Notice: No   Fee: No   HP Access: Yes

Ethel M Chocolate Factory (chocolate mfr)   SIC Code: 2066
One Sunset Way
Henderson, NV 89014
702-438-2641   Contact: Manager

On this fascinating self-guided tour you will learn all about the art of chocolate making through an informative video. This will show you virtually every step of the candy making process from the kitchen all the way to the wrapping of individual chocolates. **NOTE:** Free samples. **DIRECTIONS:** From the Las Vegas Strip, drive east on Tropicana to Mountain Vista (five and one-half miles). Take right and go two miles to Sunset Way. Turn left at the traffic light into Green Valley Business Park, then left again on to Cactus Garden Dr.

Hours: 8:30 am- 7:00 pm   Days: Monday - Sunday
Advance Notice: No   Fee: No   HP Access: Yes

Kidd Marshmallow Factory (candy mfr)   SIC Code: 2064
1180 Marshmallow Lane
Henderson, NV 89015
702-564-3878   Contact: Ann Walters

On this self-guided tour you will actually see the process that puts those delightful bits of fun in your hot chocolate. **NOTE:** Free sample. **DIRECTIONS:** Hwy 95 south to Sunset, exit left, first right on Gibson, two and one-half miles, take right on Marycrest.

Hours: 9:00 am - 4:30 pm   Days: Monday - Sunday
Advance Notice: No   Fee: No   HP Access: Yes

Numana Hatchery (hatchery)   SIC Code: 0921
Highway 447
Sutcliffe, NV 89510
702-574-0290   Contact: Manager

This is a photo-display exhibit of the Pyramind Lake Paiute Indian Reservation, with sections on the land, the lake, the people and the Fisheries Restoration Project. **DIRECTIONS:** Located about 30 miles north of Reno on Rt 445/446.

Hours: 8:00 am - 4:30 pm   Days: Monday - Friday
Guided tours 10:00 and 2:00   Saturday and Sunday
Advance Notice: No   Fee: No   HP Access: Yes

Hall Manufacturing Co., Inc. (canvas goods mfr)   SIC Code: 2394
56 Milford Street
Brookline, NH 03033
603-673-4841   Contact: Betty Hall

A guided tour of a small sewing factory where you will see the designing, cutting, stitching and silk screening of tote bags and industrial specialties. **DIRECTIONS:** Rt 13 north of Fitchburg (MA) area to Rt 130. Also 10 miles west of Nashua.

Hours:	Days:	Monday - Friday	
Advance Notice: Yes	Fee:	No	HP Access: Yes

Foster's Daily Democrat (newspaper)   SIC Code: 2711
333 Central Avenue
Dover, NH 03820
603-742-4455   Contact: Donna Mangan

In touring this newspaper facility you will see the workings of the newsroom, press, production, and advertising areas. Recommended time to see the actual press in operation is between noon and 2:00 pm. **DIRECTIONS:** Located in downtown Dover at intersection of Central, Henry Law & Washington.

Hours: 8:00 am - 5:00 pm	Days:	Monday - Friday	
Advance Notice: Yes	Fee:	No	HP Access: No

Salmon Falls Stoneware (pottery products)   SIC Code: 3269
Oak Street Engine House
Dover, NH 03824
603-749-1467 (800-621-2030)   Contact: Manager

Visit the craftsmen at the Oak Street Engine House, built by the Boston and Maine Railroad at the turn of the century. You will see the potters at their wheels and you will also see thousands of pieces of pottery. **DIRECTIONS:** From Rt 4, turn west on Oak across from bank. Look for sign at top of driveway.

Hours: 9:00 am - 5:00 pm	Days:	Monday - Sunday	
Advance Notice: No	Fee:	No	HP Access: Yes

Stonyfield Farm (yogurt)   SIC Code: 2026
10 Burton Drive
Londonderry, NH 03053
603-437-4040   Contact: Lori Doyle

Tour the yogurt works and see how yummy yogurts are made, traveling from the tropical incu-bator to the arctic coolers. **NOTE:** Enjoy a free sample of delicious frozen yogurt. Tours are on the hour. **DIRECTIONS:** Rt 93 north to exit 5. Left onto Rt 28 north two and 2/10 miles, turn left on Page Rd. Second left onto Webster Rd, left at stop sign. One mile turn right onto Burton Dr.

Hours: 10:00 am - 4:00 pm   Days: Tuesday - Saturday
Advance Notice: No   Fee: $1.00   HP Access: Yes

Amoskeag Fishways (hatchery)   SIC Code: 0921
1 Fletcher Street
Manchester, NH 03102
603-626-3474   Contact: Elizabeth L. LaRocca

Look through the "Window on the River" and see migrating salmon, shad, herring and dozens of other kinds of freshwater fish on the way to the head of Amoskeag Falls. Tour Amoskeag Hydro Station and learn how water produces electricity. Learn why the Merrimack River was important to people of earlier times. Listen as a voice from the past describes life long ago. **DIRECTIONS:** From I - 293 and Rt 3, take Amoskeag Bridge, exit 6. From 101 east, take Rt 93 south to 293 north.

Hours: Noon - 6:00 pm   Days: Monday - Friday
       10:00 am - 4:00 pm   Saturday - Sunday
Advance Notice: Yes   Fee: No   HP Access: Yes

Parker's Maple Barn & Sugar House (maple syrup)   SIC Code: 0831
1316 Brookline Road
Mason, NH 03048
603-878-2308   Contact: Ron or Sandy Roberts

Watch and learn the complete maple syrup process - from the tree sap to the table. **NOTE:** Tours are the last Friday in February to mid-April. **DIRECTIONS:** From MA, about two miles into NH on Rt 13 to Brookline Rd west and follow signs to Parker's. Approximately 10 miles west of Nashua.

Hours: 8:30 am - 2:30 pm   Days: Monday - Friday
Advance Notice: Yes   Fee: No   HP Access: Yes

Anheuser-Busch Brewery (brewery)   SIC Code: 2082
221 Daniel Webster Highway
Merrimack, NH 03054
603-595-1202   Contact: Deborah Buttemeier

Discover the special ingredients that go into the brewing of their family of fine beers. In just 90 - minutes you will learn about the long natural brewing process they have been using for more than a century. Come and stroll the lovely gardens and view the majestic Clydesdales. See the European-style courtyard and stables, home to the Budweiser Clydesdale East Coast hitch. **DIRECTIONS:** Follow Rt 3 (Everett Turnpike) to exit 10. At the end of ramp, take left. Follow for one-half mile. Take left onto Daniel Webster Hwy. Take first right.

Hours: 10:00 am - 4:00 pm   Days: Wednesday-Sunday (November-April)
        9:30 am - 5:00 pm   Monday- Sunday   (May-October)
Advance Notice: Yes   Fee: No   HP Access: Yes

Castle Springs (bottled water)   SIC Code: 2086
Route 171 - Ossipee Park Road
Moultonborough, NH 03254
603-476-8844   Contact: Tour Department

Tour the bottling facility and see the source of Castle Springs pure and natural spring water.
Visit the spectacular 5200 acre estate and turn-of-the century mansion built on a mountaintop
overlooking Lake Winnipesaukee. **NOTE:** Picnicking. Snack Bar. Gift shop.
DIRECTIONS: Rt 93 north to exit 23, Rt 104 to Rt 3 north to Rt 25 east. Follow signs.

Hours: 9:00 am - 5:00 pm   Days: Saturday - Sunday (May 13 - June 17)
       9:00 am - 4:00 pm   Monday - Sunday (Sept 4 - Oct 22)
Advance Notice: No   Fee: $4.00   HP Access: No

Granite Lake Pottery (pottery products)   SIC Code: 3269

Franklin Pierce Hwy (Route 9)
Munsonville, NH 03457
603-847-9908   Contact: Bill Laudfair

See potters at their wheel making various items. Decorators will provide an interesting
experience as different decorations are hand painted on each item. Each piece of pottery is
wheel- thrown or slab built and then hand decorated so no two pieces are exactly alike. See
their new walk-in size kiln, while making for greater production quantities, still maintains the
personal touch of hand crafted pottery and art work. **DIRECTIONS:** On Rt 9, between
Concord and Keene. Across from Granite Lake.

Hours: 1:00 - 3:00 pm   Days: Monday - Friday
Advance Notice: No   Fee: No   HP Access: No

Waste Management of NH (recycling center)   SIC Code: 5093
90 Rochester Neck Road
Rochester, NH 03837
603-332-2386   Contact: Alan L. Davis

After an overview at the Visitors Center, you will take a tour of the facility including the TLR-I and TRL-II landfills, Leachate Treatment Facility, Landfill Gas to Electricity Plant, Materials Recovery Facility and Invessel Organic Composting Facility. **DIRECTIONS:** Exit 12 off Spaulding Tnpk to Rt 125 south for two miles, left at the four-way intersection.

Hours: 8:00 am - 3:00 pm   Days: Monday - Friday
Advance Notice: Yes   Fee: No   HP Access: Yes

Seabrook Station (utility)   SIC Code: 4939
Route 1
Seabrook, NH 03874
800-338-7482   Contact Reception Desk

Visit the newest of New England's Nuclear Power Plants where there is lots to see and do. Watch reactor operations, participate in hands-on training simulated control room. Travel by bus to the observation platform near the containment building and take close-up photos. You can explore hands-on energy exhibits, see how uranium is used to make electricity and discover how many kilowatts it takes to energize New England. Observe local flora and fauna as you stroll through carefully preserved forest and salt march and even enjoy the woodside picnic area. **DIRECTIONS:** Rt 95 north to exit 1 right off ramp to Rt 1 north.

Hours: 10:00 am - 4:00 pm   Days: Monday - Friday
Advance Notice: No   Fee: No   HP Access: Yes

Hampshire Pewter Company (pewter ware)   SIC Code: 3914
43 Mill Street
Wolfeboro, NH 03894
603-569-4944   Contact: Jenine Steele

This 30 - minute tour begins with a video followed by a guided tour watching the craftsmen at work. Hampshire Pewter practices the centuries old method of hand casting pewter to produce high quality hollowware, table-top accessories and their world-famous Christmas ornaments. **DIRECTIONS:** From Portsmouth, take Rt 16 north to Ossipee, left onto Rt 28 to end. Turn right onto Main St. Take fifth right (Mill St). Company is on the right.

Hours: Call for specific times Days: Monday - Friday
Advance Notice: Yes   Fee: No   HP Access: Yes

Renault Winery (winery)   SIC Code: 2084
72 North Bremen Avenue
Egg Harbor City, NJ 08215
609-965-2111   Contact: Barbara Muller

Tour of this well-known winery includes a visit to the Antique Glass Museum which houses a
priceless champagne and wine glass collection. You will learn the unique history of Renault
Wines as well as visit the climate-controlled wine cellar and then on to the wine tasting
emporium where you will sample award-winning wine and champagne selections.
DIRECTIONS: From the Atlantic City Expressway, take exit 17 on Rt 563.

Hours: 10:00 am - 4:00 pm   Days: Monday - Saturday
Advance Notice: Yes   Fee: $2.00   HP Access: Yes

Pine Hill Poultry Farm (poultry farm)   SIC Code: 0254
Mt. Hermon Road
Hope, NJ 07844
908-459-5381   Contact: Gus Belverio or Barbara Langley

This is a one hour tour of a working farm on 32 acres which presents a park-like setting for
the young at heart. This farm raises, dresses and sells only the finest chickens. They are well
known for not adding chemicals, hormones or growth stimulants. **NOTE:** Tour is ideal for
senior citizens and children. **DIRECTIONS:** Take I - 80 to exit 12 south towards Hope and
onto Rt 521. Right onto Foundry Rd. At end, turn right to Mt Hermon Rd.

Hours: 9:00 am - 5:00 pm   Days: Wednesday - Sunday
Advance Notice: Yes   Fee: No   HP Access: Yes

Dominick V. Daniels Processing Center (postal)   SIC Code: 4311
850 Newark Turnpike
Kearny, NJ 07099-9998
201-955-9636   Contact: Joan Ann DeBlasio

A one hour tour of the U. S. Postal facility where you will follow the story of a letter using
state-of-the-art, high speed code sorters, sack sorting machines and parcel and bundle sorters.
DIRECTIONS: From the north, Garden State Pkwy south to exit 145. Take Rt 280 east to
exit 17A.

Hours: 9:00 am - 1:00 pm   Days: Monday - Friday
Advance Notice: Yes   Fee: No   HP Access: Yes

Newark Processing & Dist. Center (postal)   SIC Code: 4311
2 Federal Square
Newark, NJ 07102-9997
201-596-5354   Contact: Steve Gaitens/Malik Al

A visit to the U. S. Postal Processing & Distribution Center will give you the opportunity to see the automated and mechanized operations including the optical character readers, bar code sorters, advance facer cancellers with dual pass rough cullers, and the letter sorter machines. **DIRECTIONS:** One block from City Hall, across from Police Headquarters.

Hours: 10:00 am - 4:00 pm   Days: Monday - Friday
Advance Notice: Yes   Fee: No   HP Access: Yes

Pequest Trout Hatchery (hatchery)   SIC Code: 0921
605 Pequest Road
Oxford, NJ 07863
908-637-4125   Contact: Paul Tarlowe

A self-guided tour of a state operated trout hatchery which produces over 600,000 brook, brown and rainbow trout for the angling public. The hatchery video "Hooked on Nature" runs continuously in the auditorium. **NOTE:** Picnic grounds available. **DIRECTIONS:** From Rt 80, take exit 19 (Rt 517). Go south toward Hackettstown approximately five miles. At the first light downtown take a right onto Rt 46 west. Hatchery is approximately nine miles.

Hours: 10:00 am - 4:00 pm   Days: Monday - Sunday
Advance Notice: Yes   Fee: No   HP Access: Yes

Unionville Vineyards (winery)   SIC Code: 2084
9 Rocktown Road
Ringoes, NJ 08551
908-788-0400   Contact: Pat Galloway

Visit this old 1858 barn converted into a winery-tasting area for a tour which includes the winery, barrel/cave room and, by appointment, the vineyards. **DIRECTIONS:** 10 miles south of Flemington, off 202/31, turn east on Wertsville Rd, then proceed one and 5/10 miles to Rocktown Rd.

Hours: 11:00 am - 4:00 pm   Days: Saturday - Sunday
Advance Notice: No   Fee: No   HP Access: No

General Technology Corporation (electronics)   SIC Code: 3674
6816 Washington Street NE
Albuquerque, NM 87109
505-345-5591   Contact: Ralph H. Anderson

When visiting this company you will tour the printed circuit board fabrication and contract electronic assembly services departments. **DIRECTIONS:** I - 25 to Osuna exit, left on Osuna, cross two stop lights, take a right on Washington.

Hours: 9:00 am - 3:00 pm   Days: Monday - Friday
Advance Notice: Yes   Fee: No   HP Access; No

Levi Strauss & Company (jeans mfr)   SIC Code: 2389
8725 Pan American Freeway, NE
Albuquerque, NM 87113
505-823-2100   Contact: Sharon P. Mann

On this 90 - minute tour you will walk you through the facility having the opportunity to see the complete stage of construction of a pair of Levi Blue Jeans. **DIRECTIONS:** North on I - 25, take off ramp at Alameda.

Hours: 9:30 - 10:30 am   Days: Monday - Friday
Advance Notice: Yes   Fee: No   HP Access: Yes

Rainbo Baking Company (bakery)   SIC Code: 2051
111 Montano Road, NE
Albuquerque, NM 87107
505-345-5873   Contact: Jim Pickett

Walking tour of a large volume bakery where you will observe the equipment and watch the employees involved in the actual baking process. **NOTE:** Caution is required around the automated equipment. **DIRECTIONS:** Take Rt 448 north from exit 155 on US 40 to Montano Rd.

Hours: 8:00 am - 4:00 pm   Days: Monday, Wednesday - Friday
Advance Notice: Yes   Fee: No   HP Access: Yes

Sandia National Laboratories (research)   SIC Code: 8731
ORG 12640 (Kirkland Air Force Base)
1515 Eubank Boulevard SE
Albuquerque, NM 87185-0167
505-844-1307   Contact: Juanita Sanchez

Plan to take a general tour of this engineering research and development company. **NOTE:**
Call for appointment at least three weeks in advance. **DIRECTIONS:** Located at Kirkland
Air Force Base.

Hours: 9:00-11:00/1:00-3:00   Days: Monday - Friday
Advance Notice: Yes   Fee: No   HP Access: Yes

Sandia Shadows Vineyard & Winery (winery)   SIC Code: 2084
11704 Coronada Avenue NE
Albuquerque, NM 87122
505-856-1006   Contact: Philippe or Sylvia Littot

Tour of the winery and vineyard showing the processing of grapes to the finished product.
You will taste Cabernet, Chardonnay, Pinot Noit, Zinfandel and other classic and special
wines of the region. **NOTE:** Wine tasting. $1.00 fee per person for groups of 10 or more.
DIRECTIONS: Fwy 51 north. Go west on San Raphael.

Hours: Noon - 6:00 pm   Days: Wednesday - Sunday
Advance Notice: Yes   Fee: No   HP Access: Yes

La Vina Winery (winery)   SIC Code: 2084
Route 28
Chamberino, NM 88027
505-882-7632   Contact: Denise Stark

A 15 - 20 minute tour of this 12,000 gallon winery is all inclusive, demonstrating the process from harvest to bottling. **DIRECTIONS:** Two and one-half miles north of Gadsden, H.S. on Hwy 28, then half mile west on CR A53.

Hours: Call for appointment
Advance Notice; Yes   Fee: No   HP Access: No

Balagna Winery (winery)   SIC Code: 2084
223 Rio Bravo
Los Alamos (White Rock), NM 87544
505-672-3678   Contact: John Balagna

This winery tour will include the wine production area which demonstrates the winemakers goal to produce wines which have good fruitiness, clean flavors and show the unique characters of their New Mexico origin. Some of their wines are Zinfandel, Barbera, Chardonnay and Riesling. **DIRECTIONS:** At Sante Fe, take Hwy 84/285 to Pojoanque, and onto St Hwy 502 to the "Y" where it intersects with Hwy 4, taking you to White Rock and Bandelier.

Hours: 12 noon - 6:00 pm   Days: Monday - Sunday
Advance Notice: No   Fee: No   HP Access: Yes

Mescalero National Fish Hatchery (hatchery)   SIC Code: 0921
P. O. Box 247 202 Trout Loop
Mescalero, NM 88340
505-671-4401   Contact: Barbara Giesecke

This National Fish Hatchery is one of more than 90 hatcheries generated by the U. S. Fish and Wildlife Service. The hatchery raises approximately 400,000 fish weighing up to 95,000 pounds. **NOTE:** Appointments are necessary for groups, however the general public may walk through with explanatory visitor displays. **DIRECTIONS:** From El Paso take Hwy 54 north to Alamogordo; take Hwy 70 to Mescalero (30 miles). At end of ramp turn right on Eagle and at the "T" on Apache Dr, turn left.

Hours: 8:00 am - 4:00 pm   Days: Monday - Friday
Advance Notice: Yes   Fee: No   HP Access: Yes

Ponderosa Valley Vineyards & Winery (winery)   SIC Code: 2084
3171 Highway 290
Ponderosa, NM 87044
505-834-7487   Contact: H.K. or Mary Street

Touring the vineyards and winery will give you an opportunity to see the winemaking process. The vineyards and winery are located 5,800 feet above sea level and are on deep well drained volcanic ash deposits. **NOTE:** Wine tastings. Picnicking on site.
DIRECTIONS: Follow Rt 44 to Rt 4 to Rt 290, west of Los Alamos.

Hours: 10:00 am - 5:00 pm   Days: Tuesday - Saturday
Advance Notice: No   Fee: No   HP Access: Yes

Madison Vineyards & Winery (winery)   SIC Code: 2084
Star Route 490
Ribera, NM 87560
505-421-8028   Contact: Elise or Bill Madison

This is a small family operated vineyard and winery producing less than 5,000 gallons of wine per year. Much of the fine wines come from French hybrid grapes, creating both dry and semi- sweet wines. **NOTE:** Free tastings. **DIRECTIONS:** Mile Marker 66 at NM St Rd 3, south-west of Las Vegas.

Hours: 10:00 am - 4:00 pm   Days: Monday - Saturday
Advance Notice: Yes   Fee: No   HP Access: No

Domaine Cheurlin (winery)   SIC Code: 2084
500 Main Street
Truth or Consequences, NM 87901
505-894-0837   Contact: Patrice Cheurlin

A visit to this winery will give you an opportunity to see the Methode Champenoise techniques passed on from father to son over the years in making Chardonnay, Pinot Noir, and Pinot Blanc excellent sparkling wines. **DIRECTIONS:** Approximately 18 miles east of Truth or Consequences on Rt 25.

Hours: By appointment only   Days: Monday - Friday
Advance Notice: Yes   Fee: No   HP Access: Yes

Tularosa Vineyards (winery)   SIC Code: 2084
Star Route 2 - Box 5011
Tularosa, NM 88352
505-585-2260   Contact: Dave Wickham

This is a small operating vineyard and winery. All of the wines are produced from vinefera grapes and include most of the well-known standards as well as some very unusual varieties. **NOTE:** Wine tastings. **DIRECTIONS:** Two miles north of Tularosa on US 54.

Hours: Call for appointment
Advance Notice: Yes   Fee: No   HP Access: No

Black Mesa Winery (winery)   SIC Code: 2084
1502 Highway 68
Velarde, NM 87582
800-852-6372   Contact: Connie or Gary Anderson

Visit this small family operated winery where you will learn about the winemaking process. There will be demonstrations of current processes and barrel tastings for specific requests. **NOTE:** You are invited to sample the varietal wines that have made this famous amongst wine producers. **DIRECTIONS:** Midway between Taos and Santa Fe.

Hours: 10:00 am - 6:00 pm   Days: Monday - Saturday
Advance Notice: No   Fee: No   HP Access: Yes

Cascade Mountain Vineyard (winery)   SIC Code: 2084
Flint Hill Road
Amenia, NY 12501
914-373-9021   Contact: Michael

Tour the winery and vineyards and taste the wines that have led the east in two of America's largest and most prestigious wine national competitions. **DIRECTIONS:** From Taconic Pkwy, take Millbrook - Poughkeepsie exit, Rt 44 east to Millbrook. Continue east on Rt 44 to Amenia. Turn left on Rt 22 and follow signs.

Hours: 10:00 am - 6:00 pm   Days: Monday - Sunday
Advance Notice: Yes   Fee: $3.50   HP Access: Yes

Palmer Vineyards (vineyard)   SIC Code: 0172
108 Sound Avenue
Aquebogue, NY 11931
516-722-5364   Contact: Susan Skrezec

Self-guided tour of vineyards producing grapes for most wines, including Chardonnay, Pinot Blanc, Reisling, Cabornet and more. **NOTE:** Hay wagon rides. Country bluegrass music. Open mid-September to end of October. **DIRECTIONS:** East one and one-half miles off Rt 430.

Hours: 11:00 am - 5:30 pm   Days: Saturday - Sunday
Advance Notice: Yes   Fee: No   HP Access: Yes

Binghamton Processing & Dist. Center (postal)   SIC Code: 4311
115 Henry Street
Binghamton, NY 13902-9997
607-773-2105   Contact: Walt Terela

See the automated and mechanized processing of mail at this U. S. Postal Processing and Distribution Center. **DIRECTIONS:** Located in downtown Binghamton. Call for specific directions.

Hours: 12:00 noon - 8:00 pm   Days: Monday - Saturday
Advance Notice: Yes   Fee: No   HP Access: Yes

Buffalo News (newspaper)   SIC Code: 2711
1 News Plaza
Buffalo, NY 14240
716-849-3477   Contact: Pamela Hamilton

General tour of the press room and the entire production departments of one of New York's largest daily newspapers. You will see news as it happens and follow it through the publication process. **DIRECTIONS:** Located at the corner of Main and Scott Sts.

Hours: 10:00 and 12:00 noon   Days: Monday - Friday
Advance Notice: Yes   Fee: No   HP Access: Yes

Buffalo Processing & Dist. Center (postal)   SIC Code: 4311
1200 William Street
Buffalo, NY 14240-9998
716-846-2417   Contact: Gerry Gutauskas

A walk through tour of this U. S. Postal Service facility includes brief descriptions of the operating procedures including the automated and mechanized operations. You will watch as hundreds of thousands of pieces of mail are sorted and routed through the system. **DIRECTIONS:** Located between Bailey and Fillmore.

Hours: 9:00, 2:00,3:00,4:00   Days: Tuesday - Friday
Advance Notice: Yes   Fee: No   HP Access: Yes

QRS Music Rolls (musical instrument mfr)   SIC Code: 3931
1026 Niagara Street
Buffalo, NY 14213
716-885-4600   Contact: Judy Hoffman

This 45 - minute tour of the world's largest player piano manufacturer will include a slide presentation of the company's history and the craft of roll making. Through a wall in the manufacturing plant, you will see rolls being produced as well as hear several player pianos demonstrated. **DIRECTIONS:** Exit 9 from 190, go north on NY 266 (Niagara St) or Rt 198 to NY 266 (Niagara St), south on 266.

Hours: 10:00 am and 2:00 pm   Days: Monday - Friday
Advance Notice: No   Fee: $2.00   HP Access: No

Corning Glass Works (glassware mfrs)   SIC Code: 3229
151 Centerway
Corning, NY 14831
607-974-2000   Contact: Billie Jean Bennett

Tour of the Steuben Glass factory where you will watch skilled craftspeople up close as they use the intense heat of the furnace to turn gobs of molten glass into exquisite pieces of Steuben Glass. You will see the finishers cut, shape and polish glass forms then transform them into the magnificent crystal masterpieces that grace the collections of royalty. You will have an oppor-tunity to walk on a walkway where you will see the engraving process.
NOTE: Closed Thanksgiving, Christmas and New Years. July and August hours: 9:00 am - 8:00 pm. **DIRECTIONS**: From Rochester, take I - 390 south to Rt 17 east to exit 46. Take Corning exit and follow signs.

Hours: 9:00 am - 5:00 pm   Days: Monday - Sunday
Advance Notice: No   Fee: $5.00   HP Access: Yes

Original American Kazoo Co. (musical instrument mfr)   SIC Code: 3931
8703 South Main Street
Eden, NY 14057
716-992-3960   Contact: Dawn Carnall

A tour of the only metal kazoo factory in the world will highlight the history, amusing trivia, and demonstrate step by step information on how kazoos are made. Museum displays antique kazoos. **DIRECTIONS:** Rt 90 (NY State Thruway) to exit 57A. Go to Rt 62 in Eden.

Hours: 10:00 am - 2:30 pm   Days: Monday - Friday
Advance Notice: Yes   Fee: No   HP Access: Yes

Queens Processing & Dist. Center (postal)   SIC Code: 4311
142-02 20th Avenue
Flushing, NY 11351-9700
718-321-5109   Contact: Kuang Teng

Tour the mail processing operation of this U. S. Postal facility where you will follow the mail through the entire processing and sorting system. You will see hundreds of thousands of items of mail being routed direct to individual mail carriers. **DIRECTIONS:** Rt 95 south to White-stone Bridge, bear right at fork just over bridge onto Whitestone Pkwy. Get off at 20th Ave exit. Take a right at light.

Hours: Call for schedule
Advance Notice: Yes   Fee: No   HP Access: Yes

Fly Creek Cider Mill (cider mill)   SIC Code: 0175
RD 1 Goose Street
Fly Creek, NY 13337
607-547-9692   Contact: Barbara/Howard Michaels

Watch apple cider being made the old way and sample the fruits of autumn's harvest. This is a seasonal working water-powered cider mill, dating from 1856, using a Lesner turbine to power the Boomer & Boschert Press (1889). **NOTE:** Open mid-August - November.
DIRECTIONS: Three miles north of Cooperstown, NY, turn at blinker in Fly Creek off Rt 28/80.

Hours: No set hours   Days: Sunday - Saturday
Advance Notice: Yes   Fee: No   HP Access: Yes

Western Nassau Processing & Dist Center (postal)   SIC Code: 4311
830 Stewart Avenue
Garden City, NY 11599-9998
516-228-7502   Contact: Suzanne Franqui

This U. S. Postal Service facility will review the state-of-the-art Automation and Mechanization Systems which processes letter mail exceeding 2.2 million pieces per day.
DIRECTIONS: Meadowbrook Pkwy, exit M3 west (1/4 mile west on Stewart Ave).

Hours: 10:00 am - 4:00 pm   Days: Monday - Friday
Advance Notice: Yes   Fee: No   HP Access: Yes

Taylor Wine Company (winery)   SIC Code: 2084
Gibson Hill
Hammondsport, NY 14840
607-868-3245   Contact: Manager

Tour this well-known winery where Taylor, Great Western, Gold Seal, Lake Country and
Henry Marchant wines and champagnes are made. You will be seated in the "Theater-in-a-
Wine-Tank", which once held over 35,000 gallons of wine. Tour the grape pressing, fermentation, storage, aging and bottling facilities. **NOTE:** Wine tasting. Harvest and crushing
activities normally occur from September to mid - October. **DIRECTIONS:** From Syracuse
and the east, exit 42 from Geneva and proceed south on Rt 14 to Dresden. Take Rt 54 south
through Penn Yan to Hammondsport. Right on Main and left on Lake to the Winery Visitors
Center.

Hours: 10:00 am - 4:00 pm   Days: Monday - Sunday
Advance Notice: No   Fee: No   HP Access: yes

Remington Arms Company, Inc. (firearm mfr)   SIC Code: 3484
14 Hoefler Avenue
Ilion, NY 13357
315-895-3200   Contact: Thomas Goldin

This 3/4 mile walk-through tour of the plant takes you to the many different areas of the firearms assembly process of rifles and shotguns, and the gallery where they test fire them. The
miscellaneous machinery are where the smaller parts are made then on to the FMS area where
the computerized milling of most of the receivers are done. **NOTE:** Open for tours, June,
July, August. **DIRECTIONS:** Exit 30 off New York Thruway. Follow Main St Mohawk
through to Ilion. Company is the big red brick building on left side. Come to the Museum
entrance corner of Catherine and Hoefler Ave.

Hours: 9:30 am - 1:30 pm   Days: Monday - Friday
Advance Notice: No   Fee: No   HP Access: yes

Lamoreaux Landing Wine Cellars (winery)   SIC Code: 2084
9224 Route 414
Lodi, NY 14860
607-582-6011   Contact: Mark J. Wagner

Visit this well known wine cellar and taste some award winning wines which are the product of a lifelong commitment to growing the finest vinefera grapes. Some of the wines include Pinot Noir, Chardonnay, Riesling and Cabernet Sauvignon. **DIRECTIONS:** From exit 41 NY Thruway, take Rt 414 south for about 25 miles.

Hours: 10:00 am - 5:00 pm   Days: Monday - Saturday
Advance Notice: Yes   Fee: $4.00   HP Access: Yes

Wagner Vineyards (winery)   SIC Code: 2084
9322 Rt 414
Lodi, NY 14860
607-582-6720   Contact: Carol Voorhees

Tour the winery which includes the press deck, the tank room, the bottling line and wine cellar followed by a wine tasting in the tasting area. **NOTE:** Closed major holidays. **DIRECTIONS:** Four miles south of Lodi on Rt 414, northeast of Corning.

Hours: 10:00 am - 4:15 pm   Days: Monday - Sunday
Advance Notice: Yes   Fee: No   HP Access: Yes

Times Union (newspaper)   SIC Code: 2711
645 Albany Shaker Road
Loudonville/Albany, NY 12212
518-454-5694   Contact: Susan Radlovsky

A one hour tour of the newspaper plant will include a visit to the newsroom and production and advertising areas. You will see the workings of a newspaper in progress. **NOTE:** Must be at least 10 years of age. Tours must be scheduled two - three weeks in advance. **DIRECTIONS:** Located off exit 4 of Northway.

Hours: 10:00 am   Days: Monday - Friday
Advance Notice: Yes   Fee: No   HP Access: Yes

L. & J. G. Stickley, Inc. (furniture mfr)   SIC Code: 2519
1 Stickley Drive
Manlius, NY 13104
315-682-5500   Contact: Carolyn Audi

On this tour of the Stickley Factory, you will see how the finest quality solid cherry, oak, and mahogany furniture is made, from start to finish. **DIRECTIONS:** From Syracuse, take 481 south to exit 3 east, one mile to 92 east for three and one-half miles. Turn right at the Chase Bank.

Hours: 10:00 am   Days: Tuesday
Advance Notice: Yes   Fee: No   HP Access: Yes

Benmarl Wine Company (winery)   SIC Code: 2084
156 Highland Avenue
Marlboro, NY 12542
914-236-4265   Contact: Manager

Tour this local winery and see the production of grapes and learn how wine is made. **NOTE:** Wine tasting. Closed major holidays. **DIRECTIONS:** Located five miles north of US 84 at Newburgh on Rt 9 west to Western Ave to Highland Ave from center of Marlboro.

Hours: 12 noon - 5:00 pm   Days: Monday - Friday
Advance Notice: No   Fee: No   HP Access: Yes

Webb's Candies, Inc. (candy mfr)   SIC Code: 2064
West Lake Road - Route 394
Mayville, NY 14754
716-753-2161   Contact: Anne Straitiff

Tour includes history and process of old-fashioned candy making by hand. Famous for Goat's Milk Fudge - a unique treat. **DIRECTIONS:** Located two miles from NY Thruway exit 60.

Hours: 10:00 am - 4:00 pm   Days: Monday - Friday
Advance Notice: Yes   Fee: No   HP Access: Yes

Widmer Wine Cellars (winery)   SIC Code: 2084
1 Lake Niagara Lane
Naples, NY 14512
716-374-6311   Contact: Ed Morrison

A 30 - minute walking tour of the wine making facilities including the cellars, filtration, bottling and grounds. Come savor the flavor of the Finger Lakes on a tour of this 100-year old winery. You will stroll past massive oak casks in cool underground cellars and marvel at the museum and state-of-the-art bottling plant. **NOTE:** Wine and juice tasting.
DIRECTIONS: From US Rt 390, take exit 2 and go north to Rt 21.

Days: 10:00 am - 4:00 pm   Days: Monday - Saturday (May-October)
Advance Notice: Yes   Fee: No   HP Access: Yes

Rivendell Winery (winery)   SIC Code: 2084
714 Albany Post Road
New Paltz, NY 12561
914-255-0892   Contact: Manager

Tour the vineyards (weather permitting) followed by tour of the winery plant. Complimentary wine tastings of New York State's most awarded wines. **NOTE:** Ages 21 and older may taste wine. **DIRECTIONS:** NYS Thruway exit 18. Turn left and follow signs.

Hours: 10-00 am - 6:00 pm   Days: Monday - Friday
Advance Notice: No   Fee: No   HP Access: Yes

New York Stock Exchange (stock exchange)   SIC Code: 6231
20 Broad Street
New York, NY 10005
212-656-5165   Contact: Margret Tomere

View the New York Stock Exchange trading floor, where more than 2,500 companies list more than 141 billion shares valued at $4.4 trillion. See one of the most sophisticated, high tech working environments in the world. **NOTE:** Exhibits, video, gift shop. Tickets for self-guided tours are distributed outside the 20 Broad St entrance starting at 9:00 am as long as they are available. Easily accessible by subway. Advance notice needed for groups of 10 or more. **DIRECTIONS:** Call for specific directions.

Hours: 9:15 am - 4:00 pm   Days: Monday - Friday
Advance Notice: No   Fee: No   HP Access: Yes

Mid Hudson Processing & Dist. Center (postal)   SIC Code: 4311
99 Enterprise Drive
Newburgh, NY 12555-9997
914-567-2301   Contact: Karen Johannessen

See the mail processing operations and automated equipment of this U. S.Postal Service facility. **DIRECTIONS:** Take exit 6 off Rt 84, 17K west, to Governor Dr, left on Enterprise Dr.

Hours: 9:00 am - 6:00 pm   Days: Monday - Friday
Advance Notice: Yes   Fee: No   HP Access: Yes

Niagara Power Project Visitors Center (utility)   SIC Code: 4911
P.O.Box 277
Niagara Falls, NY 14302
716-285-3211 x6660   Contact: Community Relations Manager

Tour one of the world's largest producers of hydroelectricity and learn first hand about the use of hydrosolar, nuclear and fossil fuels as energy sources. Exciting educational hands-on exhibits on displays. **DIRECTIONS:** Take New York Thruway 90 to 290 (Youngmann Hwy) to 190 Niagara Falls. Continue across Grand Island, staying on 190. Take exit 25H, the last exit before Canada. Follow signs to Rt 104 west. Visitors Center is ahead on left.

Hours: By appointment only
Advance Notice: Yes   Fee: No   HP Access: Ye

North Salem Vineyard, Inc. (winery)   SIC Code: 2084
441 Hardscrabble Road
North Salem, NY 10560
914-669-5518   Contact: Lee Roberts

Take a tour of the winery and see the winemaking process in addition to wine tasting of Pinot Noir, Chardonnay, Reisling and other New York State wines. **NOTE:** Advance notice for groups of 10 or more. **DIRECTIONS:** Two and one-half miles east of exit 8 from Rt 684.

Hours: 1:00 - 5:00 pm   Days: Saturday - Sunday (year round)
      1:00 - 5:00 pm   Monday - Friday (Sept - December)
Advance Notice: No   Fee: No   HP Access: Yes

Syracuse Newspapers (newspaper)   SIC Code: 2711
1 Clinton Square (P.O.Box 4915)
Syracuse, NY 13202
315-470-8098   Contact: Samera Frank

On this 45 - minute tour, you will see a video explaining the newspaper operation, followed by a walk through the newsrooms where you will have an opportunity to look at the presses. **DIRECTIONS:** Downtown Syracuse at Clinton Sq, corner of Saline & West Genesee.

Hours: 10:00 am - 2:00 pm   Days: Tuesday and Thursday
Advance Notice: Yes   Fee: No   HP Access: Yes

Brown & Moran Brewing Co. (brewery)   SIC Code: 2082
417 River Street
Troy, NY 12180
518-273-2337   Contact: Garrett Brown

This is a 15 - 20 minute tour of the Brew House and the Fermenting Room. **NOTE:** Free samples. **DIRECTIONS:** I - 90 to 787, exit at downtown Troy, cross bridge, turn right on Hutton St and follow until it crosses River St.

Hours: By appointment
Advance Notice: Yes   Fee: No   HP Access: Yes

Carey Organ Company (musical instrument mfr)   SIC Code: 3931
108 Jefferson Street
Troy, NY 12180
518-273-2974 (800-836-1441)   Contact: Keith Williams

Tour this turn-of-the century brick factory building where you will see pipe and reed organ restoration and pipe organ construction. **DIRECTIONS:** Rt 787 to Rt 378 east, Rt 4 north to Jefferson St, turn right and go one-half block.

Hours: 10:00 am - 3:00 pm   Days: Monday - Friday
Advance Notice: Yes   Fee: No   HP Access: No

Icarus Furniture (furniture mfr) SIC Code: 2519
54 4th Street
Troy, NY 12180
518-274-2883 Contact: Jim Lewis

Tour this small furniture shop where Mr. Lewis will describe how made-to-order wooden furniture is made and the process for designing and building it. You will see the shop and work in progress and also see some machinery dating back to the 1920's. **DIRECTIONS:** From Albany, go north on Rt 787 to 23rd St Watervliet exit (seven miles). Take left on 23rd St to second light. Left on 2nd Ave to first light. Left on Congress St Bridge to second light. Left on 4th St to second store on right.

Hours: By appointment only
Advance Notice: Yes Fee: No HP Access: No

Marvin Neitzel Corporation (uniform mfr) SIC Code: 2389
444 River Street
Troy, NY 12181
518-272-8900 Contact: David Glerman

Take an approximate 15 - minute tour of a uniform manufacturer where you will see the cutting and sewing of garments. Limited availability. **DIRECTIONS:** Rte I -787 to Rte 7 into Troy, Hutton St exit, left onto River St. Go south one block.

Hours: 9:00 am - 3:00 pm Days: Monday - Friday
Advance Notice: Yes Fee: No HP Access: No

Brookhaven National Laboratories (research) SIC Code: 8731
William Floyd Pkwy (County Road 46)
Upton, NY 11973-5000
516-282-4049 Contact: Janet Tempel

This is a guided tour of a hands-on science museum where you will learn about Brookhaven's research and achievements. BNL is one of the nation's leading scientific research laboratories studying the laws of nature, in particular, the fields of physics, chemistry, biology, mathematics, environmental sciences and energy technology. **NOTE:** Open house on Sundays during July and August. Handicap accessible on first floor only. Advance reservations only. **DIRECTIONS:** Exit 68 off the Long Island Expressway (I - 495); one and one-half miles north on William Floyd Pkwy (County Road 46). Main gate is on the right.

Advance Notice: Yes Fee: No HP Access: No

F. X. Matt Brewing Co. (brewery)   SIC Code: 2082
811 Edward Street
Utica, NY 13502
315-732-0022   Contact: Tricia

The tour begins with a brief history of the brewery and continues into the grain room. After an elevator ride, you will enter the brew house to see the first stages of the brewing process, the fermenting cellars, and then on to the aging room. The tour ends at the bottling works. **DIRECTIONS:** Located near the corner of Court and York Sts in the west section of town.

Hours: 10:00 am - 4:00pm   Days: Monday - Saturday
Advance Notice: Yes   Fee: $3.00   HP Access: No

Utica Processing & Dist. Facility (postal)   SIC Code: 4311
100 Pitcher Street
Utica, NY 13504-9997
315-738-5371   Contact: Cathy Ducato

A visit to this U. S. Postal facility will demonstrate the new automated - mechanized processing plant procedures with a daily volume in excess of one million pieces of mail. **DIRECTIONS:** Rt 5S east to Charlestown. Right on Pitcher St. Post Office is on left.

Hours: 10:00 am - 6:00 pm   Days: Tuesday, Wednesday, Thursday
Advance Notice: Yes   Fee: No   HP Access: Yes

Farm Sanctuary (animal shelter)   SIC Code: 0752
3100 Aikens Road
Watkins Glen, NY 14891
607-583-2225   Contact: Mitch Brown

The Farm Sanctuary is the nation's only Farm Agency Rescue and Rehabilitation organization situated on a 175 - acre working farm that is home to hundreds of rescued animals. The tour includes visiting, without feeding, the pigs, turkeys, cattle, goats, and other animals. **NOTE:** The farm is located in the beautiful "Finger Lakes Region" of New York. **DIRECTIONS:** From Watkins Glen, follow Rt 409 west (up hill on Fourth St) to Rt 23, follow for eight miles to Aikens Rd, turn left. Drive on Aikens Rd for one and one-half miles until you see the Farm Sanctuary on the left.

Hours: Call for schedule   Days: Wednesday - Sunday (May - October)
Advance Notice: Yes   Fee: Donation   HP Access: Yes

Charlotte Processing & Dist. Center (postal)　　　　SIC Code: 4311
2901 South Interstate 85, Service Road
Charlotte, NC 28228-9998
704-393-4484　　　　　Contact: Andrea Davis

A tour of this U. S. Postal Processing and Distribution Center will show the mail flow process, including the entry and dispatch process. **DIRECTIONS:** I - 85 to Billy Graham exit. Facility is located on NE Service Rd.

Hours: 9:00 am - 3:00 pm　　　Days: Monday - Friday
Advance Notice: Yes　　　　　Fee:　No　　　　HP Access: Yes

Mom N Pop's Smokehouse (meat processor)　　　　SIC Code: 2013
101 Western Steer Mom N Pop Drive
Claremont, NC 28610
704-459-7626　　　　　Contact: Eugene Houston

This is a self-guided tour of a smokehouse where you will see country hams being cured as well as fresh country biscuits being made. **NOTE:** Free samples. **DIRECTIONS:** Take US Rt 40 west of Winston- Salem to exit 135. Call for further directions.

Hours: 9:00 am - 4:30 pm　　　Days: Monday - Friday
Advance Notice: No　　　　　Fee:　No　　　　HP Access: yes

Fayetteville Observer-Times (newspaper)　　　　SIC Code: 2711
458 Whitfield Street
Fayetteville, NC 28302-0849
910-323-4848　　　　　Contact: Campbell Haigh

This 90 - minute in-depth tour of a modern newspaper facility will include a complete overview of the day-to-day operations encompassing the advertising, circulation, and production departments as well as the newsroom itself. **NOTE:** Tours are available by appointment only during September - November and January - May. School tours are available for grades four and above. **DIRECTIONS:** Whitfield St runs south from US Rt 401 in the center of Fayetteville.

Hours: 10:00 am　　　　Days: Tuesday and Friday
Advance Notice: Yes　　　Fee:　No　　　　HP Access: Yes

Greensboro Processing & Dist. Center (postal)　　　SIC Code: 4311
900 East Market Street
Greensboro, NC 27498-9700
910-271-5423　　　　　　　　Contact: Bob Carter

An approximate 45 - minute tour of the U. S. Postal facility where you will observe the manual/LSM machines and the automation processing of mail. **DIRECTIONS:** From I - 40/I - 85, look for the Elm/Eugene St exit. Turn and head back towards town. Take Elm/Eugene St to downtown. Turn right on Market St (one way) and go about 12 blocks. The Processing Center will be on the right side of Market St. Look for the blue canopy.

Hours: 8:00 am - 5:00 pm　　　Days: Monday - Friday
Advance Notice: Yes　　　　　　Fee: No　　　　　　HP Access: Yes

Replacements, Ltd. (chinaware)　　　　　　　SIC Code: 3262
1089 Knox Road
Greensboro, NC 27420
910-697-3000 (800 562-4462)　　Contact: Darla Doumanian

The 30 - minute tour begins with a guided walk through the office and warehouse areas and ends with a visit to the showroom where you will learn how mystery patterns are identified by researchers, how tableware is inspected, how minor imperfections are removed from crystal, how gold or platinum trim on china is repaired, how flatware is refinished and how vintage china is restored to its original beauty. **NOTE:** Advance notice for large groups of 15 or more. **DIRECTIONS:** Off I - 85/40 at Mt. Hope Church Rd, exit 132, between Greensboro and Burlington.

Hours: 8:30 am - 5:30 pm　　　Days: Monday - Friday
Advance Notice: No　　　　　　Fee: No　　　　　　HP Access: Yes

Spring Garden Brewing Company (brewery)　　　SIC Code: 2082
714 Francis King Street
Greensboro, NC 27410
910-299-3649　　　　　　　　Contact: Christian Boos

Visit this real Bavarian style brewery where beer is brewed daily. Their lagers are aged for seven weeks before serving. **NOTE:** Free samples. **DIRECTIONS:** From I - 40, two miles north of 314 Guilford College exit.

Hours: 9:00 am - 5:00 pm　　　Days: Monday - Friday
Advance Notice; No　　　　　　Fee: No　　　　　　HP Access: Yes

Kinston Processing & Dist. Center (postal)   SIC Code: 4311
208 East Caswell Street
Kinston, NC 28501-9998
919-527-6123   Contact: June Knowles

On the tour of the U. S. Postal Processing and Distribution Center you will walk through the mail distribution, automation equipment and the sorting equipment areas. **DIRECTIONS:** Hwy 70 east to 11/55 north to Caswell St.

Hours: Call for appointment   Days: Monday - Friday
Advance Notice: Yes   Fee: No   HP Access: Yes

Rocky Mount Processing & Dist. Center (postal)   SIC Code: 4311
201 South George Street
Rocky Mount, NC 27801-9997
919-977-3123   Contact: Dennis Avent

At the U. S. Postal Processing & Distribution Center you will take a half-hour tour of the facility where you will see the automated and mechanized operations of the facility. Watch as hundreds of thousands of pieces of mail are sorted and routed through the distribution system. **DIRECTIONS:** Located in the center of the city. Call for specific directions.

Hours: 10:00 am - 7:00 pm   Days: Flexible
Advance Notice: Yes   Fee: No   HP Access: Yes

Antelope Valley Station (utility)   SIC Code: 4939
Basin Electric Power Cooperative
P.O.Box 1059
Beulah, ND 58523
701-873-4545   Contact: Manager

A view from the observation deck (320 feet) highlights the two hour tour of the power plant. You will view the inside of the boiler, stand next to an operating turbine-generator and observe activities in the plant's control room. **NOTE:** There is walking involved. Not recommended for children under age 10. **DIRECTIONS:** Junction of ND St Hwys 49 and 200, drive one and one-half miles north, then left at county road junction, drive four miles west and one mile north.

Hours: 9:00 am - 3:00 pm   Days: Monday - Friday
Advance Notice: Yes   Fee: No   HP Access: Yes

Dakota Gasification Company (natural gas)   SIC Code: 1311
Box 1149 - County Road 26A
Beulah, ND 55823
701-873-6667   Contact: Joan Dietz

The Great Plains Synfuels Plant is the only commercial-sized coal gasification plant in the US, producing an average of 160 million cubic feet of synthetic natural gas per day plus byproducts. **NOTE:** No cameras allowed. **DIRECTIONS:** Located five miles northwest of Beulah. From the junction of ND 49 and 200, drive one and one-half miles north, turn left at county road junction, drive three and one-half miles west.

Hours: By appointment   Days: Monday - Friday
Advance Notice: Yes   Fee: No   HP Access: No

Freedom Mine (coal mine)   SIC Code: 1221
The Coteau Properties Company
HC3 Box 49
Beulah, ND 58523
701-873-2281   Contact: Bill Suter

Tour the coal mine and its operations which produces 15 million tons of lignite annually, making it the seventh largest coal mine in the US and the largest lignite mine nationally. **DIRECTIONS:** 10 miles northwest of Beulah, ND.

Hours: 7:00 am - 3:00 pm   Days: Monday - Friday
Advance Notice: Yes   Fee: No   HP Access: Limited

Bismarck Processing & Dist. Center (postal)   SIC Code: 4311
2220 East Bismarck Expressway
Bismarck, ND 58504-9997
701-221-6550   Contact: Distribution Supervisor

This U. S. Postal facility offers a tour of the mail processing facility and an overview of the various mail processing operations including automation. **DIRECTIONS:** Traveling west on I - 94, take exit 162 and turn south on North Bismarck Expressway. As you continue south on the Expressway, it will curve west at which time you will be on East Bismarck Expressway.

Hours: 8:00 am - 5:00 pm   Days: Monday - Friday
Advance Notice: Yes   Fee: No   HP Access: Yes

KXMB TV (TV broadcast)   SIC Code: 4833
1811 North 15th Street
Bismarck, ND 58501
701-223-9197   Contact: Tracey Reinbold

The 20 - 30 minute tour consists of a walk through the building including the studio, news room and control room. You will get a complete explanation of the facility and all of its workings. **DIRECTIONS:** Located three blocks south of I - 94 and Hwy 83, then east on Spaulding for three blocks.

Hours: Call for appointment   Days: Monday - Friday
Advance Notice: Yes   Fee: No   HP Access: No

Super Valu Warehouse (food warehouse)   SIC Code: 5141
707 Airport Road
Bismarck, ND 58504
701-222-5600   Contact: Donna Arneson

This is a 45 - minute tour of the office and warehouse of a well-known supermarket chain. **DIRECTIONS:** From US 94 take exit 159 south to 9th St/University Dr. Airport Rd is on left.

Hours: 9:00 am - 3:30 pm   Days: Monday - Friday
Advance Notice: Yes   Fee: No   HP Access: No

Dakota Growers Pasta Company (pasta)   SIC Code: 2098
One Pasta Avenue
Carrington, ND 58421-0021
701-652-2855   Contact: Manager

This company is the world's first grower-owned pasta cooperative. This tour will take you through the mills, where you will see the processing and packaging process of this new pasta making company. **DIRECTIONS:** Take Rt 281 north of Jamestown from US Rt 84 to Rt 200. Once in Carrington, call for specific directions.

Hours: Call for schedule   Days: Monday - Friday
Advance Notice: Yes   Fee: No   HP Access: Yes

Pipestem Creek (floriculture)   SIC Code: 0181
7060 Highway 9
Carrington, ND 58421
701-652-2623   Contact: Ann Hoffert

Tour the everlasting gardens, private gardens, factory, drying facilities, production facilities, restored wooden buildings including the depot. All of the elements for the designs are cultivated in the gardens and fields of Pipestem Creek or grow wild nearby. **DIRECTIONS:** From I - 29 at Jamestown, go 33 miles north on Rt 281 and one mile east on Rt 9.

Hours: By appointment   Days: Monday - Friday
Advance Notice: Yes   Fee: $2.00   HP Access: No

Eyewear Concepts (eyeglasses)   SIC Code: 3851
446 3rd Avenue West
Dickinson, ND 58601
701-225-2020   Contact: Chuck Andrus

Tour the optical finishing department and the optical dispensary of a local retail optician. Learn how eyeglasses are made and matched to the user. **NOTE:** Grade six and up. **DIRECTIONS:** Located one-half mile south of I - 94, exit 61.

Hours: 9:00 am - 12 noon   Days: Monday - Thursday
Advance Notice: Yes   Fee: No   HP Access: No

American Crystal Sugar Company (sugar refinery)   SIC Code: 2062
Highway 2, Box 357
East Grand Forks, ND 56721
218-773-5126   Contact: Peggy Rieger

The 40 - 60 minute tour will give you a clearer idea of how sugar beets are turned into sugar. The tour will show the process of washing the beets to the end process of bagging the sugar. **DIRECTIONS:** Located on Old Highway 2.

Hours: Call for schedule   Days: Monday - Friday
Advance Notice: Yes   Fee: No   HP Access: No

Concrete, Inc. (concrete)   SIC Code: 3272
5000 DeMers Avenue
Grand Forks, ND 58201
701-772-6687   Contact: Bob Sween

In touring this manufacturer of concrete components, you will have an opportunity to see the production of precast/prestressed concrete products as well as the production of wall panels made for warehouses and retail stores. **DIRECTIONS:** Going north on I - 29, take the second exit for Grand Forks, turn left (west) and go approximately one-half mile west of DeMers.

Hours: 8:00 am - 4:00 pm   Days: Monday - Friday
Advance Notice: Yes   Fee: No   HP Access: No

U.S.Energy & Environmental Research Ctr (utility)   SIC Code: 4939
15 North 23rd Street
Grand Forks, ND 58202
701-795-8181   Contact: Patrick Miller

A one hour tour of the environmental laboratories and combustion pilot plant area where you will hear explanations and see demonstrations of how EERC research and technology prevents pollution, produces efficient energy and cleans up the environment. **DIRECTIONS:** Located on southeast corner of University of North Dakota campus.

Hours: 8:00 am - 5:00 pm   Days: Monday - Friday
Advance Notice: Yes   Fee: No   HP Access: Yes

Nash Finch Company (food warehouse)   SIC Code: 5141
1425 Burdick Expressway, West
Minot, ND 58701
701-852-0365   Contact: Dana Steinwand

Complete tour of a grocery wholesale distribution center. **DIRECTIONS:** West on Burdick Expressway West.

Hours: Call for appointment
Advance Notice: Yes   Fee: No   HP Access: Yes

Terhorst Manufacturing Company (plastic mfr)   SIC Code: 3089
615 East Burdick Expressway
Minot, ND 58701
701-852-0535   Contact: Marion Kolb

On this one hour tour you will view the molding machine operation and tool and die shop operations of this company involved in injection molded plastics. You will see a display board of the variety of their products, learn about the plant history and take part in a question and answer session. **NOTE:** Company encourages tours of their facility because of their unique process. **DIRECTIONS:** North side of viaduct, just east of St. Joseph Hospital.

Hours: 8:00 am - 4:00 pm   Days: Monday - Thursday
Advance Notice: Yes   Fee: No   HP Access: Yes

Garrison Dam, US Army Corp of Engineers (utility)   SIC Code: 4939
P.O.Box 527
Riverdale, ND 58565
701-654-7451   Contact: Sallie Pochant

The Garrison Project resource is used for electric power, flood control, irrigation, recreation, municipal water supply and downstream navigation. **NOTE:** No pets, smoking, purses, food, beverages or packages on tour. Cameras are allowed. Open Memorial Day - Labor Day. **DIRECTIONS:** Two and one-half miles southwest of Riverdale, ND, Hwy 200 below the Garrison Dam.

Hours: 8:00 am - 4:00 pm   Days: Monday - Friday
Advance Notice: Yes   Fee: No   HP Access: Yes

Leland Olds Station (utility)   SIC Code: 4939
P.O.Box 99 - Highway 200
Stanton, ND 58571
701-745-3371   Contact: Tour Department

The Leland Olds Station is a lignite-fired electric generating station operated by Basin Electric Power Cooperative. It has two units. Unit 1 is rated at 210,000 KW capacity and Unit 2 is rated at 440,000 KW capacity. You will take a guided tour of the power plant and see how coal is used to generate electricity. **NOTE:** There is walking involved and not recommended for children under 10 years of age. **DIRECTIONS:** One mile south and three and one-half miles east of Stanton, ND.

Hours: Call for appointment   Days: Monday - Friday.
Advance Notice: Yes   Fee: No   HP Access: No

Cooperative Power Association (electric company)   SIC Code: 4911
Coal Creek Station
Box 780 - Highway 83 South
Underwood, ND 58576
701-442-3211   Contact: Frank J. Mattern

On this one hour guided tour of the largest lignite-fired power plant in the country, you will see a video presentation, see the turbines, the generator, control room, furnace, pulverizers, condensor, repair shop and most of all a spectacular view from the 21st floor (outdoors). **DIRECTIONS:** On Hwy 83, 50 miles north of Bismarck.

Hours: 10:00-Noon/12:30-3:00   Days: Monday - Friday
Advance Notice: No   Fee: No   HP Access: Yes

Falkirk Mining Company (coal mine)   SIC Code: 1221
P.O.Box 1087
Underwood, ND 58576
701-442-5751   Contact: Linda G. Ash

After viewing a 10 - minute video overview of the mine operation you will go on a one and one-half hour field tour to watch the actual surface coal minings taking place. **NOTE:** 24 hours advance notice is required. Open during September - May only. **DIRECTIONS:** Four miles south of Underwood, ND.

Hours: 8:00 am - 2:30 pm   Days: Monday - Friday
Advance Notice: Yes   Fee: No   HP Access: Yes

Akron Processing & Distribution Center (postal)   SIC Code: 4311
675 Wolf Ledges Parkway
Akron, OH 44309-9997
330-996-9756   Contact: Sally Frock

Tour the mail processing facility of the U. S. Postal System and see all aspects of mail processing. **DIRECTIONS:** Rt 76 west off interchange, first exit (Grant St/Wolf Ledges), through light to second intersection, take right and facility is on the second block on the right side.

Hours: 9:00 am - 6:00 pm	Days: Monday - Friday	
Advance Notice: Yes	Fee: No	HP Access: Yes

Goodyear World of Rubber (rubber products)   SIC Code: 3069
1144 East Market Street
Akron, OH 44316
330-796-7117   Contact: Manager, World of Rubber

A one hour tour (by request) of the "World of Rubber" will include an introductory film. You will see a simulated miniature rubber plantation, several unique rubber products, exhibits of how rubber is made and processed into items including tires. **DIRECTIONS:** Located off I - 76 on the east side of Akron. Westbound - use the Goodyear Blvd/Martha Ave exit. Eastbound - use the Arlington/Kelly Ave exit.

Hours: 8:30 am - 4:30pm	Days: Monday - Friday	
Advance Notice: No	Fee: No	HP Access: Yes

Lee Middleton Original Doll Factory (doll mfr)   SIC Code: 3942
1301 Washington Boulevard
Belpre, OH 45714
740-423-1717 (800-233-7479)   Contact: Rosalee Armour

This factory invites you on a 20 - minute tour to watch artisans magically transform vinyl and clay into the collectible dolls of artist Lee Middleton. **NOTE:** Closed on national holidays. **DIRECTIONS:** From Athens, take US 50 southeast to Belpre. Turn right on Farson St at the first stoplight. At end of Farson St turn left on Washington Blvd. Look for sign.

Hours: 9:00 am - 3:00 pm   Days: Monday - Friday
Advance Notice: Yes   Fee: No   HP Access: Yes

Cooper's Mill & Jelly Factory (jams,jellies)   SIC Code: 2033
1414 North Sandusky Avenue
Bucyrus, OH 44820
419-562-4215   Contact: Manager

Your tour of the jelly factory begins when you first walk into the viewing room where all the activities of the jelly factory, apple butter making and cider mill surrounds you. You may observe firsthand, the delicious ripe fruits cooked into their irresistible products. Be sure to take time to go into the screened-in porch to watch the apple butter bubbling in open kettles over a wood fire. After the tour, you are invited to visit the country market and gift shop. **NOTE:** Free samples. **DIRECTIONS:** Located at junction of Rt 30 Bypass and Rt 4.

Hours: By appointment only   Days: Monday - Saturday
Advance Notice: Yes   Fee: No   HP Access: Yes

Boyd's Crystal Art Glass (glass mfr)   SIC Code: 3229
1203 Morton Avenue
Cambridge, OH 43725
740-439-2077   Contact: Sue Boyd

Take a tour of this glass manufacturer of dolls, bears, unicorns, trains, airplanes, tractors, mice and more. **DIRECTIONS:** I - 70, exit 178, north on St Rd 209 3/4 mile, turn right (Woodlawn) dead ends into Boyd Glass.

Hours: 7:00 am - 3:00 pm   Days: Monday - Friday
Advance Notice: Yes   Fee: No   HP Access: Yes

Degenhart Paperweight (glass mfr)   SIC Code: 3229
65323 Highland Hills Road
Cambridge, OH 43725
740-432-2626   Contact: Mrs. Erna Burris

On this self-guided tour you will see an audio visual program and exhibits focusing on glass-making techniques, midwestern pattern glass, paperweights, Degenhart Crystal Art Glass, Cambridge Glass Company Wares, novelties and other related topics. **DIRECTIONS:** I - 77 north to Rt 22, Cambridge-Salt Fork exit. Located behind the gas station.

Hours: 9:00 am - 5:00 pm   Days: Monday - Saturday
Advance Notice: Yes   Fee: No   HP Access: Yes

Chillicothe Gazette (newspaper)   SIC Code: 2711
50 West Main Street
Chillicothe, OH 45601
740-773-2111   Contact: Jane Mitten

Tour of this nearly 200-year old newspaper company includes a visit to the newsroom, the printing presses and all other aspects of the newspaper industry. **DIRECTIONS:** Coming in on US 35/50/23 go to the Main St exit. Turn west and go to the center of town to Paint & Main Sts. The Chillicothe Gazette is one-half block west of Paint St on Main St.

Hours: By appointment only   Days: Monday - Friday
Advance Notice: Yes   Fee: No   HP Access: Limited

Scherer Industrial Group, Inc. (repair shop)   SIC Code: 7699
4721 Interstate Drive
Cincinnati, OH 45246
513-874-8722   Contact: Steve

This is a 30 - minute tour of a hydraulic repair service to industry including repair and re-building of all types of hydraulic equipment. **DIRECTIONS:** Take exit 42 (Rt 747) north from Rt 275. Go left on Interstate Dr.

Hours: By appointment only
Advance Notice: Yes   Fee: No   HP Access: Yes

Anheuser-Busch Brewery (brewery)   SIC Code: 2082
700 East Shrock Road
Columbus, OH 4322
589-847-6271   Contact: Tour Department

In just 90 - minutes, you will learn about the slow, natural brewing process used for more than a century. You will be escorted into the viewing area overlooking the Brew Hall. At the end of the tour, you will see their newest addition, giant fermentation tanks four stories tall. **NOTE:** Free sample of beer and soda. **DIRECTIONS:** From downtown Columbus, take I - 71 north to SR 161 west to Busch Blvd (SR 710). Turn right and follow signs.

Hours: 9:00 am - 4:00 pm   Days: Monday - Saturday
Advance Notice: Yes   Fee: No   HP Access: Yes

Krema Nut Company (nuts)   SIC Code: 2068
1000 West Goodale Boulevard
Columbus, OH 43212
614-299-4132 (800-222-4132)   Contact: Mike or Peggy Giunta

This 30 - 45 minute tour of the country's oldest commercial peanut butter manufacturer will show you how peanut butter is made and you can watch the master roaster prepare the gourmet nuts. **NOTE:** Free tasting. No tours November or December. **DIRECTIONS:** Take the Goodale Blvd exit from SR 315 in Columbus. Go west on Goodale to Krema. Facility is on the right side.

Hours: 9:00 am - 2:00 pm   Days: Monday - Friday
Advance Notice: Yes   Fee: No   HP Access: Yes

Schwebel Baking Company (bakery)   SIC Code: 2051
1950 Newberry Street
Cuyahoga Falls, OH 44221
330-929-9822   Contact: Cheryl Richmond-Abshire

On this 45 - minute tour you will see the process of baking bread, from the mixing of the dough to the slicing and wrapping of the finished product. **NOTE:** You will be required to wear hair nets, safety glasses and ear protection, which will be provided. Please wear flat rubber-soled shoes, comfortable casual attire and no jewelry. **DIRECTIONS:** Take the Broad St exit off Rt 8. Go over railroad tracks and take a right at the next light. Schwebel's is located in the Dairy Mart building.

Hours: 9:00 am - 8:00 pm   Days: Wednesday - Thursday
Advance Notice: Yes   Fee: No   HP Access: Yes

Breitenbach Winery (winery)   SIC Code: 2084
5934 Old Route 39, NW
Dover, OH 44622
330-343-3603   Contact: Manager

This winery tour will include over 25 award-winning wines made in their cellar, including Chardonnay, Cabernet Savignon, Johannisberg Riesling plus both fruit and berry wines. **NOTE:** Free samples. **DIRECTIONS:** Three miles west of I - 77 on Old St Rt 39, between Dover and Sugarcreek. (Look for purple sign.) Located in the heart of Amish Country.

Hours: By appointment only
Advance Notice: Yes   Fee: No   HP Access: No

Longaberger Company (wood container)   SIC Code: 2449
95 North Chestnut Street
Dresden, OH 43821
740-754-6330   Contact: Manager

This tour will take you through the Gallery of Exhibits illustrating the family success story. There is a video presentation which will tell the story of the company while a Longaberger weaver demonstrates how the baskets are made. You will tour a quarter-mile mezzanine and watch thousands of weavers making Longaberger baskets, while tour guides offer fascinating details about the company and its manufacturing process. Next you will get a bird's eye view of more production processes, including staining, final quality assurance, packing, and shipping. **NOTE:** The best time to see full-scale production is Monday - Friday, 8:00 am - 1:00 pm. Gift Shop. **DIRECTIONS:** From Zanesville, take US Rt 70 to exit 60 north to traffic light at Third St in to town. Take left on Main St to Information Center.

Hours: 8:00 am - 4:30 pm   Days: Monday - Saturday
Advance Notice: No   Fee: No   HP Access: Yes

Allied Signal -Autolite Division (automotive parts mfr)   SIC Code: 3714
1600 North Union Street
Fostoria, OH 44830
419-436-5642   Contact: Jack Glenn

This is a one and one-half hour tour of a spark plug manufacturer where you will be able to view the metal working, ceramic manufacturing and assembly areas. **DIRECTIONS:** One block east of St Rt 23 at the intersection of North Union and Jones Rd.

Hours: 7:30 am - 3:00 pm   Days: Monday - Friday
Advance Notice: Yes   Fee: No   HP Access:

Costello's Candies (chocolates)   SIC Code: 2066
39 West Liberty Street
Girard, OH 44420
330-545-0325   Contact: Dorothy or Mary Ann

Tour of a chocolate and ice cream factory where you will see candy making in progress. **DIRECTIONS:** Heading eastbound on I - 76 from Akron, connect with I - 80 to Girard. Get off on Rt 422 in Girard, going north about 3/4 of a mile which will run into the city of Girard. Take a left on Liberty St and go one-half block. Located next to Bank One.

Hours: 9:00 am - 4:00 pm   Days: Monday - Saturday
Advance Notice: Yes   Fee: No   HP Access: Yes

Airstream, Inc. (motor home mfr)   SIC Code: 3716
419 West Pike Street
Jackson Center, OH 45335
937-596-6111   Contact: Tour Department

The approximate one hour tour of this well-known motor home manufacturer starts in the lobby of the service building and continues to the main production building where you will be able to see motor homes being assembled. **DIRECTIONS:** From I - 75 take exit 102. Take SR 274 for approximately 10 miles. Look for signs.

Hours: 2:00 pm   Days: Monday - Friday
Advance Notice: No   Fee: No   HP Access: No

Chalet Debonne Vineyards (winery)   SIC Code: 2084
7743 Doty Road
Madison, OH 44057
216-466-3485 (800-424-9463)   Contact: Tour Manager

Visit this family owned and operated winery which is one of the most modern wine cellars in the east. You will enjoy an interesting and leisurely tour of the underground facilities with a family member. You will see the hand hewn-oak barrels, the shiny stainless tanks and presses which are state-of-the-art equipment and contribute to the family's commitment to excellence. **NOTE:** Wine tasting. **DIRECTIONS:** From Cleveland, take I - 90 east to SR 528, south to Griswold, left on Emerson, right on Doty, and follow the signs.

Hours: 1:00 - 6:00 pm   Days: Tuesday - Saturday
Advance Notice: No   Fee: No   HP Access: Yes

Mansfield Post Office (postal)   SIC Code: 4311
200 North Diamond Street
Mansfield, OH 44901-9998
419-755-4621   Contact: Barbara Brubaker

Tour this mail processing/delivery facility and see the day-to-day operations in progress.
DIRECTIONS: From I - 71 north (exit 169), take SR 13 north into Mansfield. Follow Rt
13 through Mansfield. At the bottom of the hill go over one block. Make a left at the next
block on Diamond St. Continue north through five traffic lights and you will see the post
office on your right. Parking is available.

Hours: Call for appointment   Days: Monday - Friday
Advance Notice: Yes   Fee: No   HP Access: Yes

Rossi Pasta (pasta)   SIC Code: 2098
114 Greene Street
Marietta, OH 45750
740-376-2065 (800-227-6774)   Contact: Jennifer Grove

Actual tours in the plant are not open to the public, but the pasta-making process is visible
from the outlet store. **NOTE:** Free samples. **DIRECTIONS:** Take exit 1 from I - 77, and
go one mile west on Pike Street.

Hours: 10:00 am - 1:00 pm   Days: Monday - Friday
Advance Notice: No   Fee: No   HP Access: Yes

Rocky Shoes & Boots, Inc. (footwear mfr)   SIC Code: 3149
39 East Canal Street
Nelsonville, OH 45764
740-753-1951   Contact: Kay

On this tour you will have an opportunity to watch shoes and boots being manufactured in a
factory that has been in operation since 1932. **NOTE:** Two days advance notice. Factory
outlet store is next door. **DIRECTIONS:** From Springfield, take Rt 70 towards Columbus,
pick up Rt 270 east and then take the Rt 33 south, East Lancaster exit. Company is located
on Rt 33 in Nelsonville about 45 minutes from Lancaster.

Hours: Call for appointment   Days: Monday - Friday
Advance Notice: Yes   Fee: No   HP Access: Yes

Liberty Seed Company (seeds)   SIC Code: 0181
461 Robinson Drive
New Philadelphia, OH 44663
330-364-1611   Contact: Connie Watson

This one hour tour will take you through seven production greenhouses where you will see the inhouse germination laboratory. In addition, you will walk through the 10,000 square foot retail greenhouse as well as the retail vegetable greenhouse. **NOTE:** Garden gallery of gifts and accessories. **DIRECTIONS:** I - 77 to Rt 250 east to Rt 259 east. Take a left on Robinson.

Hours: 8:00 am - 6:00 pm   Days: Monday - Friday
Advance Notice: Yes   Fee: No   HP Access: Yes

Lafarge Corporation (cement mfr)   SIC Code: 3241
11435 Road 176
Paulding, OH 45879
419-399-4861   Contact: Jane Taft

This two hour tour begins with the showing of a 10 - minute video presentation that gives a general overview of cement manufacturing. You will tour the quarry and the cement plant where you can look through a tinted lens into a kiln's hot end. The view is flame, molten clinker and mineral crags which looks like the creation of the world. You will also tour the adjacent resource recovery facility as well. **NOTE:** Please be sure to call first. Free parting gifts. **DIRECTIONS:** Located just north of Paulding in northwest Ohio, one mile west of US Rt 127 or CR 176.

Hours: 8:00 am - 5:00 pm   Days: Monday - Friday
Advance Notice: Yes   Fee: No   HP Access: Limited

Navistar International (truck and bus mfr)   SIC Code: 3711
6125 Urbana Road
Springfield, OH 45502
937-390-2800   Contact: Tour Department

Tour one of the largest medium and heavy duty truck and school bus assembly plants in North America. You may also visit the state-of-the-art robotic plant, located adjacent to the main assembly facility. **DIRECTIONS:** From the center of town, follow Rt 4 (Lagonda Ave) north to the body plant.

Hours: By appointment only   Days: Monday - Friday
Advance Notice: Yes   Fee: No   HP Access: Yes

Scherer Industrial Group (repair shop)   SIC Code: 7699
5330 Prosperity Drive
Springfield, OH 45502
937-390-6667   Contact: George

A 30 - minute tour of an industrial electromechanical and hydraulic repair and manufacturng company involving motors, electronic components, automotive and power equipment. **DIRECTIONS:** Follow Rt 68 north of Springfield towards Urbana. Prosperity Dr is on the left just south of Urbana.

Hours: By appointment only
Advance Notice: Yes   Fee: No   HP Access: Yes

Toledo Processing & Dist. Center (postal)   SIC Code: 4311
435 South Saint Clair Street
Toledo, OH 43601-9997
419-245-6917   Contact: Tina Jones

A one hour tour of the U. S. Postal Processing and Distribution Center will show how the equipment is used to process the mail flow. **DIRECTIONS:** East or west take Rt 80/90 Tnpk to I - 75 exit 4A, north to Collingwood. North or south take I - 75 to Collingwood exit.

Hours:	10:00 am	Days:	Tuesday - Wednesday		
	6:00 pm		Monday - Friday		
Advance Notice: Yes		Fee:	No	HP Access:	No

Shamrock Vineyard (winery)   SIC Code: 2084
111 CR 25 Rengert Road
Waldo, OH 43356-830
614-726-2883   Contact: Tom and Mary Quilter

Tour the vineyard (in season) where you will have the opportunity to see the process of wine making from grape crushing to pressing, to fermentation, to the wine cellar, to the bottling plant and then to a sit down tasting of wines. **NOTE:** State Law requires a small charge for wine tasting. **DIRECTIONS:** From Columbus, take US 23 to Waldo/Fulton Rd for one and 4/10 miles, turn left on Gearhiser Rd for one and 1/10 miles and right on Reingert Rd to winery.

| Hours: 1:00 - 3:00 pm | Days: | Monday - Saturday | | |
| Advance Notice: Yes | Fee: | $1.50 | HP Access: | Yes |

Inniswood Metro Gardens (floriculture)   SIC Code: 0181
940 Hempstead Road
Westerville, OH 43081
614-895-6216   Contact: Emily Eby

Tour of the Herb Garden will last from 45 minutes to one and one-half hours (depending on group interest) which will include nature trails, rose garden, herb garden, rock garden and many general plantings. **DIRECTIONS:** I - 270 east to Hempstead Rd. Look for signs.

| Hours: 8:00 am to dusk | Days: | Tuesday - Sunday | | |
| Advance Notice: Yes | Fee: | No | HP Access: | Yes |

Schwebel Baking Company (bakery)   SIC Code: 2051
965 E. Midlothian Boulevard
Youngstown, OH 44502
216-783-2860   Contact: Karly Demko

See the whole process of making bread from the mixing of the dough to the slicing and
wrapping of the bread. **DIRECTIONS:** 1/4 mile west of Rt 680 in Youngstown.

Hours: 9:00 am - 3:00 pm   Days: Monday, Thursday, Friday
              6:30 pm   Tuesday - Wednesday
Advance Notice: Yes   Fee: No   HP Access: Yes

Youngstown Processing & Dist. Center (postal)   SIC Code: 4311
99 S. Walnut Street
Youngstown, OH 44501-9993
216-744-681   Contact: Deborah Holecko

The tour of this U. S. Postal facility follows the travel of a piece of mail from cancelling to
the carrier case. Details of each phase of processing will be explained. **NOTE:** The
afternoon hours are more interesting as that is when all the machinery and full crew are at
work. **DIRECTIONS:** Downtown Youngstown, corner of Walnut and Front Sts.

Hours: 9:00 am - 6:00 pm   Days: Monday - Friday
Advance Notice: Yes   Fee: No   HP Access: Yes

5 B''s B-Wear Sportswear (textile products)   SIC Code: 2399
1606 Moxahala Avenue
Zanesville, OH 43702-2478
740-454-8453   Contact: Tour Coordinator

On your first stop you will see a computer-controlled fabric cutting system at work. A state-
of-the-art conveyor moves garments to each machine operator who completes one step in the
process. On the next stop, you will watch as multi-head computer-controlled embroidery
machines stitch intricate designs onto jackets, shirts, hats, and many other items. As you exit
the factory, you will have an opportunity to visit the outlet store. **NOTE:** Factory tours can
be scheduled for groups of 15 or more. **DIRECTIONS:** US 70 to exit 155 south to
Moxahala Ave.

Hours: By appointment only   Days: Monday - Friday
Advance Notice: Yes   Fee: No   HP Access: Yes

Cimarron Cellars (winery)   SIC Code: 2084
Route 1 - Box 79
Caney, OK 74533
405-889-6312   Contact: Dwane Pool

When you visit this winery you will note that the sandy soil, exposure and fairly dry climate
are perfect for quality grape production. You will walk through the vineyard and the winery
where you will see the operation and wine-making process. **NOTE:** Free wine tasting.
DIRECTIONS: Located two miles south of Caney and five miles east of Hwy 69/75.

Hours: By appointment   Days: Monday - Saturday
Advance Notice: Yes   Fee: No   HP Access: No

Tulsa Port of Catoosa (transportation)   SIC Code: 4449
S. 5350 Cimarron Road
Catoosa, OK 74015
918-266-2291   Contact: Weida Young

A one hour tour of the Arkansas River Historical Society's Museum will include a talk on the
history of the McClellan-Kerr Arkansas River Navigation System. You will see a videotape
on the Port of Catoosa and participate in a driven tour of the port and industrial park.
DIRECTIONS: On US 44 east of Tulsa, take exit 240 north to Rt 167 to intersection with
Rt 266. Port of Catoosa is on the right.

Hours: 8:00 am - 4:30 pm   Days: Monday - Friday
Advance Notice: Yes   Fee: No   HP Access: Yes

4-C Ostrich Farm (ostrich farm)   SIC Code: 0291
Route 1 - Box 71A
Lawton, OK 73501
405-353-3078   Contact: Dale Coody

Take a tour of this farm where the breeding and raising of ostriches are for resale to other
breeders throughout North America. **DIRECTIONS:** Lawton is located southeast of
Oklahoma City on US Rt 44. Call for further directions.

Hours: Call for appointment
Advance Notice: Yes   Fee: No   HP Access: No

United Design (pottery products)   SIC Code: 3269
1600 North Main Street
Noble, OK 73068
405-872-7131   Contact: Phyllis Butter

A 30 - minute tour seeing all manufacturing phases of decorative figurines and collectibles at this manufacturing plant. You will see over 2,000 different figure designs being handmade by hundreds of artists and craftsmen. **NOTE:** There is a flight of stairs, with an elevator avail-able. **DIRECTIONS:** From I -35, five miles east on Hwy 9, then two miles south on Hwy 77.

Hours: 10:00 am and 1:00 pm   Days: Monday - Friday
Advance Notice: Yes   Fee: No   HP Access: Yes

Journal Record Publishing (printers)   SIC Code: 2759
621 North Robinson Avenue
Oklahoma City, OK 73102
405-278-6036   Contact: Yvonne Shanahan

Tour of the printing plant which includes the composing, pre-press, sheetfed, web and bindery departments. **DIRECTIONS:** From US Rt 40 take exit 150 to the center of the city.

Hours: 9:00 am - 5:00 pm   Days: Monday - Friday
Advance Notice: Yes   Fee: No   HP Access: Yes

Oklahoma City Processing & Dist. Center (postal)   SIC Code: 4311
320 SW 5th Street
Oklahoma City, OK 73125-9702
405-278-6371   Contact: General Clerk

On this one hour guided tour of the U. S. Postal Processing and Distribution Center, you will learn about the postal functions of automation mechanization, manual letters and flats, and the operations and mail flow will be explained. **DIRECTIONS:** Located on the corner of SW 5th and Hudson.

Hours: 8:00 am - 6:00 pm   Days: Saturday - Friday
Advance Notice: Yes   Fee: No   HP Access: Yes

The Daily Oklahoman (newspaper)   SIC Code: 2711
9000 North Broadway
Oklahoma City, OK 73114
405-475-3540   Contact: Linda Bridges

This one to one and one-half hour tour includes the production of the newspaper in various stages - editorial writing, ad production, page make-up, printing, (presses run most mornings), insertion, packaging, and paper warehouse. **NOTE:** Must be over age 10. Tour involves a lot of walking, but is wheelchair accessible. No cameras. Smoke-free facility. Tours must be scheduled at least one week in advance. **DIRECTIONS:** Britton Rd and Broadway extension. Use access road to office tower entrance.

Hours: 9:00 am - 4:00 pm   Days: Monday - Friday
Advance Notice: Yes   Fee: No   HP Access: Yes

Public Service Company of Oklahoma (utility)   SIC Code: 4939
P.O.Box 220
Oologah, OK 74053
918-581-0891   Contact: Allen Lee

A one to one and one-half hour coal-fired power plant tour with a slide presentation of power generation facilities found in electric power plants. **NOTE:** Two week advance notice is required. **DIRECTIONS:** Located at intersection of Hwys 169 and 88. Follow Rt 169 north from Tulsa, turn right (east) on Hwy 88; entrance is about two blocks on the right.

Advance Notice: Yes   Fee: No   HP Access: No

Frankoma Pottery (pottery products) SIC Code: 3269
2400 Frankoma Road
Sapulpa, OK 74066
918-224-5511   Contact: Gift Shop Personnel

Take a 25 - 30 minute guided tour through the factory showing and describing how pottery is made. **NOTE:** Visit factory museum and factory gift shop. **DIRECTIONS:** I - 44 west to 66 Hwy. Follow 66 Hwy into Sapulpa, turn right on Frankoma Rd (Old 66 Hwy) and go one mile north. Just 15 minutes from Tulsa.

Hours: 9:30 - 2:45 pm   Days: Monday - Friday
Advance Notice: Yes   Fee: No   HP Access: Yes

Audio Visuals, Inc. (photography) SIC Code: 7335
1512 East 15th Street
Tulsa, OK 74120
918-584-3396   Contact: Ernie Einsporn

A custom slide show and tour of a professional photo finishing lab where you will have an opportunity to see all aspects of black and white and color printing, and computer graphics. **NOTE:** If you bring a black and white negative, they will print one (or you may even print your own negative). **DIRECTIONS:** Three and one-half blocks east of Peoria on south side.

Hours: 8:00 am - 5:00 pm   Days: Monday - Friday
Advance Notice: Yes   Fee: No   HP Access: Yes

Tulsa Performing Arts Center (theater) SIC Code: 7922
110 East Second Street
Tulsa, OK 74103
918-596-2366 (800-364-7111)   Contact: Melanie Hunter

Take a back stage tour of four theaters. The Music Hall is home to Broadway, opera, ballet, and the Philharmonic. The lobbies house collections of modern and current art. **DIRECTIONS:** I - 44 from Oklahoma City and points west, take Tulsa exit "North Hwy 75" to Tulsa, continue across bridge, then take Seventh St exit to Boulder. Turn left onto Boulder and right onto Second St. Park in lot between Second and Third Sts along Cincinnati.

Hours: 9:00 am - 5:00 pm   Days: Monday - Friday
Advance Notice: Yes   Fee: No   HP Access: Yes

World Publishing Company (newspaper)   SIC Code: 2711
315 South Boulder Avenue
Tulsa, OK 74103
918-581-8592   Contact: Dale Ross

A 45- minute building tour of departments necessary for the production of a daily newspaper which delivers 140,000 newspapers daily, with a Sunday circulation of over 225,000. **NOTE:** Free gifts. **DIRECTIONS:** Located in downtown Tulsa.

Hours: Call for schedule   Days: Monday - Friday
Advance Notice: Yes   Fee: No   HP Access: Yes

Watonga Cheese Factory (cheese processor)   SIC Code: 2022
314 East 2nd Street
Watonga, OK 73772
405-623-5915   Contact: Joan Knudsen

A self-guided tour looking through a viewing window will show you how many types of cheese are made. **DIRECTIONS:** US Rt 40 to exit 108 to Rt 281 to Watonga. Located approximately 60 miles west of Oklahoma City.

Hours: Call for appointment
Advance Notice: Yes   Fee: No   HP Access: Yes

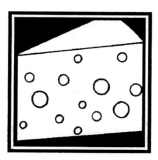

Democrat Herald (newspaper)   SIC Code: 2711
600 Lyon Street, South
Albany, OR 97321
541-926-2211   Contact: Graham Kislingberg

Tour all operations of newspaper publishing during the press run. **DIRECTIONS:** From I - 5 take Hwy 20 or 99 east /west; follow signs to City Center. Take Lyon St to 6th, turn left for Visitor's Parking.

Hours: 12:45 pm   Days: Wednesday - Thursday
Advance Notice: Yes   Fee: No   HP Access: Yes

Smoke Craft, Inc. (meat processor)   SIC Code: 2013
850 SW 30th Avenue
Albany, OR 97321
541-926-8831   Contact: Manager

Tour of a smoked meats plant where you will see and hear the process of smoking meats described. **DIRECTIONS:** US Rt 5 to exit 238 west, between Eugene and Portland. Call for further directions.

Hours: Call for appointment   Days: Monday - Friday
Advance Notice: Yes   Fee: No   HP Access: Yes

Bandon Cheese, Inc. (cheese processor)   SIC Code: 2022
680 East 2nd Street
Bandon, OR 97411
541-347-2456 (800-548-8961)   Contact: Manager

You will have an opportunity to watch cheese being made in the processing plant under the watchful eye of their Master Cheesemaker. You will also see a short video which will explain the cheesemaking process. Some of the cheeses made are: Cheddar, Monterey Jack and Colby. **NOTE:** Free samples available. **DIRECTIONS:** On Hwy 101, north end of town.

Hours: 8:30 am - 5:30 pm   Days: Monday - Saturday
Advance Notice: No   Fee: No   HP Access: Yes

Beaver Motor Coaches, Inc. (motor home mfr)   SIC Code: 3716
20545 Murray Road
Bend, OR 97701
541-389-1144   Contact: Don Trumbly

A one hour tour of the main manufacturing facility of a motor home manufacturer. **NOTE:** Children under 12 not admitted. Advance notice for large groups. **DIRECTIONS:** Go east on Empire Rd off Hwy 97. Turn right on Boyd Acres and go two miles southwest.

Hours: 10:00 am   Days: Monday - Thursday
Advance Notice: No   Fee: No   HP Access: No

Bonneville Fish Hatchery (hatchery)   SIC Code: 0921
HC 66 Box 12 Bonneville Dam
Cascade Locks, OR 97014
503-374-8393   Contact: Dan Barrett/Sue McCormick

The hatchery, operated by the State of Oregon Deptartment of Fish & Wildlife with funding through the US Army Corps of Engineers and Natural Marine Fisheries Service, is set up with kiosks for a self-guided tour of trout and sturgeon display ponds, adult salmon holding ponds, fingerling rearing ponds, fish ladder and Tanner Creek. **NOTE:** For pre-scheduled tours, call for appointment. For self-guided tours, no appointment necessary. **DIRECTIONS:** 40 miles east of Portland off I - 84.

Hours: 8:00 am to dusk   Days: Monday - Friday
Advance Notice: No   Fee: No   HP Access: Yes

Bonneville Lock & Dam (utility)   SIC Code: 4939
Cascade Locks
Cascade Locks, OR 97014
503-374-8820   Contact: Staff

Take a self-guided tour of the Visitors Center, Powerhouse and fish ladders. **NOTE:** If you desire a guided tour, you must call in advance. Visitors can view migrating salmon during spring, summer and fall months. **DIRECTIONS:** Traveling east or westbound on I - 84, take exit 40.

Hours: Call for schedule   Days: Monday - Sunday
Advance Notice: Yes   Fee: No   HP Access: Yes

Dogs for the Deaf, Inc. (pet training)   SIC Code: 0752
10175 Wheeler Road
Central Point, OR 97502
541-826-9220   Contact: Robin Dickson

After viewing a 15 - minute video, you will tour the training center and visit one of the apart-
ments where you will be able to watch an actual training session, as Hearing Dogs learn to be
the ears of their non-hearing masters. **NOTE:** Phone number above is Voice/TDD. Tours
available May 1 - September 30. **DIRECTIONS:** I - 5 north - exit 32. Right at stoplight,
left at second light, stay on Table Rock Rd for eight miles. Turn left onto Wheeler Rd at 10 -
mile marker.

Hours: 10:00 am - 2:00 pm   Days: Monday - Friday
Advance Notice: Yes   Fee: No   HP Access: Yes

Cranberry Sweets Company (candy mfr)   SIC Code: 2064
1005 Newmark Street
Coos Bay, OR 97420
541-888-6072   Contact: Manager

On a tour of this candy factory you will have an opportunity to watch candy being made
through viewing windows. **DIRECTIONS:** Coos Bay is situated on Rt 101 on the southwest coast. Call for specific directions.

Hours: Call for schedule   Days: Monday - Friday
Advance Notice: No   Fee: No   HP Access: Yes

The Oregon Connection (wood products)   SIC Code: 2499
1125 South 1st Street
Coos Bay, OR 97420
541-267-7804 (800-255-5318)   Contact: Dorothy Stearns

A guided tour through the factory where you will see master artisans turn this rare myrtlewood into unique creations. You will also be shown the various production steps of manufacturing myrtlewood from log to finished product of Wooden Touch putters.
DIRECTIONS: Located at the south end of Coos Bay, right off Hwy 101.

Hours: 9:00 am - 5:00 pm   Days: Monday - Friday (October - April)
        8:00 am - 6:00 pm   Monday - Friday (May-September)
Advance Notice : No   Fee: No   HP Access: Yes

Roseburg Forest Products Co. (lumber mill)   SIC Code: 2421
Old Highway 99 South
Dillard, OR 97432
541-679-3311   Contact: Dale Ingram/John Banducci

This is a one hour tour of a particle board plant. **NOTE:** Children must be at least 10 years old. **DIRECTIONS:** Take exit 112 from US Rt 5 near Roseburg. Call for specific directions.

Hours: 1:30 pm   Days: Wednesday
Advance Notice: Yes   Fee: No   HP Access: Yes

Weyerhaeuser Pulp & Paper Mill (paper mill)   SIC Code: 2621
785 North 42nd Street
Eugene, OR 97401
541-746-2511   Contact: Tour Department

Tour of a pulp and paper mill where you will have an opportunity to see the process of making wood products. **DIRECTIONS:** From US Rt 5, exit 194. Take Rt 126 to 42nd St. Mill is on left.

Hours: 9:00 am   Days: Monday - Friday (September-May)
Advance Notice: No   Fee: No   HP Access: No

Lakeshore Myrtlewood. Inc. (wood products)   SIC Code: 2499
83530 Highway 101 South
Florence, OR 97439
541-997-2753   Contact: Regan Crosthwaite

Take a 10 - 15 minute tour seeing the step-by-step procedure of how beautiful myrtlewood is manufactured. **NOTE:** Call to be sure factory is open. Large groups should call in advance for appointment. **DIRECTIONS:** I - 26 to coast. In Florence go left over bridge four miles south.

Hours: 9:00 am - 4:00 pm   Days: Monday - Friday
Advance Notice: No   Fee: No   HP Access: Yes

Tim Ply Co. (plywood mill)   SIC Code: 2436
125 NE Mill Street
Grants Pass, OR 97526
541-479-6822   Contact: Tour Department

Tour of a full facility plywood manufacturing mill. See rough logs become finished market-able wood products. **DIRECTIONS:** Take exit 58 from US Rt 5.

Hours: By appointment   Days: Monday - Friday
Advance Notice: Yes   Fee: No   HP Access: No

James River Corporation (paper products)   SIC Code: 2621
P.O.Box 215
Halsey, OR 97348
541-369-2293   Contact: Tour Department

Tour of a paper products manufacturing plant where you will see how paper products are made from start to finish. **NOTE:** Tours during June - August only. **DIRECTIONS:** Halsey is located two miles west of US 5, 15 miles south of Corvallis. Call for specific directions.

Hours: 9:30 am and 1:30pm   Days: Monday - Friday
Advance Notice: Yes   Fee: No   HP Access: No

Rodgers Instrument Corp. (musical instrument mfr)   SIC Code: 3931
1300 NE 25th Street
Hillsboro, OR 97123
503-648-4181   Contact: Lynn Simon or Donna Parker

This is a one hour tour of an organ manufacturing facility which will include an organ demonstration by one of the in-house organists. Most of the organists perform in concerts throughout the United States. **DIRECTIONS:** Hwy 26 west to Shute Rd/Helvetia Rd exit. Left at light, continue on Shute Rd to end of intersection with Cornell Rd. Turn right, continue to light at NE 25th St. Turn right and go 1/4 mile. Located on right side. Please park in front visitors parking area.

Hours: 9:00 am - 2:30 pm   Days: Monday - Thursday
Advance Notice: Yes   Fee: No   HP Access: Yes

Full Sail Brewing Company (brewery)   SIC Code: 2082
506 Columbia Street
Hood River, OR 97031
541-386-2281   Contact: Catherine Dutcher

Take a self-guided tour through this well-known local brewery. You will watch as special beers are being produced from hops, fermentation and finally to marketable products. **NOTE:** Appointment is necessary for large tours. **DIRECTIONS:** Exit 63 I - 84 east (one hour east of Portland).

Hours: Flexible   Days: Monday - Friday
Advance Notice: Yes   Fee: No   HP Access: Yes

Juanita's Tortilla Factory (food products)   SIC Code: 2099
2885 Van Horn Drive
Hood River, OR 97031
541-386-6311   Contact: Manager

Tour this manufacturer of tortilla, potato, corn and tortilla chips, as well as bread and other bakery products. **NOTE:** Free samples. **DIRECTIONS:** From Portland, take Hood River City Center exit 68 off I - 84. Call for further directions.

Hours: 9:00 am - 12:00 noon   Days: Monday - Friday
Advance Notice: Yes   Fee: No   HP Access: Yes

Luhr Jensen & Sons, Inc. (sporting goods mfr)   SIC Code: 3949
400 Portway Avenue
Hood River, OR 97031
541-386-3811   Contact: Brenda Kramer

Take a tour through the factory where fishing lures and electric smokers are manufactured. **NOTE:** Advance reservations for parties of five or more must call two days in advance. **DIRECTIONS:** From Portland, take Hood River City Center exit 63 off of I - 84. Take a left at the stop sign which will take you back over the freeway. At the first stop sign, take a right. Second stop sign, take a left. Continue to follow the road around the loop. First building on the right.

Hours: 11:30 am and 1:30 pm   Days: Monday - Friday
Advance Notice: Yes   Fee: No   HP Access: No

Carriage Works (transportation equipment)   SIC Code: 3799
707 South 5th Street
Klamath Falls, OR 97601
541-882-0700   Contact: Barbara Evensizer

Visit the manufacturer of expresso carts and food carts as well as horse drawn carriages. These items are built and shipped from this factory to companies all over the world. **DIRECTIONS:** Located in the south central area of the state, just north of the California border. Located near the junction of US Rt 97 and Rt 140.

Hours: 8:00 am - 5:00 pm   Days: Monday - Friday
Advance Notice: Yes   Fee: No   HP Access: No

Fleetwood Travel Trailers (travel trailer mfr)   SIC Code: 3792
62582 Pierce Lane
La Grande, OR 97850
541-963-7101   Contact: Tour Department

A one hour tour of a travel trailer manufacturer showing you the details that go into the manufacturing process. **DIRECTIONS:** From Rt 84 take exit 265. Go north on McAllister to Rt
82. Watch for signs.

Hours: By appointment only	Days: Monday - Friday	
Advance Notice: Yes	Fee: No	HP Access: Yes

The Observer (newspaper)   SIC Code: 2711
1406 Fifth Street
La Grande, OR 97850
541-963-3161   Contact: Don Powell

A 30 - minute tour of a newspaper in which you will see the newsroom, the presses and the
high-tech operations involved in printing a newspaper. **DIRECTIONS:** From I - 84, eastbound, take the first exit, 256, Adams Ave. Proceed to the second stop light, turn right onto
Fourth St and proceed several blocks up the hill. At the top of the hill, you will see a gold
building on your left. The front entrance is actually on Fifth St, one block over to your left.

Hours: By appointment	Days: Monday - Friday	
Advance Notice: Yes	Fee: No	HP Access: No

Real Oregon Gift (wood products)   SIC Code: 2499
3955 Coast Highway 101
North Bend, OR 97459
541-756-2582   Contact: Judi Larson

Tour this full line manufacturing facility and sawmill featuring products made from myrtlewood. See specialty bowls, salt and pepper shakers, candlesticks and many other myrtlewood
products being made. **DIRECTIONS:** Located five miles north of the North Bend Bridge.
Call for specific directions.

Hours: 9:00 am - 4:30 pm	Days: Monday - Friday (May-October)	
By appointment	(November - April)	
Advance Notice: Yes	Fee: No	HP Access: Yes

Pendleton Woolen Mills (woolen mill)   SIC Code: 2231
1307 SE Court Place
Pendleton, OR 97801
541-276-6911   Contact: Kathy Comstock

A 30 - minute tour of a woolen processing plant which will show you the different processes involved in wool processing. **NOTE:** Advance notice for groups. Walking type shoes must be worn. **DIRECTIONS:** From La Grande, take Rt 84 north to exit 210. Mill located beyond Murphy House.

Hours: 9:00,11:00,1:30,3:00   Days: Monday - Friday
Advance Notice: No   Fee: No   HP Access: No

Knutsons Handcrafted Clocks (clocks)   SIC Code: 3873
530 West 8th Street
Port Orford, OR 97465
541-332-1905   Contact: Lyle/Margaret Knutson

A visit to this clock manufacturer will enable you to see handcrafted mantle, wall and grandfather clocks being made by master craftsmen. These clocks are made from myrtlewood, local and exotic woods. **DIRECTIONS:** Located on 8th St between Oregon and Idaho Sts in the southern part of downtown area.

Hours: 9:00 am - 4:00 pm   Days: Monday - Saturday
Advance Notice: Yes   Fee: No   HP Access: Yes

The Wooden Nickel (wood products)   SIC Code: 2499
1205 Oregon Street
Port Orford, OR 97465
541-332-5201   Contact: Manager

A tour of the myrtlewood manufacturer will give you insight into the process of making myrtle-wood products. **DIRECTIONS:** From Eugene, take Hwy 126 to Florence, then drive down the coast approximately 100 miles to Port Orford. The facility is located in the middle of the town.

Hours: 8:00-11:30/1:00-4:00   Days: Monday - Friday
Advance Notice: Yes   Fee: No   HP Access: Yes

Portland Processing & Dist. Center (postal)   SIC Code: 4311
715 NW Hoyt Street
Portland, OR 07208-3099
503-294-2306   Contact: Nancy Nathe

A 45 - 60 minute tour of the U. S. Postal Processing & Distribution Center will include the flats and flats sorters area, the computer area, the letter sorting area, the optical character readers, the barcode sorters and the philatelic area. **DIRECTIONS:** Coming from the north, take the Broadway Bridge exit. Following road, get into far right hand lane. Cross Broadway Bridge and go through light at end of bridge. Follow to Hoyt (next light) and turn right.

Hours: 9:30 am - 12:30 pm   Days: Tuesday - Saturday
Advance Notice: Yes   Fee: No   HP Access: Yes

The Oregonian (newspaper)   SIC Code: 2711
1320 SW Broadway Drive
Portland, OR 97201
503-221-8336   Contact: Trish Rolin

A 30 - 45 minute tour of this newspaper plant will include a visit to the advertising, art and editorial departments. **NOTE:** Minimum age is 12. You will be shown how to make your own "Press Hat". No tours during the summer months. **DIRECTIONS:** From I - 5 north, take the City Center exit and continue onto Front Ave. Turn left on Clay St and continue to 6th St, turn right on Jefferson and then turn left. The plant takes up the whole block, by 6th and Broadway, Columbia & Jefferson.

Hours: 10:00 am - 12:00 pm   Days: Tuesday and Thursday
Advance Notice: Yes   Fee: No   HP Access: Limited

Pyramid Outdoor Cooking Systems (metal goods mfr)   SIC Code: 3499
3292 South Highway 97
Redmond, OR 97756
541-548-1041 (800-824-4288)   Contact: Ed Wettig

Tour the stainless steel fabricating plant where the Pyramid Outdoor Cooking System is manufactured. Included as part of the tour is a showroom demonstration. **DIRECTIONS:** Located in the center of the state about 15 miles north of Bend on Rt 97 at the junction of Rt 126.

Hours: 8:00 am - 3:30 pm   Days: Monday - Friday
Advance Notice: Yes   Fee: No   HP Access: Yes

Roseburg Forest Products Co. (plywood mill)   SIC Code: 2436
3064 Riddle By Pass Road
Riddle, OR 97469
541-874-2216   Contact: Dale Ingram/John Banducci

A two hour tour of a plywood and wood products plant. **NOTE:** Children must be at least 10 years old. **DIRECTIONS:** Located on Rt 5, south of Roseburg. Call for further directions.

Hours: 1:00 pm   Days: Tuesday and Thursday
Advance Notice: Yes   Fee: No   HP Access: Yes

Salem Processing & Dist. Center (postal)   SIC Code: 4311
1050 25th Street SE
Salem, OR 97309-5930
541-370-4700   Contact: Barb Hayden

The U. S. Postal facility tour will consist of a tour of the building with an explanation of all work stations and duties performed. **NOTE:** Call for specific hours. **DIRECTIONS:** I - 5 to Salem, east on Mission St to 25th St, north on 25th to Post Office.

Hours: Flexible   Days: Monday - Friday
Advance Notice: Yes   Fee: No   HP Access: Yes

Seven-Up Bottling Company (soft drinks)   SIC Code: 2086
2561 Pringle Road SE
Salem, OR 97302
541-585-2822   Contact: Tour Department

A tour of this well-known soft drink bottler will demonstrate the processes involved in the sterilization and filling of soda bottles. **NOTE:** Tours are from September - June only. **DIRECTIONS:** US Rt 5, exit 252 west to Balte Creek and Pringle Rd. Located near the Fairview Hospital in the south section of town.

Hours: 8:00-11:00/12:30-3:30   Days: Tuesdays
Advance Notice: Yes   Fee: No   HP Access: Yes

Weyerhaeuser Company (paper mfr)   SIC Code: 2621
785 North 42nd Street
Springfield, OR 97478
541-741-5478   Contact: Susan Oldham

This is a one and one-half to two hour paper mill tour where you will see the process from logs to finished paper. At the end of the tour you will have an opportunity to see the recycling process. **NOTE:** Advance notice necessary. **DIRECTIONS:** I - 5 exit 194 at Springfield, east to 42nd St, take right. Plant is one-half mile on left.

Hours: By appointment   Days: Monday - Friday
Advance Notice: Yes   Fee: No   HP Access: No

Latimer Quilt & Textile Center (quilt mfr)   SIC Code: 2392
2105 Wilson River Loop Road
Tillamook, OR 97141
541-842-8622   Contact: Denise Clausen

This is a self-guided tour through three exhibit and work rooms where you will see weavers, spinners and quilters at work on projects. The Latimer Center provides a hands-on learning experience with classes for weaving, spinning, dyeing, papermaking, quilting, tatting, cross stitch, needlepoint and basketry. **DIRECTIONS:** 1/4 mile east on Wilson River Loop Rd, which is one mile north of downtown Tillamook.

Hours: 10:00 am - 4:00 pm   Days: Tuesday - Saturday
       12:00 noon - 4:00 pm   Sunday
Advance Notice: Yes   Fee: $1.00   HP Access: Yes

Tillamook County Creamery (cheese processor)   SIC Code: 2022
4175 Highway 101 North
Tillamook, OR 97141
541-842-4481   Contact: Sandy

On this self-guided tour you will learn about the making of Tillamook Cheese through the large viewing windows. You will see the cheesemaking and packaging departments and videos along the way which will explain the process. **NOTE:** Free cheese samples. **DIRECTIONS:** Located on Hwy 101, two miles north of Tillamook.

Hours: 8:00 am - 6:00 pm   Days: Monday - Friday
Advance Notice: Yes   Fee: No   HP Access: Yes

U.S. Army Corps of Engineers (utility)   SIC Code: 4939
McNary Lock and Dam
P.O.Box 1441
Umatilla, OR 97882
541-922-4388   Contact: Jeff Philip

Self-guided viewing of the powerhouse, navigation lock, fish ladders and the Pacific Salmon Visitor Information Center. **NOTE:** Tours are available from June 1 - September 15. Hourly tours of powerhouse throughout the summer. Other facility tours are available upon request. **DIRECTIONS:** 35 miles south of Kennewick, WA on I - 82.

Hours: 9:00 am - 5:00 pm   Days: Monday - Friday
Advance Notice: Yes   Fee: No   HP Access: Yes

Sportsmen's Cannery & Smokehouse (seafood)   SIC Code: 2092
182 Bay Front Loop
Winchester Bay, OR 97467
541-271-3293   Contact: Mikayle Karcher

The tour of this small family company, will show the process of fish coming in off the boats, cleaning, cutting, packed in cans and the processing of cans. You will also see the hand labeling process. This company is noted for its high quality, hand packed, gourmet seafood. **NOTE:** Free samples and recipes of dips and spreads. Advance notice is requested since processing is not done on a daily basis. **DIRECTIONS:** Located just north of Coos Bay. Follow signs off Hwy 101 to cannery.

Hours: 9:00 am - 6:00 pm   Days: Sunday - Saturday
Advance Notice: Yes   Fee: No   HP Access: Yes

Clover Hill Vineyards & Winery (winery)   SIC Code: 2084
9850 Newtown Road
Breinigsville, PA 18031
610-395-2468   Contact: Patricia or John Skrip, Jr.

At this modern, state-of-the-art winery, you will sample and savor the award-winning wines and enjoy the magnificent view from the top of the hill. You will appreciate the wines through an educational wine tasting in a relaxed atmosphere. **NOTE:** Large groups should make advance reservations. **DIRECTIONS:** Rt 78/22 to Rt 100 south. At second traffic light on Rt 100, turn right onto Schantz Rd to Newtown Rd, turn left.

Hours: 11:00 am - 5:30 pm   Days: Monday - Saturday
Advance Notice: No   Fee: No   HP Access: No

Buckingham Valley Vineyards (winery)   SIC Code: 2084
1521 Route 413
Buckingham, PA 18912
215-794-7188   Contact: Kathy Forest

Take a self-guided tour of the bottling area and storage facilities of Bucks County's first and friendliest winery. You will walk through the vineyards, tour the cool wine cellars and sample the wines. Some of their wines include dry reds, whites, and roses and fruits. **DIRECTIONS:** Two miles south of Rt 202 or 9 miles north of Newtown.

Hours: 12:00 noon - 6:00 pm   Days: Tuesday - Friday
        10:00 am - 6:00 pm   Saturday
        12:00 noon - 4:00 pm   Sunday
Advance Notice: No   Fee: No   HP Access: No

Cornwall Iron Furnace (foundry)   SIC Code: 3322
Rexmont Road at Boyd Street
Cornwall, PA 17016
717-272-9711   Contact: Richard Strattan

Tour this uniquely well-preserved 1742-1883 iron-making complex with the massive stove furnace, steampowered air blast machinery and several related buildings still intact. **NOTE:** Advance notice for groups. **DIRECTIONS:** Follow signs from Rts 419, 322 or 722 in southern Lebanon County.

Hours: 9:00 am - 5:00 pm   Days: Tuesday - Saturday
        12:00 noon - 5:00 pm   Sunday
Advance Notice: No   Fee: $3.50   HP Access: No

Sand Castle Winery (winery)   SIC Code: 2084
755 River Road - Route 32
Erwinna, PA 18920
800-722-9463   Contact: Joseph Maxian

You will tour the vineyards (weather permitting) and take a tour of the underground cellar winery. You will learn about the equipment used in the process of wine fermenting. You will also learn about the art of winemaking and the patience involved of wine aging. **NOTE:** Adults only will receive complimentary wine tastings. **DIRECTIONS:** From US 95 where it enters Pennsylvania from New Jersey, follow Rt 32 about 25 miles north and look for signs to winery.

Hours: 10:00 AM - 5:30 PM   Days: Sunday - Saturday
Advance Notice: No   Fee: No   HP Access: No

Twin Brook Winery (winery)   SIC Code: 2084
5697 Strasburg Road
Gap, PA 17527
717-442-4915   Contact: Cheryl Caplan

When you visit this picturesque estate winery, you will stroll through the vines in the on-site vineyard. You will stop in the beautifully restored 19th century barn, which houses state-of-the-art winemaking facilities and a rustically styled tasting room. You will taste wines ranging from dry to sweet, sample dry oak aged Chardonnay or Chancellor, semi-dry Vidal Blanc, or try one of the seasonal wines. **DIRECTIONS:** From Lancaster, take Rt 30 to Rt 41 south to Gap Town Clock. Take left on Strasburg Rd.

Hours: 9:00 am - 5:00 pm   Days: Monday - Saturday
Advance Notice: No   Fee: No   HP Access: Yes

Lehman's Egg Service, Inc. (eggs)   SIC Code: 0259
1266 Kauffman Road West
Greencastle, PA 17225
717-375-2261   Contact: Delores Shindle

On this 30 - minute tour of one of the largest egg processing plants in the United States with an output of 300,000 dozen eggs per week, you will observe how the eggs are processed. **DIRECTIONS:** From US Rt 80, take exit 3. Call for specific directions.

Hours: 10:00- noon/1:00-2:00   Days: Tuesday - Wednesday
Advance Notice: Yes   Fee: No   HP Access: No

Hershey's Chocolate World (chocolate mfr)   SIC Code: 2066
800 Park Boulevard
Hershey, PA 17033
717-534-4900   Contact: Cathy Cain

Experience chocolate making on a free chocolate making automated tour ride. The tour will take you from the cocoa bean to the packaging of the finished product. You will see the harvesting of cocoa beans in South America, the careful blending and weighing of ingredients and you will see hundreds of chocolate bars on conveyor belts. **NOTE:** Free sample at the end of the tour. Tours are from mid - June through Labor Day. **DIRECTIONS:** From the north and east, take I - 81 and 78. From the south, take I - 83. From east or west, take the PA Tnpk.

Hours: 9:00 am - 6 45 pm   Days: Monday - Saturday
Advance Notice: No   Fee: No   HP Access: Yes

The Old Candle Barn (candle mfr)   SIC Code: 3999
Main Street
Intercourse, PA 17534
717-768-3231   Contact: Thea Althouse

Take a self-guided tour of the factory where you will watch candles being poured by hand, hand-dipped and carved with great skill by local Amish people. There is also a Quilt Room where you can watch quilting being done. **DIRECTIONS:** Rt 340, Main St.

Hours: 8:00 am - 4:00 pm   Days: Monday - Friday
        8:00 am - 2:00 pm   Saturday
Advance Notice: No   Fee: No   HP Access: Yes

Phillips Mushroom Place (mushrooms)   SIC Code: 0182
Route 1& Orchard Avenue
Kennett Square, PA 15348
215-388-6082   Contact: Marlene Giancola

Learn the history, lore and mystique of mushrooms through motion pictures, dioramas, slide presentations and fascinating exhibits. **NOTE:** Gift Shop. **DIRECTIONS:** Located on US Rt 1, one-half mile south past Longwood Gardens, about an hour drive from the Main Line.

Hours: 10:00 am - 6:00 pm   Days: Monday - Saturday
Advance Notice: Yes   Fee: $1.25   HP Access: Yes

Rodale Institute Research Center (farm research)　　　SIC Code: 0762
611 Siegfriedale Road
Kutztown, PA 19530
215-683-1400　　　　　　　Contact: Jane Fisher

A 90 - minute tour of the world's foremost organic research farm where the focus is on agricultural and horticultural field experiments. **NOTE:** Tours are conducted from May - September. Self guided tours are free. Tour by an expert guide is $4.50 adult and $2.50 children under 12. **DIRECTIONS:** Two miles south of I - 78, exit 13.

Hours:	11:00 am and 2:00 pm	Days:	Monday - Saturday	
	2:00 pm		Sunday	
Advance Notice: No		Fee:	See Note	HP Access: Yes

Anderson Bakery Company, Inc. (pretzel mfr)　　　SIC Code: 2052
2060 Old Philadelphia Pike
Lancaster, PA 17602
717-299-1616　　　　　　　Contact: Linda Yos

Enjoy a self-guided tour of this bakery where you will see the entire pretzel baking process from the overhead catwalk, including the fascinating twisting machine that gives the Dutch pretzels their unique shape. **NOTE:** Tours not conducted on major holidays. Retail store. **DIRECTIONS:** Located one block east of Rt 30 on Rt 340 in Lancaster County.

Hours: 8:30 am - 4:00 pm	Days:	Monday - Friday	
Advance Notice: Yes	Fee:	No	HP Access: Yes

Lancaster County Winery (winery)　　　SIC Code: 2084
799 Rawlinsville Road
Lancaster, PA 17584
717-464-3555　　　　　　　Contact: Todd Dickel

Tour the winery facilities where you will get a description of what is done year round in the vineyard and an explanation of the farming operation. **NOTE:** Restrooms are not handicap accessible. **DIRECTIONS:** Lancaster City south on Rt 272.

Hours: 10:00 am - 4:00 pm	Days:	Monday - Saturday	
Advance Notice: No	Fee:	$3.00	HP Access: Yes

Lancaster Newspapers Newseum (newspaper)   SIC Code: 2711
28 South Queen Street
Lancaster, PA 17603
717-291-8600   Contact: Receptionist

Take this self-guided tour where you will observe printing presses in operation through a viewing window. You will also view a large collection of old newspapers. **DIRECTIONS:** From Rt 30, take Harrisburg Pike exit to center of Lancaster. Located next to the General Hospital.

Hours: Days: Monday - Friday
Advance Notice: Yes   Fee: No   HP Access: Yes

Lancaster Postal Service (postal)   SIC Code: 4311
1400 Harrisburg Pike
Lancaster, PA 17604-9992
717-396-693   Contact: Susan Kiefer

See how the mail is processed in this U. S. Postal facility. You will follow letters through the system of bar code reading, sorting and routing as thousands of pieces of mail are handled daily. **DIRECTIONS:** From Rt 30 east or west, take Harrisburg Pike exit, go towards Lancaster City, approximately one-half mile across from Donnelly.

Hours: 10:30 am - 8:30 pm   Days: Monday - Friday
Advance Notice: Yes   Fee: No   HP Access: Yes

Weaver's Famous Lebanon Bologna (meat processor)   SIC Code: 2013
15th Avenue & Weavertown Road
Lebanon, PA 17042
717-274-6100 (800-932-8377)   Contact: Hugh B. Miller

Visit this 100 - year old commercial manufacturer of Lebanon Bologna using authentic outdoor smokehouses. You will also learn the Lebanon Bologna story. **NOTE:** Free samples. **DIRECTIONS:** From the north, follow Rt 72 south to 422 east, turn left on 15th Ave, east of Lebanon to Weavertown Rd.

Hours: 9:00 am - 4:00 pm   Days: Monday - Saturday
Advance Notice: No   Fee: No   HP Access: Yes

6Stroh Brewery Company (brewery)   SIC Code: 2082
Routes 22 & 100
Lehigh Valley, PA 18051
215-395-6811   Contact: Manager

On a tour of this modern brewery you will have an opportunity to see the brewing process and learn how their famous beer is made. **DIRECTIONS:** I - 78, exit 14A.

Hours: By appointment   Days: Monday - Friday
Advance Notice: Yes   Fee: No   HP Access: Yes

Limerick Energy Information Center (electric co)   SIC Code: 4911
298 Longview Road
Linfield, PA 19468
215-495-6767   Contact: Lisa or Frank Pennell, Jr.

This is a 30 - minute tour of displays of natural energy, electricity, nuclear power and dinosaur footprint fossils. You will have the opportunity to operate the control rods of a simulated nuclear reactor or ride a bicycle to generate electricity. Your visit may include a visit to the nearby Limerick Training Center, part of the Limerick Nuclear Power Station, to see control room operators practice on a simulator and/or vehicle tour of exterior of the plant. **NOTE:** Group reservations are encouraged. **DIRECTIONS:** Take Rt 422 (Pottstown Expressway) to the Sanatoga exit. Turn left at the end of the ramp. Turn left at the first stop sign onto Sanatoga Rd. Follow for approximately 3/4 mile and turn right onto Longview Rd. The Energy Center is located on the left.

Hours: 10:00 am - 4:00 pm   Days: Tuesday - Saturday
Advance Notice: No   Fee: No   HP Access: Yes

Julius Sturgis Pretzel House (pretzel mfr)   SIC Code: 2052
219 East Main Street
Lititz, PA 17543
717-626-4354   Contact: Michael Tshudy

Visit America's first Pretzel Bakery Museum and operating pretzel bakery. Each person will receive a piece of dough to twist your own pretzel. Learn all about the history of the pretzel and see how pretzels are baked in the old original ovens that baked the first pretzel in America. **DIRECTIONS:** Rt 772 in the town of Lititz.

Hours: 9:30 am - 4:30 pm   Days: Monday - Saturday
Advance Notice: No   Fee: $1.50   HP Access: Yes

The Martin Guitar Co. (musical instrument mfr)   SIC Code: 3931
510 Sycamore Street
Nazareth, PA 18064
610-759-2837 (800-247-6931)   Contact: Tour Department

A company guide will take you on this one hour tour that blends old world hand craftsman-ship with modern technology. You will enjoy a fascinating view of this instrument and string manu-facturing plant which will show you the steps and skills involved in the creation of high quality fretted instruments. You are invited to take advantage and visit the Martin Museum as well. **NOTE:** Tours leave promptly at 1:15 pm. Retail store. Closed all major holidays.
DIRECTIONS: Eight to ten miles north of Bethlehem, take Main St north to Broad St. Turn right on St Elmo St, left on Sycamore St.

Time: 1:15 pm only	Days: Monday - Friday	
Advance Notice: Yes	Fee: No	HP Access: Yes

New Castle Processing & Dist. Center (postal)   SIC Code: 4311
435 South Cascade Street
New Castle, PA 16108-9997
412-656-7207   Contact: Sally Baker

A general tour of this U. S. Postal facility will show how the mail arrives and is processed and how it is dispatched throughout the facility. **NOTE:** Tours are conducted by advance appointment only. **DIRECTIONS:** From US Rt 80, follow US Rt 75 south to Rt 422 west, about 11 miles. Take right at BP Gas Station.

Hours: By appointment		
Advance Notice: Yes	Fee: No	HP Access: Yes

Arrowhead Spring Trout Hatchery (hatchery)   SIC Code: 0921
Route 2
Newmanstown, PA 17073
610-589-4830   Contact: Manager

Tour the Home of the Rainbow Trout and fish for trout daily. Full services available.
NOTE: Closed during December. Senior Day each Tuesday. Free with ID.
DIRECTIONS: One mile south of Rt 419.

Hours: 9:00 am - 4:00 pm	Days: Monday - Sunday	
Advance Notice: No	Fee: $1.00	HP Access: Yes

Herr's Snack Factory (potato chips)   SIC Code: 2096
Routes 1 & 272
Nottingham, PA 19362
610-932-9330 (800-284-7488)   Contact: Jim Herr

Starting with "The Magical World of Herr's" video, followed by a guided tour of the plant, you will learn about potato chips, cheese curls, popcorn, pretzels, corn chips and tortilla. **NOTE:** You will sample snacks right out of the oven. **DIRECTIONS:** From Philadelphia, take I - 95 south to Rt 322 west to Rt 1 south. Exit at Rt 272 (Nottingham) and turn left. Travel for 50 yards, turn right onto Herr Dr and follow signs to the Herr's Visitor Center.

Hours: 9:00 am - 3:00 pm   Days: Monday - Thursday
Advance Notice: Yes   Fee: No   HP Access: Yes

Preate Winery, Inc. (winery)   SIC Code: 2084
149 Milwaukee Avenue
Old Forge, PA 18518
717-457-1555 (800-765-5346)   Contact: Greg Preate

On this visit, you will stroll past the vineyards, inspect the fermenting and bottling rooms, and experience the mystery of the winemaking process. **NOTE:** Free wine tasting of Vidal Blanc, Seyval Blanc, Chardonnay and Riesling, etc. **DIRECTIONS:** From PA Tnpk take exit 38. Follow signs.

Hours: 10:00 am - 5:00 pm   Days: Monday - Friday
        10:00 am - 3:00 pm   Saturday
Advance Notice: Yes   Fee: No   HP Access: Yes

Seltzer's Lebanon Bologna Co. (meat processor)   SIC Code: 2013
230 North College Street
Palmyra, PA 17078
717-838-6336   Contact: Aggy or Ruth

A seven minute videotape of the facility is followed by a 15 - minute tour of America's largest Lebanon bologna plant where you will see the old fashioned wooden smokehouses in use since 1902. **DIRECTIONS:** Two miles east of Hershey on Rt 522. Turn left on College St and go two blocks. Located in the heart of Pennsylvania Dutch Country.

Hours: 8:00-11:45/12:30-3:15 Days: Monday - Friday
Advance Notice: Yes   Fee: No   HP Access: Yes

Dock Street Brewing Company (brewery)　　　　SIC Code: 2082
2 Logan Square - 18th & Cherry
Philadelphia, PA 19103
215-496-0413　　　　　　　　Contact: Manager

A 30 - minute tour of Philadelphia's only full grain brewery. **DIRECTIONS:** Located in the west side of downtown Philadelphia. Call for specific directions.

Hours: 6:00 pm　　　　Days: Wednesday
　　　　3:00 pm　　　　　　　　Saturday
Advance Notice: Yes　　　Fee:　　No　　　　HP Access: Yes

Philadelphia College of Textiles (vocational svs) SIC Code: 8331
4201 School House Lane
Philadelphia, PA 19144
215-951-2851　　　　　　　Contact: Christine Foy

Plan to take a scheduled tour of the textile labs which contain handweavings, industrial Jacquard looms and knitting machines. **NOTE:** Tours are also given of tech campus art gallery. **DIRECTIONS:** Exit 32 off I - 76 (Schuylkill Expressway). Follow Lincoln Dr to Gypsy Ln (first right). Go to end and turn left on School House Ln to Henry Ave (first light).

Hours: 9:00 am - 5:00 pm　　Days: Monday - Friday
Advance Notice: Yes　　　　Fee:　　No　　　HP Access: No

WHYY - TV12 (TV broadcast)　　　　　　SIC Code: 4833
150 North 6th Street
Philadelphia, PA 19106
215-351-1200　　　　　　　Contact: Cara Schneider

This tour will include the master control room of TV 12 and 91 FM where you will learn about the interesting features of the studios. **DIRECTIONS:** Enter on 6th St between Race and Arch.

Hours: 10:00 am - 4:00 pm　　Days: Monday - Friday
Advance Notice: Yes　　　　Fee:　　No　　　HP Access: Yes

Clover Hill Vineyards & Winery (winery)   SIC Code: 2084
RD 1 - West Meadow Road
Robesonia, PA 19551
610-693-8383   Contact: Patricia or John Skrip, Jr.

Tour the tasting room which offers tasting the varietal, estate-bottled wines. An extensive wine list includes white, rose and red wines ranging from the fruity, native Labruscas to the more subtle French-American hybrids and viniferas. **NOTE:** Groups must make advance reservations. **DIRECTIONS:** From Rt 422 or Rt 183, follow the Bernville to Robesonia Rd to West Meadow Rd. Travel west 1/10 mile on West Meadow Rd to the first driveway on the right.

Hours: 11:00 am - 5:00 pm   Days: Monday - Saturday
Advance Notice: Yes   Fee: No   HP Access: No

Cherry Valley Vineyards (winery)   SIC Code: 2084
Lower Cherry Valley Road
Saylorsburg, PA 18353
717-992-2255   Contact: Mary Sorrenti

A tour of this winery is where you will learn about winemaking, bottling and wine folklore. There will be a question and answer period followed by a visit to the tasting room for a complete wine tasting of delicious award-winning wines. **DIRECTIONS:** Saylorsburg exit off Rt 33. Follow signs to winery.

Hours: 1:00 - 4:00 pm   Days: Saturday - Sunday
Advance Notice: No   Fee: No   HP Access: No

Scranton Processing & Dist. Center (postal)   SIC Code: 4311
2800 Stafford Avenue
Scranton, PA 18505-9997
717-969-5141   Contact: Marie Werner

In the U. S. Postal Processing and Distribution Center you will follow a letter through a highly automated facility which sorts one million pieces of mail a day. **DIRECTIONS:** I-81 to exit 51. Follow signs (less than two blocks).

Hours: 8:00 am - 2:00 pm   Days: Monday - Friday
Advance Notice: Yes   Fee: No   HP Access: Yes

Windgate Vineyards & Winery (winery)   SIC Code: 2084
Hemlock Acres Road
Smicksburg, PA 16256
814-257-8797   Contact: Tammy Dalessio

Situated high in the hills of Western Pennsylvania, take a one hour tour of this vineyard which produces a number of French hybrid grape varieties, including white, red, rose and blush wine. **NOTE:** Sample the estate-bottled award winning wines! **DIRECTIONS:** From PA Tnpk take exit 5 and follow signs toward Pittsburgh for one mile to Rt 910, turn right, and follow Rt 28 Expressway north signs.

Hours: 10:00 am - 5:00 pm   Days: Monday - Friday
Advance Notice: Yes   Fee: $2.00   HP Access: Yes

Straub Brewery, Inc. (brewery)   SIC Code: 2082
303 Sorg Street
St. Mary's, PA 15857
814-834-2875   Contact: Amy Jo Foote

A 30 - minute walk back into brewery nostalgia through one of the oldest breweries in the nation. Receive a thorough explanation of how Straub's process is distinctive from others and learn the fascinating family history in brewing beer for over 120 years. Finish the tour with a view of the modern packaging facilities and get a sample from the famous Eternal Tap. **NOTE:** No children under 12. **DIRECTIONS:** Located 6/10 mile from "the Diamond", PA Rt 120, downtown St. Mary's.

Hours: 9:00 am - 12 noon   Days: Monday - Friday
Advance Notice: No   Fee: No   HP Access: No

Martin's Potato Chips, Inc. (potato chips)   SIC Code: 2096
RD #1 (P.O.Box 28)
Thomasville, PA 17364-0028
717-792-3565 (800-272-4477)   Contact: Tonja McCauley

The approximately one hour tour of this family-owned company will show you the process of making potato chips from the dumping of the potatoes from the trailers to the finished product. **NOTE:** Free sample. Picnic area. Groups must make advance reservations. **DIRECTIONS:** Located on Rt 30 between York and Gettysburg.

Hours: 9:00 am - 2:00 pm   Days: Monday - Thursday
Advance Notice: Yes   Fee: No   HP Access: Yes

National Fisheries Research Lab (hatchery)　　　　SIC Code: 0921
Box 63
Wellsboro, PA 16901
717-724-3322　　　　　　Contact: Manager

A self-guided tour of the Research and Development Laboratory where you will learn about the improved methods used for producing hatchery fish. **NOTE:** Guided tours by reservation only. **DIRECTIONS:** Located in the north central part of Pennsylvania, near the PA Grand Canyon. From US Rt 180/220, take Rt 287 north about 40 miles through the beautiful Tioga State Forest Region.

Hours:8:30 am - 3:30 pm　　Days:　Monday - Friday
Advance Notice: Yes　　　　Fee:　No　　　　HP Access: Yes

Wilkes-Barre Processing & Dist. Center (postal)　　　SIC Code: 4311
300 South Main Street
Wilkes-Barre, PA 18701-9997
717-829-5459　　　　　　Contact: Philip Conrad, Jr.

A tour of the U. S. Postal Processing and Distribution Center will include the workroom floor, the carrier section and the platform operations. **DIRECTIONS:** Located in downtown Wilkes-Barre.

Hours: 9:00 am - 7:00 pm　　Days:　Monday - Friday
Advance Notice: Yes　　　　Fee:　No　　　　HP Access: Yes

Wolfgang Candy Company (candy mfr)　　　SIC Code: 2064
50 East 4th Avenue
York, PA 17405
717-843-5536 (800-248-4273)　　Contact: Dianne Freed

You will have an opportunity to tour the kitchen where peanut and cashew brittle are made. You will visit the factory production area where peanut butter puffs and peanut butter kisses are made, and you will also see the chocolate coating process, and the hand dipping of raisin clusters, in some cases using antique candy molds and other candy manufacturing items. **DIRECTIONS:** North George St to 4th Ave, convenient to I - 83 and Rt 30.

Hours: 8:00 am - 3:00 pm　　Days:　Monday - Friday
Advance Notice: Yes　　　　Fee:　No　　　　HP Access: No

Vanguard Sailboats (boat builder)   SIC Code: 3732
16 Peckham Drive
Bristol, RI 02809
401-254-0960   Contact: Manager

On this 20 - minute tour, you will watch as fiberglass boats are built from the outside in. You will see workers add the hardware and see how the decks and hulls are joined. For boat enthusiasts, you will truly appreciate being witness to the building of this high-performance racing boat. **NOTE:** Free stickers. At least five days advance notice. Gift shop. Closed holidays. **DIRECTIONS:** From Rt 114, drive over Mt. Hope Bridge toward Bristol. Take a right on Rt 136 and left at Gooding Ave. Take right at Board Common Rd and left at Peckham Dr. Factory is on right.

Hours: 9:00 am - 4:00 pm   Days: Monday - Friday
Advance Notice: Yes   Fee: No   HP Access: Yes

Watson Farm (animal farm)   SIC Code: 0212
North Road
Jamestown, RI 02835
401-423-0005   Contact: Manager

Take a self guided tour of this 280 - acre farm on Conanicutt Island which is a working farm with cattle, sheep, horses, chickens and a large garden. A two mile walking trail with alternate shorter routes provides a picturesque vista of farmland and Narragansett Bay. **NOTE:** Tours from June 1 - October 15. **DIRECTIONS:** Located in the southern part of the state on Conanicutt Island, west of Newport. Look for signs.

Hours: 1:00 - 5:00 - pm   Days: Tuesday, Thursday and Sunday
Advance Notice: No   Fee: No   HP Access: Yes

Dame Farm (farm)   SIC Code: 0191
29 Brown Avenue
Johnston, RI 02919
401-277-2632   Contact: Manager

Tour this working farm and see farm equipment used from 1870 to 1915 and farming exhibit in restored ice house. **NOTE:** Marked nature/hiking trail. **DIRECTIONS:** Located off US Rt 6 about two miles west of the intersection of US Rt 6 and Rt 295.

Hours: 10:00 am - 4:00 pm   Days: Monday - Sunday
Advance Notice: Yes   Fee: No   HP Access: No

Sakonnet Vineyards (winery)   SIC Code: 2084
162 West Main Road
Little Compton, RI 02837
401-635-8486   Contact: Manager

Take a self-guided walk of the vineyard, tour the winery and sample the award winning wines and enjoy the wonderful romance of winemaking. **NOTE:** Audio-visual presentation.
DIRECTIONS: From Newport, go north on East Main Rd (Rt 138) or West Main Rd (Rt 114) to Rt 24 north. Exit - Tiverton/Little Compton - Rt 77. Go south on Rt 77 through traffic light at Tiverton Four Corners. Sakonnet is three miles further on the left.

Hours: 11:00 am - 5:00 pm   Days: Monday - Saturday
Advance Notice: Yes   Fee: No   HP Access: No

Vinland Wine Cellars (winery)   SIC Code: 2084
909 East Main Road
Middletown, RI 02842
401-848-5161 (800-345-1559)   Contact: Rosemary Childress

Tour through the winery to see and learn how grapes are grown and wine is produced. Brief discussion of winemaking and wine tasting. **NOTE:** Advance notice for large groups.
DIRECTIONS: Winery is part of the Eastgate Mall on East Main Rd. Coming from downtown Newport, go east on Memorial Blvd, past Easton's Beach, then north of Aquidneck Ave (Rt 138A) to East Main Rd (Rt 138). Winery is on right one and one-half miles further north at the traffic signal.

Hours: 10:00 am - 5:00 pm   Days: Monday - Saturday
       12:00 noon - 5:00 pm   Sunday
Advance Notice: No   Fee: No   HP Access: Yes

Thames Glass (glass blowers)   SIC Code: 3229
688 Lower Thames Street
Newport, RI 02840
401-846-0576   Contact: Manager

On this tour you will see a team of highly skilled glassworkers through the production of designs using traditional tools and techniques. The process includes gathering the molten glass onto the end of a steel pipe, blowing and shaping the glass and decorating it with colored glass or gold and silver leaf. You will see molten glass shaped into vases, bowls, perfume bottles, plates, paperweights, goblets, mugs, and candlesticks. **DIRECTIONS:** Go south on America's Cup Dr (on the way to Ocean Dr), turn right onto Thames St, and continue 8/10 mile (past Wellington Ave) to the corner of Webster & Thames Sts.

Hours: 9:00 am - 4:30 pm   Days: Monday - Saturday
Advance Notice: No   Fee: No   HP Access: Yes

Providence Processing & Dist. Center (postal)   SIC Code: 4311
24 Corliss Street
Providence, RI 02904-9701
401-276-6800   Contact: David Gilmore

A general tour of the U. S. Postal Processing & Distribution Center where you will see the workings of a medium to large Mail Processing Facility. **DIRECTIONS:** Rt 95 north to State House exit, take second right into parking lot.

Hours: 9:00 am - 1:00 pm   Days: Tuesday, Wednesday,Thursday
Advance Notice: Yes   Fee: No   HP Access: Yes

Perryville Trout Hatchery (hatchery)   SIC Code: 0921
2426 Post Road
Wakefield, RI 02879
401-783-5358   Contact: Fred Chiarini

This hatchery raises trout for Rhode Island streams and ponds. Depending upon the time of year, you may see fish from eggs, up to two years old and older. **DIRECTIONS:** Old Post Rd, Perryville exit off Rt 1 South Kingston. Hatchery is approximately one mile on left.

Hours: 9:00 am - 3:00 pm   Days: Monday - Friday
Advance Notice: Yes   Fee: No   HP Access: Yes

Cruse Vineyards & Winery (winery)   SIC Code: 2084
Route 4 - Woods Road - Box 404
Chester, SC 29706
803-377-3944   Contact: Susan Cruse

On your visit to this vineyard you will see how red, white and blush wines are produced from both the classic grapes of the Old World and new varieties of the French hybrids. **NOTE:** Groups by appointment only. **DIRECTIONS:** Located four and one-half miles from exit 65, I - 77.

Hours: 3:30 - 6:00 pm   Days: Friday
        Noon - 6:00 pm   Saturday
Advance Notice: No   Fee: No   HP Access: No

Blenheim Bottlers, Inc. (soft drinks)   SIC Code: 2086
901 Brookwood Drive
Columbia, SC 29201
803-779-3688 (800-270-9344)   Contact: Carla

This is a 20 - minute tour of a new modern soft drink bottling plant. You will see the state-of-the-art new process for filling bottles at a high rate of speed. **NOTE:** Free samples. **DIRECTIONS:** Hwy 301 and I - 95 at South of the Border.

Hours: 8:00 am - 5:00 pm   Days: Monday - Friday
Advance Notice: Yes   Fee: No   HP Access: Yes

Florence Processing & Dist. Center (postal)   SIC Code: 4311
1901 West Evans Street
Florence, SC 29501-9997
843-679-2440   Contact: Supervisor on duty

A tour of this U. S. Postal facility will include a detailed explanation of mail flow and the methods used for processing mail as well as specific information pertaining to each of the manual, mechanized and automated operations. In addition, dispatch and delivery operations will be shown and explained. **DIRECTIONS:** Exit 160 east from US Rt 95 to Evans St. Call for further directions.

Hours: By appointment only   Days: Monday - Saturday
Advance Notice: Yes   Fee: No   HP Access: Yes

Oshkosh Truck Corp. (truck mfr)   SIC Code: 3711
552 Hyatt Street
Gaffney, SC 29341
803-487-1700   Contact: Jack Folk

On this tour you will have the opportunity to see the assembly of commercial and Class A RV chassis. **DIRECTIONS:** I - 85 north to exit 90 (Hyatt St). Take right on Hyatt. Go approximately one mile. Plant is on the left.

Hours: 9:30 am and 2:00 pm   Days: Monday - Friday
Advance Notice: Yes   Fee: No   HP Access: Yes

Greenville Processing & Dist. Center (postal)   SIC Code: 4311
600 West Washington Street
Greenville, SC 29602-9997
864-282-8414   Contact: Terri Massie

See the various stages of mail processing at the U. S. Postal Processing and Distribution Center. You will see the loading dock, the cancelling machines, computerized mail sorting equipment, and manual letter cases. **DIRECTIONS:** From I - 85, take Rt 385 to downtown Greenville. At fifth stop light turn left onto Academy St. Take a right on West Washington St. Post Office is several blocks down on the right.

Hours: 9:00 am - 1:00 pm   Days: Monday - Friday
Advance Notice: Yes   Fee: No   HP Access: Yes

Park Seed Company (seeds)   SIC Code: 0181
Cokesbury Road - Highway 254
Greenwood, SC 29647
803-223-8555   Contact: Bill Cook

The external tour of the trial gardens is self-guided and the internal tour, in and around the mailing facilities, is led by Mr. Cook. **DIRECTIONS:** Northeast of Greenwood on Hwy 254.

Hours: 10:00 am - 2:00 pm   Days: Monday- Friday
Advance Notice: Yes   Fee: No   HP Access: Yes

Mohawk Industries (carpet mfr)   SIC Code: 2273
300 Landrum Mills Road
Landrum, SC 29356
803-457-3391   Contact: Anne Culbreth

This plant, the largest carpet weaving facility under one roof in the world, is where you will take a one hour tour to view the process from production through to the finished carpet. **DIRECTIONS:** Rt 85 north or south to Rt 26 west to exit 5. Turn left on Hwy 11 and right on Frontage Rd for two and one-half miles to plant.

Hours: 9:00-noon/1:00-4:00   Days: Monday - Friday
Advance Notice: Yes   Fee: No   HP Access: Yes

Clemson Apparel Research (apparel)   SIC Code: 2389
500 Lebanon Road
Pendleton, SC 29670
803-646-8454   Contact: Tour Department

Tour this advanced apparel manufacturing research facility using state-of-the-art technology and equipment to manufacture men's dress shirts and other products. The facility was established with a grant from the Government which authorizes the facility to make men's short sleeve military shirts for demonstration purposes. **DIRECTIONS:** From I - 85, take exit 19B onto US 76 in Clemson. After third traffic light, six miles from I - 85, turn right onto Westinghouse Rd. Go one mile to stop sign. Turn left onto Lebanon Rd.

Hours: 8:00 am - 4:30 pm   Days   Monday - Friday
Advance Notice: Yes   Fee: No   HP Access: Yes

Duke Power's World of Energy (utility)   SIC Code: 4939
7812 Rochester Highway
Seneca, SC 29672
803-885-4600 (800-777-1004)   Contact: Lynn Peak

A tour of the World of Energy will show you a fun way to learn how nuclear energy is
created. The Center features computer games to test your knowledge of energy and shows
how to use it more efficiently. Exhibits demonstrate how natural resources are used to make
electricity. **NOTE:** Advance notice for groups. **DIRECTIONS:** Located on Hwy 130 and
183 - nine miles north of Seneca. Call for visitor schedule.

Hours: 9:00 am - 5:00 pm   Days: Monday - Saturday
Advance Notice: No   Fee: No   HP Access: Yes

American Classic Tea (tea)   SIC Code: 5149
Charleston Tea Plantation
6617 Maybank Highway
Wadmalaw Island, SC 29487
803-559-0383   Contact: Sarah Fleming McLester

You will visit the only tea plantation in America where you will listen to the staff tell about
the exciting world of tea production. After a stroll down the oak-lined drive, you will enjoy a
complimentary glass of American Classic Tea in the gazebo. **NOTE:** Open House is first
Saturday of each month during May - October. The tour is cancelled in case of rain. Tours
are on the half hour. **DIRECTIONS:** From Hwy 17, take either Main Rd or Hwy 171 to
Hwy 700, Maybank Hwy. Distance from Church Creek Bridge to entrance is 11 miles.
Plantation is on left side.

Hours: 10:00 am - 1:30 pm   Days: Saturday
Advance Notice: Yes   Fee: No   HP Access: Yes

Campbell Farms (potato chips)   SIC Code: 2096
Dakota Style Chips
Route 1 - Box 85
Clark, SD 57225
605-532-5271(800-446-2779)   Contact: Betty Campbell

A 30 - minute tour of a potato chip manufacturing facility where you will be able to see honey mustard potato chips, pretzels, popcorn, and sunflower seeds being processed right before your eyes. **NOTE:** Free samples. **DIRECTIONS:** Mile marker 351 or Hwy 212, then follow directions on sign to facility.

Hours: 9:00 am - 12:00 noon   Days: Vary
Advance Notice: Yes   Fee: No   HP Access: No

Dakota Central Processing & Dist. Center (postal)   SIC Code: 4311
555 15st Street NW
Huron, SD 57399-0001
605-352-9835   Contact: Eileen Nenaber

A one hour tour of the U. S. Postal Processing & Distribution Center will include the entire mail process demonstrating the automated and mechanized operations. You will see how thousands of pieces of mail are sorted and distributed daily. **DIRECTIONS:** Located next to the Huron Airport.

Hours: By appointment
Advance Notice: Yes   Fee: No   HP Access: Yes

Homestake Gold Mine Surface Tours (gold mine)   SIC Code: 1041
160 West Main Street
Lead, SD 57754
605-584-3110   Contact: Shari Bloxham

This is a one hour guided tour through the surface workings of the largest operating underground gold mine in the Western hemisphere. See giant hoists, ore crushing and milling of gold-bearing ore, Homestake's Waste Water Treatment Plant and open cut surface mine. **NOTE:** Free ore samples. Gift shop. Advance notice for large groups. **DIRECTIONS:** Located on Lower Main St in the New City Park.

Hours: 8:00 am - 5:00 pm   Days: Monday - Friday (Sept - May)
        10:00 am - 5:00 pm   Saturday - Sunday (June -August)
Advance Notice: No   Fee: $4.25 adults   HP Access: Yes

Heartland Consumer Power District (utility)   SIC Code: 4911
203 West Center Street
Madison, SD 57042
605-256-6536   Contact: Manager

On this tour you will learn what Heartland does and the purposes of a public power district and you will also see how electricity is generated and transmitted to the customers.
DIRECTIONS: Follow US Rt 29 north of Sioux Falls to exit 109. Then take Rt 34 to center of town. Call for further directions.

Hours: 8:00 am - 5:00 pm   Days: Monday - Friday
Advance Notice: Yes   Fee: No   HP Access: Yes

Dacotah Cement (cement)   SIC Code: 3241
501 North St. Onge Street
Rapid City, SD 57709
605-394-5200   Contact: Bonnie Lemay

Take a tour of this cement manufacturing facility which is owned by the citizens of South Dakota. The facility produces six types of cement dependent on customer requirements.
NOTE: Driving tours available for handicapped individuals, but access to some buildings is limited. **DIRECTIONS:** Exit 55 off I - 90, two miles south on the right side of the road.

Hours: 9:00 am - 2:00 pm   Days: Monday - Friday
Advance Notice: Yes   Fee: No   HP Access: No

Landstrom's Black Hills Gold (jewelry mfr)   SIC Code: 3911
405 Canal Street
Rapid City, SD 57709
605-343-0157   Contact: Sandra Hammond

You will see a 45 - 60 minute film and take a tour of the jewelry production in a designated area. A question and answer period is provided by tour director. **DIRECTIONS:** From I - 90, take exit 58 to Canal St.

Hours: 8:00 am - 4:30 pm   Days: Monday - Friday
Advance Notice: Yes   Fee: No   HP Access: Yes

Mount Rushmore Jewelry (jewelry mfr)   SIC Code: 3911
2707 Mount Rushmore Road
Rapid City, SD 57709
605-343-2226   Contact: Betty Lambert

This tour takes you on the floor of the most modern jewelry manufacturing facility in the midwest. You will learn about the ancient art of lost wax casting, wax injection, investment, bright cutting, wriggling, and more. You will also visit with the skilled craftspeople. **NOTE:** Retail outlet available. **DIRECTIONS:** From I - 90 go south on Rt 16 to Mount Rushmore Rd.

Hours: 8:00 am - 5:00 pm   Days: Monday - Friday
Advance Notice: No   Fee: No   HP Access: Yes

Sioux Pottery & Crafts (pottery products)   SIC Code: 3269
2209 Highway 79 South
Rapid City, SD 57701
605-341-3657 (800-657-4366)   Contact: Rob or Jeff

This is a 20 - 30 minute tour showing the casting, sanding, painting and designing of Lakota made pottery by Sioux Indians. **NOTE:** Advance notice for large groups. **DIRECTIONS:** One mile past School of Mines towards Drivers License Bureau.

Hours: 11:00 am   Days: Monday, Wednesday, Friday
Advance Notice: No   Fee: No   HP Access: Yes

Sioux Falls Processing & Dist. Center (postal)   SIC Code: 4311
320 South Second Avenue
Sioux Falls, SD 57102-9300
605-332-3300   Contact: Rainier Van Bemmel

A tour of the U. S. Postal Processing & Distribution Center will demonstrate what happens to your letter or package once it gets to the post office. **DIRECTIONS:** Located in downtown Sioux Falls.

Hours: 8:00 am - 8:00 pm   Days: Monday - Saturday
Advance Notice: Yes   Fee: No   HP Access: Yes

Basin Electric Power Cooperative (utility)   SIC Code: 4911
Spirit Mound Station
Highway 19 North (P.O.Box 393)
Vermillion, SD 57069
605-624-4981   Contact: Manager

This is an oil-fired electric generating station with two units, each unit rated at 60,000 KW capacity. You will take a one-hour guided tour of the power plant and see how industrial combustion turbines are used to generate electricity. **NOTE:** There is walking involved and not recommended for children under 10 years of age. **DIRECTIONS:** Eight and one-half miles north on Hwy 19 and two miles west of Vermillion.

Hours: By appointment   Days: Monday - Friday
Advance Notice: Yes   Fee: No   HP Access: No

Watertown Monument Works, Inc. (granite)   SIC Code: 1411
1007 5th Street, SE
Watertown, SD 57201
605-886-6942 (800-843-3305)   Contact: Sue Grist

Tour of a granite manufacturer where you will see sawing, polishing, shaping, memorial design, art work, stencil cutting, shaping, flowers and sandblasting. Depending on current production schedule, you may also see counter tops and furniture being manufactured.
DIRECTIONS:
I - 29 to Hwys 212 and 81.

Hours: 9:00 am - 3:30 pm   Days: Monday - Thursday
Advance Notice: Yes   Fee: No   HP Access: Limited

Ardmore Cheese Company (cheese processor)   SIC Code: 2022
State Highway 7 - 200 West Main Street
Ardmore, TN 38449
423-427-2191   Contact: Manager

Tour of a large cheese manufacturing plant which produces a variety of cheddar cheeses.
DIRECTIONS: Take exit 1 from US Rt 65 east. Located on the Tennessee/Alabama border.

Hours: By appointment   Days: Monday - Saturday
Advance Notice: Yes   Fee: No   HP Access: No

Dale Hollow National Fish Hatchery (hatchery)   SIC Code: 0921
Fish Hatchery Road (P.O.Box C)
Celina, TN 38551
423-243-2443   Contact: Dudley R. Korth

Self-guided tour of this U.S. Department of the Interior trout hatchery facility and small aquarium which features several common fish found in Dale Hollow Lake. Hatchery provides rainbow, brown and lake trout to trout waters in TN, AL and GA. Annual average production is 200,000 pounds. **DIRECTIONS:** Three miles north of Celina on Hwy 53.

Hours: 7:00 am - 4:00 pm   Days: Monday - Sunday
Advance Notice: No   Fee: No   HP Access: Yes

Morris Winery & Vineyard (winery)   SIC Code: 2084
352 Union Grove Road
Charleston, TN 37310
423-479-7311   Contact: Manager

At Tennessee's largest pick-your-own-vineyard you will pick blueberries in July, grapes in July and August and muscalines in September and October. Wines include Concord, White Riesling, Muscadine, Niagara, and Catawba. **DIRECTIONS:** From Chattanooga, follow US Rt 75 to exit 33 east to Rt 11 north. Look for signs.

Hours: 8:00 am - 8:00 pm   Days: Monday - Saturday
Advance Notice: Yes   Fee: No   HP Access: No

Cordova Cellars Winery & Vineyard (winery)   SIC Code: 2084
9050 Macon Road
Cordova, TN 38018
901-754-3442   Contact: Manager

Cordova Cellars is a full production winery and vineyard located in a beautiful rural setting.
The tour guide will describe all phases of grape growing and wine making operations.
NOTE: Advance notice for groups. **DIRECTIONS:** From Memphis, take I - 40 north
toward Nashville to Germantown south exit, (exit 16, Rt 177). Turn right onto Germantown
Pkwy and proceed south two and 7/10 miles. Turn left at the traffic light onto Macon Rd.
Proceed another two and 2/10 miles where you will see the sign on the left side of the road.

Hours: 10:00 am - 5:00 pm   Days: Tuesday - Saturday
Advance Notice: No   Fee: No   HP Access: Yes

Stonehaus Winery, Inc. (winery)   SIC Code: 2084
Genesis Road at I - 40
Crossville, TN 38555
423-484-9463   Contact: Kathy Wheeler

This is a guided 20 - minute educational tour showing the winemaking process from the
crushing of the grapes to the final step of bottling. **NOTE:** Picnic facilities are available.
Limited winter hours. **DIRECTIONS:** Located at exit 320, Genesis Rd at I - 40 (across
the interstate from Vanity Fair Shopping Mall).

Hours: 10:00 am - 6:00 pm   Days: Monday - Saturday
Advance Notice: No   Fee: No   HP Access: Yes

Erwin National Fish Hatchery (hatchery)   SIC Code: 0921
1715 Johnson City Highway
Erwin, TN 37650
423-743-4712   Contact: Andrew L. Currie

On this self-guided tour you will visit the hatchery where six strains of rainbow trout are
raised, producing 15 million disease-free eggs annually to support the National Broodstock
Program. The Broodstock operations are performed in a manner that will preserve or
optimize the genetic diversity of the hatchery fish. **DIRECTIONS:** Rt 181 south from
Johnson City. Exit 19 turn left at light (one-half mile on left).

Hours: 7:30 am - 4:00 pm   Days: Monday - Friday
Advance Notice: Yes   Fee: No   HP Access: Yes

Knoxville Processing & Dist. Center (postal)   SIC Code: 4311
1237 East Weisgarber Road
Knoxville, TN 37950-9997
423-558-4536   Contact: Norimi Bradner

On a tour of the U. S. Postal Processing & Distribution Center you will follow the flow of mail from entry to the Postal Service to the dispatch bound for distribution. **DIRECTIONS:** Take exit 383, west on Paper Mill, right at light. At Weisgarber Rd turn right and the Center will be about one and one-half miles on your left.

Hours: 2:00 - 10:30 pm   Days: Monday - Friday
Advance Notice: Yes   Fee: No   HP Access: Yes

Jack Daniel Distillery (distillery)   SIC Code: 2085
Route 1
Lynchburg, TN 37352
423-759-4221   Contact: Roger Brashears

This is a 70 - minute tour in which you will observe every step of the sour mash whiskey making art, including Jack Daniel's charcoal-mellowing process used at this distillery for more than a century. **NOTE:** Tour involves walking and stairs. Closed holidays.
DIRECTIONS: Exit I - 24 via Rt 55 or I - 65 by way of Rts 64 and 50. Entrance to distillery is right off Hwy 55 next to the Mulberry Creek Bridge.

Hours: 8:00 am - 4:00 pm   Days: Monday - Saturday
Advance Notice: Yes   Fee: No   HP Access: No

Agricenter International (farm research)   SIC Code: 0762
7777 Walnut Grove Road
Memphis, TN 38120
901-757-7777   Contact: Jamey Hatley

A self-guided tour of America's premier showcase for agricultural technology, a 1000-acre complex demonstrating the latest agricultural products, equipment and practices. **NOTE:** Exhibition pavilion and 575 - seat amphitheater. Closed major holidays. **DIRECTIONS:** In Memphis, go east from I - 240 on Walnut Grove exit, or I - 40 at Germantown Pkwy.

Hours: 9:00 - 4:00 pm   Days: Monday - Friday
Advance Notice: No   Fee: No   HP Access: Yes

Coors Brewery (brewery)   SIC Code: 2082
5151 East Raines Road
Memphis, TN 38118
901-375-2100   Contact: Scott Eggleston

You will be taken on a 40 - minute walking tour where you will see the brewhouse, packing operations and the power plant. **NOTE:** Adult guests can sample products (soft drinks are provided as well). **DIRECTIONS:** I - 240 to Mt. Moriah exit. Go south on Mt. Moriah, and stay in right lane to Mendenhall Rd. Turn right to the visitors parking lot on the left.

Hours: 10:00 am - 4:00 pm   Days: Monday - Saturday (June - August)
            Noon to 4:00 pm   Monday - Saturday (September-May)
Advance Notice: Yes   Fee: No   HP Access: Yes

Memphis Processing & Dist. Center (postal)   SIC Code: 4311
555 South Third Street
Memphis, TN 38136-9009
901-521-2182   Contact: Carol McKinnie

On the tour of the U. S. Postal Processing and Distribution Center you will observe the workroom floor operations, the optical character reader, which sprays bar codes on letters, and bar code sorters, which sorts letters according to Zip Codes after bar codes have been sprayed on letters. **DIRECTIONS:** South on Second St to Calhoun, left on Calhoun to Third St. Turn right.

Hours: 9:00 - 10:00 am   Days: Monday - Friday
Advance Notice: Yes   Fee: No   HP Access: Yes

Nashville Processing & Dist. Center (postal)   SIC Code: 4311
525 Royal Parkway
Nashville, TN 37230-9998
615-885-9127   Contact: Bobby Miller or Charles Massey

This busy U.S. Postal Processing and Distribution Center tour will show you state-of-the-art automated equipment, including sack sorter, bundle sorter, flats sorter, optical character readers and bar code sorters - all geared to process your mail with speed, accuracy and efficiency. **DIRECTIONS:** From I - 40, take exit 216-C (Donelson Pike), turn left at Royal Pkwy (second light).

Hours: 24 hours per day   Days: Monday - Sunday
Advance Notice: Yes   Fee: No   HP Access: Yes

Tennessee Valley Authority (Norris Dam) (utility) SIC Code: 4939
Route 441 North (P.O.Box K)
Norris, TN 37828
423-632-1825 Contact: Public Safety Officer

The first flood control structure built by TVA was completed in 1936. The dam overlooks on both sides. After an overview of history of the Dam, you will tour through the electrical generating/flood control area of the Dam. **NOTE:** By appointment only. **DIRECTIONS:** US Hwy 441 off of I - 75 (Anderson County, TN).

Hours: 8:00 am - 3:00 pm Days: Monday - Sunday
Advance Notice: Yes Fee: No HP Access: Yes

Tennessee Walking Horse Museum (horses) SIC Code: 0272
Corner Calhoun & Evans Streets
Shelbyville, TN 37160
423-684-5915 Contact: Tour Director

This exciting family exhibit covers the history of the breed, its specialized training, the breed registry, one-night horse shows, the Tennessee Walking Horse National Celebrities and its reigning World Grand Champion in the heart of Tennessee's horse country. You will learn about the only horse to be named after the state in which it was bred. Also included is a seven minute video. **DIRECTIONS:** From I - 24 south, take the Shelbyville exit. Turn left on Madison St. The Center is 1/8 mile on the left.

Hours: 9:00 am - 5:00 pm Days: Monday - Saturday
Advance Notice: No Fee: $3.00 HP Access; Yes

Sequoyah Energy Connection (utility) SIC Code: 4939
2000 Igou Ferry Road
Soddy-Daisy, TN 37379
423-843-4098 Contact: Dick Salisbury

Visit the Energy Connection's 2,000 sq. ft. exhibit area and learn about energy, the Sequoyah Nuclear plant and the TVA. Computer-touch screens make it family fun. **NOTE:** Closed major holidays. **DIRECTIONS:** US 27 north to Soddy-Daisy Sequoyah Rd exit. It is approximately five and 8/10 miles to Igou Ferry Rd to the facility.

Hours: 10:00 am - 4:00 pm Days: Monday - Saturday
Advance Notice: No Fee: No HP Access: Yes

Dutch Maid Bakery (bakery)   SIC Code: 2051
111 Main Street
Tracy City, TN 37387
423-592-3171   Contact: Peggy

Tour this old, well established bakery located in the mountains of Tennessee where you will
hear a brief history of the bakery and then tour the mixing room operations, the work up
areas, and see an oven demonstration. This bakery produces Old World baked specialties
using recipes from the late 1800's. **DIRECTIONS:** From Nashville on I - 24, take
Monteagle exit and follow Hwy 41 (not 41A) to Tracy City. Turn right at the second traffic
light. Brick building is one-half block away on the left..

Hours: 10:30 am - 3:30 pm   Days: Monday - Saturday
Advance Notice: Yes   Fee: No   HP Access: No

Mountain Lakes Glass (glassblowing)   SIC Code: 3229
340 Lake Road - Box 850
Tracy City, TN 37387
423-592-5252   Contact: Sally or Ed Russell

On this visit, you will watch glass blowing demonstrations in the classical style. Vases,
goblets, paperweights and ornaments are made from 100% recycled glass. Products are
sold worldwide to a very select market. **DIRECTIONS:** On US 41, look for Monteagle
Mountain between Chattanooga and Nashville. Tracy City is six miles from the Interstate.

Hours: By appointment only
Advance Notice: Yes   Fee: No   HP Access: Yes

George Dickel Distillery (distillery)   SIC Code: 2085
1950 Cascade Hollow Road
Tullahoma, TN 37388
423-857-3124   Contact: Barbara J. Moore

See how Tennessee Sour Mash Whisky is still made the same way George Dickel did over
100 years ago. Souring the mash and charcoal mellowing the Whisky is the magic that makes
superb George Dickel. **NOTE:** Gift shop. **DIRECTIONS:** From Nashville, take I - 24 east
to exit 105. Turn right at end of the ramp to Rt 41 for two miles to Blantons Chapel Rd.
Turn right and proceed four miles to Lyndell Bell Rd. Take left to Normandy Dam sign, turn
right and travel three and 2/10 miles to Normandy.

Hours: 9:00 am - 3:00 pm   Days: Monday - Friday
Advance Notice: No   Fee: No   HP Access: Yes

New York (Texas) Cheesecake (bakery)   SIC Code: 2051
122 North Palestine
Athens,TX 75751
903-675-3665 (800-225-6982)   Contact: Manager

Delicious, mouth-watering cheesecake made in New York, Texas (pop. 12) on a farm overlooking East Texas hills. This popular cheesecake is distributed throughout the United States
and at Neiman Marcus department stores. **DIRECTIONS:** Located in downtown Athens at
the junction of US Rts 175 and 31.

Hours: 3:00 - 6:00 pm   Days: Monday - Friday
Advance Notice: Yes   Fee: No   HP Access: Yes

Austin American Statesman (newspaper)   SIC Code: 2711
305 South Congress Avenue
Austin, TX 78704
512-445-3559   Contact: Christina Fajardo-Ethridge

Take a 30 - 45 minute tour of the advertising, editorial, layout and press room of this daily
newspaper. **NOTE:** Tours must be scheduled from one - two months in advance. Children
must be at least eight years of age. **DIRECTIONS:** Barton Springs Rd dead ends into their
parking lot, just south of the river.

Hours: By appointment   Days: Monday - Friday
Advance Notice: Yes   Fee: No   HP Access: Yes

Austin Processing & Dist. Center (postal)   SIC Code: 4311
8225 Cross Park Drive
Austin, TX 78710-9997
512-929-1205   Contact: Beverly Reed

See how this U. S. Postal facility processes incoming and outgoing mail. You will see automated, manual and mechanized operations direct, sort and distribute hundreds of thousand of
pieces of mail per day using state-of-the-art automated equipment. **NOTE:** Advance notice
is required. **DIRECTIONS:** Cross Park Dr runs between Cameron Rd and Hwy 290.
Located in Walnut Creek Business Park.

Hours: By appointment only
Advance Notice: Yes   Fee: No   HP Access: Yes

Celis Brewery, Inc. (brewery)   SIC Code: 2082
2431 Forbes Drive
Austin, TX 78754
512-835-0884   Contact: Peter Camps

Make it a point to take this 30 - minute tour to visit Belgian brewmaster Pierre Celis' brewery which produces three brews: Celis White, Celis Pale Bock, and Celis Golden. This brewery is known as the fastest growing brewery in America. **NOTE:** Free samples. **DIRECTIONS:** I - 35 to 290 east, proceed for two and one-half miles, left on Cross Park Dr, 1/4 mile down on left.

Hours: 2:00 pm and 4:00 pm   Days: Tuesday - Saturday
Advance Notice: No   Fee: No   HP Access: Yes

National Wildflower Research Center (floriculture)   SIC Code: 0181
2600 F.M. 973
Austin, TX 78725
512-929-3600   Contact: Manager

Established in 1982 and donated by Lady Bird Johnson, the Center is created to simulate research and education about preservation, propagation and use of wildflowers throughout the nation. Especially colorful during the Spring. **DIRECTIONS:** Farm Road 973 intersects Rt 71 at the northeast corner of Bergstrom Air Force Base, southeast of Austin.

Hours: 9:00 am - 4:00 pm   Days: Monday - Friday
Advance Notice: Yes   Fee: No   HP Access: Yes

Blue Bell Creameries (ice cream mfr)   SIC Code: 2024
1000 Horton Street
Brenham, TX 77833
409-836-7977 (800-327-8135)   Contact: Cynthia Robinson

A 40 - minute tour of the manufacturing plant which produces 20 million gallons of ice cream per year. **NOTE:** Prior arrangements must be made for all tours in March and April. Groups of 15 or more must make an appointment. No charge for children under age six. Children age 6 - 14 and senior citizens $1.50. **DIRECTIONS:** Off US 290 - Loop 577.

Hours: 10:00,11:00,1:00,2:00   Days: Monday - Friday
Advance Notice: No   Fee: $2.00   HP Access: Yes

Messina Hof Wine Cellars (winery)   SIC Code: 2084
4545 Old Reliance Road
Bryan, TX 77808
409-778-9463   Contact: Paul Bonarrigo

Tour of an historic winery building, barrel room and vineyards, with insight as to how wine is produced. **NOTE:** Free wine tasting. **DIRECTIONS:** Exit Hwy 6 at Old Reliance Rd, turn right and follow signs to Messina Hof.

Hours: 1:00 pm   Days: Monday - Friday
            12:30, 2:30, 4,00 pm   Saturday
            12:30, 2:30 pm   Sunday
Advance Notice: Yes   Fee: No   HP Access: Yes

Taylor Made Saddles (saddlery)   SIC Code: 3199
Highway 55 - P.O.Box 667
Camp Wood, TX 78833
830-597-2255   Contact: Tom or Peggy Taylor

Watch custom made saddlery and harnesses being built on this tour. **NOTE:** There will be time for questions. **DIRECTIONS:** Hwy 55 north to downtown Camp Wood.

Hours: By appointment only
Advance Notice: Yes   Fee: No   HP Access: Yes

Golden Gals' Pralines (candy mfr)   SIC Code: 2064
1001 South Donoho Street
Clarksville, TX 75426
903-427-3148   Contact: Manager

Cottage industry specializing in gourmet pralines, handmade with finest Texas pecan halves. **DIRECTIONS:** Clarksville is located in the northeast corner of the state. From Rt 30 take exit 198. Follow Rt 82 to town. Call for further directions.

Hours: 9:00-noon/1:00-4:00   Days: Monday - Friday
Advance Notice: No   Fee: No   HP Access: Yes

Marshall Pottery (pottery products)   SIC Code: 3269
1137 Conveyor Lane #118
Dallas, TX 75247
214-638-7578   Contact: Manager

You will see hundreds of kinds of decorative and utility pots, plaques, figurines and bowls. You will also see a regular demonstration of pottery making and firing. **DIRECTIONS:** Take the Inwood Rd exit north from US Rt 35, just north of downtown. Follow to Conveyor Ln.

Hours: 9:00 am - 6:00 pm   Days: Monday - Saturday
Advance Notice: No   Fee: No   HP Access: Yes

The Dallas Morning News (newspaper)   SIC Code: 2711
508 Young Street
Dallas, TX 75202
214-977-7069   Contact: Keith Austell

This one hour tour includes an historical overview of The Dallas Morning News, from its beginnings in Galveston, TX in 1885 to today; and a physical tour of the various departments including the newsroom, photo desk, news art, photography and composing. **NOTE:** Children must be at least 10 years old and in the fifth grade. No sandals, cut-offs or tank top shirts. Tennis shoes are strongly suggested. **DIRECTIONS:** Located near the Hyatt Hotel in the downtown area.

Hours: 9:00 am - 4:00 pm   Days: Monday - Friday
Advance Notice: Yes   Fee: No   HP Access: Yes

Denton Record-Chronicle (newspaper)   SIC Code: 2711
314 East Hickory Street
Denton, TX 76201
940-381-9514   Contact: Kelly Harrison

On your visit to this newspaper you will get a complete tour and explanation of the day-to-day workings of the newspaper. **DIRECTIONS:** East off the downtown square.

Hours: 9:00 am - 4:00 pm   Days: Monday - Friday
Advance Notice: Yes   Fee: No   HP Access: No

Fort Worth Star-Telegram (newspaper)   SIC Code: 2711
685 John B. Sias Memorial Parkway
Fort Worth, TX 76101
817-551-2212   Contact: DeAnna Howard

This approximate one hour tour begins with a video, showing the Star-Telegram (past and present) and then you will have a guided tour of the production facility. You will see offset presses and robots in action. **NOTE:** Reservations are required. Age limit is six years of age or older. **DIRECTIONS:** Exit Hemphill St south off I - 20. Turn left onto John B. Sias Memorial Pkwy. You must enter from Hemphill St. Drive to the main entrance and unload passengers before parking in the designated areas.

Hours: By appointment   Days: Wednesday - Friday
Advance Notice: Yes   Fee: No   HP Access: Yes

Dulcimer Factory (musical instrument mfr)   SIC Code: 3931
715 South Washington Street
Fredericksburg, TX 78624
830-997-6704   Contact: John or Shirley Naylor

Take a tour of the factory where the oldest original American stringed instrument are made from a variety of woods. Tours and history of the dulcimer are conducted by the owner. **NOTE:** Tours are every half hour. Closed from noon to 1:00 pm. **DIRECTIONS:** US Rt 10 north of San Antonio to Rt 16 northeast.

Hours: 10:00-noon/1:00-4:00   Days: Monday - Friday
Advance Notice: No   Fee: No   HP Access: Yes

Anheuser-Busch Brewery (brewery)   SIC Code: 2082
775 Gellhorn Drive
Houston, TX 77029
713-675-2311   Contact: Tour Department

In just one and one-half hours, you will stroll through the scenic gardens for an outdoor escalator ride to the Brew Hall. There you will enjoy a fascinating look at the century-old brewing process. Then you will see the high-speed packaging equipment fill an assortment of bottles and cans. After the tour, you can relax with complimentary samples of beer and snacks. **DIRECTIONS:** From downtown Houston, take I - 10 east to Gellhorn.

Hours: 9:00 am - 4:00 pm   Days: Monday - Saturday
Advance Notice: Yes   Fee: No   HP Access: Yes

Borden, Inc. (ice cream mfr)   SIC Code: 2024
4494 Campbell Road (NW Houston)
Houston, TX 77041
713-744-3700   Contact: Brenda Reed

From the viewing area at this ice cream plant, you will be able to look down on the production floor and watch the packing, boxing and filling processes. You will also see a video explaining the history of Borden and the Elsie and Elmer dolls. **NOTE:** Free ice cream treat. **DIRECTIONS:** Near Clay & Campbell in NW Houston.

Hours: 9:00 and 10:00 am   Days: Tuesday and Thursday
Advance Notice: Yes   Fee: No   HP Access: Yes

The Houston Chronicle (newspaper)   SIC Code: 2711
801 Texas Avenue
Houston, TX 77002
713-220-7904   Contact: Florence Stuchly

A 45 - minute tour of this daily newspaper called "The Daily Miracle" will include the production, editorial, advertising and circulation departments. **DIRECTIONS:** Located at the corner of Texas Ave, Milam and Travis.

Hours: 9:00 am - 1:00 pm   Days: Tuesday - Thursday
Advance Notice : Yes   Fee: No   HP Access: Yes

Marshall Pottery (pottery products)   SIC Code: 3269
4901 Elysian Field Avenue
Marshall, TX 75670
903-938-9201   Contact: Manager

You will see hundreds of kinds of decorative and utility pots, bowls, plaques and figurines. See regular demonstrations of pottery making and firing. **DIRECTIONS:** Marshall is located along US Rt 20, just west of Shreveport, LA at the junction of Rts 20 and 59. Call for specific directions.

Hours: 9:00 am - 6:00 pm   Days: Monday - Saturday
Advance Notice: No   Fee: No   HP Access: Yes

Exell Helium Plant (natural gas)   SIC Code: 1311
U. S. Interior Department
Highway 287
Masterson, TX 79058
806-935-9670   Contact: Stephen Urbanczyk

This is a two hour plant tour which consists of a walk through the entire plant where you will see a cryogenic demonstration with liquid nitrogen. **NOTE:** Two week advance notice is required. **DIRECTIONS:** 35 miles north of Amarillo, one mile west from Hwy 287.

Hours: 9:00 am - 3:00 pm   Days: Monday - Friday
Advance Notice: Yes   Fee: No   HP Access: No

Samuell Farm (animal farm)   SIC Code: 0291
100 East Highway 80
Mesquite, TX 75149
972-670-8263   Contact: Steve Norden/Maynelle Cheney

Take a self-guided tour of a 340 - acre farm which features a wide variety of animals to experience life on a working farm. Maintained to recall farming days of 1800's to early 1900's, the farm's many features include antique tractors, ponds for fishing, picnic sites, petting area, hay-rides, hiking and nature areas. **DIRECTIONS:** Located 14 miles east of downtown Dallas.

Hours: 9:00 am - 5:00 pm   Days: Monday - Saturday
Advance Notice: No   Fee: $3.00   HP Access: Yes

Eilenberger's Butternut Bakery (bakery)   SIC Code: 2051
512 North John Street
Palestine, TX 75801
903-729-2253   Contact: Theresa Bambeck

Famous since 1898 for fruit cakes baked from an Old World recipe, you will receive a complete tour of the bakery including the history of the bakery. **NOTE:** Free samples. **DIRECTIONS:** Palestine is located southeast of Dallas where Hwys 79, 187and 84 meet. Call for further directions.

Hours: 10:00 am - 3:00 pm   Days: Monday - Saturday
Advance Notice: Yes   Fee: No   HP Access: Yes

The Dallas Morning News (newspaper)   SIC Code: 2711
3900 West Plano Parkway
Plano, TX 75074
972-977-7069   Contact: Keith Austell

A one hour tour of the production facility of this newspaper will include an historical overview as well as a walk through the paper warehouse, where you will see the paper handling, plate-making, pressroom and distribution operations. **DIRECTIONS:** From downtown Dallas follow the North Tollway or the Central Expressway to Plano Pkwy at Coit Rd.

Hours: 9:00 am - 4:00 pm   Days: Monday - Friday
Advance Notice: Yes   Fee: No   HP Access: Yes

Spoetzl Brewery (brewery)   SIC Code: 2082
603 East Brewery Street
Shiner, TX 77984
512-594-3383   Contact: Bernadette Fikac

A guided tour through each facet of the brewery which is one of a few remaining breweries whose product is made, bought and consumed entirely in Texas; almost all of the annual 25,000 barrels marketed in surrounding area. **NOTE:** Free tasting. Gift shop/Museum. **DIRECTIONS:** From San Antonio, take I - 10 east to Rt 183 south. In Gonzalas go left on Hwy 90A (Alt 90). This road takes you into Shiner. At stop light (the only one in town) go left on Hwy 95. Brewery is on left after bridge.

Hours: 11:00 am & 1:30 pm   Days: Monday - Friday
Advance Notice: Yes   Fee: No   HP Access: Yes

Imperial Holly Company (sugar refinery)   SIC Code: 2062
198 Kempner Street
Sugar Land, TX 77478
713-491-9181   Contact: Tour Line

During this one hour tour, you will observe the complete sugar manufacturing process in one of the nation's largest and most up-to-date sugar refineries. **NOTE:** Gift shop. No cameras. Stairs involved. **DIRECTIONS:** Take I - 59 south to Hwy 6 exit in Sugar Land, turn right. At Alt 90, turn right, then left onto Ulrich. Building is on right.

Hours: 10:00 am and 2:00 pm   Days: Monday - Friday
Advance Notice: Yes   Fee: No   HP Access: No

Southwest Dairy Center (vocational school)   SIC Code: 8331
1210 Houston Street
Sulphur Springs, TX 75482
903-439-6455   Contact: Jodie Morris, Director

A video production will illustrate the dairy industry today. The exhibit tour will illustrate early dairy product production, augmented with cream separation demonstrations and butter churning demonstrations. Five Mobile Dairy Classrooms travel a six-state area with a cow, calf and milking equipment for milking demonstrations and instructions in the care and feeding as well as facts about the dairy industry. **NOTE:** Advance notice is required for groups. **DIRECTIONS:** I - 30 to exit 122 (Hwy 19), north to Hwy 11 east.

Hours: 9:00 am - 4:00 pm   Days: Monday - Saturday; Sunday pm only
Advance Notice: No   Fee: No   HP Access: Yes

Dr. Pepper Seven-Up (soft drinks)   SIC Code: 2086
300 South Fifth Street
Waco, TX 76701
800-922-6386   Contact: David Beaty (Curator of Education)

Housed in the 1906 Home of Dr. Pepper, the Center is dedicated to telling the story of the soft drink industry, with a focus on Dr. Pepper where you will learn about the invention, production and advertising of America's oldest major soft drink. The one hour tours are guided by trained docents and end with a visit to the antique operating soda fountain. **DIRECTIONS:** I - 35 to Waco, exit 4th St toward town, four blocks to Mary Ave, one block left to 5th St.

Hours: 10:00 am - 4:00 pm   Days: Monday - Saturday (Sunday pm only)
Advance Notice: Yes   Fee: $3.00   HP Access: Yes

Kennecott Utah Copper Mining (copper mine)   SIC Code: 1021
8362 W 10200 S
Bingham Canyon, UT 84006
801-322-7300   Contact: Public Affairs

On this tour you will have an opportunity to learn how copper is produced and how it serves
your daily needs in so many important ways. You will also have an overlook view which will
allow you to easily see the mining operations. You will then take a stroll through the Visitors
Center - a step back in time - and a look into the future. At the end of the tour, you will see a
dramatic video presentation which will bring to life the production of copper at Kennecott.
NOTE: Tours April 1 through October 31. All admission fees collected are donated to local
charities and non-profit organizations. **DIRECTIONS:** From Salt Lake City, south on Rt 15
to 7200 south exit. Follow signs to Visitors Center.

Hours: 8:00 am - 8:00 pm   Days: Monday - Sunday
Advance Notice: No   Fee: $2.00   HP Access: Yes

Intermountain Power Project (utility)   SIC Code: 4939
850 West Brush Wellman Road
Delta, UT 84624
435-864-4414   Contact: Terry Hyde

Take this two hour tour in which you will have the opportunity to view the outside facilities,
the converter station and the generating station. **DIRECTIONS:** Located 12 miles southeast
of Delta.

Hours: 8:00 am - 3:00 pm   Days: Monday - Friday
Advance Notice: Yes   Fee: No   HP Access: Yes

Space Dynamics Laboratory (USU) (space research)   SIC Code: 9661
1695 North Research Park Way
Logan, UT 84341-1942
435-755-3202   Contact: Paul Huber

You will spend approximately 20 - minutes receiving an historical overview of the facility and then go on a 25 - minute tour where you will view the laboratories, clean rooms, see space craft being developed, machine shop, and computer aided designing area. **DIRECTIONS:** 17 blocks north, five blocks east of Center and Main.

Hours: 9:00 am - 4:00 pm   Days: Tuesday - Friday
Advance Notice: Yes   Fee: No   HP Access: Yes

Geneva Steel (steel mill)   SIC Code: 3312
10 South Geneva Road
Orem, UT 84058
435-227-9178   Contact: George Wright

A two hour tour where you will see molten steel pour from the oxygen furnace and 2,400 degree steel rolled in the rolling mill. All the components of steel making are explained and shown. **NOTE:** There are no set schedules, all tours must be scheduled in advance. Minimum age: 12. **DIRECTIONS:** I - 15 to exit 274, or the Orem Center St exit. Go west off the freeway and follow the road straight. The tour begins just south of the administration building in the Human Resource Building.

Hours: By appointment only
Advance Notice: Yes   Fee: No   HP Access: Yes

NuSkin International (toiletries mfr)   SIC Code: 2844
75 West Center Street
Provo, UT 84601
801-345-8687   Contact: Tour Department

Tour of the Visitors Center where you will learn and observe how NuSkin products are made. In addition you will visit the order processing department and the computer room. **NOTE:** Tour may include the Distribution Center. Advance notice for parties of 10 or more. Tours are given on the hour and half-hour. **DIRECTIONS:** Located in downtown Provo. Call for specific directions.

Hours: 8:30 am - 4:30 pm   Days: Monday - Friday
Advance Notice: Yes   Fee: No   HP Access: Yes

Rock of Ages Quarries, Inc. (granite quarry)   SIC Code: 1411
Quarry Hill
Barre, VT 05641
802-476-3119   Contact: Janet Cross/Todd Paton

A delightful, informative 60 - 90 minute guided tour beginning at the Visitors Center with a video presentation explaining quarrying and the manufacturing of granite. You may also take a shuttle tour to the spectacular Upper E. L. Smith Quarry at 500 feet deep. From the safety of the observation platform, you will be able to watch quarriers far below as they cut the granite. You may even see giant blocks of granite being hoisted from the quarry depths by a mammoth derrick. Shuttle tour is available Monday through Friday from June until mid October (9:30 am - 3:00 pm). There is a charge for the shuttle tour of $4.00 for adults and $1.50 for children age 6 - 12. **NOTE:** Bring your camera. Free granite specimen souvenirs. Picnic area available. **DIRECTIONS:** From I - 89, take exit 6 and follow signs.

Hours: 8:30 am - 5:00 pm   Days: Monday - Saturday
Advance Notice: No   Fee: See above   HP Access: Yes

Rock of Ages (Manufacturing Div.) (granite quarry)   SIC Code: 1411
Box 482
Barre, VT 05641
802-476-3119   Contact: Janet Cross/Todd Paton

From the newly remodeled observation deck which spans two football fields, you can observe the sawing, shaping and lettering of granite products. Depending upon the production schedule, you may even see a sculptor transform the granite into beautiful and enduring art work. The facility is the most modern and up-to-date in the country. **NOTE:** Bring your camera. Free granite samples. Picnic area available. Closed July 4. **DIRECTIONS:** From I - 89, take exit 6 and follow signs.

Hours: 8:00 am - 3:30 pm   Days: Monday - Friday
Advance Notice: No   Fee: No   HP Access: Yes

Auger's Sugar Mill Farm (maple sugaring)   SIC Code: 0831
Grover Road - Route 16 South
Barton, VT 05822
802-525-3701 (800-688-7978)   Contact: Norman or Mike Auger

A complete wagon tour of the farm will include a demonstration of the revolution of maple sugaring. **NOTE:** Free samples. Self-guided tour of facility is also available. **DIRECTIONS:** Off exit 25 on I - 91. 1/10 mile to Rt 16 south, first farm on right.

Hours: 8:00 am - 6:00 pm   Days: Monday - Sunday
Advance Notice: No   Fee: No   HP Access: Yes

Tom & Sally's Handmade Chocolates (candy mfr)   SIC Code: 2064
6 Harmony Place
Brattleboro, VT 05301
802-254-4200   Contact: Thomas Fegley

A 30 - minute tour where you will observe the various methods of making chocolates by hand. **DIRECTIONS:** Exit 2 off I - 91 to downtown Brattleboro. Left at the fork. Right turn into the Harmony parking lot just before Main St.

Hours: By appointment only   Days: Monday - Sunday
Advance Notice: Yes   Fee: No   HP Access: No

Cabot Creamery Corp. (cheese processor)   SIC Code: 2022
Main Street
Cabot, VT 05647
802-563-2231   Contact: Manager

On this tour, you will see a short video on the history of the creamery and learn how products are processed. The staff will take you into the plant and show you the magic of cheese-making. You will see how special varieties of aged cheddar cheese are prepared, as well as their low fat cheeses and dairy products. **NOTE:** Free samples. **DIRECTIONS:** From I - 89 at Mont-pelier, take Rt 302 to Rt 3 east. At Marshfield, go left on Rt 215, then five miles to Cabot Village. (From I - 91, take exit 21 at St. Johnsbury to Rt 2 west. At Marshfield, go right on Rt 215, five miles to Cabot Village.)

Hours: 9:00 am - 4:00 pm   Days: Monday - Friday (June - October)
        9:00 am - 4:00 pm   Saturday (winter hours)
Advance Notice: Yes   Fee: $1.00   HP Access: Yes

Bragg Farm Sugarhouse (maple sugaring)   SIC Code: 0831
Route 14 North
East Montpelier, VT 05651
802-223-5757   Contact: Manager

Tour this family operated sugarhouse and walk maple woods where they hang 2,000 buckets. You will hear how sap is collected, boiled, and turned into maple products. Free taste and test with explanation of different grades of syrup. **DIRECTIONS:** From Montpelier, follow Rt 2 to East Montpelier and Rt 14 north. Look for signs.

Hours: 8:30 - 6:00   Days: Mon - Sun
Advance Notice: No   Fee: No   HP Access: Yes

Dakim Farm (foods)   SIC Code: 2099
Route 7
Ferrisburg, VT 05456
802-425-3971   Contact: Sam Cutting IV

See Vermont's finest cob-smoked ham, pure maple syrup, aged cheddar cheese and other specialty foods being made. Tour the smokehouses, the maple syrup cannery and cheese cutting operations. **NOTE:** Free samples. **DIRECTIONS:** 30 minutes south of Burlington on Rt 7 (Midway between Burlington and Middlebury).

Hours: 8:00 am - 5:00 pm   Days: Monday- Sunday
Advance Notice: Yes   Fee: No   HP Access: No

Crowley Cheese, Inc. (cheese processor)   SIC Code: 2022
Healdville Road
Healdville, VT 05758
802-259-2340   Contact: Manager

You are welcome to watch colby cheese being made the same way as it was when Winfield Crowley began making it in 1882. The factory is believed to be the oldest in the western hemisphere. **NOTE:** Call ahead to be sure cheese is being made that day. Gift shop. **DIRECTIONS:** Healdville is a tiny, rural community of a few dozen people on a paved town highway two miles from Rt 103, five miles north of Ludlow and 20 miles south of Rutland.

Hours: 8:00 am - 4:00 pm   Days: Monday - Friday
Advance Notice: Yes   Fee: No   HP Access: Yes

North River Winery (winery)

SIC Code: 2084

Route 12 - River Road
Jacksonville, VT 05342
802-368-7557

Contact: Manager

The 1850's farmhouse and barn which house the winery are filled with the charm of an age when wines were made by local residents. This is an interesting and informative tour of the winemaking facilities and you will have an opportunity to sample some of the various wines. **DIRECTIONS:** From Brattleboro, take exit 2. On Rt 9 travel west for about 17 miles to Rt 100 south for six miles. At Jacksonville Center, take right at "T" intersection, then take an immediate left onto Rt 112 south for 1/4 mile. Winery on the left.

Hours: 10:00 - 5:00
Advance Notice: No

Days: Sunday - Saturday (Late May - Dec)
Fee: No
HP Access: Yes

Morse Farm (maple sugaring)

SIC Code: 0831

County Road
Montpelier, VT 05602
802-223-2740 (800-242-2740)

Contact: Manager

Watch how maple sugaring is done from the trees to finished product. **NOTE:** Maple trail walk. Free sugarhouse tour, syrup tasting and slide show. **DIRECTIONS:** In Montpelier take Main St and follow the signs.

Hours: 8:00 am - 6:00 pm
Advance Notice: No

Days: Sunday - Saturday
Fee: No
HP Access: Yes

New England Maple Museum (maple sugaring)   SIC Code: 0831
Route 7
Pittsford, VT 05763
802-483-9414   Contact: Manager

You will experience the dramatic process involved in cooking 40 gallons of sap to yield a single gallon of maple syrup. You will learn the complete history of maple sugaring. You will observe antiques, paintings, slide show and exhibits displaying entire process from sap to syrup and see today's modern equipment producing maple syrups and candies. **NOTE:** Gift shop. Closed January and February. **DIRECTIONS:** From Rutland, take Rt 7 to Pittsford. Follow signs.

Hours: 8:30 - 5:30   Days: Monday - Friday
Advance Notice: No   Fee: No   HP Access: Yes

Vermont Marble Exhibit (granite)   SIC Code: 1411
5 PSI Plaza - 62 Main Street
Proctor, VT 05765
802-459-2300   Contact: Manager

Visit the world's largest marble museum and learn about the mining, processing and marketing of this natural mineral resource. Learn the complete history of this fascinating Vermont industry. **DIRECTIONS:** From Rutland, take Rt 4 west and Rt 3 north into town. Watch for signs.

Hours: 9:00 am - 5:30 pm   Days: Monday - Friday
Advance Notice: No   Fee: No   HP Access: Yes

Shelburne Farms (cheese processor)   SIC Code: 2202
102 Harbor Road
Shelburne, VT 05482
802-985-8686   Contact: Hilary Sunderland

This one to one-half hour tour begins with an award-winning slide show. You will then board an open-air wagon with a tour guide to visit the gardens at the Inn and see the cheesemaking facility in the Farm Barn. You will return to the Visitor's Center for cheese tasting. Tours given mid - May through mid - October. Tour is not handicap accessible, however, handicapped visitors may drive to the Farm Barn to see the cheesemaking process.
DIRECTIONS: From I - 89 take exit 13. Drive south on Rt 7 for five miles. Turn right at Bay Rd and follow to entrance to the property.

Hours: 9:00 am - 5:00 pm   Days: Monday - Friday
Advance Notice: No   Fee: $5.50   HP Access: No

Vermont Teddy Bear Company (stuffed toys)   SIC Code: 3944
2031 Shelburne Road
Shelburne, VT 05482
802-985-1319   Contact: Allison Coyne/Tom Shamponis

Visit this very special factory and take a hands-on-tour to see how a teddy bear is born and handcrafted with pride. You will see how each piece of material is cut, sewn and stuffed so each bear has just the right firmness. **DIRECTIONS:** Three and one-half miles south of Burlington on Rt 7 south.

Hours: 10:00 am - 4:00 pm   Days: Monday - Saturday
        1:00 - 4:00 pm   Sunday
Advance Notice: No   Fee: No   HP Access: Yes

Maple Grove Farms of Vermont, Inc. (candy mfr)   SIC Code: 2064
167 Portland Street
St. Johnsbury, VT 05819
802-748-5141 (800-525-2540)   Contact: Phil Jenkins

A guided tour of one of Vermont's largest attractions where you will see maple candy and their famous salad dressings being made. **NOTE:** Closed major holidays. **DIRECTIONS:** Rt 2 east of town.,

Hours: 8:00 am - 4:00 pm   Days: Monday - Friday
Advance Notice: No   Fee: $1.00 adults   HP Access: No

Ben & Jerry's Ice Cream (ice cream mfr)   SIC Code: 2024
Route 100 & Rt 2
Waterbury, VT 05676
802-244-5641   Contact: Tour Department

Included in this fun and educational guided tour, is a 10 - minute video presentation about the Ben & Jerry Story which is followed by a 20 - minute tour to the mezzanine where you will get a great view of the action in the Production Room with detailed information on the steps taken to make Vermont's finest ice cream and yogurt. **NOTE:** Fresh made sample.
DIRECTIONS: Exit 10 off I - 89. Go north on Rt 100, towards Stowe. One mile on the left.

Hours: 9:00 am - 5:00 pm   Days: Monday - Saturday
          9:00 am - 8:00 pm   Monday - Saturday (July-August)
Advance Notice: No   Fee: $1.00   HP Access: Yes

Cabot Creamery (cheese processor)   SIC Code: 2022
Route 100
Waterbury, VT 05676
802-244-6334   Contact: Manager

On this self-guided tour, you will view a video about the cheesemaking process and learn about Vermont's agricultural heritage. You will be able to sample a complete selection of Cabot's award-winning cheeses along with many other Vermont-made specialty items.
NOTE: Free samples. **DIRECTIONS:** Located on Rt 100 just north of I - 89.

Hours: 9;00 am - 5:00 pm   Days: Monday - Friday
Advance Notice: No   Fee: No   HP Access: Yes

Cold Hollow Cider Mill (cider mill)   SIC Code: 0175
Route 100
Waterbury Center, VT 05677
802-244-8771   Contact: Manager

You will learn the history of the cider mill as well as see a demonstration on how cider is made. A video will be shown with a question and answer period to help you understand the complicated process. **NOTE:** Free samples. **DIRECTIONS:** Located on Rt 100, just north of I - 89.

Hours: 8:30 - 4:30   Days: Monday - Sunday
Advance Notice: No   Fee: No   HP Access: Yes

Green Mountain Chocolate Co. (chocolate mfr)   SIC Code: 2066
Rt 100
Waterbury, VT 05676
802-244-1139

You will see the Master Pastry Chef's chocolate sculptures and memorabilia and be able to watch the chocolate making demonstrations during the season. They also feature Green Mountain Coffee. **NOTE:** You may enjoy a cup of coffee while you savor a complimentary taste of quality chocolates. **DIRECTIONS:** I - 89 to exit 10. Go north on Rt 100. Located halfway between Ben & Jerry's and Cold Hollow Cider Mill.

Hours: 9:00 am - 6:00 pm   Days: Monday - Saturday
Advance Notice: No   Fee: No   HP Access: Yes

Simon Pearce Glass, Inc. (glass blowers)   SIC Code: 3229
Route 5 North
Windsor, VT 05089
802-674-6280   Contact: Tammi or Darlene

Visitors can observe glass blowers at work from an ideal vantage point - a catwalk viewing gallery above the factory floor. **DIRECTIONS:** North on I - 91, take exit 9, bear right on US 5, go one mile. Simon Pearce is on the left.

Hours: 9:00 am - 5:00 pm   Days: Monday - Sunday
Advance Notice: Yes   Fee: No   HP Access: Yes

Afton Mountain Vineyards, Inc. (winery) SIC Code: 2084
R R 3
Afton, VA 22920
540-456-8667 Contact: Shinko or Tom

A self-guided tour of the vineyards and a guided tour of the winery describing the processes of winemaking from the crush through bottling. **DIRECTIONS:** From Charlottesville, VA, take I - 64 west to exit 107, US 250 west to SR 151, south on 151, three miles to Rt 6, west on Rt 6, one and 8/10 miles to Rt 631, south one and 2/10 miles to Winery on left.

Hours: 10:00 am - 6:00 pm Days: Wednesday - Monday
Advance Notice: No Fee: No HP Access: Yes

Burnley Vineyards & Winery (winery) SIC Code: 2084
Route 1- 4500 Winery Lane
Barboursville, VA 22923
540-832-2828 Contact: Manager

Tour of small winery and vineyard which includes wine tastings of some of their wine including Chardonnay, Riesling, Cabernet Sauvignon and Spicy Rivanna. **DIRECTIONS:** From Barboursville, go south on Rt 20 for two miles. Turn right on Rt 641 for 1/4 mile, entrance to the winery is on the left.

Hours: 1:00 am - 5:00 pm Days: Wednesday - Sunday
Advance Notice: No Fee: No HP Access: No

Oakencroft Vineyard & Winery (winery) SIC Code: 2084
Route 5, Barracks Rd.
Charlottesville,VA 22901
804-296-4188 Contact: Carolyn Graves

You will tour the loading/grape processing area, the cellar, the barrel room and return to the antique filled tasting room to sample some of Virginia's best wines. In addition, you will find one of the most beautiful farm wineries in the state with vistas of the Blue Ridge Mountains stretching beyond the vineyards and a lake with Virginia water fowl fronting the winery. **NOTE:** Gift shop. Open April - December. **DIRECTIONS:** From I - 64, take exit 118B, then take third exit which is Rt 654 (Barracks Rd). At stop sign turn left for approximately three miles. Winery sign on left.

Hours: 11:00 am - 5:00 pm Days: Monday - Sunday
Advance Notice: Yes Fee: $1.00 HP Access: Yes

Stonewall Vineyards (winery)   SIC Code: 2084
Route 2 (Box 107A)
Concord, VA 24538
804-993-2185   Contact: Sterry Davis

On a tour of the vineyard, you will walk the sunny fields of pampered grapes, ideally matched to the microclimate and selected for flavor excellence. On the winery tour, you will observe the age-old art of wine making perfected in compact, modern facilities. Some of the wines produced here are Chardonnay, Vidal Blanc, Cayuga, Mist and Mirage. **DIRECTIONS:** 15 miles east of Lynchburg. From Rt 460 in Concord, go north six miles on Rt 608, left on Rt 721, first farm on left.

Hours: 11:00 am - 4:00 pm   Days: Wednesday - Sunday
Advance Notice: Yes   Fee: $3.00   HP Access: Yes

Union Camp (paper mfr)   SIC Code: 2621
34040 Union Camp Drive
Franklin, VA 23851
804-569-4321   Contact: Nancy Brown

The one hour tour will take you through the plant to view the processing of paper and paper products in a paper mill. You will see the largest paper machine and visit the sheet finishing area, after a short orientation of the operation. **NOTE:** Children must be 12 years or older. You must wear sturdy leather shoes. No sneakers or sandals. **DIRECTIONS:** Located on Business 58 west of the Norfolk - Virginia Beach area. Call for specific directions.

Hours: 7:30 pm only   Days: 3rd Wednesday of every month
Advance Notice: Yes   Fee: No   HP Access: Yes

Richmond Newspapers, Inc. (newspaper)   SIC Code: 2711
5555 Chamberlayne Road
Hanover, VA 23069
804-649-6901   Contact: Barbara Smith

The tour is approximately one-and-a-quarter hours and will show you the inner workings of a large daily newspaper. **NOTE:** Children must be 10 years old or in the fourth grade. **DIRECTIONS:** From the north, go south on I - 95, east on I - 295 to US 301 exit; north on US 301 approximately 1/4 mile. Plant entrance on right.

Days: By appointment only   Days: Monday, Thursday, Friday
Advance Notice: Yes   Fee: No   HP Access: Yes

Loudoun Times-Mirror (newspaper)   SIC Code: 2711
9 East Market Street
Leesburg, VA 22075
540-777-1111   Contact: Marie Curran or Charlotte Howard

This is a complete tour of a newspaper plant which includes watching the press when it is running. **DIRECTIONS:** 30 miles west of Washington, DC, eight miles from Dulles Airport.

Hours: By appointment only
Advance Notice: Yes   Fee: No   HP Access: No

Tarara Winery (winery)   SIC Code: 2084
13648 Tarara Lane
Leesburg, VA 22075-5236
540-771-7100   Contact: Margaret Hubert

The winery, of 6,000 square feet, is built in the caves to provide a perfect temperature and humidity controlled environment for barrel-aging the premium wines. On this visit you will have the opportunity to sample Chardonnay, Cabernets, Charval, Terra Rouge, or Cameo wines. **NOTE:** Tours on Tuesday and Wednesday by appointment only. **DIRECTIONS:** From Washington, DC go west on Rt 7 to Leesburg, north on Rt 15 approximately eight miles to Lucketts, right on 662. Three miles to sign on driveway on left.

Hours: 11:00 am - 5:00 pm   Days: Thursday - Monday (March-December)
Advance Notice: No   Fee: No   HP Access: Yes

WAGE Radio (radio broadcast)   SIC Code: 4832
711 Wage Drive SW
Leesburg, VA 22075-5236
540-777-1200   Contact: Julia Bobbitt/Program Director

See how a small market radio station operates. **DIRECTIONS:** Located on Wage Dr off of Catactin Circuit, adjacent to Loudoun County High School.

Hours: 10:00 am - 6:00 pm   Days: Monday - Friday
Advance Notice: Yes   Fee: No   HP Access: Yes

Willowcroft Farm Vineyards (winery)   SIC Code: 2084
Route 2
Leesburg, VA 22075
540-777-8161   Contact: Dave Collins

Tour this family owned winery and vineyard located high on Mount Gilead in a rustic, quaint barn setting. Grapes are grown on the premises and 4,000 gallons are produced annually. **DIRECTIONS:** From Leesburg, exit from bypass on Rt 15 south to Rt 704 (Harmony Church Rd). Turn right and immediate left onto Rt 797 (Mount Gilead Rd) and enjoy the three and 1/10 mile country road to the entrance.

Hours: 12:00 noon - 5:00 pm   Days: Saturday - Sunday
Advance Notice: No   Fee: No   HP Access: No

Mountain Cove Vineyards (winery)   SIC Code: 2084
Route 1
Lovingston, VA 22949
804-263-5392 (800-489-5392)   Contact: Al Weed

Take a complete tour of this winery facility and vineyard. You will receive a detailed explanation of how grapes are grown and wine is made. **DIRECTIONS:** Located 32 miles south of Charlottesville or 32 miles north of Lynchburg, just three and one-half miles west of US 29 at Lovingston on SR 651.

Hours: 1:00 - 5:00 pm   Days: Wednesday - Sunday
Advance Notice: No   Fee: No   HP Access: Yes

Lynchburg Processing & Dist. Center (postal)   SIC Code: 4311
3300 Odd Fellows Road
Lynchburg, VA 23501-9997
804-528-8956   Contact: Gayle Taylor

When you tour this U. S. Postal Service facility you will see mail processing, including automation, the letter-sorting machine, the flat-sorting machine, manual casing, the dock area, carrier section and the entire general mail facility. **DIRECTIONS:** Odd Fellows Rd exit from Rt 29 North.

Hours: 9:00 - 11:00 am   Days: Tuesday and Thursday
Advance Notice: Yes   Fee: No   HP Access: Yes

Misty Mountain Vineyards, Inc. (winery)   SIC Code: 2084
RR 2
Madison, VA 22727
540-923-4738   Contact: Manager

Take a complete tour of this winery facility and learn how grapes are grown for the production of premium wines, Chardonnay, Merlot, Cabernet Sauvignon and Reisling. **DIRECTIONS:** From Charlottesville, follow Rt 29 north about 25 miles. Call for further directions.

Hours: By appointment only
Advance Notice: Yes   Fee: No   HP Access: No

Chateau Morrisette Winery (winery)   SIC Code: 2084
P.O. Box 766
Meadows of Dan, VA 24120
540-593-2865   Contact: Rain Lutz

Tour of winemaking areas, processing equipment, storage tanks and bottling areas. Visit the beautiful winery and grounds. **NOTE:** Tours are given hourly. **DIRECTIONS:** Mile Post 172 - Blue Ridge Parkway.

Hours: 11:00 am - 4:00 pm   Days: Monday - Sunday
Advance Notice: No   Fee: $1.00   HP Access: Yes

Rowena's Jam & Jelly Factory (jams, jellies)   SIC Code: 2033
758 West 22nd Street
Norfolk, VA 23527
757-627-8699 (800-627-8699)   Contact: Cameron Foster

Tour the kitchen and store where jams and sauces are made and sold. You will then proceed to the bakery where Rowena's famous pound cakes are made. **NOTE:** Tours from January to September only. **DIRECTIONS:** From the Virginia Beach Expressway, take I - 64 or I - 264 to Waterside Dr (becomes Boush St). Continue on Boush St to 22nd St. Turn left to almost the end of the street.

Hours: 10:00 am - 2:00 pm   Days: Monday - Thursday
Advance Notice: Yes   Fee: No   HP Access: Yes

Ingleside Plantation Winery (winery)   SIC Code: 2084
Route 638
Oak Grove, VA 22443
804-224-8687   Contact: Cindy Eason

Tour and see permanent exhibits, colonial wine bottles and seals. Taste award-winning wines including red, white and blush wines, as well as Virginia champagne. **NOTE:** Advance notice for large groups. Picnic in the courtyard pavilion. **DIRECTIONS:** Two and one-half miles south of Oak Grove on Rt 638.

Hours: 10:00 am - 5:00 pm   Days: Monday - Saturday
          12 noon - 5:00 pm   Sunday
Advance Notice: No   Fee: No   HP Access: Yes

Rockbridge Vineyards (winery)   SIC Code: 2084
Route 1, Exit 205 off I-81
Raphine, VA 24472
540-377-6204   Contact: Jane Rouse

Farm owner operated winery featuring White Riesling, St. Mary's Blanc, Chardonnay, Pinot Noir and Tuscarora White wines. Tour of vineyards (5 acres) renovated barn (dairy barn/barn to winery) in high pastoral setting (2000 feet) of the Shenandoah Valley. **DIRECTIONS:** West on 606, one mile off I - 81 exit 205, midway between Lexington and Staunton, VA.

Hours: 12:00 am - 5:00 pm   Days: Thursday - Saturday
Advance Notice: No   Fee: No   HP Access: No

Richmond Newspapers, Inc. (newspaper)   SIC Code: 2711
333 East Grace Street
Richmond, VA 23293
804-649-6901   Contact: Barbara Smith

The tour is approximately one-and-a-quarter hours and will show you the inner workings of a large daily newspaper. **NOTE:** Children must be in the fourth grade. **DIRECTIONS:** Located in the center of town. Call for further directions.

Days: By appointment only   Days: Wednesday
Advance Notice: Yes   Fee: No   HP Access: Yes

Joyner of Smithfield Ham Shop (meat processor)   SIC Code: 2013
315 Main Street
Smithfield, VA 23430
757-357-2162   Contact: Manager

There are no scheduled tours but you are welcome to visit and hear a talk on ham processing with photographs used to illustrate the process. Smithfield is the Ham Capital of the World. **NOTE:** Plan to visit the gift shop and the plant outlet store. **DIRECTIONS:** Rt 17 west to Rt 10. Follow signs to Smithfield center. Shop is located next to large hardware store on Main St.

Hours: By appointment only   Days: Monday - Saturday
Advance Notice: No   Fee: No   HP Access: Yes

Lake Anna Winery (winery)   SIC Code: 2084
5621 Courthouse Road
Spotsylvania, VA 22553
540-895-5085   Contact: Manager

Enjoy a complete tour of the winemaking facility and Oak Hill Vineyard. All Lake Anna
Wines are made from grapes grown at Oak Hill Vineyard or from grapes grown locally. You
will hear an explanation of how wine is made followed by wine tasting. **DIRECTIONS:**
From Fredericksburg, (about 30 minutes) take Rt 1 bypass south to Four Mile Fork. Turn
right on Rt 208 (Courthouse Rd). Continue on Rt 208, turn left at Spotsylvania Courthouse,
turn right at Snell, and left at Post Oak. Go seven miles to winery, entrance is on the left.

Hours: 11:00 am - 5:00 pm   Days: Wednesday - Saturday
            1:00 pm - 7:00 pm   Sunday
Advance Notice: No   Fee: No   HP Access: No

S. Wallace Edwards & Sons, Inc. (meat processor)   SIC Code: 2013
11455 Rolfe Highway
Surry, VA 23883
757-294-3121 (800-222-4267)   Contact: Amy Harte

A 15 - minute tour showing how Virginia Hams are smoked and cured. You will visit the
smokehouse, the curing rooms and the aging rooms. **NOTE:** Tours are every hour on the
half-hour and are from March 1 - September 30. Bus tours please call ahead for scheduling.
DIRECTIONS: Located on Rts 10 & 31 on the west side of the Village. A short pleasant
ferry ride from the Jamestown/Williamsburg area.

Hours: 9:30 am and 4:30 pm   Days: Monday - Friday
Advance Notice: No   Fee: No   HP Access: No

Christian Broadcasting Network, Inc (TV broadcast)   SIC Code: 4833
977 Centerville Turnpike
Virginia Beach, VA 23463-0001
757-579-2745   Contact: Margaret Kidd

Experience the excitement of live TV with Pat Robertson, Ben Kinchlow and Terry
Meeuwsen on the 700 Club, a morning television program, which is live most weekdays from
10:00 - 11:30 am. Tours of Studio Building may not include live television program.
DIRECTIONS: I - 64 to exit 286B (Indian River Rd) CBN is at the Interchange.

Hours: 11:30 am, 2:00,3:00 pm Days: Monday - Friday
Advance Notice: Yes   Fee: No   HP Access: Yes

Loudoun Valley Vineyards (winery)   SIC Code: 2084
RFD 1, P.O. Box 340
Waterford, VA 22190
540-882-3375   Contact: D. Tucker

Tour the gently sloping vineyards which cover fields where Mosby's Raiders once roamed. There are 25 planted areas on a 90 acre property. Also visit the winery with breathtaking views and award-winning wines. **DIRECTIONS:** From Leesburg, VA, take Rt 7, west two miles to Rt 9 west. Proceed five miles to the winery on the right.

Hours: 11:00 am - 5:00 pm   Days: Saturday - Sunday
Advance Notice: No   Fee: No   HP Access: No

Anheuser-Busch Brewery (brewery)   SIC Code: 2082
One Busch Gardens Boulevard
Williamsburg, VA 23187
757-253-3039   Contact: Tour Department

In just one hour, you will take a leisurely self-guided tour and see the brewhouse and high-speed packaging operations. You can also stroll through the newest beechwood aging cellar. **DIRECTIONS:** From Washington, DC, take I - 95 to I - 295 south at Richmond to I - 64 east to Exit 242A.

Hours: 9:00 am - 4:00 pm   Days: Monday - Saturday
Advance Notice: Yes   Fee: No   HP Access: Yes

The Candle Factory (candle mfr)   SIC Code: 3999
7521 Richmond Road
Williamsburg, VA 23188
757-564-3354   Contact: Tour Department

While in the observation room, you will have an opportunity to see how soaps and candles are manufactured. An educational video presentation will give you a closer look at their products and how they are made. **DIRECTIONS:** From I - 64, take exit 231A (Hwy 607 to Norge) directly to The Candle Factory.

Hours: 9:00 am - 5:00 pm   Days: Monday - Sunday
Advance Notice: No   Fee: No   HP Access: Yes

Williamsburg Winery (winery)   SIC Code: 2084
5800 Wessex Hundred
Williamsburg, VA 23185
757-229-0999   Contact: Drew Haynie

Award-winning winery, graciously guided tour through the underground barrel cellars which explain the winemaking process. Adults only will enjoy a taste of five wines in the unique Wine Shop. **NOTE**: No tours January 15 - February 15. People under age 21 are free. **DIRECTIONS:** I - 64 exit 242A, west on 199 to third traffic light, left, then left at first intersection.

Hours: 11:00 am - 5:30 pm   Days: Tuesday - Saturday
             12:00 noon   Sunday
Advance Notice: No   Fee: $5.00 adults   HP Access: Yes

Commonwealth Gin (cotton gin)   SIC Code: 0724
25165 Buckhorn Drive
Windsor, VA 23487
757-242-3566 (800-695-2655)   Contact: Ora C. Saunders

This tour entails a visit through one of two "cotton gins" in the state in which you will see how cotton is processed. **NOTE:** Tours may be scheduled with two days notice during the months of October and November. **DIRECTIONS:** From Portsmouth, take Rt 58 west to Petersburg exit to Rt 460 west to Windsor. Take left at first light, cross tracks, onto Buckhorn Dr. Follow one mile. Gin is on the left.

Hours: By appointment only
Advance Notice: Yes   Fee: No   HP Access: Yes

KLKI Radio Island Broadcasting (radio broadcast)   SIC Code: 4832
25th & Commercial
Anacortes, WA 98221
360-293-3141   Contact: William T. Berry

Tour the complete operations of a local radio station where you will have an opportunity to observe behind the scene activities as well as the broadcasting equipment. **NOTE:** Minimum age: six years. **DIRECTIONS:** Main street of Anacortes. Call for specific directions.

Hours: 9:00 am - 4:00 pm   Days: Monday - Sunday
Advance Notice: Yes   Fee: No   HP Access: Yes

Safeway Stores Distribution Ctr. (food warehouse)   SIC Code: 5141
224 124th Avenue, NE
Bellevue, WA 98009
206-455-6453   Contact: Terry Gerber

You will go on a 30 - minute tour through each warehouse, grocery, produce, and bakery departments. **NOTE:** There are various tours available, please call ahead for times and schedules. **DIRECTIONS:** Located south of Hwy 520 on the east side. From Seattle, take I - 90 or 520 east. From I - 90 head north on I - 405 to 520. Head east on 520 and take the 124th St exit. Go straight through. You will pass the Metro bus station. The Distribution Center is on your right as you come up the hill.

Hours: Mornings only   Days: Tuesday - Wednesday
Advance Notice: Yes   Fee: No   HP Access: No

Bellingham Cold Storage (food warehouse)   SIC Code: 5141
2825 Roeder Avenue
Bellingham, WA 98310
360-733-1640   Contact: Manager

A tour of the facilities relating to fin fish and shellfish processing, freezing and storage; vegetable freezing and storage; and shipping and receiving. **NOTE:** Age six and over. **DIRECTIONS:** Located in the northwest corner of the state. Take exit 255 from US Rt 5 to city. Call for further directions.

Hours: By appointment only   Days: Monday - Friday
Advance Notice: Yes   Fee: No   HP Access: No

Bellingham Herald (newspaper)   SIC Code: 2711
1155 North State Street
Bellingham, WA 98225
360-676-2600   Contact: Janette Michael

This is a one hour tour of the newsroom, composing room, paste up, camera and letterflex plate deparments of Whatcom County's daily newspaper plant. **NOTE:** Prefer groups of 10 to 20 people. **DIRECTIONS:** Located at the corner of State and Chestnut Sts. Call for further directions.

Hours: 9:00 am - 4:00 pm   Days: Monday - Friday
Advance Notice: Yes   Fee: No   HP Access: Yes

Munroe Wool Company (woolen mill)   SIC Code: 2231
1450 Island View
Bellingham, WA 98225
360-734-3373   Contact: John Munroe

On this one hour tour you will see the process of washing, drying, picking and carding of wool fleece made into batts or roving. You will have an opportunity to see wool-filled comforters which are made in Shop #2. **DIRECTIONS:** West on Marine Dr to Bancroft. Go south one block - west one block.

Hours: 9:00 am - 5:00 pm   Days: Monday - Saturday
Advance Notice: Yes   Fee: No   HP Access: Yes

KBFW Radio (radio broadcast) SIC Code: 4832
1919 Broadway
Bellingham, WA 98225
360-734-8555 Contact: Steven Smith

Tour of the studio, offices, control room, and production facilities of this small country AM radio station. **DIRECTIONS:** From I - 5, take the Guide Meridian exit, get in left lane. At stop light turn left, go back under the Interstate. Follow Meridian until you get to the corner of Meridian, Broadway and Girard. You will be in the Foundation District. Station is located above Dewitt's Furniture.

Hours: 9:00 am - 3:00 pm Days: Monday - Friday
Advance Notice: Yes Fee: No HP Access: Yes

The Seattle Times (newspaper) SIC Code: 2711
19200 120th Avenue NE
Bothell, WA 98011
206-489-7015 Contact: Kate Palmer

Tour a state-of-the-art newspaper printing and distribution plant, complete with robots. **DIRECTIONS:** Exit 24 off I - 405. Go east three blocks.

Hours: 9:00 am, Noon, 1:30 Days: Monday, Wednesday, Friday
Advance Notice: Yes Fee: No HP Access: Yes

The Sun Newspaper (newspaper) SIC Code: 2711
545 5th Street
Bremerton, WA 98337
360-377-3711 Contact: Mischa Lanyon

This one hour newspaper tour begins with a brief talk on duties from managing editor to paper carrier and proceeds to the step-by-step production process of a daily newspaper including various departments, the composing room and press room. **NOTE:** No children under five years of age. **DIRECTIONS:** Located on 5th St between Park and Pacific in downtown Bremerton, four blocks up from ferry.

Hours: 11:30 am - 4:30 pm Days: Monday, Tuesday, Thursday, Friday
Advance Notice: Yes Fee: No HP Access: Yes

Carnation Farm (dairy farm)   SIC Code: 0241
28901 NE Carnation Farms Road
Carnation, WA 98014
206-788-1511   Contact: Denise Beebe

Take this 40 - minute self guided walking tour of a modern milking facility with calf and
maternity barn, "The Birth of a Calf" video, petting area, and milking parlor. You will also
visit the stable museum, the Kitty Barn, and the Labrador Retrievers in the farm kennels. A
view of the beautiful flowering gardens is a must. **NOTE:** Steep hills may be difficult for
wheelchairs. Tour from March 1 - October 31. Closed holidays. **DIRECTIONS:** Located
15 miles north of North Bend on Rt 203. From US Hwy 90, a short distance east of Seattle.

Hours: 10:00 am - 3:00 pm   Days: Monday - Saturday
Advance Notice: Yes   Fee: No   HP Access: Yes

Wind River Nursery (trees)   SIC Code: 5261
1262 Hemlock Road
Carson, WA 98610
509-427-3200   Contact: Frani Thompson

This nursery currently grows six million conifers and native non-conifers on 180 acres. They
grow over 25 species of shrubs and plants that are largely used for watershed restoration
projects. The tour goes into the field and greenhouses, and into the processing plant (in
spring and fall). You will see an arboretum initially planted in 1912 that still exists. **NOTE:**
Tours by advance reservation. **DIRECTIONS:** Located eight miles north of Carson on
Wind River Hwy, turn left on Hemlock Rd, go about 1/4 mile to the Wind River
Administrative Office on the right.

Advance Notice: Yes   Fee: No   HP Access: No

Aplets & Cotlets Candy (candy mfr)   SIC Code: 2064
117 Mission Street
Cashmere, WA 98815
509-782-2191   Contact: Tour Department

This guided tour will show you the nut sorting, candy kitchen and packaging line. You will also hear a short talk on the history of the company and see how this favorite confection is made. **NOTE:** Tours are conducted every 20 minutes. Adults must accompany children. Free samples. **DIRECTIONS:** Located just one minute off Hwy 2 in Cashmere.

Hours: 8:00 am - 5:00 pm   Days: Monday - Friday
Advance Notice: No   Fee: No   HP Access: Yes

Centralia Knitting Mills, Inc. (apparel)   SIC Code: 2389
1002 West Main Street
Centralia, WA 98531
360-736-3994   Contact: Manager

Tour includes the letter and emblem department, knitting department, sewing and cutting areas, and all phases of manufacturing of award jackets and sweaters. You will also be shown how chenille letters and screen printing are done. **DIRECTIONS:** Centralia can be reached from exit 81 off US Rt 5, about 20 miles south of Olympia. Call for specific directions.

Hours: 7:00 am - 4:30 pm   Days: Monday - Friday
Advance Notice: Yes   Fee: No   HP Access: No

Kulien Hand Made Shoes Factory (boots)   SIC Code: 3149
611 North Tower Street
Centralia, WA 98531
360-736-6943   Contact: Tour Department

Guided tour of factory specializing in hand-made work boots, hiking boots, logging boots and riding boots as well as leather shoes. The factory is family-owned and has been in operation since 1877. **DIRECTIONS:** From Tacoma on I - 5, take exit 82 and go east. Take Harrison Ave east into town. Harrison Ave turns into Main St. Follow straight until you come to Tower Ave and take a left. Look for building with a large shoe on top.

Hours: 8:00 am - 5:00 pm   Days: Tuesday - Friday
      8:00 am - 4:00 pm   Saturday
Advance Notice: Yes   Fee: No   HP Access: No

Pacific Power & Light Company (electric company)   SIC Code: 4911
913 Big Hanaford Road
Centralia, WA 98531
360-736-9901   Contact: Nikki Blakley

This one to two hour tour includes basic orientation on the plant, main transformers, emergency diesel generators, coal storage yard, coal silo, coal conveyors, ash handling equipment and pollution control equipment. **NOTE:** Age 13 and older. **DIRECTIONS:** I - 5 north take Centralia exit 82 left onto Harrison Ave. Follow Johnson Rd to stop sign, go right onto Reynolds Ave to traffic light and left on North Pearl St to Big Hanaford Rd, right 4 miles.

Hours: 9:00 am and 12:45 pm   Days: Tuesday and Thursday
Advance Notice: Yes   Fee: No   HP Access: No

The Chronicle (newspaper)   SIC Code: 2711
321 North Pearl Street
Centralia, WA 98531
360-736-3311   Contact: Teresa Wollan

Tour the pressroom (where newspaper is actually printed), composing room, ad layout, and newsroom (reporters, and AP wire stories, classified area, ad taking). Newspaper has a daily circulation of 16,000. **NOTE:** If there is time, you will learn how to make pressmen hats. Free gifts. **DIRECTIONS:** From Tacoma, take I - 5 south, left off exit 82 on Harrison Ave through three stop lights and take a left over the bridge onto First Ave about one mile, take a right at light onto Pearl St. Plant is located at corner of Pearl and Maple Sts.

Hours: 10:00 am - 4:00 pm   Days: Monday - Friday
Advance Notice: Yes   Fee: No   HP Access: Yes

Moduline Industries, Inc. (mobile home mfr)   SIC Code: 2451
Sturdevant Street - Chehalis Industrial Park
Chehalis, WA 985320
360-748-8881 (800-325-0807)   Contact: Michael Ervin

The 45 - minute tour includes stations in manufacturing mobile homes, beginning with the production line, starting with the chassis, and continue on through to the finished home and shipment. **NOTE:** Age 16 and over. Three days notice required. **DIRECTIONS:** I - 5 to exit 76 east. Go right at first light (Interstate Ave). Go to end at Bishop Rd. Turn right and take first left on Sturdevant Rd. The factory is about two blocks up on the left.

Hours: 8:00-11:00/3:00-4:00   Days: Monday - Friday
Advance Notice: Yes   Fee: No   HP Access: No

Turnbull National Wildlife Refuge (preserve)   SIC Code: 0971
26010 South Smith Road
Cheney, WA 99004
509-235-4723   Contact: Refuge Manager

Tour of 2,200 acres of protected area for migratory waterfowl. Take a self-guided auto tour of five miles through refuge with wildlife oriented opportunities available. Staff is available to present a one-half hour slide show and a talk about the refuge. **DIRECTIONS:** From US Rt 90, south of Spokane, take exit 270 south to Cheney. Call for specific directions.

Hours: Dawn - Dusk   Days: Monday - Sunday
Advance Notice: Yes   Fee: No   HP Access: Yes

Washington Dept. of Fish & Wildlife (hatchery)   SIC Code: 0921
390 North Hofstetter
Colville, WA 99114
509-684-7424   Contact: Jim Ebel

A 30 - minute guided tour and slide show presentation of large rainbow trout in a natural pond. Inside hatchery tours vary with season. **DIRECTIONS:** From Hwy 395, turn east on Hwy 20 then north on Hofstetter.

Hours: 8:00 am - 5:00 pm   Days: Monday - Friday
Advance Notice: Yes   Fee: No   HP Access: Yes

Nooksack State Salmon Hatchery (hatchery)   SIC Code: 0921
State of Washington Dept. of Fish & Wildlife
5048 Deming Road
Deming, WA 98244
360-592-5140   Contact: Bob Molony

This guided tour includes the entire hatchery operation with an oral presentation. From September through November you will observe adult salmon and fish egg taking operation. **DIRECTIONS:** 22 miles east of Bellingham, WA.

Hours: 8:00 am - 4:30 pm   Days: Monday - Friday
Advance Notice: No   Fee: No   HP Access: Yes

Boeing Commercial Airplane Co. (aircraft mfr)   SIC Code: 3721
3003 West Casino Road
Everett, WA 98206
425-342-2121   Contact: Staff

This 90 - minute tour features a slide-tape and movie on the history of Boeing and an overview of the products. You will also have an opportunity to visit the major assembly building and flight line. **NOTE:** Minimum age: 10. Reservations should be made three to six months in advance. **DIRECTIONS:** I - 5, exit 189, west three and one-half miles.

Hours: 9:00 am - 1:00 pm   Days: Monday - Friday
Advance Notice: Yes   Fee: No   HP Access: Yes

Ro-Dar Farms (dairy farm)   SIC Code: 0241
6343 Church Road
Ferndale, WA 98248
360-384-3363   Contact: Rod, Darlene or Kent

Visit this modern dairy handling a 300 cow herd on 150 acres which is located on the edge of a fast growing residential area. See the Herringbone Double 8 Parlor using Westfalia's computerized state-of-the-art milking system. Visualize how a modern dairy facility merges with the challenges of urban growth, environmental pressures, and economic constraints to produce quality products. **NOTE:** Certain aspects of the tour are not handicap accessible. **DIRECTIONS:** On I - 5 exit off 262, turn right, go through Main St, Ferndale until Church Rd, exit on right.

Hours: 10:30 am - 5:00 pm   Days: Monday - Friday
Advance Notice: Yes   Fee: No   HP Access: Limited

Trout Fish Hatchery (hatchery)   SIC Code: 0921
Ford Indian Reservation
Ford, WA 99013
509-258-4269   Contact: Manager

The guided tour includes an explanation of the species of fish, age and the various stages of the fish hatchery program, including a question and answer period. **DIRECTIONS:** Located in the southeast part of the Spokane Indian Reservation. From Rt 2, west of Spokane, follow Rt 231 north about 15 miles.

Hours: 9:00-noon/1:00-4:00   Days: Monday - Sunday
Advance Notice: Yes   Fee: No   HP Access: Yes

Shapes of Clay (pottery products)   SIC Code: 3269
25717 126th Avenue East
Graham, WA 98338
253-847-6454   Contact: Michael Manavie

On this tour, you will watch skilled artisans form and mold the clay sculptures using their customized (secret) process. **DIRECTIONS:** Located about 15 miles southeast of Tacoma on Rt 161.

Hours: 8:00 am - 4:30 pm   Days: Monday - Friday
Advance Notice: Yes   Fee: No   HP Access: Yes

Grand Coulee Dam (utility)   SIC Code: 4939
National Park Service
Grand Coulee, WA 99133
509-633-0881   Contact: Tour Department

Take this guided tour in a glass enclosed incline elevator which travels down the face of Forebay Dam 465 feet. You will learn about the third power plant, artifact room, spillway shows, movies and photographic displays are involved. **DIRECTIONS:** Located at the intersection of Rts 174 and 155 about 75 miles west of Spokane.

Hours: 9:00 am - 5:00 pm   Days: Monday - Friday
Advance Notice: Yes   Fee: No   HP Access: Yes

Boehm's Homemade Swiss Candies (candy mfr)   SIC Code: 2064
255 NE Gilman Boulevard
Issaquah, WA 98027
206-392-6652   Contact: Manager

A 45 - minute tour which includes an art gallery visit to Mr. Boehm's home, where you will watch hand-dipped chocolates being made in an authentic chapel. Escorted tours by appointment only. **DIRECTIONS:** Take exit 17 from eastbound I - 90. Turn right off the exit, then left onto Gilman Blvd.

Hours: 10:30 am and 2:15 pm   Days: Monday, Tuesday, Friday
Advance Notice: Yes   Fee: No   HP Access: Yes

Good Thunder Arts/Blue Earth (pottery products)   SIC Code: 3269
2307 Tuttle Lane
Lummi Island, WA 98262
206-758-7121   Contact: Ria Nickerson or Basil Atkinson

This is a tour of a pottery studio and sandblasting facility where you will see a demonstration of the crafts produced and tour the facility. **DIRECTIONS:** Exit 260 off I - 5, follow directions to Lummi Casino, 10 minute ferry ride to Lummi Island.

Hours: By appointment only
Advance Notice: Yes   Fee: No   HP Access: No

Edaleen Dairy (dairy farm)   SIC Code: 0241
9593 Guide Meridian Road
Lynden, WA 98264
360-354-5342   Contact: Laura Morgan

Tour includes visiting calf barn, watching cows being milked, and the milk bottling process. **NOTE:** Free sample cone of Edaleen Dairy ice cream. **DIRECTIONS:** Take exit 256 (Hwy 539) off I - 5 Fwy north. Go 14 miles north. Located one mile south of Canadian border.

Hours: 9:00 am - 4:00 pm   Days: Monday - Friday
Advance Notice: Yes   Fee: No   HP Access: Yes

Seattle City Light (electric company)   SIC Code: 4911
Boundary Road
Metaline Falls, WA 99153
509-446-3083   Contact: Tour Department

This guided 30 - 45 minute tour includes the underground powerhouse and through cavelike tunnels onto the 340 foot high dam itself. You can also enjoy the panoramic view from the Vista House, perched 500 feet above the Pend Oreille River. **NOTE:** Open Memorial Day to Labor Day. **DIRECTIONS:** Go north from Metaline on Hwy 31, turn on County Rd 62, drive for 11 1/2 miles and turn right on the access road.

Hours: 10:00 am - 5:30 pm,   Days: Thursday - Monday
Advance Notice: No   Fee: No   HP Access: Yes

Miller Art Products (manufacturing)   SIC Code: 3999
Hidden Hollow Ranch
Mica, WA 99023
509-926-5133   Contact: Manager

View custom-made artificial trees, plants and floral arrangements as they are being produced. **NOTE:** Minimum age is 12. **DIRECTIONS:** Mica is southeast of Spokane on Rt 27. Call for further directions.

Hours: 10:00 am - 4:00 pm   Days: Tuesday and Saturday
Advance Notice: Yes   Fee: No   HP Access: Yes

KBRC Radio Station (radio broadcast)   SIC Code: 4832
2222 Riverside Drive
Mount Vernon, WA 98273
360-424-4278   Contact: Station Manager

A 40 - minute walk-through tour of a radio station to observe equipment in use. Schedule your visit in time to watch a live broadcast from the studios. **DIRECTIONS:** From Rt 5 take exit 533 in the northeast corner of the state.

Hours: By appointment only   Days: Monday - Friday
Advance Notice: Yes   Fee: No   HP Access: yes

L.T. Mike Webster Nursery (floriculture)   SIC Code: 0181
9805 Bloomberg Street
Olympia, WA 98504
360-753-5305   Contact: Manager

This one-half hour tour includes seed extraction, bare root, forest nursery seedlings and green-houses. Learn about the entire process from their expert staff. **DIRECTIONS:** Follow US Rt 5 to exit 99 to Bloomberg. Take left and follow signs.

Hours: 8:00 am - 4:30 pm   Days: Monday - Friday
Advance Notice: Yes   Fee: No   HP Access: No

The Olympian (newspaper)   SIC Code: 2711
1268 East 4th Avenue
Olympia, WA 98506
360-754-5416   Contact: Tour Department

This guided tour will take you through the newspaper departments including advertising, composing, press, news, accounting and circulation. The tour guide will explain the function of each department and answer any questions. **DIRECTIONS:** Fourth Ave runs through the center of town just north of US Rt 5.

Hours: 1:00 - 4:00 pm   Days: Wednesday
Advance Notice: Yes   Fee: No   HP Access: Yes

Pasco General Mail Facility (postal)   SIC Code: 4311
3500 West Court Street
Pasco, WA 99301-9998
509-547-8481   Contact: Connie Beutler

The tour consists of an overview of the mail processing operation using new automated mechanized equipment. Follow hundreds of thousands of pieces of mail being routed through this central distribution facility. **DIRECTIONS:** From Richland, go south on George Washington Way, staying in the right lane. Take exit marked "Pasco" which is I - 182. Stay on I - 182 to exit 12A. As you come around the curve, exit off onto Court St. Take a right at the stop light. After the next light you will see the Post Office on your left.

Hours: By appointment only
Advance Notice: Yes   Fee: No   HP Access: Yes

Columbia Crest Winery (winery)   SIC Code: 2084
Columbia Crest Drive - Highway 221
Paterson, WA 99345
509-875-2061   Contact: Linda Mercer

A self-guided tour of the winemaking areas where you will see the processing equipment used. The winery is surrounded by 2,000 acres of estate vineyard. **NOTE**: You will have the opportunity to taste Chardonnet red and white wines as well as many other wines. **DIRECTIONS:** Located 26 miles south of Prosser on Hwy 221 in the eastern part of the state.

Hours: 10:00 am - 4:30 pm   Days: Monday - Sunday
Advance Notice: No   Fee: No   HP Access: Yes

Fax Flux Test Facility (research)   SIC Code: 8731
1100 Jadwin Avenue
Richland, WA 99352.
509-376-3026   Contact: Jan Larkin/Denise Connor

Slide show and guided tours of exhibits and scale models of the Fax Flux Test Facility. The sodium-cooled test reactor is located nearby. **NOTE:** Junior high age and up is preferred. **DIRECTIONS:** From US Rt 82 take exit 102. Follow Rt 182 for approximately six miles. Richland is located in the south central part of the state.

Hours: 10:00 am - 4:00 pm   Days: Monday - Friday
Advance Notice: Yes   Fee: No   HP Access: Yes

Westinghouse Hanford Company (utility)   SIC Code: 4939
P.O.Box 1970 B3-27
Richland, WA 99352
509-376-5995   Contact: Denise Conner

A three hour bus tour of the Hanford Site with an escort on board to explain the operations at the 560 square mile site. **NOTE:** Must call a week in advance. US citizens only and must have valid photo identification. Minimum age is 15 for the Hanford Site. Tours begin at the Federal Building near the Red Lion Motor Inn. **DIRECTIONS:** Richland is located in the southern part of the state midway between Spokane and Seattle on the Columbia River.

Hours: 8:00 am - 5:00 pm   Days: Monday - Saturday
Advance Notice: Yes   Fee: No   HP Access: Yes

Wilcox Farms, Inc. (dairy farm)   SIC Code: 0241
40400 Harts Lake Valley Road
Roy, WA 98580
306-458-7774 (800-568-6456)   Contact: Tricia Buti

This is a two hour guided tour through the dairy barns where the herds are, to the milking parlor and on to the packaging plant. You will also tour the egg packaging plant where everything is fully automated. Farm includes over 1,000,000 laying hens and pullets and more than 54,000 eggs are processed each hour and packaged for supermarkets and restaurants. **DIRECTIONS:** I - 5 south of Tacoma to exit 127 (Hwy 512 east) two and a half miles to the Pacific Ave exit (Hwy 7). Go right five miles to the "Roy Y". Take right fork through Roy to McKenna and turn left at the BP Gas station. Take Harts Lake Rd about four and one-half miles to Harts Lake Valley Rd. The office is on the right.

Hours: By appointment only   Days: Monday - Friday
Advance Notice: Yes   Fee: No   HP Access: No

Northwestern Glass (glass mfr)   SIC Code: 3229
5802 East Marginal Way South
Seattle, WA 98134
206-762-0660   Contact: Manager

This 45 - minute tour includes viewing the manufacturing process of glass containers from raw material to finished product, packed in cartons ready for shipment to customer.
DIRECTIONS: Located in the downtown area, south of the King Dome.

Hours: By appointment only   Days: Monday - Friday
Advance Notice: Yes   Fee: No   HP Access: Yes

Roffe Company (apparel)   SIC Code: 2389
808 Howell Street
Seattle, WA 98101
206-622-0456   Contact: Manager

Tours are intended for adults and students in advanced education where they will be able to observe the manufacturing of ski wear. **DIRECTIONS:** Located at the corner of 8th and Howell in the downtown section of city.

Hours: 9:00 am - 5:00 pm   Days: Monday - Friday
Advance Notice: Yes   Fee: No   HP Access: Yes

Seattle Goodwill Facilities Tour (vocational tng)   SIC Code: 8331
1400 South Dearborn Street Lane
Seattle, WA 98144
206-329-1000   Contact: Lorraine Weeks

The tour includes a close-up look at the processing plant which handles over 6,300 tons annually of donated clothing and household items. You will be able to trace the production route that donated items travel before being sold in the stores, from dock unloading to sorting to cleaning to packaging to pricing. If desired, you can also visit the store and vocational and adult education classrooms. **DIRECTIONS:** I - 5 to Dearborn St exit, head east on Dearborn.

Hours: 8:30 am - 3:30 pm   Days: Monday - Friday
Advance Notice: Yes   Fee: No   HP Access: Yes

West Point Treatment Plant (water treatment)   SIC Code: 4941
Fort Lawton Discovery Park
Seattle, WA 98199
206-447-6801   Contact: Manager

This is a one hour tour of a treatment plant facility where you will follow the progress from the time sewage enters the plant to outfall; influent channel, sedimentation and aeration tanks, digesters, engine rooms, dewatering facility and generators for methane power. **NOTE:** Ages 10 and over. **DIRECTIONS:** Take Fairview exit west from US 5, just north of the downtown area to Nickerson St. Follow signs to Discovery Park.

Hours: 9:00 am - 3:30 pm   Days: Tuesday - Friday
Advance Notice: Yes   Fee: No   HP Access: Yes

Weyerhaeuser Sequim Seed Orchard (floriculture)   SIC Code: 0181
445 Kitchen-Dick Lane Road
Sequim, WA 98382
425-683-6710   Contact: Manager

Tour covers the orchard operation of the grafting, and flower stimulation cultural practices. **DIRECTIONS:** Located in the Olympic Mountains National Park, west of Seattle on Hwy 101 near Port Townsend.

Hours: 8:00 am - 2:00 pm   Days: Monday- Friday
Advance Notice: Yes   Fee: No   HP Access: No

City of Spokane Upriver Plant (utility)   SIC Code: 4939
East 914 North Foothills Drive
Spokane, WA 99207
509-625-6641   Contact: Leon Sproule

Tour will consist of a view of the aquifer in well, the pumping plant and the hydroelectric
generating plant. **NOTE:** Must call in advance to arrange tour. Groups welcome up to 20
people. **DIRECTIONS:** From the center of town, follow Trent Rd east 1/4 mile beyond
junction with Mission 15 waterworks, take left.

Hours: 8:00 am - 3:00 pm   Days: Monday - Friday
Advance Notice: Yes   Fee: No   HP Access: No

KHQ-TV Studios (TV broadcast)   SIC Code: 4833
South 4202 Regal Street
Spokane, WA 99223
509-488-6000   Contact: Manager

A 30 - 60 minute tour includes newsroom, news and production studios, AM and FM radio
stations, master control, film and office area. May be able to meet air talent if they are in the
building. **DIRECTIONS:** Located south of Lincoln Park off of 29th Ave.

Hours: By appointment only
Advance Notice: Yes   Fee: No   HP Access: Yes

National Weather Service (weather forecast svs)   SIC Code: 8999
2601 North Rambo Road
Spokane, WA 99224-9164
509-244-0110 x 222   Contact: John S. Livingston

View weather measuring devices, facsimile receivers, teletypes and charts used in weather
forecasting. **NOTE:** Third grade and older. **DIRECTIONS:** From the Interstate, take exit
275 (Spokane Airport exit). When road divides, take road away from airport. You will go
through a little town 'Airway Heights' about four miles from the exit. Turn right on Rambo
Rd (one mile from the Texaco Gas Station). Go past railroad tracks for two miles.

Hours: Noon - 3:00 pm   Days: Monday - Friday
Advance Notice: Yes   Fee: No   HP Access: No

Joseph T. Ryerson & Sons (metal good mfr)   SIC Code: 3499
207 North Freya Street
Spokane, WA 99202
509-535-1581   Contact: Manager

View activities of a multi-product service center for metal electric-eye burning equipment, shears, hacksaws, and fabrication of reinforced steel. **NOTE:** Junior high age and older **DIRECTIONS:** Take exit 283 north from US Rt 90. Call for further directions.

Hours: By appointment only
Advance Notice: Yes   Fee: No   HP Access: No

Safeway Stores, Inc. (food warehouse)   SIC Code: 5141
5707 North Freya
Spokane, WA 99207
509-482-4023   Contact: Manager

A walking tour of over seven acres of various warehouses including Perishable Goods, Frozen Foods and Groceries. You will observe the receiving, storing and distribution of retail food store merchandise. **NOTE:** Minimum age: 10. Bring coats. **DIRECTIONS:** Take exit 283B north from US Rt 90. Go east on Francis and left back onto Freya.

Hours: 10:00 am - 1:00 pm   Days: Monday - Friday
Advance Notice: Yes   Fee: No   HP Access: No

Spokane Wastewater Treatment Plant(water trmt)   SIC Code: 4941
4401 North Aubrey I. White Parkway
Spokane, WA 99205-4600
509-625-4600   Contact: Doreen Summers

On this one and one-half hour tour you will walk with a tour guide through the modern activated sludge Wastewater Treatment Plant. Plant operation and process will be explained using a model of the plant. **DIRECTIONS:** Take the Maple St exit off I - 90. Go north, cross bridge, take a left at the second light (Maxwell St). Go west on Maxwell and as the road bends it will become Pettet Dr. Go down the hill and under the bridge. Continue to follow the river for approximately two and 4/10 miles. Stay to the left of the "Y". Go to main office.

Hours: By appointment only
Advance Notice: yes   Fee: No   HP Access: Yes

Yakima Gourmet Cheese Co. (cheese processor)   SIC Code: 2022
105 South First Street
Sunnyside, WA 98944
509-837-6005   Contact: Manager

Tour the factory aging rooms specializing in Dutch Gouda cheese. **NOTE:** Free samples.
DIRECTIONS: From US Rt 82 take exit 67. Sunnyside is located in the south central part
of the state.

Hours: 9:30 am - 5:00 pm   Days: Monday - Saturday
Advance Notice: No   Fee: No   HP Access: Yes

The Suquamish Tribe (hatchery)   SIC Code: 0921
Indianola Road NE
Suquamish ,WA 98392
360-589-3142   Contact: Gary Ives, Manager

A 30 - 45 minute tour of a small salmon hatchery which has indoor holding tanks and a
holding pool. Spawning season: mid - September through mid - October (Chinook); late
October through mid - December (Chum); and mid - October through mid - November
(Coho). **NOTE:** Closed noon to 1:00 pm. **DIRECTIONS:** Located northwest of Seattle in
the Bremerton area. Call for specific directions.

Hours: 8:00 am - 4:00 pm   Days: Monday - Friday
Advance Notice: Yes   Fee: No   HP Access: Yes

McFarland Cascade (lumber treating)   SIC Code: 2491
1640 East Marc Street
Tacoma, WA 98421
253-572-3033   Contact: Manager

A 60 - 90 minute tour of a wood treating plant, where you will learn about wood preservation
and lumber treatment. **DIRECTIONS:** Please call for specific directions.

Hours: By appointment only
Advance Notice: Yes   Fee: No   HP Access: No

Parker Paint Manufacturing Co. (paint products)   SIC Code: 2851
3101 South Tacoma Way
Tacoma, WA 98503
253-473-1122   Contact: Manager

Brief talk on marketing and the manufacture of paint, followed by a tour of the actual making, packaging and storing of paint. **DIRECTIONS:** Located between Pine and 38th near Costco in the center of the city.

Hours: By appointment only   Fee: No   HP Access: No

The Tacoma News Tribune (newspaper)   SIC Code: 2711
1950 South State Street
Tacoma, WA 98405
253-597-8511   Contact: Joan - Marketing Department

A one hour tour is conducted through the production and newsroom departments, usually coinciding with that day's printing of the paper. A tour guide will provide a short description of production techniques before the tour begins. **DIRECTIONS:** Located in the heart of the city near the famous Tacoma Dome and at the intersection of 19th and State Sts.

Hours: 1:00 pm   Days: Monday, Wednesday, Thursday
Advance Notice: Yes   Fee: No   HP Access: Yes

The Columbian (newspaper)   SIC Code: 2711
701 8th Street, West
Vancouver, WA 98666
360-694-3391   Contact: Jeanne Peters

A tour of Vancouver's daily newspaper will take you through the various departments.
NOTE: Children must be in the fourth grade and older. No tours in August or December.
DIRECTIONS: From downtown City Hall area, follow Broadway south to 8th St west.

Hours: By appointment only
Advance Notice: Yes   Fee: No   HP Access: Yes

Pendleton Woolen Mills (woolen mill)   SIC Code: 2231
2 17th Street
Washougal, WA 98671
360-835-2131   Contact: Tour Department

A one hour tour of the mill will show you the process firsthand from the state-of-the-art dye
house, through spinning and weaving, to the finishing of their distinctive Indian blankets.
NOTE: Mill store. Large groups by advance reservations. **DIRECTIONS:** From I - 5 or
I - 205, take Hwy 14 east to the 15th St/Washougal exit. Turn left and proceed one block
north to A St. Turn right and proceed two blocks to 17th St. Turn right and enter parking lot.

Hours: 9:00,10:00,11:00 am   Days: Monday - Friday
Advance Notice: Yes   Fee: No   HP Access: No

Spokane Tribal Kokanee Hatchery (hatchery)   SIC Code: 0921
P.O.Box 100
Wellpinit, WA 99040
509-258-7297   Contact: Delbert Brown or Tim Peone

Guided tour through the fish rearing facility by hatchery personnel which will also include
information on local Indian tribal artifacts and a history of the area. **DIRECTIONS:** Three
miles west, one-half mile south of Ford, WA. West on Ford/Wellpinit Hwy, south on Martha
Boardman Rd.

Hours: 9:00 am - 4:00 pm   Days: Monday - Friday
Advance Notice: Yes   Fee: No   HP Access: Yes

Rocky Reach Dam (utility)   SIC Code: 4939
P.O.Box 1231
Wenatchee, WA 98807
509-663-7522   Contact: Bonnie Brawley

A one hour self-guided tour will consist of an informative walk from the Visitors Center to
the generator floor and spillway viewing areas; and a hard hat tour down to the shaft of a
generating unit. **NOTE:** For maintenance reasons, tours are subject to cancellation
periodically. **DIRECTIONS:** Located on the Columbia River on Hwy 97A just seven miles
north of Wenatchee.

Hours: 9:00 am - 5:00 pm   Days: Monday - Sunday
Advance Notice: Yes   Fee: No   HP Access: No

Chateau Ste. Michelle Winery (winery)   SIC Code: 2084
14111 NE 145th Street
Woodinville, WA 98072
206-488-1133   Contact: Judy Hilton

Tour of the winery facilities, which includes the cellar and bottling line. Wines include
Merlot, Cabernet, Sauvignon and Chardonnay. **NOTE:** Tasting is also included in the tour.
DIRECTIONS: Traveling north or south on I - 405, take exit 23 east (SR 522, Monroe-
Wenatchee). Follow SR 522 to the Woodinville exit. At stop sign turn right. Continue to
NE 175th St, turn right. Go over railroad tracks to the stop sign, turn left onto Hwy 202 for
approximately two miles.

Hours: 10:00 am - 5:00 pm   Days: Monday - Friday
Advance Notice: Yes   Fee: No   HP Access: Yes

Boise Cascade Corporation (lumber mill)   SIC Code: 2421
805 North 7th Street
Yakima, WA 98901
509-453-3131   Contact: Tour Department

Tour two sawmills, planing and shipping (one hour) or tour a plywood plant (one and one-
half hours). **NOTE:** Must make reservations a few days in advance. Long pants must be
worn and no open toed shoes are allowed. You will be required to wear goggles, hard hats
and ear protection during the tour. Minimum age: Eight years. **DIRECTIONS:** Located in
the center of town. Please call for specific directions.

Hours: 9:00 am and 12:30 pm   Days: Monday - Friday
Advance Notice: Yes   Fee: No   HP Access: No

Capitol Theatre (theater)   SIC Code: 7922
19 South Third Street
Yakima, WA 98901
509-575-6267   Contact: Manager

This tour highlights a rare look behind the curtain, the exquisite hand painted dome ceiling and a visit with "Shorty" the theatre's ghost. Tour meets in the main lobby on Third St.
DIRECTIONS: On I - 82 Hwy, take the Yakima Ave/Terrace Heights exit (from the north exit 33B), from the south (exit 33). Go west on Yakima Ave, towards the city center, continue (approximately eight blocks) to Third St, turn left. The theatre is in the middle of the block on the left.

Hours: By appointment only
Advance Notice: Yes   Fee: No   HP Access: No

Dowty Aerospace Corp. (aircraft parts)   SIC Code: 3728
2720 West Washington Avenue
Yakima, WA 98909
509-248-5000   Contact: Tour Department

A 30 - minute tour on design, prototype, engineering test, manufacturing and quality control areas of the latest state-of-the-art aerospace hydraulic component manufacturer. **NOTE:** Minimum age: 16. **DIRECTIONS:** Located at the air terminal.

Hours: 8:00 am - 5:00 pm   Days: Monday - Friday
Advance Notice: Yes   Fee: No   HP Access: Yes

Pepsi Cola Bottling Company (soft drinks)   SIC Code: 2086
1001 South 1st Street
Yakima, WA 98901
509-248-1313   Contact: Manager

This is a 45 - minute walking tour of the Pepsi Cola Bottling and Noel canning plants.
DIRECTIONS: Located in the center of town. Please call for specific directions.

Hours: 10:00 am - 3:00 pm   Days: Monday - Friday
Advance Notice: Yes   Fee: No   HP Access: No

Western Recreation Vehicles (trailer mfr)   SIC Code: 3792
3401 West Washington Avenue
Yakima, WA 98903
509-457-4133   Contact: Tour Department

This 45 - minute tour shows exactly how an Alpenlite trailer camper is made, from frame
work to completed assembly. You will observe the quality control standards used to produce
this high quality product. **DIRECTIONS:** Located just south of the center of town.

Hours: 1:00 pm   Days: Monday - Friday
Advance Notice: Yes   Fee: No   HP Access: Yes

WSWP-TV (TV broadcast)   SIC Code: 4833
Airport Road & Industrial Drive
Beckley, WV 25801
304-255-1501   Contact: Cindy Martin

A tour of this television facility will include the graphics, audio production, editing areas, as well as the master control room and studio. **NOTE:** Mainly geared towards students, but adults are welcome. Must be scheduled in advance. **DIRECTIONS:** Airport Rd exit, off I - 64, one mile straight ahead.

Hours: 9:00 am - 5:00 pm   Days: Monday - Friday
Advance Notice: Yes   Fee: No   HP Access: Yes

Pilgrim Glass Corporation (glass mfr)   SIC Code: 3229
64 Airport Road
Ceredo, WV 25507
304-453-3553   Contact: Lori Watts

You are promised VIP treatment when you visit this company where you will view glass-blowers producing glowing exotic colors in the making of Cameo and Cranberry glassware. You will tour from an observation deck which overlooks the entire work area, or if available, you may take a guided tour. **DIRECTIONS:** From I - 64, take exit 1 (Kenova exit) and follow signs to airport. Facility is located approximately one mile.

Hours: 9:00 am - 5:00 pm   Days: Monday - Thursday
Advance Notice: Yes   Fee: No   HP Access: Yes

National Radio Astronomy Obs. (observatory)   SIC Code: 8733
Route 28/92
Green Bank, WV 24944
304-456-2011   Contact: Sue Ann Heatherly

See where cosmic history is studied through interstellar impulses captured on radio telescopes. **DIRECTIONS:** Located on Rt 28/92 in the Monongahela National Forest. This is due east of Charleston, near the Virginia border.

Hours: By appointment only
Advance Notice: Yes   Fee: No   HP Access: Yes

Huntington Processing & Dist. Center (postal)   SIC Code: 4311
1000 Virginia Avenue West
Huntington, WV 25704
304-526-9600   Contact: Debbie Wolfe

A tour of the U.S. Postal facility will show you the mail processing floor and the carrier section. **DIRECTIONS:** 11th St west, towards the river.

Hours: 10:00 am - 3:00 pm   Days: Monday - Friday
Advance Notice: Yes   Fee: No   HP Access: Yes

Glass Swan, Inc. (glass mfr)   SIC Code: 3229
Main Street
Jane Lew, WV 26378
304-884-4014   Contact: Manager

This is an outlet for West Virginia glass which also features a glass blowing studio for you to watch craftsmen at work. **DIRECTIONS:** From Morgantown in the north, follow US Rt 79 south to exit 105, about 45 miles.

Hours: 9:00 am - 3:30 pm   Days: Monday - Friday
Advance Notice: No   Fee: No   HP Access: No

Potomac Highland Winery (winery) SIC Code: 2084
Route 1 - Fried Meat Ridge Road
Keyser, WV 26726
304-788-3066 Contact: Charles Whitehill

Come tour and taste the award-winning wines, see the vineyard and the great Potomac Highland view. Wines include Chardonnay, Riesling, Seyval Blanc, Pinot Noir and Seyval Blush. **DIRECTIONS:** From Keyser, take Rt 46 east for four miles, turn right on Knobley Rd for 8/10 mile, bear left on Fountain-Headsville Rd for one and 2/10 miles, turn right on Fried Meat Ridge Rd for one and one-half miles and look for vineyard and sign on left.

Hours: By appointment only
Advance Notice: Yes Fee: No HP Access: Yes

Blenko Glass Company (glass mfr) SIC Code: 3229
Fairground Road
Milton, WV 25541
304-743-9081 Contact: Manager

World famous for hand blown glassware and stained glass, this visit will take you to the observation area where you will observe the various steps in handcrafting glass; the furnace where silica sand, combined with other materials, is fueled under intense heat; the gatherer who takes from this mass a small "gob" of glass which he delivers to a blower, who blows the gob into a form or shape, using tools similar to those used centuries ago. **NOTE:** Not open first two weeks in July and week between Christmas and New Years. **DIRECTIONS:** From I - 64, exit 28 towards Milton, right at Rt 60 and left onto Fairground Rd.

Hours: 8:00-noon/12:30-3:15 Days: Monday - Friday
Advance Notice: No Fee: No HP Access: No

Brown's Creation in Clay (pottery products) SIC Code: 3269
Route 10
Morgantown, WV 26505
304-296-6656 Contact: Anna Brown

Visit the studio and see demonstrations of hand built stoneware pottery using herb imprints in clay. Seasonal tour of herb garden and drying shed. **NOTE:** Gift shop. **DIRECTIONS:** From I - 68 get off at exit 1, turn right. Go about one and one-half miles on Rt 119 south. Turn right after hardware store and continue for 7/8 mile to second house on left.

Hours: 4:00 - 5:00 pm Days: Monday - Saturday
Advance Notice: Yes Fee: No HP Access: No

Fork's of Cheat Winery (winery)   SIC Code: 2084
Rt 4 - Stewartstown Road
Morgantown, WV 26505
304-598-2019   Contact: Jerry Deal

Tour this family owned vineyard and winery producing wines from American varietals and French hybrid grapes and see the process involved in creating these fine wines.
DIRECTIONS: Located six miles north of Morgantown.

Hours: 10:00 am - 5:00 pm   Days: Monday - Saturday
Advance Notice: Yes   Fee: No   HP Access: No

Gentile Glass Company (glass mfr)   SIC Code: 3229
425 Industrial Avenue
Morgantown, WV 26505
304-599-2750   Contact: John Gentile

This tour features a great selection of hand-cut lead crystal, tableware, handmade paperweights, art glass and antique reproductions. You will visit the cutting department where items of crystal is hand-cut. See the very interesting processes from beginning to end.
DIRECTIONS: Exit 155 from I - 79 to WV Rt 7 east and Rt 19 south over bridge. Left at first stop light, one block to University Ave, left down hill one block to Industrial Ave, turn right, one half-block to factory.

Hours: 8:00-11:00/12:30-2:30   Days: Monday - Friday
Advance Notice: No   Fee: No   HP Access: No

Mt. Storm Power Station (utility)   SIC Code: 4939
HC 76, Box 430
Mt. Storm, WV 26739
304-259-5272   Contact: Louanna Carr

A two hour tour of the General Station, Coal Yard area and the new Scrubber Facility.
DIRECTIONS: Rt 93, approximately 25 miles west of Canaan Valley Resort.

Hours: By appointment only
Advance Notice: Yes   Fee: No   HP Access: Yes

Dalzell Corp. (glass mfr)   SIC Code: 3229
802 Parkway
New Martinsville, WV 26155
304-455-2900   Contact: Debbie Roberts

A knowledgeable guide will take you through the working factory to show the various steps
in producing all hand-pressed glassware. This company is noted for its ruby colored glass,
Viking features glass bowls, plates and other pieces of delicate, handcrafted glassware.
NOTE: Retail store. Advance notice for groups. **DIRECTIONS:** WV Rt 2 south (or
north). Turn at first light south of Ohio Rt 7. Right on First St, next to factory.

Hours: 9:00-10:45;12:15-3:45   Days: Monday - Friday
Advance Notice: Yes   Fee: No   HP Access: No

Homer Laughlin China Company (chinaware)   SIC Code: 3262
Harrison Street - State Route 2
Newell, WV 26050
304-387-1300   Contact: Sue Watson

Creators of the brightly colored, collectible Fiesta dinnerware, the company reintroduced the
popular line in 1986, marking its golden anniversary. On this tour you will see china being
made and decorated in the largest restaurant china manufacturing facility in the United States.
DIRECTIONS: Newell is located at the northernmost tip of the state between the Ohio and
Pennsylvania borders. From Wheeling in the south, follow Rt 7.

Hours: 10:30 am and 1:00 pm   Days: Monday - Friday
Advance Notice: No   Fee: No   HP Access: Yes

Robert F. Pliska & Company Winery (winery)   SIC Code: 2084
101 Piterra Place
Purgitsville, WV 26852
304-289-3900   Contact: Manager

Come tour the winery and taste the award-winning Seyval, Foch, Chandler and Cabernet
wines. **NOTE:** Picnic area. **DIRECTIONS:** Purgitsville is located in the eastern pan-
handle south of Cumberland and Keyser on Rt 220. Take Rt 50 to US 220 south.

Hours: 1:00 - 4:00 pm   Days: Tuesday - Saturday
Advance Notice: No   Fee: No   HP Access: No

Schneider's Winery (winery) SIC Code: 2084
Jersey Mountain Road
Romney, WV 26757
304-822-7434 Contact: Steve Snider

See every aspect of the winemaking process with hands on demonstration at West Virginia's largest winery. Specialty wines include Foch, Seyval and fruit wines, Niagara and Concord. **NOTE:** Wine tasting, picnic area. **DIRECTIONS:** Two miles north of US Rt 50 on Rt 5 (Jersey Mountain Rd).

Hours: 12 noon - 6:00 pm   Days: Wednesday - Sunday
Advance Notice: No   Fee: No   HP Access: Yes

Brooke Glass Company (glass mfr) SIC Code: 3229
6th and Yankee Streets
Wellsburg, WV 26070
304-737-3461 Contact: Lorraine DeWitt

Operating along the Ohio River since 1879, you will see production from molten glass to the finished product, including hand painting of glassware by the artists. Specialties include lamp and lighting fixture parts, candle accessories and colored glass. **NOTE:** Factory shutdown first two weeks in July. Gift shop. **DIRECTIONS:** Take Rt 2, 15 miles north of Wheeling; 12 miles south of Weirton.

Hours: 10:00 am and 2:00 pm   Days: Monday- Friday
Advance Notice: No   Fee: No   HP Access: No

Reynolds Sugar Bush, Inc. (maple syrup)   SIC Code: 0831
W 18850 Maple Road
Aniwa, WI 54408
715-449-2057   Contact: Juan Reynolds

See the world's largest single sugarbush and see the processing of pure maple syrup. **NOTE:** Tours are best during sugaring when the sap is being gathered in late March and early April. **DIRECTIONS:** Intersection of Hwy 45 and 52.

Hours: 9:00 am - 3:00 pm   Days: Monday - Friday
Advance Notice: Yes   Fee: No   HP Access: Yes

Appleton Brewery (brewery)   SIC Code: 2082
1004 S. Olde Oneida St.
Appleton, WI 54915
920-735-0507   Contact: John Jungers

Take a 15 - minute tour and see a restored brewery built in 1869 which produces Adler Brau Beer. **NOTE:** Small charge for beer samples and snacks. **DIRECTIONS:** Southeast end of Skyline Oneida St Bridge. Take Appleton St south.

Hours: Afternoons   Days: Monday - Saturday
Advance Notice: Yes   Fee: $3.00   HP Access: Yes

Mossholder Cheese Factory (cheese processor)   SIC Code: 2022
4017 North Richmond Street
Appleton, WI 54915
920-734-7575   Contact: Manager

Visit this small, family-operated cheese factory and see some of Wisconsin's finest cheese being made and taste the results. **DIRECTIONS:** Located in the eastern part of the state on beautiful Lake Winnebago. Call for specific directions.

Hours: 9:00 am - 5:00 pm   Days: Monday - Friday
Advance Notice: Yes   Fee: No   HP Access: Yes

Vande Walle's Candies (candy mfr) SIC Code: 2064
400 Mall Drive
Appleton, WI 54915
920-738-7799 Contact: Don Vande Walle Sr.

A self-guided tour through the manufacturing plant where you will see how homemade confections are made, as well as delicious bakery items and smooth, creamy ice cream. **NOTE:** Free samples. **DIRECTIONS:** From Hwy 41, take exit 125 west one block and then go north two blocks.

Hours: 9:00 am - 4:00 pm Days: Monday - Friday
Advance Notice: No Fee: No HP Access: No

Foremost Farms, USA (cheese processor) SIC Code: 2022
300 Hwy 14
Arena, WI 53503
608-753-2661 Contact: Manager

Through a viewing area, you will watch as some of Wisconsin's finest cheese is being made. **NOTE**: Sample their tasty Co-Jack, Colby, Pepper Jack and Vegetable Jack cheeses. **DIRECTIONS:** From Milwaukee take I - 94 to I - 90 into Madison. Stay on Rts 12 and 18 to Hwy 14. Take a right at the stop sign. Follow Hwy 14 to Arena. Plant is on left. Look for the large mouse on the sign.

Hours: 8:00 am - 3:00 pm Days: Monday - Saturday
Advance Notice: No Fee: No HP Access: Yes

Honey Acres (honey) SIC Code: 0279
Highway 67 North
Ashippun, WI 53003
800-558-7745 Contact: Kay Diehnelt

Tour of this honey processing plant where you will see liquid honey filling, and honey gift pack assembly lines. You will also tour "Honey of a Museum". See a slide show on beekeeping, displays of beekeeping around the world, pollination and beeswax, and a live bee tree. **NOTE:** Honey tasting. Tours on Saturday and Sunday from May 15 through October 30. **DIRECTIONS:** Hwy I - 94 from Milwaukee or Madison exit Hwy 67 north 13 miles north of Oconomowee on Hwy 67.

Hours: 9:00 am - 3:30 pm Days: Monday - Friday
Noon - 4:00 pm Saturday - Sunday
Advance Notice: Yes Fee: No HP Access: Yes

Carousel Creations (wood products)   SIC Code: 2499
Highway 63
Barronett, WI 54814
715-822-4189   Contact: Ron Helstern

This 45 - minute guided tour will take you behind the scenes where you will watch wood-carvers create carousel animals (weighing up to 250 pounds) in the same fashion used a century ago. **NOTE:** Individuals can walk around the showroom. Guided tours are for groups of 15 or more. There is no fee for self-guided tour. **DIRECTIONS:** From I - 90 go to Baldwin and take Hwy 63 to Barronett. Look for western style front porch sign on left.

Hours: 8:00 am - 5:00 pm   Days: Monday - Friday
Advance Notice: No   Fee: $2.00   HP Access: Yes

Booth Cooperage (wood products)   SIC Code: 2499
1 Washington Avenue
Bayfield, WI 54814
715-779-3400   Contact: Manager

Watch a local cooper at work assembling barrels around the huge open hearth. This is an interesting and educational tour. **NOTE:** Tours from Memorial Day to early October. Guided tours upon request for large groups. Buses welcome. A slide presentation is available for viewing when the cooper is not at work. **DIRECTIONS:** Located on Washington Ave and the Lake Shore (across from the Madeline Island Ferry landing).

Hours: 9:30 am - 5:30 pm   Days: Monday - Friday
Advance Notice: No   Fee: No   HP Access: Yes

Alto Dairy (cheese processor)   SIC Code: 2022
307 North Clark Street
Black Creek, WI 54106
920-984-3331   Contact: Manager

A visit to this dairy which show you how Cheddar, Colby, Brick and Edam cheese are made. **NOTE:** You will be able to sample some of each. **DIRECTIONS:** Located at the junction of Rts 47 and 54, west of Green Bay.

Hours: 8:00 am - 5:00 pm   Days: Monday - Friday
Advance Notice: No   Fee: No   HP Access: Yes

Cedar Creek Winery (winery)   SIC Code: 2084
N 70 W 6340 Bridge Road
Cedarburg, WI 53012
414-377-8020 (800-827-8020)   Contact: Connie Niebauer

On this tour of a 130 year old woolen mill building, you will hear the history of the building, and an explanation of how the wines are made and bottled. This will be followed by wine tasting with cheese and crackers. **DIRECTIONS:** Located in downtown Cedarburg, 17 miles north of Milwaukee, WI. Call for specific directions.

Hours: 10:00 am - 5:00 pm   Days: Monday - Sunday
Advance Notice: No   Fee: $2.00   HP Access: No

Leinenkugel Brewing Co. (brewery)   SIC Code: 2082
1-3 Jefferson Avenue
Chippewa Falls, WI 54729
715-723-5557   Contact: Karla Rubenzer

This 30 - minute tour will include a brief history and viewing of the brew house, the fermenting room, bottling/can viewing and packaging areas. **NOTE:** Gift shop. **DIRECTIONS:** Located on Hwy 124 north.

Hours: 9:30 am - 3:30 pm   Days: Monday - Saturday (June, July, August)
       11:00 am and 1:00 pm   Monday - Friday (September - May)
Advance Notice: Yes   Fee: No   HP Access: No

Eau Galle Cheese Factory Inc. (cheese processor)   SIC Code: 2022
N6765 State Highway 25
Durand, WI 54736
715-283-4211   Contact: Carol Buhlman

On this 45 - minute tour you will have the opportunity to walk through the plant and get a first
hand look at cheesemaking. There is also a viewing window and a video presentation.
NOTE: Tours given Memorial Day - Labor Day. Please call ahead for large groups.
DIRECTIONS: Located on St Hwy 25 (north of Durand) and 20 minutes south of
Menomonie. Call for specific directions.

Hours: 11:00 am   Days: Saturdays
Advance Notice: Yes   Fee: No   HP Access: Yes

Otter Rapids Hydroelectric Dam (utility)   SIC Code: 4939
Highway 70 West
Eagle River, WI 54521
715-479-3183 (800-450-7260)   Contact: Manager

Take this self-guided tour of the generating plant which you will view through a glass
window. **DIRECTIONS:** Located north of Wausau and Rhinelander, continue on Rt 17 to
town. Call for specific directions.

Hours: By appointment only
Advance Notice: Yes   Fee: No   HP Access: No

Duesenberg Motors (automobile mfr)   SIC Code: 3711
1006 Academy Street
Elroy, WI 53929
608-462-8100   Contact: Tour Department

See reproductions of this famous automobile being made. **NOTE:** Tours by appointment
only. **DIRECTIONS:** From US Rt 90/94 take exit 61 Rt 80 or exit 60 Rt 82 to Elroy.

Hours: 8:00 am - 3:30 pm   Days: Friday - Sunday
Advance Notice: Yes   Fee: No   HP Access: Yes

School Grove Cheese Factory (cheese processor)   SIC Code: 2022
W 2346 US Highway 10
Forest Junction, WI 54123
414-989-1073   Contact: Carl or Julie Ruedinger

You will tour the processing facility and learn the procedure for making cheese and see the equipment in operation. **DIRECTIONS:** Corner of Hwy 10 and Hwy 57 in Forest Junction.

Hours: By appointment only
Advance Notice: Yes   Fee: No   HP Access: No

Union Star Cheese Factory (cheese processor)   SIC Code: 2022
7742 Highway 110
Fremont, WI 54940
920-836-2804   Contact: Manager

On this tour you will see cheese being made every morning except Sunday. The best time to watch is from 9:00 to 10:00 am. **NOTE:** Sample some of the best cheese curds in the world. **DIRECTIONS:** Five miles southeast of Fremont on St Rd 110 or 22 miles northeast of Oshkosh on St Rd 110.

Hours: 6:00 am - 5:00 pm   Days: Monday - Saturday
Advance Notice: No   Fee: No   HP Access: Yes

Green Bay Processing & Dist. Center (postal)   SIC Code: 4311
300 Packerland Drive
Green Bay, WI 54303-9997
920-498-3969   Contact: Gloria K. Shermo

At this U. S. Postal Office Distribution Center, after viewing a 15 - minute video "A History of the United States Postal Service", you will go on a walking tour of the mail processing work area. **DIRECTIONS:** Hwy 41, west on Mason St to Packerland Dr, go north to facility.

Hours: 9:00 am - 3:00 pm   Days: Monday - Friday
Advance Notice: Yes   Fee: No   HP Access: Yes

AMPI-Morning Glory Farms (cheese processor)   SIC Code: 2022
186 A Madison Street
Hillsboro, WI 54630
608-489-2651   Contact: Richard Glick

Watch the production of Muenster cheese, a specialty of this plant. The best time to see cheesemaking is in the early afternoon. **DIRECTIONS:** Travel on Hwy 33 and 80, one block south on the east edge of town.

Hours: 9:00 am - 4:30 pm   Days: Monday - Friday
Advance Notice: No   Fee: No   HP Access: Yes

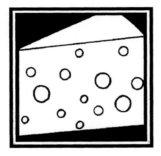

Radloff's Cheese (cheese processor)   SIC Code: 2022
500 East Griffith Street
Hustisford, WI 53034
920-349-3266

On this tour, you will be able to watch cheese being made and sample the products. Some of their cheeses are Muenster, Mozzarella, Monterey Jack, Cheddar, Colby, Provolone, Swiss, etc. **NOTE:** Please call ahead for schedule to be sure cheese is being made that day. Retail store. **DIRECTIONS:** Take Hwy 151 north off I - 90 in Madison to Columbus. Take 16/60 east and stay on Hwy 60 until Hwy E. Turn left and follow into Hustisford.

Hours: 8:00 - 11:00 am   Days: Monday - Friday
Advance Notice: No   Fee: No   HP Access: Yes

Krause Publications (publisher)   SIC Code: 2721
700 East State Street
Iola, WI 54990
715-445-4612   Contact: Julie Ulrich

When you tour the world's largest publisher of periodicals and books on hobbies, outdoors, rural construction trade, and farming, you will have the opportunity to see the 75,000 square foot main offices, which house the business, editorial, advertising and production departments. **NOTE:** You may pick up sample copies of publications on coins, antique autos, comic books, sports cards, toys, firearms and record collecting. **DIRECTIONS:** From Green Bay, take Hwy 54 west to Waupaca, then Hwy 49 north to Iola. Take a right on Hwy 161 and Krause is about 1/4 mile on the right.

Hours: By appointment only.
Advance Notice: Yes   Fee: No   HP Access: Yes

Bieri's Cheese Mart & Factory (cheese processor)   SIC Code: 2022
3271 County P
Jackson, WI 53037
920-677-3227   Contact: Tour Department

Tour this cheese factory where you can watch them make prize-winning Brick, Muenster and Baby Swiss cheese. **DIRECTIONS:** One and one-half miles south of Hwy 60 on Mayfield Rd.

Hours: 8:00 am - 4:00 pm   Days: Monday - Friday
Advance Notice: Yes   Fee: No   HP Access: Yes

General Motors North American Truck (truck mfr)   SIC Code: 3711
1000 Industrial Avenue
Janesville, WI 53546
608-756-7681   Contact: Karen Puerner

On this 90 - minute tour, you will see how skilled workers and high-tech robotics combine to build top-quality vehicles such as the Chevrolet Suburban and the Blazer. **NOTE:** Call for mid-summer model change dates. Reservations are required for groups of 10 or more. Closed first two weeks in July. **DIRECTIONS:** I - 90 east to Hwy 11 west for 1/4 mile. Turn left on Palmer Dr. Turn left on Beloit Ave. Turn right at Delavan Dr (first light, turn left at plant).

Hours: 9:30 am and 1:00 pm   Days: Monday - Thursday
Advance Notice: Yes   Fee: No   HP Access: Yes

Kohler Company (plumbing fixture mfr)   SIC Code: 3261
444 Highland Drive
Kohler, WI 53044
920-457-4441   Contact: Eric Gottesman

On this tour of the world's leading manufacturer of bath fixtures you will visit the manufacturing and packing areas. **NOTE:** Must be 14 years or older. No cameras allowed.
DIRECTIONS: Located one hour north of Milwaukee off I - 43, east on Hwy 23 west
(exit 126). Proceed 2/3 mile to County Trunk Y (Kohler exit). Once on Highland Dr, go
one mile and the Design Center will be on your left.

Hours: 9:30 am - 5:00 pm   Days: Monday - Friday
Advance Notice: Yes   Fee: No   HP Access: Yes

G. Heileman Brewing Company (brewery)   SIC Code: 2082
1111 South 3rd Street
La Crosse, WI 54601
608-782-2337 (800-433-2337)   Contact: Scott Ziebell

This 45 - minute tour will put you in touch with both the rustic past and the high-tech future
of brewing. You will visit the state-of-the-art brewhouse with its computer control center as
well as the 1858 brewhouse. You will see a variety of interesting sites including the World's
Largest Six-Pack; a 15 foot statue of King Gambrinus; and the historic Victorian-style home
of Gottlieb Heileman built in 1870. You will have an opportunity to visit the fermentation
cellars. **NOTE:** Free beer tasting or soft drinks. **DIRECTIONS:** Five miles south of I - 90
and onto Hwy 35.

Hours: 10:00 am - 3:00 pm   Days: Monday - Saturday
Advance Notice: No   Fee: No   HP Access: No

Flambeau Mine Center (copper mine)   SIC Code: 1021
N 4100 Highway 27
Ladysmith, WI 54848
715-532-6690   Contact: Greg Fauquier

At the Public Visitors Center which overlooks the open-pit mining operations, you will learn about Wisconsin's only active copper mine. **NOTE:** Center is open between Memorial Day and Labor Day. **DIRECTIONS:** One and one-half miles south of Ladysmith on St Hwy 27.

Hours: 10:00 am - 6:00 pm   Days: Monday - Sunday (weather permitting)
Advance Notice: Yes   Fee: No   HP Access: Yes

Lakewood Fish Hatchery (hatchery)   SIC Code: 0921
14865 Hatchery Lane
Lakewood, WI 54138
715-276-6066   Contact: Raoul Schottky

At this facility you will have an opportunity to view its 26 tanks, seven raceways and six ponds, and you will see how small fish are first raised indoors in tanks. At about four inches they crowd themselves and must be spread to outdoor raceways and ponds which you will visit. **DIRECTIONS:** East on Cty Rd F, two miles, right on John Lake Rd to Hatchery Ln.

Hours: 9:00 am - 4:00 pm   Days: Monday - Friday
Advance Notice: Yes   Fee: No   HP Access: No

Carr Valley Cheese Company (cheese processor)   SIC Code: 2022
53797 County Road G
LaValle, WI 53941
608-986-2781 (800-462-7258)   Contact: Elizabeth

Come and watch them make rind ripened Cheddar wheels the genuine, old-fashioned way. Then taste their Fresh Curd which comes out daily after 9:00 am. **NOTE:** Best time to observe cheesemaking is from 8:00 am to 1:00 pm. **DIRECTIONS:** Hwy 33 west through Reedsburg to LaValle, turn left on Hwy 58 through Ironton to County G, turn left.

Hours: 8:00 am - 4:00 pm   Days: Monday - Saturday
Advance Notice: No   Fee: No   HP Access: Yes

Simon's Specialty Cheese (cheese processor)   SIC Code: 2022
Highway 51 and County Trunk N
Little Chute, WI 54140
920-788-6311   Contact: Dave or Judy Simon

See some of Wisconsin's finest cheese being made. **NOTE:** Tasting. **DIRECTIONS:** Take
US Hwy 41 to Little Chute exit. Turn left on County Trunk N. Store is located at the corner
of Hwy 51 and County Trunk N. Located five miles north of Appleton.

Hours: 8:00 am - 6:00 pm   Days: Monday - Friday
Advance Notice: No   Fee: No   HP Access: Yes

Bountiful Harvest Winery (winery)   SIC Code: 2084
W 9061 State Road 60
Lodi, WI 53555
608-592-5254   Contact: Manager

Learn about the painstaking art of champagne-making from the vineyard to the bottle.
NOTE: Free samples. **DIRECTIONS:** From Madison, follow US Rt 90 about 15 miles to
Rt 60 west.

Hours: 9:00 am - 5:00 pm   Days: Monday - Friday
Advance Notice: No   Fee: $2.00   HP Access: Yes

Natural Ovens of Manitowac (bakery)   SIC Code: 2051
4300 County Trunk CR
Manitowoc, WI 54221
920-758-2500 (800-558-3535)   Contact: Paul or Barbara Stitt

After a short history of the company is given, you will view the mixing and baking of breads, rolls, etc. The brick oven bakes 20,000 loaves of bread per day. **NOTE:** Animal petting area. Heirloom Apple Orchard. Children can have fun in the Farm Machinery Building. **DIRECTIONS:** From the south, I - 43 north to exit 144 (Hwy C), take right on Hwy C to stop sign, left on CR, two and one-half miles to bakery.

Hours: 9:00,10:00, 11:00 am   Days: Monday,Wednesday,Thursday,Friday
Advance Notice: Yes   Fee: No   HP Access: Yes

Nasonville Dairy, Inc. (cheese processor)   SIC Code: 2022
10898 Highway 10 West
Marshfield, WI 54449
715-676-2177   Contact: Ken Heiman

Tour this dairy and see the process from milk to cheese. They produce both domestic and foreign type cheeses. **DIRECTIONS:** West of Marshfield on Hwy 10 and Cht 'B-B'.

Hours: By appointment   Days: Monday - Friday
Advance Notice: Yes   Fee: No   HP Access: No

Harley-Davidson, Inc. (motorcycle mfr)   SIC Code: 3751
11700 West Capitol Drive (Highway 45)
Milwaukee, WI 53203
414-535-3544   Contact: Tour Director

Begin by viewing a video on the history of the company along with the current operations. Then take a one hour tour and see the assembly process of Harley-Davidson transmissions and engines from start to finish. **NOTE:** 14 days advance notice required. Children must be 12 years of age or older. .No cameras allowed. Closed-toed shoes are required. Gift shop. **DIRECTIONS:** Exit Capitol Dr off Hwy 45. See the plant from the Freeway.

Hours: By appointment only
Advance Notice: Yes   Fee: No   HP Access: Yes

Miller Brewing Company (brewery)   SIC Code: 2082
4251 West State Street
Milwaukee, WI 53208
414-931-2337   Contact: Gilbert Llanas

The tour begins with a video presentation of the history, founder and the beer making process. From there you will go through the packaging and shipping departments, followed by stops at the Brew House and Caves Museum and then on to product sampling at the Miller Inn. **DIRECTIONS:** Located on the west side of Milwaukee, less than five minutes from I - 94.

Hours: 10:00 am - 3:30 pm   Days: Monday - Saturday
Advance Notice: Yes   Fee: No   HP Access: No

Pabst Brewing Company (brewery)   SIC Code: 2082
915 West Juneau Avenue
Milwaukee, WI 53201
414-223-3709   Contact: Kristine Richter

The 35 - minute tour will include direct viewing of the Brew House, with its magnificent hand-wrought copper brew kettles dating back to the 1890's; the Packaging Center; and the vast ultramodern Shipping Center. **NOTE:** Free samples. **DIRECTIONS:** Located northeast of junction of Rts 94, 794 and 43. Take the Broadway exit from Rt 43 to free parking at 9th Ave and Juneau.

Hours: 10:00 am - 3:00 pm   Days: Monday - Friday (June - August)
         10:00,11:00,1:00-3:00 pm   (September - May)
Advance Notice: No   Fee: No   HP Access: No

Alp and Dell Cheese (cheese processor)   SIC Code: 2022
657 Second St.
Monroe, WI 53566
608-328-2122 (800-257-3355)   Contact: Penny or Kay

This is a self guided 15 - 25 minute tour in a large hall where actual cheesemaking can be observed. Some of the specialty cheese made here are Grand Cru Gruyere, Fontina, several kinds of Ostenborg Havarti, Muenster and Edam. **DIRECTIONS:** From Madison, cheesery is located on Hwy 69 south by-pass.

Hours: 8:00 am - 4:30 pm   Days: Monday - Friday
Advance Notice: No   Fee: No   HP Access: Yes

Mt. Sterling Cheese Coop (cheese processor)   SIC Code: 2022
103 Diagnol Street
Mt. Sterling, WI 54645
608-734-3151   Contact: Kent Salmon

Tour this small plant where they make cheese from goat's milk. **NOTE:** Since cheese is not made every day, be sure to call first. **DIRECTIONS:** From Milwaukee, take I - 94 into Hwy 14 then to Hwy 27 south. Plant is one block east of intersections of Hwy 27 and 171.

Hours: By appointment only
Advance Notice: Yes   Fee: No   HP Access: Yes

Nelson Cheese Company (cheese processor)   SIC Code: 2022
Highway 35 South
Nelson, WI 54756
715-673-4725   Contact: Ed Greenheck

On a tour of this cheesemaking facility you will be able to watch the process of making cheese. **DIRECTIONS:** Located on Wisconsin Scenic Hwy 35 - across Mississippi River Bridge at Waukasha Hwy 61.

Hours: 9:00 am - 5:00 pm   Days: Monday - Sunday
Advance Notice: No   Fee: No   HP Access: Yes

Swiss Miss Lace Factory (lace fabric mfr)   SIC Code: 2241
1100 Second Street (Highway 69 south)
New Glarus, WI 53574
608-527-2515   Contact: Robert Wieser

Tour the factory where Swiss lace and embroideries are manufactured on 20 ton Swiss imported sewing machines. **NOTE:** Closed noon hour. **DIRECTIONS:** Take I - 90 to Janesville, then Hwy 11 west to Monroe. Take Hwy 69 north to New Glarus. Factory is located directly behind the store on 11th Ave and Second St.

Hours: 8:30 am - 4:00 pm   Days: Monday - Friday
Advance Notice: Yes   Fee: No   HP Access: Yes

Springside Cheese Corp. (cheese processor)   SIC Code: 2022
7989 Arndt Road
Oconto Falls, WI 54154
920-829-6395   Contact: Licia Hintz

Viewing from three large windows, this 30 - minute tour will enable you to watch cheddar cheesemaking as well as a large variety of other cheeses. **DIRECTIONS:** From Green Bay, take US Rt 141 approximately 25 miles to Rt 22 west. Look for signs.

Hours: 9:00 am - 4:00 pm   Days: Monday - Friday
Advance Notice: Yes   Fee: No   HP Access: No

Oshkosh Processing & Dist. Center (postal)   SIC Code: 4311
1025 West 20th Avenue
Oshkosh, WI 54901-9998
920-236-0236   Contact: Greg Robinson

The U. S. Postal facility personnel will demonstrate automated and mechanized equipment including the advanced facer cancelling system, micro-mark cancelling machines, multi-line optical character readers, bar code sorters, delivery bar code sorters, multi-position letter sorting machine and flat sorting machines. **DIRECTIONS:** Hwy 41 to Hwy 44 exit. Follow Hwy 44 northeast to 20th Ave, go east on 20th Ave to Post Office.

Hours: 8:00 am - 9:00 pm   Days: Monday - Friday
Advance Notice: Yes   Fee: No   HP Access: Yes

Cedar Grove Cheese, Inc. (cheese processor)   SIC Code: 2022
E 5904 Valley View Road
Plain, WI 53577
608-546-5284   Contact: Robert Wills

When touring this facility you will learn about the history and process of cheesemaking. You will also be able to observe actual cheesemaking. **DIRECTIONS:** On the Beltline heading west, take Hwy 14 to Spring Green. Go north approximately eight miles. Located one-half mile east of Plain (Hwy 23) to Mill Rd.

Hours: 9:00, 10:00, 11:00 am   Days: Monday - Friday
Advance Notice: No   Fee: No   HP Access: Yes

Georgia-Pacific Corporation (paper mfr)   SIC Code: 2621
100 Wisconsin River Drive
Port Edwards, WI 54469
715-887-5076   Contact: Craig Timm

The one and one-half hour guided plant tour will show how wood fiber is turned into finished paper products including uncoated bonds, printing grades and specialty grades. **NOTE:** Minimum age is seven. Age 12 and under must be accompanied by an adult. It is recommended that flat comfortable shoes be worn. **DIRECTIONS:** Located on Hwy 54 approximately four miles south of Wisconsin Rapids. From Tomah, take Hwy 173 through Nekoosa. On the far side of town, Hwy 173 meets Hwy 54. Turn right at the intersection and continue to the stop sign which faces the river. Turn right.

Hours: 1:00 pm   Days: Monday - Friday (June - August)
Advance Notice: No   Fee: No   HP Access: No

St. John Mine Ltd. (lead mine)   SIC Code: 1031
129 South Main Street
Potosi, WI 53820
608-763-2121   Contact: Harry D. Henderson

Visitors are guided through the lead mine that was opened in 1828. You will have an opportunity to view the equipment and mining techniques used nearly 160 years ago. **NOTE:**
Tours conducted May - October. **DIRECTIONS:** From Chicago, take I - 90 to Rockford to
US 20 to Hwy 61 north to Potosi/Tennyson. Take a left on Cty O to stop sign in downtown
area. St. John's Mine is located about 1/4 mile on the right.

Hours: 9:00 am - 5:00 pm   Days: Monday - Friday (May - October)
Advance Notice: Yes   Fee: No   HP Access: No

Jung Garden Center (seeds)   SIC Code: 0181
333 South High Street
Randolph, WI 53956
920-326-3121   Contact: Brenda

Visit this famous seed company which distributes 2.5 million seed and garden catalogs
annually. **NOTE:** No tours in April or May. **DIRECTIONS:** From US Rt 90 take exit 108
to Rt 33 east for approximately 25 miles and then south on Rt 73.

Hours: 8:00 am - 5:00 pm   Days: Monday - Saturday (except January-February)
Advance Notice: No   Fee: No   HP Access: Yes

Rhinelander Paper Company (paper mfr)   SIC Code: 2621
515 West Davenport Street
Rhinelander, WI 54501
715-369-4100   Contact: William Vancos

On this tour you will learn how paper is made - from wood pulp to finished product. **NOTE:**
No children under 12. Number of stairways involved. No cameras. No open sandals, high
heels or canvas shoes. Tours are conducted June through August. **DIRECTIONS:** Coming
from the south, turn off Business Hwy 8 at the Chamber of Commerce Center. Follow Sutliff
Ave to end. At stop sign, turn left. Mill will be on your right. Look for smoke stacks.

Hours: 10 am-11,1:30 pm-2:30   Days: Tuesday - Friday
Advance Notice: No   Fee: No   HP Access: No

Wisconsin Dairy State Cheese (cheese processor)   SIC Code: 2022
Highway 34 C
Rudolph, WI 54475
715-435-3144   Contact: Mike Moran

On a tour of this cheese factory, you will see cheese being made in a very modern cheese plant. There will also be a movie presentation. **DIRECTIONS:** Located seven miles north of Wisconsin Rapids on Hwy 34.

Hours: 9:00 am - 4:00 pm   Days: Monday - Friday
Advance Notice: Yes   Fee: No   HP Access: Yes

Bass Lake Cheese Factory (cheese processor)   SIC Code: 2022
598 Valley View Trail
Somerset, WI 54025
715-247-5586   Contact: Julie or Scott Erickson

A very informative tour with a guide who will explain the process through a viewing window. This is the only plant producing cows milk, goats milk and sheeps milk, all at one plant. **NOTE:** Free samples. **DIRECTIONS:** I - 94 to exit 4. Go four miles to Cty U (turns into a right-of-way) to left on Cty I (crossover E) Stay on Cty I to left.

Hours: 10:00 am - 5:00 pm   Days: Monday- Saturday
Advance Notice: Yes   Fee: No   HP Access: Yes

Cloverleaf Cheese, Inc. (cheese processor)   SIC Code: 2022
W10911 County Road North
Stanley, WI 54768
715-669-3145   Contact: William and Arlene Marten

Visit this small family-owned plant making award-winning Colby and Cheddar cheese in open vats and hoop it by hand, which proves to be quite interesting to viewers. **DIRECTIONS:** Three and one-half miles east of Stanley on Hwy 29 to Koser Rd. Right (south) one and one-half miles.

Hours: By appointment only   Days: Monday - Friday
Advance Notice: Yes   Fee: No   HP Access: Yes

Herrschners, Inc. (mail order)   SIC Code: 5961
2800 Hoover Avenue
Stevens Point, WI 54481
715-341-4554   Contact: Ann Zdroik

Tour of the operations of a 160 million foot mail order crafts processing plant. Some of their crafts include needlecraft items, rug kits, yarn, Christmas crafts, etc. **DIRECTIONS:** One mile off Hwy 10 east on Country Club Dr.

Hours: 9:00 am - 3:00 pm   Days: Monday - Friday
Advance Notice: Yes   Fee: No   HP Access: Yes

Stevens Point Brewery (brewery)   SIC Code: 2082
2617 Water Street
Stevens Point, WI 54481
715-344-9310 (800-369-4911)   Contact: Mae Nachman

A guided tour of one of Wisconsin's oldest breweries in existence since 1857. You will see the brewhouse and packaging lines where the finest malted barley, corn, pure Wisconsin water and European Hops are transformed into the award-winning brews you will come to love: Point Special, Point Bock, Point Light, Spud Premier, and Point Classic Amber. Each batch is craft brewed with care and aged the traditional old-world way. **NOTE:** Free samples. **DIRECTIONS:** From I - 90/94 take Hwy 51 north. Nearing Stevens Point, take Rt 10 west (Main St), follow to Water St past two stop signs and see the brewery on left.

Hours: 11:00 am - 2:00 pm   Days: Monday - Saturday (June - August)
Advance Notice: Yes   Fee: $2.00   HP Access: Limited

Cherryland Brewing brewery)   SIC Code: 2082
341 North 3rd Avenue
Sturgeon Bay, WI 54235
920-743-1945 (800-880-1945)   Contact: Mark Feld

In this microbrewery tour, which is housed in a turn-of-the-century railroad station, you will see the production of three main beers, Silver, Golden and Cherry Rail Beer. You will also sample a frosty local brew while watching the brewmaster at work. **DIRECTIONS:** From the south, take the Sturgeon Bay Business District exit (Green Bay Rd) north across the down-town bridge. Turn left on First Ave (four blocks). Brewery is on the right.

Hours: 9:00 am - 5:00 pm   Days: Monday - Sunday
Advance Notice: No   Fee: No   HP Access: Yes

Door Peninsula Winery (winery)　　　　　　　SIC Code: 2084
5806 Highway 42
Sturgeon Bay, WI 54235
920-743-7431　　　　　　Contact: Bob Pollman

This 20 - minute tour includes a trip to the wine cellar, a short video presentation, history of winemaking, and tastings of wines made from local cherries, apples, cranberries and plums. **NOTE:** Free wine tasting. **DIRECTIONS:** Hwy 42/ 57 from Green Bay through Sturgeon Bay. At split, stay on Hwy 42. Winery is about eight miles north of Sturgeon Bay on right.

Hours: 9:00 am - 6:00 pm　　Days:　Monday - Sunday
Advance Notice: Yes　　　　Fee:　$1.00　　HP Access: No

Fruit of the Woods Wine Cellar (winery)　　　SIC Code: 2084
6971 Gogebic Street
Three Lakes, WI 54562
715-546-3080　　　　　Contact: Scott McCain

A 20 - minute tour of the winemaking area, where you will see Wisconsin's original cranberry wine being made and the bottling area. See a video of the cranberry harvest. **NOTE:** Wine tasting. Guided tours on the hour. Tours from late May to mid - October. **DIRECTIONS:** Located at the corner of Hwy 45 and Cty Hwy A in downtown Three Lakes.

Hours: 10:00 - 4:00　　Days:　Monday - Friday
Advance Notice: No　　Fee:　No　　HP Access: Yes

Genesse Woolen Mill (woolen mill)　　　　　SIC Code: 2231
S40 W28178 Highway 59
Waukesha, WI 53188
414-521-2121　　　　Contact: Manager

On a tour of this mill, you will watch wool being processed as it was 100 years ago. **DIRECTIONS:** I - 94 to exit Hwy 18 west. Continue on Hwy 59/164. Stay on Hwy 59 for two miles. Mill is two driveways west of town line on right side of Hwy 59. Watch for deer crossing sign by the driveway.

Hours: 10:00 am - 4:00 pm　　Days:　Monday, Tuesday, Thursday, Friday
Advance Notice: No　　　　Fee:　No　　HP Access: Yes

Hsu's Ginseng Enterprises (ginseng)   SIC Code: 0831
T6819 County Road W
Wausau, WI 54401
715-675-2325   Contact: Dolores

On this tour you will learn about the cultivation of this mysterious root crop. **NOTE:** There is a $35.00 fee for large groups. **DIRECTIONS:** From Hwy 51, take exit 197 to Cty Rd W.

Hours: By appointment only
Advance Notice: Yes   Fee: No   HP Access: Yes

Langlade Fish Hatchery (hatchery)   SIC Code: 0921
W1260 Fish Hatchery Road
White Lake, WI 54491
715-882-8757   Contact: Hatchery Manager

A 30 - minute tour where you will see German brown trout being raised. **DIRECTIONS:** Located in the southern end of the Nicolet National Forest. From Wausau, follow US 51 north approximately 15 miles to Rt 64 east. Watch for signs.

Hours: 7:45 am - 4:30 pm   Days: Monday - Friday
Advance Notice: Yes   Fee: No   HP Access: Yes

Wild Rose Fish Hatchery (hatchery)   SIC Code: 0921
Highway 22 North
Wild Rose, WI 54984
920-622-3527   Contact: Supervisor

On this 45 - minute tour you will be shown how German brown trout, chinook salmon, lake sturgeon, and musky are raised. This is the only hatchery to experimentally raise north pike. **NOTE:** Hike or cross country ski on the trail. **DIRECTIONS:** From Fond du Lac, take Hwy 41 north to Oshkosh, then Hwy 21 west to Wautoma. Take Hwy 22 north to Wild Rose, proceeding through town. Hatchery is one-half mile north of Wild Rose on Hwy 22.

Hours: 8:00 am - 3:030 pm   Days: Monday - Sunday
Advance Notice: No   Fee: No   HP Access: Yes

Cady Cheese Factory, Inc. (cheese processor)   SIC Code: 2022
126 Highway 128
Wilson, WI 54027
715-772-4218   Contact: Wendy or Dave Marcott

You will be able to see through four viewing windows how colby and cheddar cheese is made. **NOTE:** Free samples of Colby and cheese curd. **DIRECTIONS:** Three and one-half miles south on Hwy 128, off I - 94, or right off Hwy 29 at the intersection of Cty Rd T and Hwy 128.

Hours: 9:00 am - 5:00 pm   Days: Monday - Friday
Advance Notice: Yes   Fee: No   HP Access: Yes

Consolidated Papers (paper mill)   SIC Code: 2621
231 First Avenue
Wisconsin Rapids, WI 54495-8050
715-422-3373   Contact: Bob Walker

A two and one-half hour guided papermaking tour of the manufacturer of enamel printing paper used for magazines and catalogs. **NOTE:** Children must be accompanied by adult. **DIRECTIONS:** Enter on Fourth Ave. Call for specific directions..

Hours: 10:00 am   Days: Wednesday, Thursday, Saturday
Advance Notice: No   Fee: No   HP Access: Yes

Consolidated Papers Forest Tour I (forestry)　　　SIC Code: 0811
P.O.Box 8050
Wisconsin Rapids, WI 54495-8050
715-422-3373　　　　　　　Contact: Bob Walker

This is a 16-mile, two hour self-guided auto tour designed to acquaint you with modern forest management techniques. You will see how various forest regeneration methods work with nature to properly utilize this renewable resource. **NOTE:** Be alert for wildlife because the forest management methods produce quite a variety of forest inhabitants. Tours only from late May through mid - October. **DIRECTIONS:** Call for specific directions.

Hours: By appointment only
Advance Notice: Yes　　　　　Fee:　No　　　　　HP Access: Yes

Consolidated Papers Forest Tour II (forestry)　　　SIC Code: 0811
P.O.Box 8050
Wisconsin Rapids, WI 54495-8050
715-422-3373　　　　　　　Contact: Bob Walker

This two hour, one and one-half mile, self-guided walking tour was developed to expand your understanding of modern forest management techniques. **DIRECTIONS:** Call for specific directions.

Hours: By appointment only
Advance Notice: Yes　　　　　Fee:　No　　　　　HP Access: No

Teton Homes (travel trailer mfr)   SIC Code: 3792
3283 North 9 Mile Road
Casper, WY 82604
307-235-1525   Contact: Tour Department

A one hour tour with an explanation of components that go into the making of fifth wheel trailers. You will be able to view work in progress and examine the interior of a finished trailer. **NOTE:** No children under age 16. **DIRECTIONS:** Located on Rts 20/26 about one mile west of the airport.

Hours: 11:30 am   Days: Monday - Friday
Advance Notice: Yes   Fee: No   HP Access: No

Eagle Bronze, Inc. (foundry)   SIC Code: 3322
130 Poppy Street
Lander, WY 82520
307-332-5436   Contact: Manager

On this tour you will see how bronze sculptures and monuments are manufactured using the 2,000 year old lost wax process. **DIRECTIONS:** Exit I - 80 at Rawlins, WY. Follow Hwy 287 to Lander from Rawlins which will be approximately 130 miles.

Hours: 10:00 am and 2:00 pm   Days: Tuesday - Thursday (September-May)
        1:30 pm   Tuesday, Thursday (June- August)
Advance Notice: Yes   Fee: No   HP Access: Yes

Missouri Basin Power Project (utility)   SIC Code: 4939
Laramie River Station
347 Grayrocks Road
Wheatland, WY 82201
307-322-9601   Contact: Kathy Jones

This is a coal-fired electric generating station. The station has three units, each rated at
550,000 KW capacity. You will take a guided tour of the power plant and see how coal is
used to generate electricity. **NOTE:** There is walking and heights involved and not recommended for children under 13 years of age. **DIRECTIONS:** Seven miles northeast of
Wheatland. Look for green directional signs near both exits to Wheatland on I - 25.

Hours: By appointment only   Days: Monday - Friday
Advance Notice: Yes   Fee: No   HP Access: No

Thunder Basin Coal Company (coal mine)   SIC Code: 1221
Box 406
Wright, WY 82732
307-939-1300   Contact: Kord Babcock

Take a coal mine tour which meets at the guard shack. You will have to sign a release form
to take the tour. **NOTE:** Tours are only conducted during the summer and end in mid-
August. **DIRECTIONS:** From Gillette on US 90, take Hwy 89 to WY 450 exit.

Hours: 8:00 am - 1:00 pm   Days: Monday - Friday
Advance Notice: Yes   Fee: No   HP Access: No

INDEX-1

INDEX-2

Standard Industrial Classification

The Standard Industrial Classification (SIC) system was devised by the U.S. Government Office of Management & Budget to ease the comparison of statistical data on the nation's economy. The classification scheme is also used in the private sector to present business data. It covers most economic activity in the United States. Where a company has more than one code number, the more predominant one has been selected for these listings.

Order Form
(tear out or photocopy)

Please Send:

Inside America - The Great American Industrial Tour Guide

_____ Copies at $21.95 each =   _____

Mass residents add 5% sales tax   _____

Shipping & handling; $3.00 for first book
$1.50 each additional   _____

Total enclosed .... _____

Name ....

Address ....

City .... **State**..... .... **Zip** ....

Send check or money order to:

Heritage Publishing
P.O. Box 4320
Peabody, MA 01961-4320

phone (800) 624-4961

Call or write for quotations on quantity purchases